IN LONDON

The comprehensive guide to drinking in the capital

B

Published by John Blake Publishing Ltd,
3 Bramber Court, 2 Bramber Road,
London W14 9PB, England

www.johnblakepublishing.co.uk

This edition published in 2009

978 184454 707 4

British Library Cataloguing-in-Publication Data:

A catalogue record for this book is available from the British Library.

Design by www.envydesign.co.uk

Printed in Great Britain by Scotprint

1 3 5 7 9 10 8 6 4 2

Papers used by John Blake Publishing are natural, recyclable products made from wood grown in sustainable forests. The manufacturing processes conform to the environmental regulations of the country of origin.

A-Z of London Underground Stations

A few tube stations are very close together so we have combined them in one map. The index below will guide you to the appropriate section. Where necessary, pointers have been placed throughout the book to direct you to the correct map.

Please note the maps are not to scale.

A-Z OF LONDON UNDERGROUND STATIONS

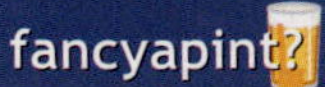

Acknowledgements

Fancyapint.com (and this book) would not be possible without the help of these people – all of whom have contributed in some way:

Harriet Brown, Gordon Butler, Mark Coaten, Stacey Collins, James Cone, Michael Crossland, Bill Dornan, Robert Dunnett, Dee Fancett, Pat Fanning, Dean Fetzer, Debra Fetzer, Neil Foston, Bernd Goettert, Valerie Gonet, Michelle Grayson, Ken Grint, Phoebe Harkins, Dominic Heaney, Adam Hickford, David Little, Ben Locker, Simon Luker, Gerry Lynch, Jennie Lynch, Ross MacFarlane, Doug McCarthy, Jim McKenzie, Robert Moody, Stephen O'Dea, Arthur Rabatin, Sean Robinson, Ellie Seaward, Fiona Stevens, Mary Tills, Steve Watson, Dan Wilson

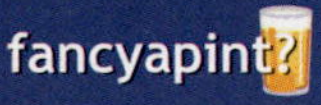

Contents

CONTENTS

Fancyapint? – about this book

Welcome to the second edition of Fancyapint? in London. We've updated and expanded the book to include new pubs, the London overground line, new reviews and new photographs. Every pub in the book was photographed and visited at least once by a Fancyapint? reviewer in 2008 and often many more times than that. And any changes to pubs that occur after the book has been published will be listed on special pages on the internet – fancyapint.com/book and fancyapint.mobi/book so you can be sure that you're always up to date.

This book is a selection of the best and a few of the worst pubs on Fancyapint.com. We've created this selection to help visitors and people who live in London find somewhere decent for a drink, just about anywhere in central London and a couple of outlying parts. We may have missed out your favourite – we've missed out some of our own – and, much as we'd like to, there just isn't space in a book to include all our reviews from Fancyapint.com.

The pubs in this book are organised by nearest their underground, overground and DLR station and these are listed in alphabetical order. All stations in travel zones one and two are included, plus some popular, outlying districts (e.g. Richmond and Wembley). Some of the stations are very close to each other so we have combined them on one map. Where they are combined, a pointer will direct you to the correct map. There is also an alphabetical listing of pubs at the back of the book.

In this guide, as on the Fancyapint? website, you'll find our entirely subjective opinions and observations about the pubs we've been to. If you're like us, you'll love the same pubs, and, if you're not, you won't – but that's life. The only points there shouldn't be any dispute about are the factual items: the pub's name, its location etc. The rest is up for (sometimes heated) debate.

When it comes down to it, at Fancyapint? we only really care about two things: that you should enjoy our guide and have a great time down the pub. Cheers – the Fancyapint? team.

About pubs

'As soon as I enter the door of a tavern, I experience an oblivion of care, and a freedom from solicitude; when I am seated, I find the master courteous and the servants obsequious to my call, anxious to know and ready to supply my wants; wine there exhilarates my spirits and prompts me to free conversation, and an interchange of discourse with those whom I must love; I dogmatise and am contradicted; and in this conflict of opinions and sentiments I find delight.'

Dr Samuel Johnson

An almost uniquely British institution, the pub has been at the heart of our communities for centuries. The pub has had a long and often chequered history, but it remains an important part of our society – even in multicultural, multimedia, stay-at-home, jet-off-to-foreign-parts, 21st-century Britain. The pub is still the focus of many people's social lives; it is often a microcosmic mirror of its community and of the country as a whole. Changes in pub culture reflect changes in larger society – changes such as the increase in the consumption of wine, the marked improvement in the quality and variety of food and the increasing number of women who visit pubs. The pub's image is changing but its importance hasn't diminished.

They've been around for a long time, but pubs have not always been in the form familiar today. They're the bastard offspring of at least four parents, combining elements of alehouses and taverns with coaching inns and coffee houses. Over the centuries, as the significance of ale and wine (and other forms of alcohol) has changed in our society, the essence of these forerunners has been distilled and mutated until we have a distinct presence in our neighbourhoods known as the 'public house'. One thing, however, is constant: pubs have had an important place in society for a long, long time – read Pepys or Johnson, Dickens or Orwell and you won't have to read for long before you find a mention of a tavern or two – they are important both socially and personally.

Over the years, the pub has developed its own rituals, etiquette and foibles, that often appear to be quaint and impenetrable to people from other cultures – we know, because we get the emails to prove it. We do odd things in pubs: we line up at bars to order drinks, instead of having them brought to us; we don't tip the bar staff when we buy a drink; we buy a round of drinks for eight of our mates and expect the same in return, knowing damn well we can't possibly manage them; and the list goes on. There's no logic to it, it's just how things are. Like most things in life, experience is the best way to learn about anything: to truly get to know pubs, you have to visit them, and that's what this book is about.

At Fancyapint? we're all great fans of the pub, all pubs, from 16th-century half-timbered alehouses to sleek bars; if you can get a pint in it and socialise with good friends, we'll be there.

This book and Fancyapint.com are a celebration of pubs. We want you to share our enjoyment of them experiencing them at their best and avoid the worst – we've already done that for you. And, if we do seem overly critical, it's only because we care – if your best friend can't tell you you're a hopeless case, who can?

About Fancyapint?

Fancyapint? is a collaborative effort. We have a team of more than thirty reviewers – all volunteers, aged 20–55+, female and male, straight and gay, smokers and nonsmokers, from all walks of life. A disparate, and often dissipated, bunch, what we have in common is a love of pubs.

Every pub listed on the site has been visited by a Fancyapint? reviewer, and the review he or she writes has to answer one simple question: 'What's it like?' The aim is to capture what we feel about a pub in 150 words or so and, while we might mention ales and food, we don't go into these in depth – there are plenty of other guides for that. It's a bit like asking a knowledgeable friend about it: you want a quick answer, not a life story, so that you can make your mind up about where you want to go. To speed that process there is our pint rating system too, so that, with a few words, a rating and a picture, you should be able to decide pretty quickly where you're going next for a drink.

Of course, we don't get it right every time: pubs change (sometimes in a single day); sometimes there's an atypical bad or good experience upon which we have based our review; we sometimes make mistakes – we're only human; or there's simply a difference of opinion. So a word of caution: if you're planning something special at a pub, check with the pub first. We'd hate you to turn up for a big celebration only to find you'll be drinking in someone's living room because the pub's been converted into apartments.

A short history of Fancyapint?

Fancyapint? started life as a personal database written in HyperCard on an Apple Mac in the 1980s. Distributed on a tiny local network and on floppy disk, it provided the answer to that vital after-work question: 'Where are we going tonight?' Even at that early stage, all the necessary ingredients, including our 'pint' rating system, were in place; so, when the Web came along in the 1990s, it was an obvious next step.

Fancyapint.com, in its current form, launched in 1999 and has grown considerably since then, listing around 2,500 London pubs (and now expanding to cover the rest of the UK). The site gets more than 3,000,000 visitors per year.

We'd always wanted to do a book of the site and the first edition was published in 2006. Sure, we have mobile versions of Fancyapint.com, but even with 3G mobiles you don't always have access to the internet and often it can be slow. A book is portable, its batteries don't go flat and you can still read it when you've dropped it in a pint of beer. (Try doing that with your mobile! Or rather – don't.)

So here you have it, the latest Fancyapint? book, updated, expanded and ready to get you to that first, fine pint of the day.

FAQs – the Fancyapint? guide to drinking in London

Here are the answers to questions we frequently get asked by visitors to London.

Drinking age in the United Kingdom

You can buy an alcoholic drink in the UK if you're over the age of 18. A few words of advice: if you look young, you may be asked for identification – your passport should do the trick. Some pubs run identity-card schemes, but if you're a visitor you probably won't have one of these cards.

What may be somewhat confusing to visitors is the fact that some pubs, clubs and bars operate their own minimum age limit, a limit that's above the minimum legal age. This can be 21, 23 or 25 and is entirely down to the discretion of the management. If they refuse to allow you in, don't argue: it won't get you anywhere other than chucked out into the street. There are plenty of other places to go. In any case, regardless of age, admittance to any establishment is at the discretion of the management – if they don't want you in the place, there's no legal obligation for them to let you in.

UNDERAGE DRINKING

It is illegal for anyone under the age of 18 to buy an alcoholic drink or for anyone knowingly to purchase a drink for someone underage. It is also against the law for anyone running licensed premises (or their employees) to sell a drink to someone underage. There is an exception: it is not an offence to buy a drink for a sixteen- or seventeen-year-old in conjunction with a table meal in a restaurant as long as the meal is not in the bar area. Similarly, a sixteen- or seventeen-year-old can purchase a drink in a restaurant with a table meal under these restrictions.

Some pubs allow families in for meals and some don't, it depends on their licence. Some even have areas where children can play, but they will still require parents to supervise their offspring. Children under fourteen years of age are allowed into pubs that hold a children's certificate. They must be accompanied by an adult and are restricted to those areas that have been certified suitable for young children. Pubs holding such a certificate must serve meals and non-alcoholic drinks, normally until 9 p.m.

The Visit Britain website has more information at www.visitbritain.com.

Opening and closing times

Pub opening and closing times are down to the licence that applies to the establishment, although most pubs stick to a pretty standard schedule. See below for late-night drinking.

'Normal' times are as follows for England and Wales. Scotland is slightly different, it has had more liberal opening times for some time and as a consequence there's less of a pattern. We expect the same will happen in England and Wales over time.

	Opening	Closing
Monday to Saturday	11 a.m.	11 p.m.
Sunday	12 noon	10.30 p.m.

Pubs usually call 'last orders' ten minutes before closing time and this is often indicated by ringing a bell. It's merely a warning and you can continue to buy drinks until closing time. When time is called – by ringing the bell again or calling 'Time, please, ladies and gents' – that's it: drink sales are closed; you can't buy booze to take home at this point either. What follows next is 'drinking-up time', when the pub will allow you up to twenty minutes to finish your drink. Some pubs do this more aggressively than others. But, if you find a more relaxed one, they will often let you finish up at your own pace. 'Lock-ins' (drinking beyond the times allowed by the pub's licence) are illegal, even with the new laws, but they do happen in some instances. If you find yourself locked in a pub after last orders and still getting a drink you may count yourself lucky, but be warned: you could get into trouble with the law.

LATE-NIGHT DRINKING

The law changed in 2005 to allow pubs to apply for a licence to serve outside 'normal' hours, theoretically at any time in a 24-hour period. This means pubs can now open at the hours they would like to rather than the rather restrictive 11 a.m. to 11 p.m. they had to previously (except where licence extensions had been permitted). However, not every pub's application has been successful and, even when they are successful, it is often difficult to find out which pubs do have late opening hours. And in any case sometimes pubs will close when the landlord feels like it.

Three years after the introduction of the new licensing regime, we find that pubs tend to cluster late-night opening at the end of the week, primarily Thursday, Friday and Saturday nights. This often means they're open just a few extra hours, say to 1 or 2 a.m. on those nights, or simply until midnight.

There are alternative places to go for a late-night drink, but they are more likely to be clubs and bars than pubs, and there are a few things to consider before trying to get into one:

- Most of these establishments have gentlemen on the door for the express purpose of keeping pissed, aggressive or unwanted punters from entering. If you are too drunk, you won't get in.
- Some pubs and clubs charge an entry fee later in the evening. However, getting there early can often avoid a charge. Some clubs levy an entry fee at all times.
- Clubs and bars tend to have music, often making it difficult to have a conversation – if that's what you wanted to do. Some are obviously better than others for this sort of thing, but the venues can be variable as can the music.

Public transport should also be taken into consideration if you're out drinking late, since underground, rail and daytime bus services start closing down around 11.30 to midnight. Read the section *Getting there and back again* on page xvii for more information.

A few pointers on pub etiquette

Pubs are usually pretty relaxed and informal places, so there are not too many rules, but visitors do sometimes get caught out, so here are a few pointers.

ORDERING DRINKS

Generally, you order your drink from the bar and take it to where your friends are sitting or standing. You often order food from the bar, too, although food will usually be brought to you after you've ordered; if it's not clear, ask the person behind the bar. One common exception is when you're sitting down and eating – you may be able to ask the waiter or waitress for more drinks while you eat.

When you go to the bar to order drinks and there's a group of you, don't all go together, since there won't be room. One or two of you should go (if it's more than one person can carry) to order the drinks and bring them back to your table.

Don't order drinks one by one, the person behind the bar can usually remember a few drinks at a time. And an important word of advice: when you order a round of drinks that includes Guinness, order the Guinness first!

If there are lots of other people standing at the bar drinking and they are not waiting to order a drink, ask someone to let you get to the bar so you can order your drink – don't push in. When you've got your drinks, leave the bar. Don't stay where you are, because it will annoy the people who let you in. If people are queuing to order drinks, wait your turn. A good way to start a fight in a pub is to try to push to the head of a queue two minutes before closing time. If the bar staff have seen you waiting, they'll serve you.

There are a growing number of pubs in London that are offering Continental table service: you don't have to go to the bar because someone comes and takes your order! While not traditional pub behaviour, it is convenient, and we find that the atmosphere in these pubs is often more convivial than in pubs that still make you join a scrum at the bar.

PAYING FOR DRINKS

You usually pay for the drink when you order. If you're using a debit/credit card, then you can probably run a tab. Often there's a minimum order amount of £5 or £10 – not difficult to achieve in London – but you'll often have to leave your card behind the bar for security. Some places add a surcharge to your drinks bill to cover the bank charges.

With technology the way it is, some even offer cashback if you use your card! Others have cash machines (ATM) inside the pub, but these usually charge a fee for withdrawing your money! These are both dangerous developments, because they often lead to staying in the pub, headaches, memory loss and empty bank accounts. Be careful.

TIPPING

In pubs, you rarely tip at the bar, even when the bar staff give you your change on a platter – this is a ploy to extract even more money from customers, who are often already paying exorbitant prices for the drink.

However, if you feel someone working in the pub has provided exceptional service you can offer to buy him or her a drink. Sometimes, he or she will actually take the drink (and drink it with you), but more often than not will take money equivalent to the price of a drink – usually a half. This is acceptable.

A few pubs provide table service for drinks, especially if they do food, and, where you get this, it's OK to tip for good service (around 10–12.5 per cent).

DRINKING OUT OF DOORS

It's actually illegal to drink on the street in most places, unless an area outside the pub is part of, or owned by, the pub. Local authorities are very sensitive about this, so, if you are asked to stay inside a particular area by the staff or even to move indoors, please do so. If you don't, the pub could possibly lose its licence.

TO SMOKE OR NOT TO SMOKE

It is illegal to smoke in all indoor workplaces and this includes pubs, clubs, bars and restaurants – the tide has definitely turned against the recreational pint and a fag.

Most pubs have some kind of outside area where you can smoke and these should be signposted. In some, you may not be able to take your drink with you, for example if the smoking area is outside in the street and in some pubs areas that appear to be external areas are still no-smoking areas. The rule is only to smoke in designated outdoor areas, or you (and the pub) can risk a fine.

If there is nothing to say you CAN smoke, you should assume you cannot. You should also note that throwing your cigarette ends into the street could incur a fine for littering – use the ashtrays provided, you'll save yourself money and it makes the place look a lot tidier.

Getting there and back again

Except for driving – and of course we wouldn't want you to drink and drive anyway – getting around London is usually pretty easy, although sometimes it can be slow. There are plenty of public transport options, covering the whole of the capital, for you to choose from – the main choices are described below.

UNDERGROUND/OVERGROUND

In London, the obvious way to get anywhere is to use the underground (the Tube); the tube map is a London icon and, of course, this book is organised around it. The underground network is run by Transport for London (TFL) and now the Tube has an overground counterpart that integrates with it and connects areas previously not part of the network.

A major extension to the East London line is under construction and as a result all the existing stations on it are currently closed. It will connect even more areas in London, but it won't be open until 2010. You can use your tube season tickets and Oyster cards (TFL's electronic ticketing system) on the whole of this network.

DOCKLANDS LIGHT RAILWAY (DLR)

The Docklands Light Railway is a relatively new network in East London, covering from the City east to Docklands (including City Airport) and over the river to Greenwich and Lewisham. It is part of TFL's network and your tube tickets and Oyster cards are valid. The DLR doesn't have ticket barriers like the Tube and rail, but uses a validation system; if you have a prepay Oyster card (the best value way of getting around London in our opinion), you must touch your card on one of the validation machines located near the station entrance.

RAIL

If you're coming into London from a further-flung location, chances are you'll be using the rail network. The rail network is huge and links up with the Tube network. However, you must be aware that a number of different companies run the rail network and not all tickets are valid on them. Oyster cards are valid on only a small portion of the rail network, so you may have to buy a combined ticket that allows travel on all networks.

BUSES

In recent years, there's been a huge investment in the bus network in London and (unlike most cities in the UK) you can get almost anywhere by bus, even late at night and some routes operate throughout the night. It's true that bus journeys can be slow and it's better if you're pretty familiar with where you're going – a lot of Londoners don't use them for fear of getting lost – but if you've got the time you'll find them cheap (especially if you have a pre-pay Oyster card) and convenient and you get to see a lot more of London than you will deep underground.

Unfortunately, the extremely convenient Routemaster buses that were once a favourite feature of London have now been withdrawn and only operate a limited service on a couple of routes – 9 and 15.

TAXIS

Another familiar London sight is the black cab. If you've got the money, this is easily the best way to get around the capital. There are plenty of black cabs around, but, if you travel any distance, you'll find they are quite expensive and you might feel the need to get a second mortgage just to pay the fare. The fare is always shown on the meter in the cab and cabbies (cab drivers) can often be useful sources of local information.

Licensed minicabs (usually ordinary family cars or people carriers) are another option, cheaper than taxis and will take you from door to door, the same as black cabs. Minicabs cannot be hailed in the street, they must be booked through their respective cab companies, of which there are many. Minicabs have a special licence disc displayed on their front and rear windows.

You should never get into a car that stops and asks if you want a cab, or a car being touted by a person in the street. These cars are unlicensed and illegal – you'll not be covered by any insurance (not even your own travel insurance) and they can be dangerous. We call them scab cabs for very good reasons.

RIVER BOAT SERVICES

Nowadays, the Thames has been put to good use and London River Services (LRS) provide a reliable and fun way of getting around the capital. There are two types of service available: commuter services offering faster trips between key commuter stops and leisure services that putt-putt their way between a good number of London's tourist attractions. Services stretch from Woolwich in the east to Hampton Court in the west.

However, it's not possible to do this in a single trip – journeys run shorter routes, it's a little complicated, but the TFL journey planner can help you work it out. The scheduled leisure services don't run much later than 18:00 (although chartered boats can) and the commuter services stop at about the same time as the Tube.

LATE-NIGHT TRAVEL (AFTER MIDNIGHT)

Public transport should also be taken into consideration when you're drinking late, since the Tube and normal bus services start closing down around 11.30 to midnight. There may still be the odd tube after midnight (usually from central London outwards on Friday and Saturday), but it's a good idea to check the last-train listings before you leave the station on the way to the pub. Apart from a few late night trains, rail services finish around the same time as the underground and some commuter stations close early in the evening and are not open at the weekend. Night buses operate all night along most major bus routes and, while fairly dependable, can also be crowded (often so packed you can't get on) and full of people in the same state as you!

It's notoriously difficult to find a cab in some parts of London (West End and City) between 23:00 and midnight. Black cab fares go up significantly after 20:00 and even more after 22:00. However, there are lots of options for finding a taxi and having a few numbers stored in your mobile makes it much easier to get one. If you're stuck and have a mobile phone, simply text the word HOME to 60835 (60tfl) and the phone numbers for two local licensed minicab operators plus the taxi one-number will be sent direct to your mobile phone. This service is available 24 hours a day.

JOURNEY PLANNERS

There are two very good online journey planners that can help get you to and from the pub with the minimum of fuss. Transport for London has a journey planner that covers the underground, overground, DLR, river services and bus routes.

Transport Direct is a new door-to-door journey planner, funded by government. It allows you to plan your journey from wherever you are (not just London) to wherever you want to go (and your return journey) using any available means of transport – including tube, bus, rail and car. The website is at www.transportdirect.info, and you can find more information about the service on the next page.

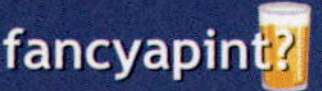

How to get there with Transport Direct

So how do you get to the pub and, importantly, back home afterwards? For directions to anywhere in Britain – not just pubs – Transport Direct (www.transportdirect.info) is the only website you'll need.

Unless you're planning to stick to soft drinks all night, you'll want to know what public transport is available. Transport Direct joins up timetable information for all modes of transport – rail, bus, underground, even ferry – giving you a complete journey plan right from your starting point to your destination.

Transport Direct journey plan – Bar Story's happy hour ends at eight, remember?

If it's going to be a late one, don't forget to use Transport Direct to plan your return journey. Knowing your route home and when the last train or bus departs can help prevent an enjoyable evening from ending with an expensive taxi journey or a long cold walk.

It's all very well knowing what bus to take, but where do you catch it from? Transport Direct's maps are particularly useful for showing the exact location of the bus stop you need. With Transport Direct, you can print a map of your whole journey or any part of it – don't forget to take the map with you, though!

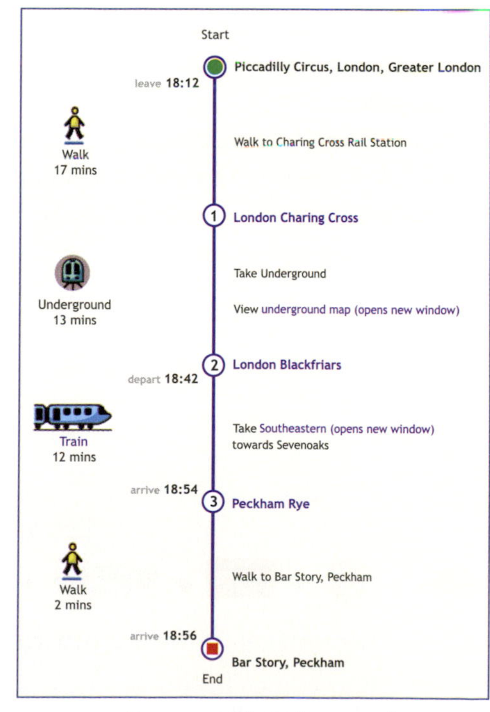

Transport Direct journey plan

If you're lucky enough to be getting a lift or have a designated driver, Transport Direct offers driving directions as well. You can even get a list of the nearest car parks to your destination. Unlike some route planners, Transport Direct's driving directions take predicted traffic levels into account, depending on the time of day you're travelling, rather than assuming freeflowing traffic conditions at all times. You can even check the CO2 emissions for your journey and compare them with those of a public transport journey – handy for when the pub conversation gets round to the topic of climate change.

For some, popping 'down the local' is the quintessential pub experience. It's convenient, familiar and can give you a warm feeling of belonging in the place where you live. If you're reading this book, chances are you enjoy making new discoveries too. Visiting a highly rated pub is a great way of exploring a new area of town. With Transport Direct, you can stride out, confident in the knowledge that you know where you're going and how to get there. And maybe even how to get back to your local in time for last orders.

That URL again: www.transportdirect.info. And, should you forget that, there's a link on every Fancyapint pub page which opens Transport Direct with the pub you're viewing pre-set as the destination. To link, perchance to drink. Aye, there's the pub.

Guide to the pint ratings

Every pub we review has a Fancyapint? 'pint' rating. It's intended to show at a glance what we feel about a pub. Here's what the ratings mean:

A five pint rated pub is worth a special effort to visit. It will be in a good location, architecturally interesting and offer a good range of well-kept beers and food of a high standard in a pleasant atmosphere. This combination of unique features and high standards makes this something we award very occasionally.

Whilst a four pint rating may be awarded more often than five, this still only goes to special pubs. It is usually awarded for having a combination of some (but not all) of the features listed above. A four pint pub is worth a detour.

Three pints are awarded to decent pubs, that offer reasonable beer and food, have a pleasant atmosphere and are easy enough to get to. Whilst you might not go too far out of your way to get to one, if you're in the vicinity of a three pint pub, don't miss it.

Two pint pubs may not have any outstanding features but are competent in most of the key areas. They have sometimes let us down in a small way – often not their fault – but nevertheless we feel they could be better. Two pint pubs are usually good, honest boozers and are often frequented by regulars.

One pint pubs cover the basics, but there are significant issues that let them down. It could be poor beer (or selection of beers), poor service (a common failing) or just frequented by a crowd of regulars that resent the presence of outsiders on their patch (another common occurrence). We usually end up going to these pubs if we're really thirsty and there's no nearby alternative.

Zero pint rated pubs pubs should be avoided until significant improvements are made.

We like or dislike pubs for all kinds reasons and we often want different things from pubs at different times. Maybe a quiet pint in cosy surroundings or a full-on games pub, or fantastic food, whatever. It should be clear from our reviews why we give a pub a particular rating.

We also know pubs change and ratings can go up or down, so be aware that any rating is based on our experiences to date. If you feel a pub's rating has changed let us know by email to editor@fancyapint.com.

Guide to the feature symbols

GOOD BEER/REAL ALE

This icon signifies that the pub has very good real ales, unusual beers, regular guest ales or Cask Marque status. As Fancyapint? is not intended to be a good beer guide, we don't normally go into a lot of detail.

TV

The pub has at least one TV showing Sky TV, Freeview, Setanta etc, sometimes all or sometimes just one. The review will describe this in more detail if it's a major attraction for the pub (e.g. a large projector screen, showing major sporting events). If a sports event you would like to see is only showing on a particular channel (especially if it's pay-per-view) check with the pub you want to visit first.

FUNCTION ROOM

The pub has a designated function room, or part of the pub can be reserved for private parties or the whole pub can be hired (quite often this happens with central pubs at weekends).

ALFRESCO DRINKING

The pub has space for outdoor drinking. This can be anything from an enclosed beer garden to a couple of tables on the street. We usually specify what kind of space is available, so, if you're looking for somewhere to have a barbecue, for instance, you should be able to find one. Don't forget that in the UK it's usually illegal to drink in the street and, at the slightest hint of sun, pubs with outdoor space will get mobbed – so get there early.

POOL TABLE

The pub has at least one pool table (we say if there are more than one). We don't mention the cost, as it's something that can change.

WATERSIDE

The pub is by water, or has waterside views. Usually, in London, it will be by the Thames, but there are also nice pubs by canals, lakes and ponds. Not all pubs with waterside views have outdoor seating (hence the distinction). Check the review for more info.

MUSIC

The pub features music – often live – and, if it's a specific kind of music, then we'll say. We don't list events: you need to call the pub for that information, although the review usually gives more information if there's something of interest. We include karaoke, jukeboxes and DJs in this category, but we will say so in the review.

PLAY AREA/CHILD POLICY

These pubs either have an area set aside for children – it's not something you get very often in central London, more often it's in the suburbs – or let children into specific areas of the pub at certain times of the day.

QUIZ NIGHT

The pub hosts a quiz night or nights – if it's a regular weekly occurrence, we usually say. Some pubs hold quizzes less frequently, sometimes monthly. Pubs can host quizzes for fun and some offer prizes such as drink or cash. You may have to pay to enter some quizzes, check this with the pub.

RESTAURANT

Most pubs do some kind of food, so we don't mention that fact here (it's rare nowadays if they don't). We use this feature to indicate pubs that have separate restaurants or eating areas, distinct from the drinking areas. We indicate any speciality food on offer here, e.g. Thai, French, Czech.

ACCOMMODATION

A few pubs in London have rooms. You should call the pub for prices and availability.

THEATRE/COMEDY

A few pubs have theatres attached; others have comedy evenings and cabaret in function rooms, or even in the main bar. Quite often, these pubs are where some now very well-known comedians honed their material over the years, so a visit to a comedy night now might well be an opportunity to see future stars. We don't include pubs near, or next door to, theatres, only pubs that actually host these kinds of event.

TRADITIONAL PUB GAMES

Some pubs still have traditional games available for you to play – e.g. darts, bar billiards, shove ha'penny, skittles, table footy and pinball. Fruit machines and video games (even Space Invaders, Asteroids and Defender) don't count.

GUIDE TO THE FEATURE SYMBOLS

DISABLED FACILITIES
Shows pubs with disabled facilities. Where we have more detail – e.g. access ramps – we will say. However, it usually means there's at least disabled access and a disabled toilet on the premises.

COUNTRY THEME
This indicates that a pub is themed on a country – e.g. Irish, Canadian, Scottish, Dutch. You may find people from these countries congregating here, or it may mean you can consume produce from the country in question here. The appropriate flag for the country will be displayed in the features of the review.

OPEN LATE
Now the licensing laws allow more flexible opening, we will list, where we can, the pubs that are open after 11 p.m. This information can change very quickly, so, if your night out depends on a pub being open (at any time), check first with the pub.

ATM
Signifies pubs with an ATM on the premises. Be warned: there's usually a charge for using these machines – usually about £1.50. Many pubs will give you cashback with a debit card (if you buy more than a minimum amount of drink). We don't list pubs that happen to be near to ATMs.

WIFI
Some of you can't bear to be away from the web for very long, so we've listed the pubs that offer WiFi access. Some charge for this, others don't – you'll need to check with the bar staff what you have to do to get logged on.

GAY/GAY-FRIENDLY
These pubs are either gay pubs or welcome gays. We don't go into any kind of detail about what kind of gay pubs they might be or any special events – there are plenty of other places for that kind of information.

DOGS WELCOME
Many pubs don't let our canine friends accompany us for a pint, but there are some that do. These you will find marked with a doggy icon.

Top Ten pubs

To help you, if you're looking for something in particular, we've created a few lists of our favourite ten pubs for a range of topics (with the exception of the Top Ten attractions, where we've listed our closest favourite pub to an attraction). Some lists could easily go on for much longer, but, for the sake of brevity and clarity, we've limited the choices to ten. All the pubs here are listed in alphabetical order.

FANCYAPINT? TOP TEN

Our Top Ten pubs in the book – these you must see.

- Colton Arms (Barons Court)
- George and Dragon (Acton)
- The Grapes (Westferry)
- Jerusalem Tavern (Farringdon)
- Lamb (Holborn)
- The Royal Oak (Borough)
- Victoria (Lancaster Gate)
- Windsor Castle (Edgware Road)
- Ye Olde Mitre Tavern (Farringdon)

TOP TEN THAMES-SIDE PUBS

- Angel (Bermondsey)
- Captain Kidd (Shadwell/Wapping)
- Dove (Ravenscourt Park)
- Founders Arms (Blackfriars)
- The Narrow (Limehouse DLR)
- Mayflower (Rotherhithe)
- Old Thameside Inn (London Bridge)
- Prospect of Whitby (Shadwell/Wapping)
- White Cross (Richmond)
- The Yacht (Greenwich)

TOP TEN PUBS FOR ALFRESCO DRINKING

- 1802 (West India Quay DLR)
- The Albion (Highbury & Islington)
- The Banker (Cannon Street)
- Clifton (Kilburn Park)
- Duchess (Vauxhall)
- Fentiman Arms (Oval)
- Pilot Inn (North Greenwich)
- Richard I (Greenwich DLR)
- Spurstowe Arms (Hackney Central)
- Windsor Castle (Notting Hill Gate)

TOP TEN PUBS FOR FOOD

- The Atlas (West Brompton) – modern
- The Camel (Bethnal Green) – fabulous pies
- Cock Tavern (Farringdon) – meat, loads of it
- Coopers Arms (Sloane Square) – modern and unpretentious
- Czechoslovak National House (West Hampstead) – Czech
- George and Dragon (Acton) – modern pub grub
- The Grapes (Westferry) – fine fish
- The Narrow (Westferry) – modern
- Newman Arms (Goodge Street) – excellent pies
- Princess of Wales (Chalk Farm) – Sunday roast

TOP TEN PUBS FOR WATCHING SPORT

- Alexandra (Clapham Common)
- Carpenters Arms (Marble Arch)
- The Cockpit (Blackfriars)
- Elgin (Ladbroke Grove)
- F3K (Barons Court)
- The Gun (Liverpool Street)
- The Morrison (Fulham)
- Pakenham Arms (Russell Square)
- One Tun (Goodge Street)
- Rob Roy (Edgware Road) – Scotland matches

TOP TEN INTERESTING PUB INTERIORS

- Blackfriar (Blackfriars)
- Cittie of York (Holborn)
- The George Inn (Borough)
- Holly Bush (Hampstead)
- Nag's Head (Knightsbridge)
- Princess Louise (Holborn)
- Seven Stars (Chancery Lane)
- The Warrington Hotel (Maida Vale)
- Ye Olde Cheshire Cheese (Fleet Street)
- Ye Olde Mitre Tavern (Holborn)

TOP TEN PUBS NEAR VISITOR ATTRACTIONS

- Buckingham Palace, The Mall – Buckingham Arms (St James's Park)
- Houses of Parliament, Parliament Sq. – St Stephen's Tavern (Westminster)
- London Eye, South Bank – King's Arms (Southwark)
- London Zoo, Regent's Park – Windsor Castle (Marylebone)
- Old Royal Observatory, Greenwich – Plume of Feathers (Cutty Sark)
- Sir John Soane's Museum, Lincoln's Inn' Fields, Holborn – Seven Stars (Chancery Lane)
- Tate Modern, Bankside – Founders Arms (Blackfriars)
- Tower of London, Tower Hill – Bridge House (Tower Hill)
- Wallace Collection, West End – Golden Eagle (Bond Street)
- Westminster Abbey, Parliament Sq. – Two Chairmen (St James's Park)

TOP TEN PUBS FOR BEER

- Bridge House (Tower Bridge)
- The Castle (Chancery Lane)
- Dovetail Bar (Farringdon)
- Jerusalem Tavern (Farringdon)
- Market Porter (London Bridge)
- Priory Arms (Stockwell)
- Quinns (Camden Road)
- The Rake (London Bridge)
- The Royal Oak (Borough)
- Wenlock Arms (Old Street)

TOP TEN JUKEBOXES

- Boogaloo (Highgate)
- Bradley's Spanish Bar (Tottenham Court Road)
- Good Ship (Kilburn)
- Half Moon (Putney Bridge)
- Mucky Pup (Angel
- New Rose (Angel)
- Prince George (Dalston)
- The Social (Oxford Circus)
- T-Bird (Arsenal)
- Vauxhall Griffin (Vauxhall)

TOP TEN PUBS FOR LIVE MUSIC

- Ain't Nothin' but the Blues Bar (Oxford Circus) – mostly blues
- Filthy McNasty's Whiskey Café (Angel), live music, DJs and poetry
- Golden Eagle (Bond Street), singalong around the Joanna
- The Hare (Bethnal Green) – jazz
- Hope & Anchor (Highbury & Islington), hosted some of the greats
- New Inn (St John's Wood)
- Old Blue Last (Old Street), grubby and loud – just how we like it
- Palm Tree (Mile End), traditional East End music nights
- The Red Cow (Richmond) – rock
- Wenlock Arms (Old Street) – jazz

TOP TEN PUBS FOR QUIZZES

- Charles Dickens (Southwark)
- Cleveland Arms (Paddington)
- Lord Nelson (Island Gardens)
- Nobody Inn (Dalston Kingsland)
- Old Eagle (Camden Town)
- One Tun (Goodge Street)
- Richard I (Greenwich)
- Sutton Arms (Barbican)
- Victoria (Lancaster Gate)
- Wenlock Arms (Old Street)

TOP TEN PUBS FOR GAMES

- Dog and Bell (Deptford) – bar billiards
- The Duchess (Vauxhall) – table footy
- Café Kick (Farringdon) – table footy
- Coborn Arms (Mile End) – darts
- Electricity Showrooms (Old Street) – bar billiards
- Ferry House (Island Gardens) – darts, London Fives
- Intrepid Fox (Tottenham Court Road) – pinball
- Lord Clyde (Borough) – darts
- Owl & Pussycat (Shoreditch) – bar billiards
- Queen's Head (Limehouse DLR) – darts, London Fives

TOP TEN PUBS FOR POOL

- The Banker (Cannon Street)
- Big Red (Holloway Road)
- F3K (Barons Court)
- Good Mixer (Camden Town)
- Hope & Anchor (Highbury & Islington)
- The Horseshoe (Farringdon)
- King's Arms (Chancery Lane)
- King Harold (Leyton)
- The Landor (Clapham North)
- Water Poet (Whitechapel)

The Fancyapint? 2008 pub awards

Each year, around 19 October, we celebrate the anniversary of Fancyapint.com by presenting awards to the best pubs we've visited in the previous twelve months.

These awards showcase the best pubs in London and are a small thank you to all the people who have worked so hard over the year providing an enjoyable drinking experience for everyone. And our visitors' awards are our way of saying thanks on behalf of our users. Millions of people visit Fancyapint.com each year to find the best pubs to visit and, from the feedback we get, it is clear what kind of pubs our visitors enjoy.

The Awards

There are five best London pub awards in each of two categories: the reviewers' awards and the visitors' awards, with overall winners of each.

The reviewers' awards are decided by the Fancyapint.com review team and are based on the pubs reviewed and visited over the past twelve months.

The visitors' awards are based on the most popular pubs on Fancyapint.com. These pubs are not just the most popular reviews seen on the site, they have also had the most visits arranged to them through Fancyapint.com.

There are also a number of special awards made by our reviewers. These special awards are not made every year, but go to the pubs that we feel have performed particularly well in the categories of best newcomer, best refurbishment and most improved. The fifteen awards we have made this year represent the cream of the 3,000+ pubs in our database.

Reviewers' awards

This year, to celebrate the fifth anniversary of our awards, we have created a special, one-off award for our favourite pub over the last five years.

REVIEWERS' SPECIAL AWARD – BEST LONDON PUB OVER THE LAST FIVE YEARS

The Grapes, Limehouse (page 419)

We've known and loved the Grapes for a few decades and, whilst the docks declined and Docklands emerged from the rubble, whilst properties and business roundabout boomed and bust, this pub has quietly and steadfastly maintained the values that make the British pub great. Long may it last.

REVIEWERS' AWARDS

Princess of Wales, Primrose Hill – reviewers' overall winner (page 97)

The Princess of Wales is a relaxed and affable pub – the perfect antidote to the stresses and strains of 21st-century living.

Vauxhall Griffin, Vauxhall (page 406)

The Vauxhall Griffin is one of those rare pubs that successfully appeals to everyone – not an easy thing to do.

King Edward VII, Stratford (page 385)

King Eddie's can be described as a modern pub in an old, old building that demonstrates traditional pub values such as great beer, good food and good service are never out of fashion.

Windsor Castle, Marylebone (page 138)

The Windsor Castle is possibly one of the most idiosyncratic pubs you're likely to come across. It's also one of the friendliest – it's always a pleasure to visit here.

Sir Richard Steele, Primrose Hill (page 98)

The Sir Richard Steele is a characterful and relaxed pub, where you can enjoy good beer with a varied crowd.

BEST RENOVATION

The Princess Louise, Holborn (page 205)

The Princess Louise was already famous for its magnificent interior and the recent renovation has seemingly achieved the impossible and made it even more appealing. This pub has to be on every pub fan's London itinerary.

MOST IMPROVED

North Nineteen, Archway (page 19)

North Nineteen shows that by providing quality food and drink along with unfailingly friendly service you can create a strong community local.

The Duchess, Vauxhall (page 404)

By putting back all the elements which make a great all-round pub, the Duchess has managed to turn around a tired old boozer and entice a mixed crowd of locals.

BEST NEWCOMER

Carpenters Arms, Bethnal Green (page 47)

The Carpenters Arms is a delight; when the old pub closed, we were expecting apartments to go up in its place, but instead we got another pub. And what a pub – great beer and wine, tasteful decor and excellent service. It proves if you get the basics right, you can have a great pub from day one.

Visitors' awards

The Lamb, Holborn – visitors' overall winner (page 344)

It's nice to know our visitors like it as much as we do. For those in the know, it's no surprise that the Lamb regularly receives acclaim – it's a pub that gets everything just right.

Water Poet, Spitalfields (page 361)

Perched 'twixt the City and trendy Shoreditch, the Water Poet appeals to everyone.

King's Arms, Waterloo (page 372)
For the third year in a row the King's Arms has won a visitors' award. The location, ambience and quality of service add up to a pub Fancyapint.com users just can't get enough of.

Prince Regent, Marylebone (page 24)
Informal, relaxed and funky, one of the first pubs to demonstrate that a traditional boozer doesn't have to look old-fashioned.

Counting House, Bank (page 30)
A magnificent banking hall sympathetically converted into a great pub. A splendid place to meet for a social occasion.

Fancyapint? on the move

Technology is changing all the time and we're constantly on the lookout for more ways to bring Fancyapint? to you. As a result, in addition to the super-portable, cordless, battery-free version you're holding, we also have a mobile application and our mobile internet site for your convenience.

Snaptu mobile application

Fancyapint? has partnered with Snaptu to provide the ultimate mobile-phone pub companion. With Snaptu, you can search for a suitable watering hole wherever you are and see what we have to say about it. You can build your own list of favourites, for future reference, or check out the icon index to see what each pub has to offer. And if you want to know more choose 'call pub' to talk directly to the pub.

Click on www.snaptu.com/a/fancyapint to find out more or enter m.snaptu.com into your mobile phone browser and follow the instructions.

This service is free to use, but you should check with your mobile operator to check data tariffs for your phone plan.

And, in addition to the Fancyapint? information, you'll find a selection of free, top-notch next-generation mobile services to help you live the mobile life ... in style!

Fancyapint.mobi

Fancyapint.mobi is a simpler version of the Fancyapint.com. It's designed to be read on small screens, has fewer and smaller graphics and is designed to load and run very quickly. It will run on any mobile phone with a web browser and works especially well on a slow connection. All the pub reviews, ratings, locations and contact details are there, but a lot of the extra information (e.g. maps, comments and features) has been excluded to speed things up.

Either way, along with the book, when you're on the move, it means you don't have to be without your Fancyapint? companion.

Best Bar None

Best Bar None is an award scheme supported by the Home Office aimed at promoting responsible management and operation of licensed premises. Currently running in over eighty locations across the UK, Best Bar None is now being taken up in parts of Europe, USA, New Zealand and Australia.

The composition of each local scheme varies, to meet local needs, but generally is run by partnership of police, local authority and fire safety officials who assess licensed establishments to a national standard. Premises that meet the standard receive a Best Bar None award and there is fierce competition between establishments to achieve the highest scores and gain a 'gold' award. A number of London boroughs – notably Brent (Wembley), Camden and Kensington & Chelsea – now operate Best Bar None schemes, with more starting all the time. Participation is voluntary, not all pubs and bars have the time or resources to take part in the comprehensive assessment, but more and more do apply each year. If you're visiting a borough that operates a Best Bar None scheme, qualified pubs and bars will display a plaque bearing the Best Bar None logo and the year and level of the award.

Here at Fancyapint? we feel anything that helps pubs to improve the way they are managed and operated is a good thing. It encourages improving standards and reassures us, the pub-goers, that we're in a safe and well-run environment. We have supported Best Bar None schemes for the last three years and continue to be involved closely with the scheme on national and local levels.

Best Bar None schemes are generally run annually and at different times of the year depending on the local scheme – the list of qualifying pubs is never static. For this reason we do not label qualified pubs in the book, however, you can find which are Best Bar None pubs on the Fancyapint.com website. You can also find more information about the scheme at www.bestbarnone.com.

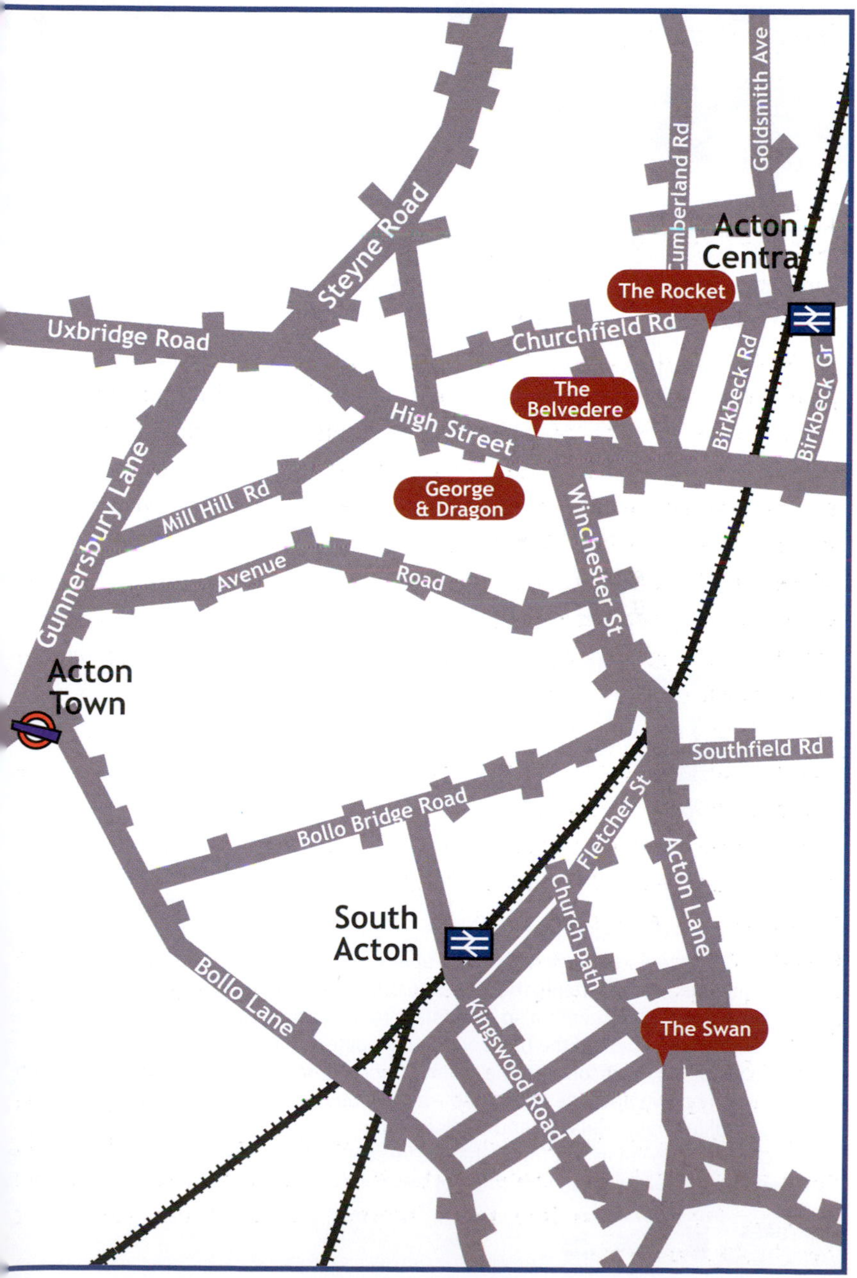

ACTON CENTRAL/ACTON TOWN/SOUTH ACTON

Goldsmith Ave
Cumberland Rd
Acton Central
The Rocket
Steyne Road
Uxbridge Road
Churchfield Rd
Birkbeck Rd
Birkbeck Gr
The Belvedere
High Street
George & Dragon
Gunnersbury Lane
Mill Hill Rd
Winchester St
Avenue Road
Acton Town
Southfield Rd
Bollo Bridge Road
Fletcher St
Acton Lane
Church path
South Acton
Bollo Lane
Kingswood Road
The Swan

The Belvedere

RATING:

106 High Road
W3 6QX

From the flurry of excited articles accompanying the opening of the Belvedere – described as London's first Polish pub – you'd be forgiven for thinking it might feel something like a Polish pub. Unfortunately, it doesn't: the decor is bog-standard pub-chain territory, while the dominating drinks include Carling and Guinness. On the food side of things, the menu is filled with un-Polish fare like Cajun Chicken and Asian Prawns. OK, perhaps we're being slightly unfair – there's Okocim on tap, while a token handful of Polish specialities can be found on the blackboard, but it's hardly out of the ordinary. Sure, there're some Polish staff here, but that's not unique. London boasts at least three or four Eastern European watering holes, but this isn't one of them – it's simply a clean, comfortable, modern, generic pub. One day, we hope to review a genuine Polish free house, rather than reporting on the exploits of a pub company that seems to be claiming the glory with something feeling like a contrived cash-in.

FEATURES: 

The Rocket

RATING: 

11-13 Churchfield Road
W3 6BD
020 8993 6123

When we first reviewed this pub, there were too many shortcomings for us to recommend it, but a change of management and substantial refurbishment has transformed it. The red walls that characterised the old pub and the large bar are still there, but furniture and fittings have been upgraded. The overall effect is simple and sophisticated and complements the food and drink on offer – good beer, decent wine and good, simple food. There's also a separate room for more serious dining, with more than enough people behind the bar, and they're polite and friendly with it. The terrace must be one of the most comfortable of any London pub, with squashy benches under a large awning down one side of the pub – an obvious draw for those who have yet to kick the smoking habit. Relaxed and civilised during the day, we've yet to experience the Rocket in the evening, but from what we've seen it should be good. With the George & Dragon up the road we can now think of two good reasons for visiting Acton.

FEATURES:   

George & The Dragon

RATING:

183 High Street
W3 9DJ
020 8992 3712

The Remarkable Restaurants group run pubs which usually get a good reception on Fancyapint? so we're happy to report their new effort tops them all. After being closed for a while, they were lucky to have taken over a building with a centuries-old history, and they make the most of the opportunity – and who could blame them. We particularly liked the wintry nooks and crannies panelled in dark wood, which features a fantastic 17th-century fireplace, rediscovered after being boarded up for years. None of it, however, feels twee or overbearing and for contrast there's also a bright and airy back room, its high ceilings tempered with a couple of art nouveau statues and a huge mural. Indeed, every aspect of the décor is well thought out and designed – as is the food, which was top notch. It was also nice to be served by people who actually seemed to be having a good time working – a rarity these days. This pub illustrates that, when thought and time are put into a pub, the results speak for themselves. This is, hands down, the best pub in Acton or indeed the surrounding area.

FEATURES:    

The Swan

1 Evershed Walk, 119 Acton Lane
W4 5HH
020 8994 8262

The Swan is an example of how to do a gastropub properly – that is don't shout about it. No tablecloths, eating-only areas or reserved signs here – just a pleasant, wood-panelled pub which happens to make a deal about its good food. Apart from the small kitchen hatch off to one side, this is a normal, chilled-out local where we were able easily to enjoy ourselves with one of their well-kept ales; we even spied a drinking bowl by the door indicating dogs were welcome. Its position on a back street between South Acton and Chiswick means it's predominantly one for the locals, but it probably attracts fans from further afield too, judging by the lack of free seats by 8pm on a Tuesday night. A gastropub which places as much emphasis on the 'pub' as the 'gastro' has to be applauded and, even if the food is a little expensive, this is still a good-quality pub worth stopping for.

FEATURES:   

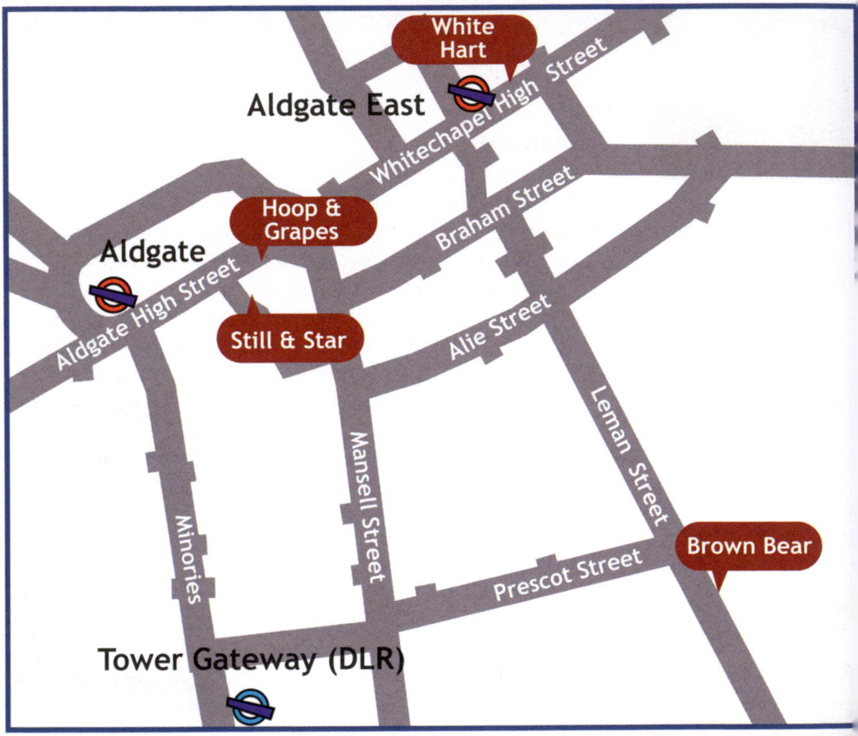

White Hart
Aldgate East
Whitechapel High Street
Hoop & Grapes
Aldgate
Aldgate High Street
Braham Street
Still & Star
Alie Street
Leman Street
Mansell Street
Minories
Brown Bear
Prescot Street
Tower Gateway (DLR)

Brown Bear

RATING:

139 Leman Street
E1 8EY
020 7481 3792

You'll be hard pressed to find much of Aldgate that hasn't been turned over and relaunched, but in amongst the warehouse flat conversions you'll find the Brown Bear – an unpretentious pub seemingly untouched by modern pub trends. Of note on our visit were a good range of real ales (nothing too out of the ordinary, but all decently kept), a dart board and a very easy-going atmosphere. The most modern touch was an MP3 jukebox on random, but even that didn't disrupt things too much (it added to the charm, if anything). This one feels like it hasn't changed much in years – an increasingly rare thing in this part of town.

FEATURES:    

HANDY FOR: Whitechapel Gallery

Hoop & Grapes

RATING:

47 Aldgate High Street
EC3N 1AL
020 7481 4583

Thanks to careless bakers and the Luftwaffe, this is one of a very tiny number of medieval timber-framed buildings – the pub claims it's the only one – left in the City. It's changed hands over the years, but never quite served up a pub experience to match its undoubted heritage. Its latest incarnation is as part of the Nicholson's brand, and the resultant 'historical' adjustment to the furnishings – some Chesterfield sofas here, a couple of chandeliers there – have helped to produce a better pub than many of the others that have stood on this site over the last 20 or so years. It's a rather safe and sound pub all told – regular beers and pub grub available – but it's also an instance where a move to the Nicholson's chain has helped rather than hindered.

HANDY FOR: Whitechapel Gallery

Still & Star

RATING: 

1 Little Somerset Street
E1 8AH
020 7702 2899

Tiny, rather quaint pub that becomes a haven for a mixed bunch of punters post clocking off. It would be unremarkable in other parts of town but in this location becomes something more rare and precious as the years go by. It's a solid, traditional old boozer – the sort of place that folk take for granted until it closes, then they start complaining. We've already lost too many of them so give this one a look if you're passing, before it's too late. Open at the usual City hours, for beer, banter and sausage rolls from the hot plate.

FEATURES: 

HANDY FOR: Whitechapel Gallery

White Hart

RATING:

89 Whitechapel High Street
E1 7RA
020 7247 1546

This pub has had its ups and downs over the years, but it's still going strong. Even though the pub was opened up a little (with the removal of a partition wall some time ago), the unwritten rule of City types in the back and local drunks in the front seems still to be observed – at least during the day. (We usually end up in the front part, there are often fewer people there.) The service is OK, the beer on offer is pretty decent, although only two of the six hand pumps were in operation and your wine-drinking companions may find choice limited. It's a relief from the bravado of many of the nearby City pubs, the grimness of some of the other local hostelries and the relentless trendiness of Shoreditch. It's open at the weekends too, just keep an eye out for the odd Ripper tour or two, interspersed with a handful of Hoxtonites.

FEATURES:  

HANDY FOR: Whitechapel Gallery, Petticoat Lane Market

The Resolute

RATING: 

210 Poplar High St
E14 0BB
020 7987 1429

It's nice to know that not all pubs in Poplar have slipped into no-go local zones. The Resolute is a well-kept house with friendly staff and bantering punters; any night of the week it's an amiable place, but, on a Saturday early-evening visit, the place was just kicking off and the lively atmosphere made us want to stay. There's decent ale on the hand pumps, including the not so easy to find (nowadays) Tetleys plus Adnam's. There'll probably be sport on at least one of the TVs (there are five of them plus a projector, sometimes showing different sports on each), but that doesn't detract from the air of conviviality. One question though – we can understand an East End pub having darts trophies in its cabinet, but how on earth did they get the one for golf around here?

FEATURES:  

HANDY FOR: Museum in Docklands

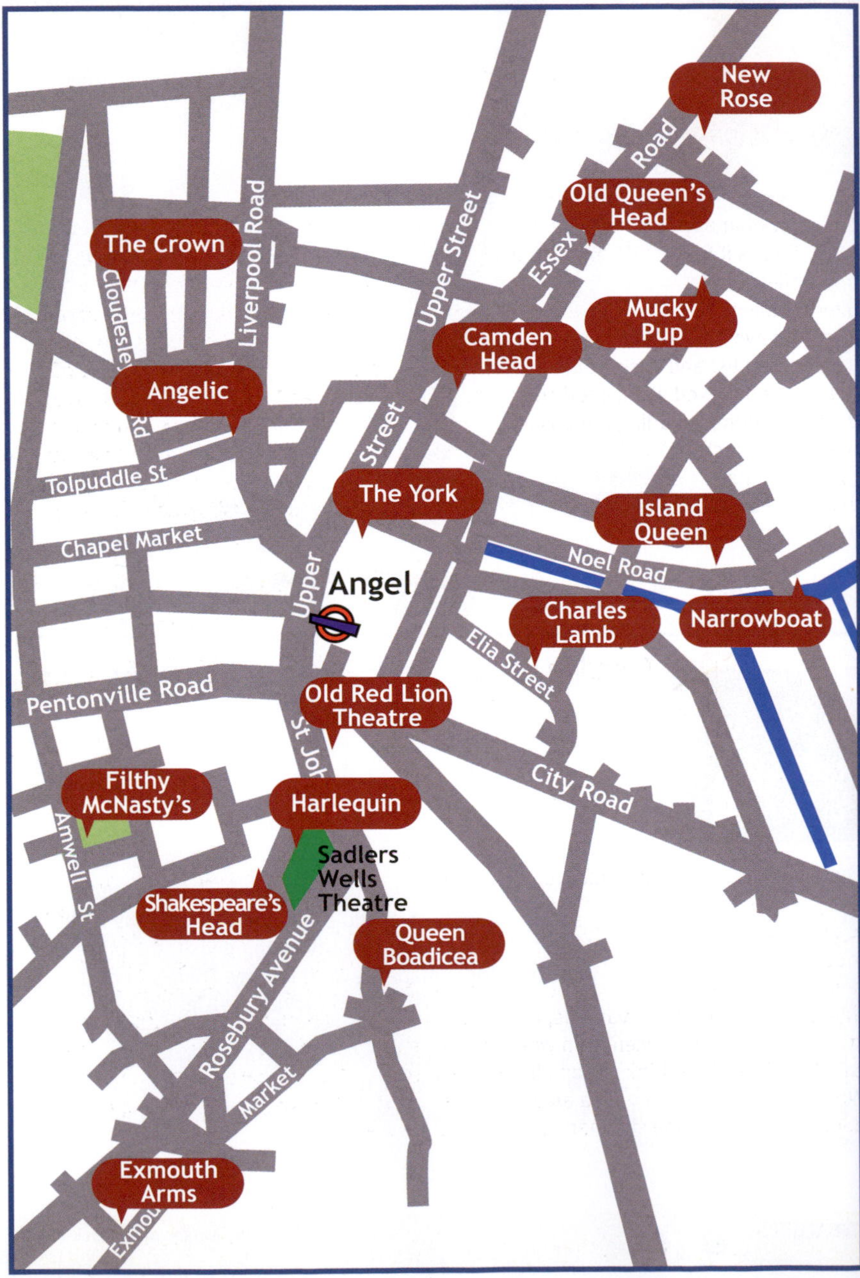

New Rose
Old Queen's Head
Mucky Pup
The Crown
Camden Head
Angelic
The York
Island Queen
Charles Lamb
Narrowboat
Old Red Lion Theatre
Filthy McNasty's
Harlequin
Shakespeare's Head
Queen Boadicea
Exmouth Arms
Angel
Sadlers Wells Theatre
Road
Essex
Upper Street
Liverpool Road
Cloudesley Rd
Tolpuddle St
Chapel Market
Street
Upper
Noel Road
Elia Street
Pentonville Road
St John
City Road
Amwell St
Rosebury Avenue
Market
Exmou

The Angelic

RATING: 3

57 Liverpool Road
N1 0RJ
020 7837 5370

This gastrobar apparently works, as it's usually busy – even on Saturday afternoons. In a lot of ways it feels more like a club inside than a pub. Maybe it's the comfy sofas, the high ceilings or the iron circular staircase descending into hell... the dungeon... the dimly lit toilets (and they are – though we were slightly worried about the door marked 'gimps' down there). That said, it still manages to have decent beer on to go with the decent wine list and cocktail menu. The food's good quality, if a bit pricey – the rib of beef for two looked like a good choice for the carnivores, and there's quite a selection to choose from, including a Tapas menu. The clientele in the evenings are a good mix of people just chillin' and having a few drinks and those that actually feel a bit peckish the food. It has a very 'grown-up' feel to it, a bit of class which doesn't pander to youfs getting smashed on alcopops. It's a refreshing oasis from normal Islington pub life and a little off the beaten track, which is probably why it's the way it is.

FEATURES:     

HANDY FOR: Business Design Centre

Camden Head

RATING: 3

2 Camden Walk
N1 8DY
020 7359 0851

The Camden Head is an attractive, ornate and well-preserved Victorian pub tucked away amongst the antiques shops of Islington and has been thoroughly reliable for as long as we can remember. There are a couple of ales on tap, some average pub fare food and a good mix of punters. It's also a pub well known for the comedy nights it hosts upstairs on numerous days of the week. One of the first to do the 'pub comedy' thing, the quality can be variable, but choose the right acts on the right night and it's still great. With a late licence on weekends, it can also provide a good place for a last couple of late-night drinks as an alternative to some other (louder) nearby venues. While a lot of pubs in the area are losing their heads in the quest for a more upmarket demographic, this one still manages to stay the same.

FEATURES:   

HANDY FOR: Business Design Centre

The Charles Lamb

RATING:

16 Elia Street
N1 8DE
020 7837 5040

The Charles Lamb boasts a good back-street setting and a distinctly French influence and feels pretty continental, all in all. Having kept the original two-room layout, old advertising signs are scattered about and flowers and candles adorn the tables. Add a great choice of ales on the hand pumps along with bottles of St Peter's Organic Best and Breton cider and it all seems rather idyllic. We've commented on its diminutive size before, but they seem to have addressed the crowding issues – it feels like a lot of bars on the continent. Its popularity does mean that getting a seat can be difficult at times, but it's worth the effort for the beer alone. And if you're feeling peckish, the lamb pasty is spot on for a snack – it is a snack, we could easily have eaten two of them when we were there last. The only confusion we've got is that, with so many continental influences, it still calls itself a 'traditional pub'. Nonetheless, it's worth a look.

FEATURES:     

HANDY FOR: Sadler's Wells Theatre

The Crown

RATING:

116 Cloudesley Road
N1 0EB
020 7837 7107

One of Fuller's more upmarket efforts and clearly aiming at the N1 demographic, this is a grand Victorian pub in a very picturesque part of Barnsbury. Apart from the blander back lounge room, much of the ornate decoration remains, with plenty of etched glass and dark-wood panels in evidence. If you're lucky enough to grab the seats in front of it, there's even a real fire for the winter evenings. Add to this a great selection of international bottled beers, mostly Fuller's beers on the hand pumps – the excellent London Porter was on last time we were in – plus a pretty extensive wine list. It gets hard to fault the place. The service is good and the well-made food is deservedly popular, though the chips we ordered last time were a bit on the soggy side. Even with the perfectly acceptable Islington Tap and Albion both a few minutes away, it's still easily the best of the lot and, unlike some other pubs in the area, isn't remotely pretentious. Recommended.

FEATURES:   

HANDY FOR: Business Design Centre

Exmouth Arms

RATING: 3

23 Exmouth Market
EC1R 4QR
020 7837 5622

Here's a pub that has completely failed to get with the programme. There's nowhere to plug in your iPod for a start and you have to leave your skateboard outside. The people playing darts in the back appeared not to be doing so ironically. There was no absinthe behind the bar either. It's stubbornly persisting as a high-street boozer. Disgraceful. And a blessed relief. It's not too busy, there are no frills and no gimmicks, except for very good ale (Harvey's Sussex), and the service is prompt and friendly. Most of the punters look like they've been there all day and don't see any compelling reason why they should go home either. For anyone else trying to avoid home it is good to know that the Exmouth stays opens until 1:30am. A refuge for those who just can't keep up with modern life (which Damon Albarn always told us was rubbish anyway).

FEATURES:     

HANDY FOR: Sadler's Wells Theatre

Filthy McNasty's

RATING: 4

68 Amwell Street
EC1R 1UU
020 7837 6067

Any pub that has pulled a pint for Nick Cave can't be doing much wrong. A short stagger to Angel tube, Filthy McNasty's is a bit of a hidden gem in the cesspit of Islington theme and chain bars. Offering a cracking range of whiskies, as well as the ubiquitous Guinness and Caffrey's, McNasty's offers welcome relief from the cold winter evenings with a homely red interior (well, homely if you reside in a bordello), comfy chairs, slouchy sofas you'll want to nod off on, and in summer it's got plenty of outside tables for you to enjoy your pint. A range of Thai food is available during the week, and roasts on Sundays keep you well fed. A lively events programme offers gigs, DJ nights and book launches, readings and even the odd poetry slamdown.

FEATURES:  

HANDY FOR: Sadler's Wells Theatre

Harlequin

RATING:

27 Arlington Way
EC1R 1UY
020 7837 9035

This pub, being next to Sadler's Wells, used to be the haunt of the backstage techies and members of the orchestra escaping from the theatre. There even used to be a phone from the backstage area. Sadly, with the demolition of the old theatre, some of that character seems to have gone, but it hasn't really changed otherwise. Never mind though, it's friendly and far enough off Islington's main drag to be very civilised, and the last refurb didn't hurt it, either. It's got regular ales on the taps, including Timothy Taylor's Landlord and Black Sheep, and the food looks good too – seasonal home-made pies are definitely something to look forward to. Combined with a welcoming landlady, friendly regulars, board games like Jenga and Connect 4, great music and occasional DJ nights, this one is definitely worth going out of your way for – and practically perfect if you're going to see a show at Sadler's Wells.

FEATURES:          

Island Queen

RATING:

87 Noel Road
N1 8HD
020 7704 7631

After a long period in the wilderness, the Island Queen's decline was reversed a few years back when Mitchells & Butlers took the time, care and patience to make this a pub to be proud of. The beer line-up is up to the good usual M&B standard: Pride, Landlord and Deuchars on the hand pumps, with Kolsch, Fruli, Leffe, Hoegaarden, Staropramen etc all on draft. The wine list is small but perfectly formed, whilst the food is good, standard upmarket pub fare. Architecturally, it's fantastic here – high ceilings, etched glass and dark, worn wood are the hallmarks of this quality establishment. The pub's popularity makes it tricky to find a seat at the usual times – Friday after work is particularly bad – but upstairs hosts extra seating to take the strain. It's in need of a lick of paint now, though; we're not sure why they changed the previous exterior of black and gilding to an odd shade of badly sun-faded red instead, but they did. Still, this is certainly a grand pub that we at Fancyapint? can heartily recommend.

FEATURES:    

HANDY FOR: Business Design Centre

Mucky Pup

RATING:

39 Queen's Head Street
N1 8NQ
020 7226 2572

The Mucky Pup was a lovely surprise when it opened a few years back and after a change of ownership last year we can happily report that the factors that made this pub stand out from its local competition remain. Along with beers kept in good nick and a free jukebox featuring some wonderfully left-field selections (The Jesus Lizard, Melvins, Can), the pool table and dart board in the back room provide good distractions. As the jukebox hints, the pub has moved in a somewhat alternative direction and Sunday's post-rock, post-punk and psyche music night provides a wonderfully esoteric foray into the outer reaches of music. With a late licence, mixed crowd and a bijou back garden, what we said of the old pub still applies: it's the sort of boozer you want to keep just for you and your mates.

FEATURES:         

The Narrowboat

RATING: 

119 St Peter's Street
N1 8PZ
020 7288 0572

After a refit a while back, it wasn't exactly surprising to discover that the Narrowboat now featured stripped floorboards and leather sofas. Still, it's not overdone and large windows give an airy feel to the place, as well as offering views straight from an estate agent's brochure of the canal. On tap are up to four real ales and emerging from the kitchen is a plentiful supply of tasty and reasonably priced modern pub grub. Two screens at the front and back of the pub mean the sport is never far away, though on the evidence of our last visit not too many punters involve themselves with the efforts of the Premiership's finest. The one final bonus is that on a warm summer's day you can go and relax outside on the canal path – just watch out for the kamikaze cyclists. A consistently solid effort in a pub crawl-able stretch of N1 that we've yet to have a bad time in.

FEATURES:    

HANDY FOR: Business Design Centre

New Rose

RATING: 

84–86 Essex Road
N1 8LU
020 7226 1082

This has settled into a decent pub after starting out as a trendy Essex Road bar – still sporting the name of our favourite Damned tune. The moody interior's not changed, still lots of exposed brick, candles and uplighters; if anything, it's just a bit more worn in. And the toilet signs however, titled 'George' and 'Mildred' are probably a joke lost on anyone under 25. Good beer and friendly service seem to be making sure the locals come back, and they are. It's a good place to watch the footy on their big screens, and the pizzas on offer look and smell fantastic. It's worth a look if you're in the area and miles better than some around it. We're fascinated by the name of its film club – The Cosmic Film club – so we'll have to pop along and see what that's all about.

FEATURES:     

HANDY FOR: Business Design Centre

Old Queen's Head

RATING:

44 Essex Road
N1 8LN
020 7354 9993

This one has changed in some ways, in others not at all – it's much the same sort of clientele it had when we first came here, it's just that it's more trendified than it used to be. Now that's not a bad thing, and it's obvious the punters like it here and we can see why. It's comfortable and pretty friendly, with a selection of lager and wine and cocktail lists that compete pretty well with nearby bars – and no, it hasn't really got much beer to speak of, barring Guinness and John Smith's. The antler chandelier over the massive (and original as far as we can tell) fireplace gives it a somewhat eclectic feel, but which fits well with the comfy sofas. There is a small patio area out the back that usually hosts smokers, but is a nice place to be in good weather, if you can avoid the smoke. There's a good food menu and plenty of seating – essentially it's a good, laid-back pub. With the benefit of a late licence, the upstairs frequently plays host to an interesting selection of live music along with various DJs, with an entry fee when something interesting is happening later in the evening. Also be warned – our recent night-time weekend visit found queues to get in, which is a clue to how busy it can get in here.

FEATURES:        

Old Red Lion Theatre Club

RATING:

418 St John Street
EC1V 4NJ
020 7837 7816

The ideal spot to sink your life savings in producing and premiering the play wot you wrote – and then drown your sorrows on the proceeds of the handful of tickets you actually managed to sell. The little theatre upstairs probably seats no more than 50 but is a lively, vibrant venue. Some great stuff and some mind-blowing rubbish gets put on there. The whole place has a theatrical, arty air but it is also a first-class local boozer. So you'll find the bottle-nosed middle managers from the big offices across the road necking it down at one end of the bar while actor wannabes giggle and shrill down the other – all interspersed with locals of all types enjoying the draft Pride, Broadside, Abbot, Leffe and Staropramen. The décor could come from a set-designer's template – that heavy old embossed wallpaper with generations of dull-red (for the walls) and essence of nicotine (for the ceiling) paint layers, comfortable benches running round, a scattering of tables and chairs and plenty of space for those who prefer to stand and bray at one another.

FEATURES:    HANDY FOR: Sadler's Wells Theatre

Queen Boadicea

RATING: 

292-294 St John Street
EC1V 4PA
020 7354 9993

This one's settled in nicely under new management. We're rather taken with the ship's figurehead of the warrior Queen that looms over the entrance and the exposed exterior tilework positively glows. True, it is almost identical to its sister pub, the Old Queen's Head on Essex Road, with a similar deficit of choice behind the bar: Guinness, Kronenbourg and John Smith's are hardly a cause for excitement these days. The atmosphere, though, does help make up for things, pulling in a mixed crowd of local workers, local, er, locals and students from City University across the road. The menu does look good and reasonably priced. It's also got a private bar at the back, called the Stag's Head Room (for obvious reasons), which can be hired, and there are regular music nights with DJs to look forward to. While not a great one for beer, this one is doing well with the local community – and you could do a lot worse.

FEATURES:       HANDY FOR: Sadler's Wells Theatre

Shakespeare's Head

RATING: 4

1 Arlington Way
EC1R 1XA
020 7837 2581

Going by the exterior, it's easy to write this one off as a grim estate pub, but actually crossing the threshold reveals not a fight over the pool table but a friendly boozer, decorated with signed photos of numerous thespians. The traditional pub grub on offer may not be too tempting to the dancers of Sadler's Wells Theatre over the road, but it caught our eye. There's some decent beers, great service, a sleepy pub cat, friendly punters (sometimes too friendly) and a lovely beer garden out the back. It's a singular little place that stands out from the average modern-day pub.

FEATURES:   

HANDY FOR: Sadler's Wells Theatre

The York

RATING: 3

82 Islington High Street
N1 8EQ
020 7247 5163

One of the few proper pubs left on Islington's main drag, it's now a Nicholson's and does everything to the standards we've come to expect from them. The beer is good – Pride, Bombardier and guests on the many hand pumps, supported by a decent wine list and the usual spirits – and it's promptly and pleasantly served. It's a big pub, so there's usually plenty of room, although it does get crowded at the times you'd expect: towards the end of the week and especially after the antique market closes. There are a few screens dotted around the place, so it's also a popular spot for watching sport and, as it's almost the closest pub to Angel tube, it is a favourite meeting place, before heading north up Upper Street. It's a decent pub, when it's not overly crowded. However, unlike most of the clientele, we don't feel the outside seating is particularly enticing – unless you're really into NO_x, particulates and avant-garde poetry (as practised by some of the local street residents).

FEATURES:   

HANDY FOR: Business Design Centre

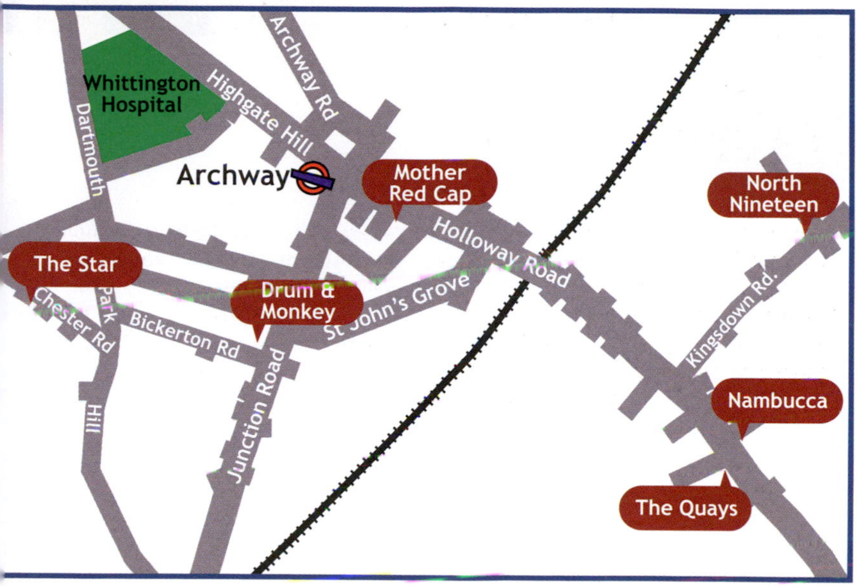

Drum & Monkey

RATING: 3/5

86 Junction Road
N19 5QZ
020 7281 2414

In days gone by, we could imagine this might have been a rather terrifying place for the uninitiated. Inside it's an unreconstructed locals pub, with predominantly Irish, predominantly male clientele. The people seemed friendly enough and the service was certainly agreeable. A recent refurbishment hasn't ripped the heart out of this pub, as they have simply painted the old wooden features white, added in a couple of couches, some plants and one of those infinite choice jukeboxes (we were thankful those choosing the songs on our visit had good taste). Jazz, DJs and comedy nights all feature at various points during the month, showing what pubs can offer if they put their minds to it. If nothing else, it's worth popping in for a couple of pints of the black stuff and to look back into the mists of time to see how pubs used to be, refurbishment notwithstanding. It also acts well as a respite and counterbalance to the studied, stilted cool of the St John's Tavern over the road.

FEATURES:     

Mother Red Cap

RATING:

665 Holloway Road
N19 5SE
020 7263 7082

Curtains drawn, door shut. From the outside it's easy to assume the worst, lump this one in with Holloway's hardcore Irish boozers and walk past. Fear not though, step inside and you'll be hit by a glorious pub interior: wall mirrors, intricate tile work, fitted banquettes – the full Victorian Monty. The stark exterior probably puts a few off but when we last looked in there was still a fairly wide representation of N19 filling this one up. What with a pool table, darts, enough screens for the sport (oh, and a decent drop of Guinness) it's easy to see why. There's regular live music upstairs in Phelan's Bar, too. Throw in friendly and efficient staff and you have one of the best pubs in the area. Seems it's been that way for a while...

FEATURES:     

Nambucca

RATING: 

596 Holloway Road
N7 6LB
020 7272 7366

Nambucca, sitting on a fairly unremarkable stretch of Holloway Road, appears at first glance to lack many distinctive features. It is, though, not the decor which attracts the punters but the variety and quality of music on offer. You're guaranteed a live performance every night over the weekend and regularly during the week too, including the twice-monthly Wonk Wednesdays, with DJs providing additional entertainment. Depending on when you visit it could be anything from indie, electro, rock or hip-hop that provides the soundtrack to your night. It seems the Holloways make fairly regular appearances too, but perhaps that is no surprise considering it's where they formed the band. The stage is at the back of the pub on a raised area, with well-worn sofas at the front. Of course, depending on the day and time, there may be a charge for entry.

FEATURES:    

North Nineteen

RATING:   

194-196 Sussex Way
N19 4HZ
020 7281 2786

A pleasant refurbished pub off the Holloway Road. The post-war building is attractive enough and the refurbishment considerate: two separate bars remain, while a back area with heavy flock wallpaper adds character. Stripped floorboards – stock in trade of any refurb – give a light and airy, but not unpleasant feeling. Being sandwiched between council estates and Holloway's Victorian flatshareland, there was a genuinely (and surprisingly) mixed crowd. It helps that both the landlord and everyone else who works there are consummate hosts and clearly trying their best to make this a comfortable pub. There's a tasty, home-made menu on offer and usually a couple of ales on, as well as regular music nights. A recent mini-ale festival also seemed to be successful. Due to its location we wonder if this place will receive the wider audience it deserves, but for the time being, the residents of N19 have a cracking community local on their hands.

FEATURES:          

Reviewers' Award – Most Improved 2008

The Quays

RATING: 

471 Holloway Road
N7 6LE
020 7272 3634

The exterior of The Quays is certainly interesting. Views are blocked by shelves of old bottles, while uplighters illuminate walls in a tacky alternating spectrum of colour. The interior is unusual, with three areas, including a front bar adorned with etched mirrors and ornate woodwork, a balcony bar and a back section featuring a huge ten-foot screen. Coupled with two plasma screens it verged on 'sports bar' territory, but also has regular live music and DJs – apparently until 4 in the morning on weekends. On our last visit it was fairly quiet barring a few regulars and friendly staff. Conversely, on weekend nights a young crowd descends and it gets lively, as it does when big matches are shown. Ultimately, this pub appeals to different people at different times for different reasons – so time your visit well. The only thing that put us off was the sign on the door exhorting us to 'remove all hats' before entering.

FEATURES:    

The Star

RATING:

47 Chester Road
N19 5DF
020 7263 9067

The previous incarnation of the Star was a particularly unwelcoming boozer, but a change of ownership gave the place a new lease of life. Even better, the change hasn't transformed it into a pseudo-restaurant: its still a bona fide pub. Thought has been put into the renovation and many original features have been kept, such as the tilework next to the bar. Exposed brickwork is complemented with understated wood panelling and we also spied a real fireplace crackling away. There's a trio of very well-kept ales, a good wine list and an interesting-looking daily menu, complemented by a fantastic jukebox worth exploring and a gravelled back garden. A TV lurks in a little nook next to the bar, with capacity for about a half-dozen punters. It's not the cheapest place, but we guess that's the price you pay for the overheads of a 'proper' freehouse. Our visits have found friendly staff looking after a scattering of locals, happy – and possibly surprised – to have a good pub in their neighbourhood.

FEATURES:   

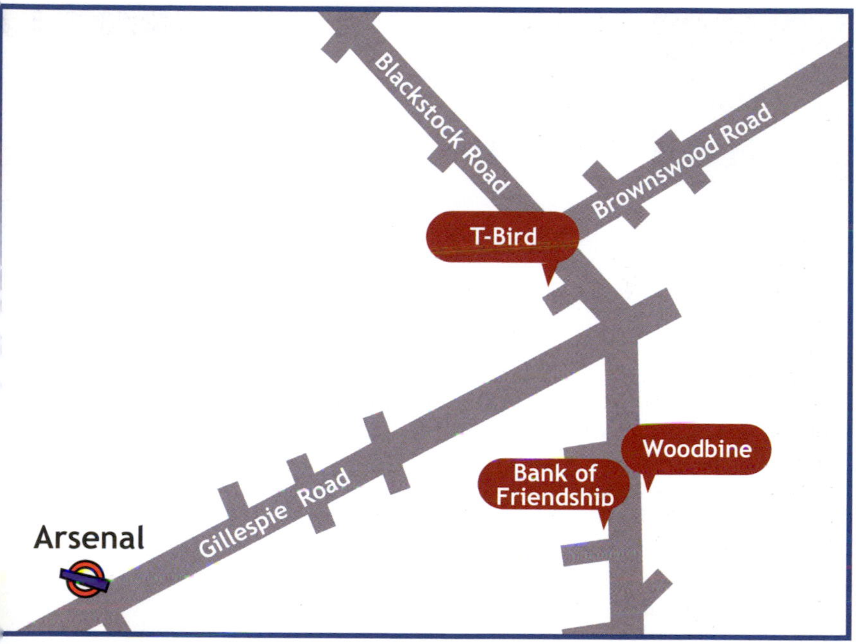

Blackstock Road
Brownswood Road
T-Bird
Woodbine
Bank of Friendship
Gillespie Road
Arsenal

Bank of Friendship

RATING: 3 pints

224 Blackstock Road
N4 3NG

It's always a pleasure to have a drink at this venerable boozer. There are no quiz machines or one-armed bandits to spoil enjoyment of fine draught Guinness, so those who prefer conversation to noise will be at home here. The place has a relaxed and friendly atmosphere and, unlike the nearby Arsenal Tavern or Gunners pubs, is not generally frequented by beery football fans. It can still get extremely busy on match days and seems to do a fairly brisk trade at other times. The coal fires are really cosy on winter days, and a nice rear terrace opens during the summer months. When you come here, just make sure Arsenal aren't playing at home.

T-Bird

RATING:

132 Blackstock Road
N4 2DX
020 7503 6202

Finsbury Park can offer a lot more than old man's boozers these days (though is still well served in that department), which means T-Bird doesn't stand out as much as when it first arrived. Comfortably worn sofas nestle with an assortment of other chairs to make this long, thin venue appear less like a corridor, but unless you get a seat it is hard to find anywhere to stand out of the way – especially with the smoking ban increasing traffic through the middle. The décor probably needs a bit of a lift now and the beer selection shows a distinct lack of imagination unless extra-cold bland lager is your tipple of choice, though we still think it's worth a visit. The jukebox has an indie flavour, and is free on a Monday, while regular DJ slots and open mic nights provide further stimulation for your ears. Hopefully the comedy night we stumbled upon a couple of years ago is no longer a regular feature – we were almost reduced to hammering rusty nails into our eyeballs to escape the pain.

FEATURES:  

Woodbine

RATING:

215 Blackstock Road
N5 2LL
020 7354 1061

The Woodbine, with its chandeliers, mirrors and swish wallpaper, offers a rather different drinking experience to the nearby Gunners haunts. Perhaps the owners think that, with Arsenal's move down the road, there is room for a different sort of crowd. Certainly catch it when there's not a match on and you may (as we have) stop off for longer than you expect. There's a decent selection of drinks including Leffe and Staropramen, while there's a decent jukebox should you feel the need to part with your hard-earned change. A screen at the back keeps you informed of sporting developments but this one feels the sort of place you could easily pass the time in without recourse to Sky Sports News. Its look and feel may seem par for the course in London nowadays, but add it to the T-Bird, Bank of Friendship and even the King's Head and you'll find that Blackstock Road's got itself a pleasant little pub crawl. Now serves Thai food.

FEATURES:  

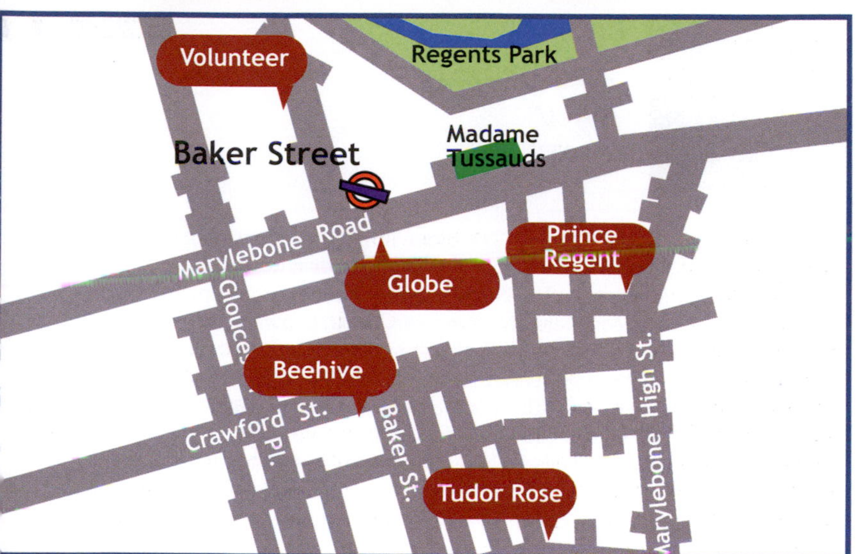

The Beehive

RATING: 3/3

126 Crawford Street
W1U 6BF
020 7487 4863

This pub's been closed for the best part of two years now and its latest incarnation on reopening is something of a shock – it's gone upmarket. And gone is the operative word. Gone is the sticky carpet. Gone are the cosy booths and pub tables. Gone are the tellys. Gone is the massive bar in the centre of the room. Gone... well, you get the picture. It's altogether more an eating place with drink, though not necessarily in a bad way – they apparently brew their own beer, Beehive Ale, and have a selection of beers from Greenwich's Meantime available too. We say 'apparently', as it was off when we were in last – we'll have to pop in another time to try it. Interestingly, the wine list is all French – not a new-world wine in evidence. The menu's an interesting cross of traditional and modern cooking with a selection of mezes and Thai fishcakes (very nice) amongst the choices. Don't get us wrong, the old Beehive had it's good points, but this one has its merits, too. Being asked if you're eating or drinking when you come through the door could be a bit off-putting, particularly as the drinkers appeared to be exiled to the back corner behind the bar. That said, the staff are very friendly and table service is a very continental way to be.

FEATURES:     HANDY FOR: Madame Tussauds, Wallace Collection

The Globe

RATING:

43 Marylebone Road
NW1 5JY
020 7935 6368

How prescient of someone to build The Globe in 1735. And how patient to wait a century and a half and more for Baker Street tube to be constructed underneath and thus create the meeting point for Wembley-goers just two stops up the Metropolitan line. With the stadium complete, this place can switch in a moment from commuters' beer-stop to heavy metal heaven or reds'r'us, depending on the North London schedule. But the place copes. It's unpretentious and businesslike. Dickens, William Pitt (the younger, of course) and Conan Doyle are claimed as past regulars. Decent, honest plain tables and chairs, oldish floorboards and panelling, and well-kept beers make for a pleasant enough West End oasis. There are tables outside for those who want copious carbon monoxide and ear-shattering traffic noise with their beer. It's easy to mock (no it's not really; we work at it) but The Globe has been getting it more or less right for nearly two centuries and shows no signs of getting it substantially wrong.

FEATURES:     

HANDY FOR: Madame Tussauds

Prince Regent

RATING: 

71 Marylebone High Street
W1U 5JN
020 7467 3811

The last refit put a fair bit of the Victorian charm back in, albeit with a twist. Another pub in the growing number of Mitchells & Butlers pubs in London to be remodelled, this one's interior now matches up fairy lights, frilly brollies and chandeliers with soft furnishings and dark-wood walls. As with other M&B pubs, it heavily promotes continental beers, though there are some good traditional English ales on tap too. The pub food is decent – there's plenty of it and there's something for all appetites, but it doesn't dominate, like it does in so many pubs nowadays. The overall effect of this one is of an elegant and swish drinking den, with the 'Opium Lounge' taking this notion even further. Add live music and it shows that you can modernise a pub yet avoid turning it into a bare-boarded gastropub or an over-designed style bar. We're impressed and, with The Prince Regent's newfound popularity with the locals, it seems that the Mitchells & Butlers' formula is a winner.

FEATURES:      

Visitors' Award Winner 2008

Tudor Rose

RATING:

44 Blandford Street
W1U 7HS
020 7935 5963

This one's not changed in years, which probably means it's due for demolition and reincarnation as a block of horrible and expensive flats. It's not a bad place at all, with decent beer on the hand pumps and proper pub grub served downstairs (upstairs there's a restaurant) including such delights as Spam fritters. Being in a Marylebone backwater, this place hardly ever gets crowded, although there's a weekday lunchtime trade, so, if you need a place for a quiet pint in the area, this place will do nicely. The service is prompt and friendly and the prices are par for the area. Whilst you wouldn't make a special effort to seek this place out, if you're in the locale, do drop in. Oh, except on a Sunday – it's closed.

FEATURES:   

HANDY FOR: Madame Tussauds, Wallace Collection

Volunteer

RATING: 

247 Baker Street
NW1 6XE
020 7486 4090

Just a few doors down from 221b, you'd expect The Volunteer to be a pub in honour of Conan Doyle's detective. It's not (you have to go to Charing Cross for that). A few years back when we first reviewed this one, we had it pigeon-holed as 'a seemingly nondescript pub' and, though it still has an unassuming exterior, the inside has been altered to something rather more extravagant. All leather settles and beaded curtains, this pub is one of the growing number owned by the Mitchells & Butlers group that opts for a loungey décor and a drink selection heavy on the Belgian beers. The changes suggest a growing market for the high-powered brews of the Low Countries. But the more we visit places like The Volunteer, with their ever-so slightly contrived feel (M&B also own the All Bar One, O'Neill's and Scream chains), the more we're sensing some clever branding and marketing at work. We've not got a problem with the quality food and drink, it's just the thought of a massive warehouse filled with beaded curtains and leather pouffes (à la the O'Neill's sheds ready to dispatch potato sacks and road signs to bars from Buenos Aires to Beijing) that gives us the fear. But if you can put such thoughts out of your mind you'll have a fine time at this one.

FEATURES:  

HANDY FOR: Madame Tussauds, Wallace Collection

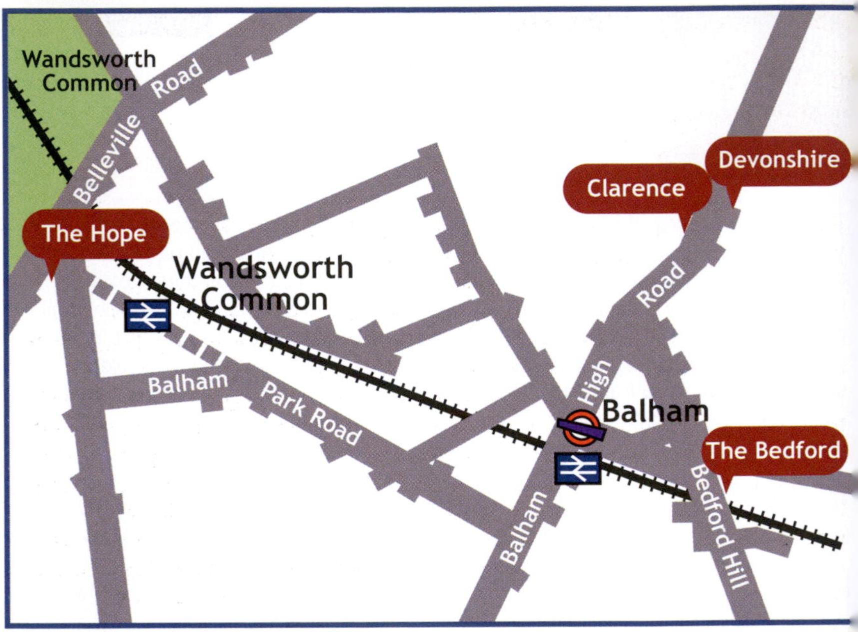

Wandsworth Common
Road
Belleville
The Hope
Wandsworth Common
Devonshire
Clarence
Road
High
Balham
Balham Park Road
The Bedford
Bedford Hill
Balham

The Bedford

RATING:

77 Bedford Hill
SW12 9HD
020 8682 8940

The Bedford is big. In another world it could be an army barracks. A huge slab of a building containing a ballroom, a theatre, umpteen function rooms, various bars, stairs, half landings and various mysterious doors. A bartender could probably work downstairs and never meet the upstairs employees. And this is so much more than just a place to drink in – although the choice isn't bad with up to half a dozen real ales promised and food is available. There was a play on in the theatre the night we were in and regular comedy and cabaret nights are on offer, too. Young, vibrant and lively is, for once, an accurate description – and, although we are not quite sure why, it seems to be summed up by the bicycles double and triple banked and chained to the railings outside. Not a place for the quiet contemplative pint and a relaxed chat but if you want full-on entertainment, noise and activity look no further.

FEATURES:      

The Clarence

RATING: 

90–92 Balham High Road
SW12 9AG
020 8772 1155

It appears the last makeover has held up pretty well. Owned by the people behind The Bishop (East Dulwich) and The Castle (Camberwell), they dropped the chess theme for canines – Clarence, it seems, is the owner's four-legged friend. It's settled in nicely, and the fact it's still here suggests it has a draw for the locals and has a comfortable atmosphere The Devonshire over the road distinctly lacks. It is hard to quibble with its drink offerings: beers and wines from all over the world will keep all but the most picky of punters from complaining. What strikes us as odd, though, is the location of the TV: there only seemed to be one screen but it was tucked away in the alcove next to the table footy at the back, almost as a preserve for those lucky enough to nab the seats around it. When the sport is on, what develops is a queue of punters pushing in to see the screen. All most odd, and not in keeping with the laidback air this one mostly pulls off. Quibbles aside, it looks to have a solid regular clientele, and for its range of drinks alone deserves a three pint rating. We were just a bit bemused that a pub named after a dog comes across as rather too stylish to have a pub dog.

FEATURES:    

The Devonshire

RATING: 

39 Balham High Road
SW12 9AA
020 8673 1363

The Young's makeover juggernaut rolls into Balham and this is the result. Not too long ago the Duke of Devonshire was a large, adept community boozer: one that could play host with equal conviction to older locals in the front bar and a younger crowd in the back. Now, it's something different – yet rather familiar if you've been to any of the many new-look Young's pubs which are sprouting up across London. The Devonshire's now a more sedate, respectable drinking hole, with traces of the old pub wiped away as succinctly as its former name – so farewell to the TV and the games machines; hello to an open plan kitchen and a Botticelli reproduction. One standfast from the old regime: they still serve you a decent pint of Young's. It's the sort of place that's perfect for aspirational, gentrified Balham – but it's one that's hard to get excited about.

FEATURES:     

The Hope

RATING:

1 Bellevue Road
SW17 7EG
020 8672 8717

This one's settled in nicely after its refurb, making it a classy and comfortable place to go with superb beers and great, good-value food. The corner site provides a triple aspect onto Wandsworth Common and the big windows and high ceilings contribute to the light airy feel of the place. Furnishing is an eclectic mix of squashy and arty sofas, traditional wood and just-this-side-of-practical modern stuff, mixed with features like traditional butchers' chopping tables. It's bigger than it looks with an airy lounge area and a few steps up to the bar area with a couple of smaller areas just off that. Beers are well kept and change regularly – there's an Ale Club on Thursdays, so there's obviously something in it. There's a decent wine list, probably prompting the Tuesday Wine Society. Pricing reflects the aspirational nature of the area – it is virtually next door to the Michelin-starred Chez Bruce. They cater for all sorts, too – as shown by the pet snacks on the sideboard.

FEATURES:    

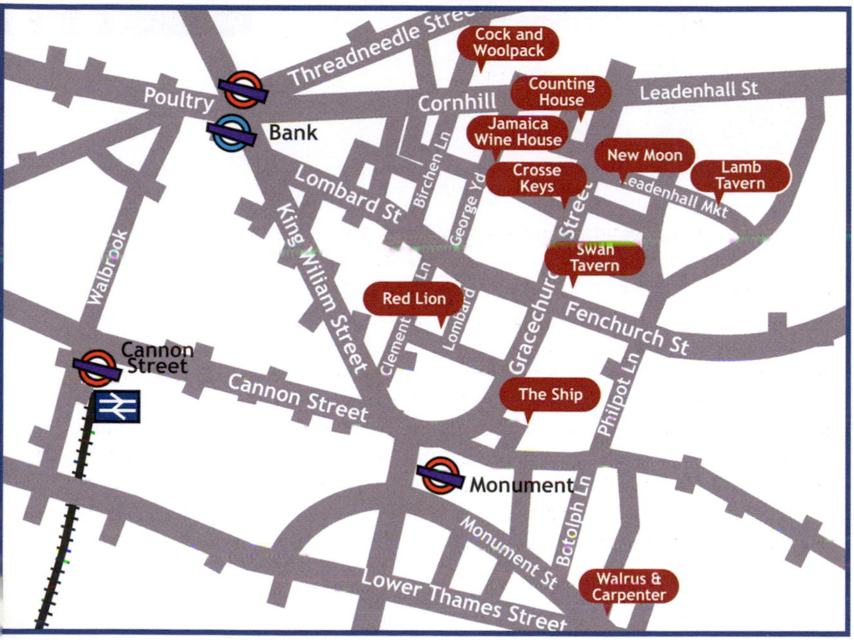

The Cock and Woolpack

RATING:

6 Finch Lane
EC3V 3NA
020 7626 4799

This unobtrusive pub is something of a City institution and, thanks to its location, is generally only frequented by those lucky few in the know or when felicity smiles upon the unwary commuter in search of a short cut (given its size, this is not such a bad thing). When Mr. Wetherspoon came up with the concept of a pub where one could go, sit in plush surroundings, drink a nice pint of ale and converse without being interrupted by loud jukeboxes, we've no doubt that the Cock and Woolpack was the sort of pub he had in mind. The difference, however, between the cavernous JD establishments and this rather pleasing Shepherd Neame snug is that the conversation actually generates an atmosphere, rather than being lost in the commodious ceilings of the former. A good pub for a quick pint on the way home (if you can find it).

FEATURES: 

HANDY FOR: Bank of England

Counting House

RATING:

50 Cornhill
EC3V 3PD
020 7283 7123

NatWest really has got it the wrong way round: the Counting House demonstrates just how much better suited a city cathedral is for drinking and dining than, in its previous guise, yet another bank. If you step inside this cavernous, soaring basilica and a 'wow' doesn't form on your lips then you truly deserve a life as a bank clerk. From the colossal island bar to the huge glass domed roof at stratospheric levels, beautiful wood, brass and marble fittings abound – wherever the eye settles, it is magnificent. The pub absorbs regiments without excessive crush (even at Friday lunchtime) at stools and tables, in a collection of smaller rooms at the back, in the many dining tables running round the mezzanine. Fuller's classic beer range is of course available, but the smart, friendly and plentiful staff also have the pick of a dizzying range of other taps running up and down the bar counter to tempt you with. Food matches the overall standard too. Not just the eponymous pies – excellent though they are, other classic dishes are supported by the adventurous traditional such as corned beef hash or Welsh rarebit with a poached egg. We could stay here all day... err, we nearly did.

FEATURES:    

Visitors' Award Winner 2008

The Crosse Keys

RATING: 

9 Gracechurch Street
EC3V 0DR
020 7623 4824

Another gigantic Wetherspoon conversion, this one of a monumental banking hall. And whilst this one doesn't have the aesthetic charm of some nearby competitors, this place impresses with its Stalinist proportions (note too the giant TV screen, in accordance with the grandiose scale of the pub). There's the usual Wetherspoon range of drink and food on offer at the usual unbeatable Wetherspoon prices, which probably explains the advanced state of inebriation of the clientele when we arrived late one evening here – apparently we're just not used to cheap drink in the City. With Wetherspoon's excellent (some might say challenging) range of beers, it's a pretty reasonable pub for the area (though we've never seen this one when there's been a game on the big screen).

FEATURES:  

HANDY FOR: Bank of England

Jamaica Wine House

RATING:

St Michaels Alley, Cornhill

EC3V 9DS

020 7929 6972

Located in the myriad courtyards and alleyways off Cornhill, this venerable City watering hole came under the ownership a few years back of the people who brought you Tup pubs. But fear not, over 300 years of atmosphere weren't traded in for stripped pine and Jamiroquai CDs. Always a popular pub, this one is often full to bursting, particularly as now the downstairs is a separate lunchtime dining space, cramming all the evening drinkers into the bar upstairs. That bar still retains an old-fashioned feel, with nooks and crannies aiming to satisfy the most furtive of drinkers (though they have to turn up early to guarantee a seat). It's a popular pub and one that can fill up quickly, usually for the duration. Quaint touches include a self-service, coin-operated humidor, but this setting surely deserves a real butler for this. A five-pint setting, then, but still only a three-pint pub.

FEATURES:  

HANDY FOR: Bank of England

Lamb Tavern

10–12 Leadenhall Market

EC3V 1LR

020 7626 2454

This splendid Young's pub has a very fine Victorian interior, with marvellous tilework and all the fixtures and fittings you'd expect of a pub in such dazzling surroundings. The pub's location, the beer and its visual appeal, we guess, make it staggeringly popular just after work and at lunchtimes, thronged with the suits from the surrounding City institutions. So at these times it's tricky to see the décor, let alone admire it and trying to sample the pub's produce can be quite taxing. However, a visit outside the busy times is well worth the effort, to enjoy the pub and its unique surroundings accompanied by Young's excellent beer.

FEATURES:    

HANDY FOR: Bank of England

New Moon

RATING:

88 Gracechurch Street
EC3V 0DN
020 7626 3625

This is a very popular pub, thanks to its location – in the heart of the City and inside the grand old Leadenhall Market. You can stand outside in the covered market when it's not too cold and that's what many people choose to do. But, even with the very long bar and plenty of staff, this pub's popularity still means getting served at peak times can be a bit of an ordeal. Now under the ownership of Greene King, the range of beer might not take your breath away and there's also everyday pub grub at lunchtimes.

FEATURES:  

HANDY FOR: Bank of England

Red Lion

RATING:

8 Lombard Court
EC3V 9BJ
020 7929 2552

Another hidden gem in the City, the wrought iron above the door hints at some of the details within. While not all original (what pub is, these days?), there's quite a few nice features about this pub to reassure us that it's not a new build. Most of the action takes place in the 'Main bar', downstairs, with its nooks and crannies for parties or quiet conversations, and Karaoke on Thursday nights at 7, if you're interested. Where it is does influence its clientele – City workers during the week, not a sniff on the weekend. Gets busy at commuting times and Thursday's a sell-out. Hot food at lunchtimes, a good range of beers and a decent wine list make this a good all-rounder. It's also quiet in the afternoons, if you need someplace for that chat or rendezvous. Worth a look.

FEATURES:    

HANDY FOR: Bank of England

The Ship

RATING:

11 Talbot Court
EC3V 0BP
020 7929 3903

You could pass Talbot Court – an essay in concrete that looks like a loading bay – a hundred times and never notice The Ship tucked on an inside corner just a hundred yards down where the slabwork gives way to a traditional London yard. It's a gem. Rebuilt in the 17th century after the original ale house was incinerated in the Great Fire, it's smallish, simple and comfortable, offering decent ales and a wide food menu. The spiral wooden staircase leads up to the narrowish upper bar where – perhaps a trick of the eye – the limited space seems to have been enhanced by installing slightly undersized tables and chairs and a tiny serving area in the corner. Perhaps it is the location, but we are told you can nearly always get a seat upstairs. Not the most happening of pubs but a splendid place for local workers to catch up on the gossip or for a relaxing one if you are passing. Closed weekends – but open until 11pm during the week.

FEATURES:  

HANDY FOR: Bank of England

The Swan Tavern

RATING:

77–80 Gracechurch Street
EC3V 0AS
020 7283 7712

A solid pub, this is the sort of miniature boozer that would fit a few times over into a Wetherspoon bank conversion. Give it a look if you fancy a change from large-scale City bars. Sure, the narrow bar becomes pretty impossible to navigate if more than a few suits start to hold court. If so, head upstairs to the confines of a slightly larger bar, the presence of which sometimes eludes the other drinkers here.

FEATURES: 

HANDY FOR: Bank of England

BANK/MONUMENT

The Walrus & Carpenter

RATING:

45 Monument Street
EC3R 8BU
020 7626 3362

Nowadays, the Walrus and Carpenter is a Nicholson's pub and, thankfully, when they took it over they sorted out the ground-floor arrangement so that it's now all one room. Previously, you could have arranged to meet friends at the pub and been blissfully unaware of the others' presence in the unconnected room. So what what else have they done? The usual extensive and well-kept range of Nicholson's ale is now on the hand pumps, there's a champagne bar downstairs and the Lewis Carroll bar and dining room created upstairs. The service is friendly, there's plenty of choice and there's decent pub grub if you need solid sustenance. The clientele is typically City and the atmosphere is solid British pub – it won't excite a young crowd, but at the same time it's not depressing and staid. It's all very Nicholson's which is generally a good thing and, in an area where there aren't many pubs to speak of, it's a very good thing.

FEATURES:   

HANDY FOR: Bank of England

BARBICAN

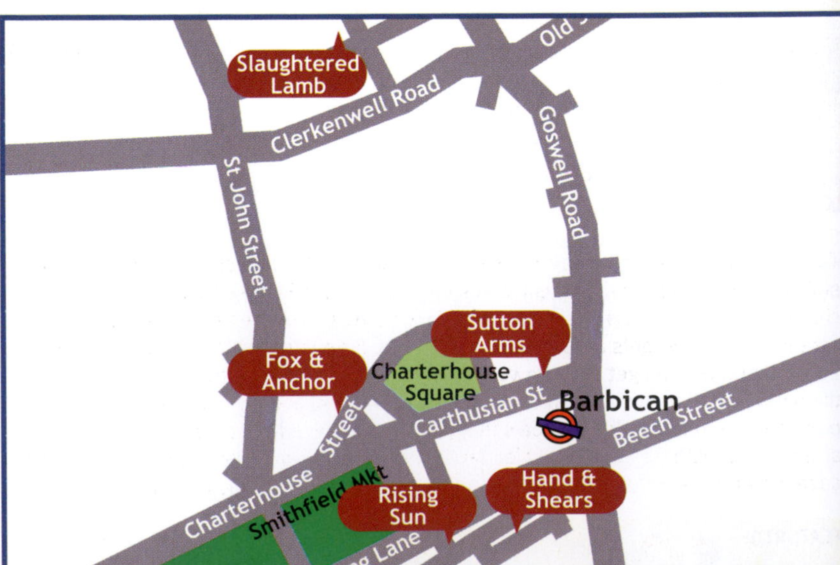

Fox & Anchor

RATING:

115 Charterhouse Street
EC1M 6AA
020 7012 3700

Having known this historic pub for more than two decades, it's finally back. Photos of Smithfield's meat market workers on the walls notwithstanding, this pub has made a move upmarket (more pinstripe, far less bloodstained apron) and no longer has the multicultural feel we loved about the old place. There's a good range of beers on the six hand pumps and the menu's gone gastro with an accompanying price hike. The new owners, Malmaison, have kept the pub largely intact (the exterior is listed anyway) and the snugs are still there and there's been a general tidy up of the old place – the most obvious change a zinc-topped bar. The friendly staff work hard, and the addition of six bedrooms must keep them on their toes. It's a good effort, especially if you're looking for a well-run gastropub, but for us it's much of a muchness. Smithfield is a unique and historic locale that's celebrated its diverse appeal over many centuries. If we get more developments like this, we'll lose that uniqueness – you might as well be in midtown Manchester, Edinburgh or Glasgow – not the historic heart of an old, old city, where close by there's a 12th-century priory, a Victorian meat market and the site of William Wallace's execution.

FEATURES:    **HANDY FOR:** Museum of London, Barbican Centre

Hand & Shears

RATING: 

1 Middle Street, Cloth Fair
EC1A 7JA
020 7600 0257

The Hand & Shears is a great little pub, which, despite its diminutive proportions, is still divided up into public, private and saloon bars – a rarity these days. It hasn't changed in years, though we guess it's only a matter of time before some well-meaning developer gets around to mucking it up. It's got a great old-fashioned pub atmosphere, but can get a bit crowded, which is possibly the secret of its avoidance of the renovator's hammer. It hasn't been neglected though, and feels just like an English pub should – and the olde-worlde setting around St Bart's Church just adds to the atmosphere. With well-kept real ales on the hand pumps and traditional pub grub, it's a real drinker's pub that just happens to get rather busy on Friday nights.

FEATURES:   **HANDY FOR:** Museum of London, Barbican Centre

The Old Red Cow

RATING:

71 Long Lane
EC1A 9EJ
020 7726 2595

We're really pleased to see the Old Red Cow return after it closed post a somewhat disastrous sojourn as the Long Lane. Ye Olde Red Cow (as it once was) has stood here for many years and was a favourite of the late great Sir Peter Ustinov when he was in town and it was one of ours too. It's a pleasant old pub – it claims to be the oldest pub in Smithfield – on a busy thoroughfare in a bustling part of the City. The upstairs room has to be one of our favourite pub rooms in the City. The Old Red Cow offers excellent beer, with Timothy Taylor's Landlord and Deuchars on the hand pumps last time we were in (they appear to change regularly) and there's a reasonable wine list, too. The food is also good here, freshly prepared, you'll have to wait a little while, but it's worth it and it's good value – we'll be coming back soon to try the Sunday roasts. It also offers WiFi and a free jukebox with a good mix of contemporary music and classics to suit just about any mood. The locals and office types who work around here are still finding out about the new Old Red Cow (huh?), so it's often a little quiet, but, from what we've experienced, it deserves to be a great success.

FEATURES:     **HANDY FOR:** Museum of London, Barbican Centre

Rising Sun

RATING:

38 Cloth Fair
EC1A 7JQ
020 7726 6671

The Rising Sun is an old and well-worn, but attractive, traditional-style pub hidden away on a slightly Dickensian-looking alley. Unlike other nearby establishments popular with besuited chaps from the City, this pub seems to attract an interesting mix of regulars, including students and designery types. It's a pretty comfortable place with darts and fruit machines up at one end, courteous service and a Tuesday quiz night. With well-priced, well-kept Sam Smith's beers, it's a good pub if you happen by, and also one of the few places open at weekends in Smithfield.

FEATURES:    **HANDY FOR:** Museum of London, Barbican Centre

Slaughtered Lamb

RATING:

34–35 Great Sutton Street
EC1V 0DX
020 7253 1516

The Slaughtered Lamb is a relatively recent remodelling of old gallery space – so it's ideal for an area with so many loft-converted flats. Equipped with a slouchy style similar to many pubs in the capital there's the slight air of this pub existing in ironic quotation marks: it's the sort of pub where the dart board is artily displayed in a cabinet, rather than actually available for play. As for its name, the pub doesn't go silent like its namesake in *American Werewolf in London*, though the too-cool-for-school attitude of the bar staff is just as chilly. Having said all that, this one's grown on us. For a start, the (rather rare) Sleeman Honey Brown Lager slipped down a treat and the varied music mix (Stones to Pink Floyd via trance and dub) suggested a great MP3 player stuck on random. We were fully expecting to be flicking through our gastronglish-english translation dictionaries, but the choices were simple and clear and mostly under a tenner. It's enormously popular so don't expect to wander in for a quiet pint and a fireside chat, you'll be hard pressed even to see a seat.

FEATURES:     HANDY FOR: Museum of London, Barbican Centre

Sutton Arms

RATING: 

6 Carthusian Street
EC1M 6EB
020 7253 0723

A while ago now, this handsome pub was given the refurbishment it deserved and was brought up to 21st-century standards with a bit of style and the right sort of attention to detail. On tap there's a decent range of beers and lagers, there's a decent wine list and a pretty imaginative and well-presented food menu. The décor is a little eclectic with its plaster busts etc, but the place feels much more comfortable than its previous incarnations and is more in keeping with the building (and its environs) – and for this we salute the owners. The upstairs restaurant has now taken on the role of lounge/restaurant, hinting at a more leisurely approach to the excellent menu, but judging from how busy it was last time we were in it's not hurt business. And now it's open for Sunday lunch.

FEATURES:     HANDY FOR: Museum of London, Barbican Centre

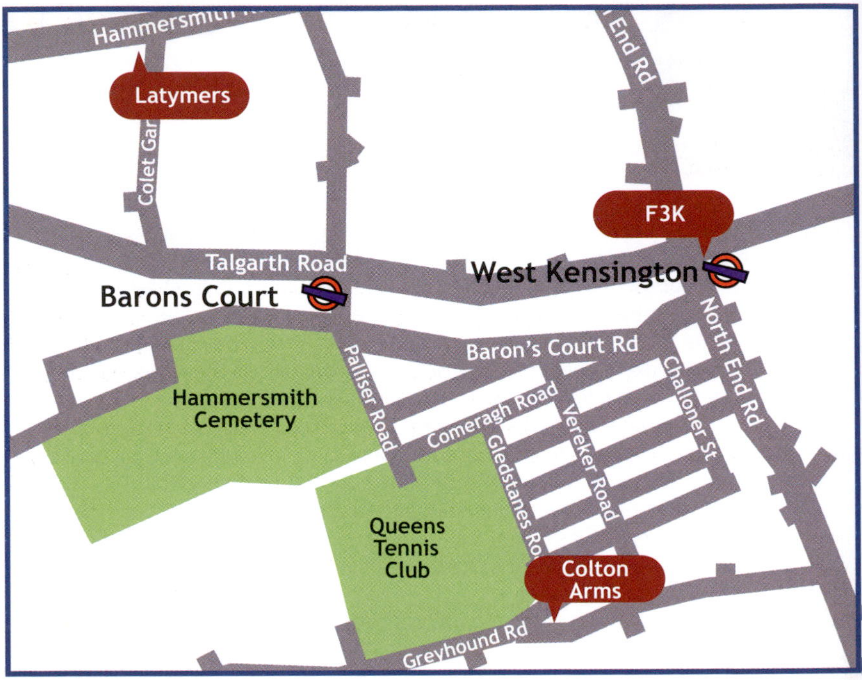

Colton Arms

RATING:

187 Greyhound Road
W14 9SD
020 7385 6956

Secreted away in the suburban no-man's land of Barons Court, this pub has the feel of a village local. A small affair with a main bar and two tiny back alcoves and a wee patio garden at the rear, the rural feel stems as much from its original oak furniture and handled pint glasses as from the courteous bar staff. Such behaviour could easily result in a faux and touristy atmosphere, but there's nothing contrived here. With excellently kept beers – and the sort of warm and homely atmosphere gastropubs strive for yet seldom attain – the pub enjoys a mixed clientele and surely your patronage as well (and while we're at it, a preservation order wouldn't go amiss). A classic boozer.

FEATURES:  

HANDY FOR: Earl's Court

F3K (Famous 3 Kings)

RATING:

171 North End Road
W14 9NL
020 7603 6071

Can't find a pub showing the match? Don't give up and go home until you've tried here. With about 15 different screens and feeds from sports channels across the globe, it's a pretty fair bet they'll be showing your game of choice. And on big nights, one of the staff comes around regularly to tell you the scores of other matches, too. If that wasn't enough to keep you occupied, a pool table, air hockey table, a labyrinthine layout and a video jukebox are there to amuse too. It's like a pub based on the inside of a teenage boy's brain. Although there are always some guest ales, it's hardly a place for the quiet contemplation of them. If it's your cup of tea, it's a full-on, hyperactive sort of place and one of the best sports bars around. Oh, it also has a late licence.

FEATURES:        **HANDY FOR:** Earl's Court

Latymers

RATING: 

Hammersmith Road
W6 7JP
020 8748 3446

Though maybe not the first pub in London to have its own Thai restaurant, Latymers is certainly one of the best, both for quality, service and value for money. The pub itself is late-80s modern and a bit too shiny for our liking (it replaced the Red Cow where the Jam and the Stranglers first played London, and was also the 'local' in *The Sweeney*) but the beer is always very well looked after and the service is excellent. It also has a nice relaxed atmosphere on weekends, being far enough away from Hammersmith station to avoid concert-goers, even with the footy on the tellies. But the food is the real draw – if you want to make your eyebrows sweat, make sure you order the Homok Talay to start.

FEATURES:   **HANDY FOR:** Olympia, Riverside Studios

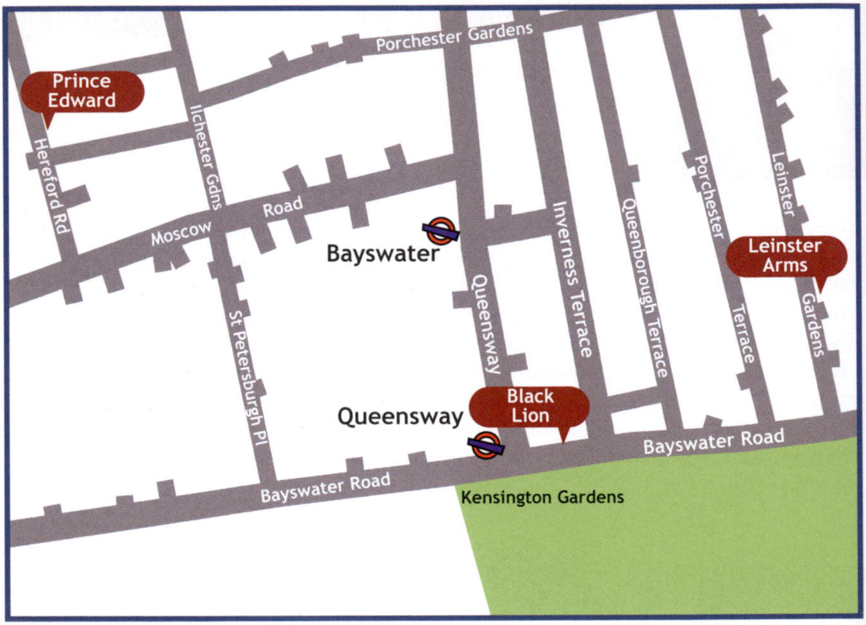

Black Lion

RATING: 

123 Bayswater Road
W2 3JH
020 7229 0917

Apparently built in 1720, the Black Lion retains some attractive features today. Its ornate original brickwork, and later Victorian ceiling and columns, are lovely. However, the elegant surroundings are somewhat compromised by the pub of today. Sure, there's enough selection to keep you sufficiently fed and watered, but the big TV doesn't really add anything. You can well imagine that this was a charming pub in bygone centuries, but today it's marred by the heavy traffic on Bayswater.

FEATURES:  

HANDY FOR: Kensington Palace

Leinster Arms

RATING:

17 Leinster Terrace
W2 3EU
020 7402 4670

Leinster Terrace has a group of independent shops and restaurants, so it's perhaps not too much of a surprise that the local pub has a similar, slightly free-spirited air. Saying that, we don't often come across pubs in such touristy parts of town (like Bayswater) that have a devoted band of regulars, nor that have such reasonably priced food (£4.50 for Sunday lunch here). This one also promotes its selection of pies and, although we didn't indulge, we can certainly say the beers hit the spot (Pride, Landlord and the guest when we visited, Inferno). It's a decent enough spot for a couple of jars: the sort of non-showy, dependable boozer you'd love as a local.

FEATURES:  

HANDY FOR: Kensington Palace

Prince Edward

RATING:  

73 Princes Square
W2 4NY
020 7727 2221

A decent, no-nonsense boozer with none of the pretensions of some of the places not so far away from here. It's a big, well-looked-after place, with good, Hall & Woodhouse ales (e.g. Badger, Tanglefoot and Fursty Ferret) and fast and very friendly service. The food is pretty pub-grub ordinary, but it can be a relief from some of the painful gastro twaddle on offer around – though a Kobe steak burger is verging on that territory – and far more economical if all you need is a fuel stop. It's got a good local feel and the warming coal fire is a great draw in the colder months. The upstairs function room is available for hire and you can find a variety of activities on there, including the odd bit of theatre. Not a bad place at all.

FEATURES:      

HANDY FOR: Portobello Road Market

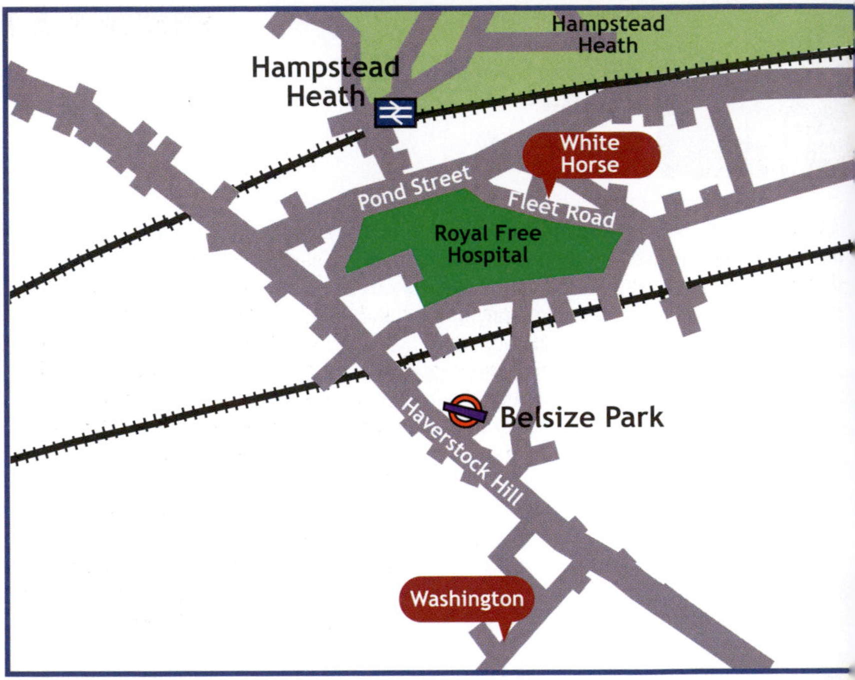

Hampstead Heath
Hampstead Heath
White Horse
Pond Street
Fleet Road
Royal Free Hospital
Belsize Park
Haverstock Hill
Washington

The Washington

RATING: 

50 Englands Lane
NW3 4UE
020 7722 8842

'The Wash', as it now nicknames itself, has veered back from the precipice of gastrodom. It's been taken over by the Mitchells & Butlers group as part of their continually expanding, non-themed, upmarket chain of pubs. As such, emphasis is on a good choice of beer, wine and well-made food. In contrast with the bland exterior, the Victorian interior is splendid, with original etched glass, wood panelling and high ceilings all intact and an eclectic mix of tables and couches, all laid out with thought. On our Sunday-afternoon visit a pianist was playing some easy listening jazzy music and the whole atmosphere was equally easy. Despite being part of a clever M&B marketing plan to cater to a specific socio-economic group, it would be churlish to do anything except recommend this place highly.

FEATURES:    

The White Horse

RATING:

154 Fleet Road
NW3 2QX
020 7485 2112

This place held out for a long time against the trend of pub refurbishments and modernisations which swept over North London (spool back to the early 1990s and this one was a venue for fledgling indie bands). A major renovation a few years back did for the mankier aspects of this place, without destroying some of its finer architectural features (most notably the ceiling). A feature of the pub's location – at a sharp road junction with large windows running the length of two almost parallel sides around an island bar – means that much of the pub is rather too exposed for the comfort of some. (There are two rooms at the back that are the exception to this rule, however.) On the plus side, there are a few real ales on hand pumps, a decent selection of (principally new-world) wines and Thai food that can be eaten in or ordered as a takeaway. Best of all, it's a friendly pub, and it gives the impression that it goes that extra mile for its customers (who, on our visit, were a wide cross-section of NW3 life). If you wanted to be picky, you could say that this one feels too smart to be the pub opposite both George Orwell's former flat and Joe Orton's favourite pick-up joint, but on our most recent visit it seemed a pub perfectly at ease with itself.

FEATURES:  

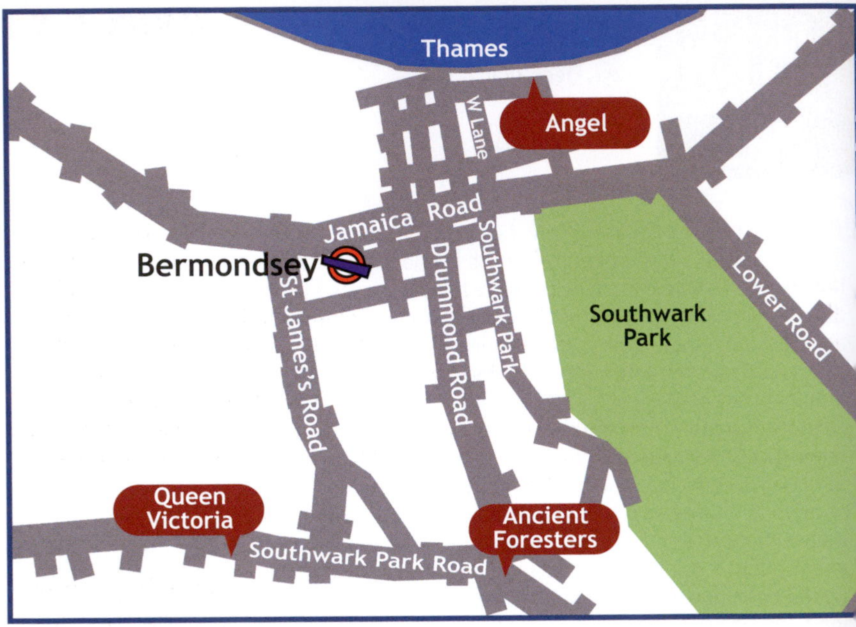

Thames
Angel
W Lane
Jamaica Road
Bermondsey
St James's Road
Drummond Road
Southwark Park
Southwark Park
Lower Road
Queen Victoria
Southwark Park Road
Ancient Foresters

Ancient Foresters

RATING: 3

282 Southwark Park Road
SE16 2HB
020 7394 1633

Should you find yourselves in need of musical accompaniment in SE16, the Ancient Foresters must be the place to visit. The side room – with backdrop incorporating Sammy, Deano and Frank – brings the air of the Sands Hotel to Bermondsey and hosts a range of bands and karaoke nights. Otherwise, this one's a fairly dependable pub: the sort of place where locals are always up for a bit of banter with the staff. Expect it to fill up when Millwall are at home, but as pubs (fairly) close to the New Den go, this one certainly makes the grade.

FEATURES:  

Angel

RATING:

101 Bermondsey Wall East
SE16 4TY
020 7394 3214

After a period of closure, the Angel is serving once more. It's had a comprehensive refurbishment which is thankfully sympathetic to the history of the place. Perhaps this pub is now ready to capitalise on its superb location. Whether you're sitting outside on the terrace or inside near a window, the Thames is impossible to ignore. Passing river traffic of various types and eras will catch your attention, as well as the very fine view towards Tower Bridge and beyond. There are a couple of pleasant (and fairly private) rooms near the bar downstairs and a handsome upstairs room with sofas, comfy chairs and historical pictures on the walls. A varied menu of main courses is available for less than a tenner, and the beer is Samuel Smith's usual range. After a dubious past, things are looking up for the Angel.

FEATURES:     **HANDY FOR:** Tower Bridge, Design Museum

Queen Victoria

148 Southwark Park Road
SE16 3RP
020 7237 9904

The Queen Victoria is a pub of such a vintage that the sign outside lists 'day trips' as one of the facilities on offer (it also offers raffles and golf). We're not sure if the charabanc still heads off to Margate nowadays; it certainly didn't the day we were in, as the pub was packed. Venerable bar staff keep an eye on proceedings, as the punters watch the sport on TV or indulge in a bit of it themselves – pool table at the front, dart board at the side. One for the locals perhaps, but judging from our visit newcomers won't have any problems, aside from finding a seat.

FEATURES:   

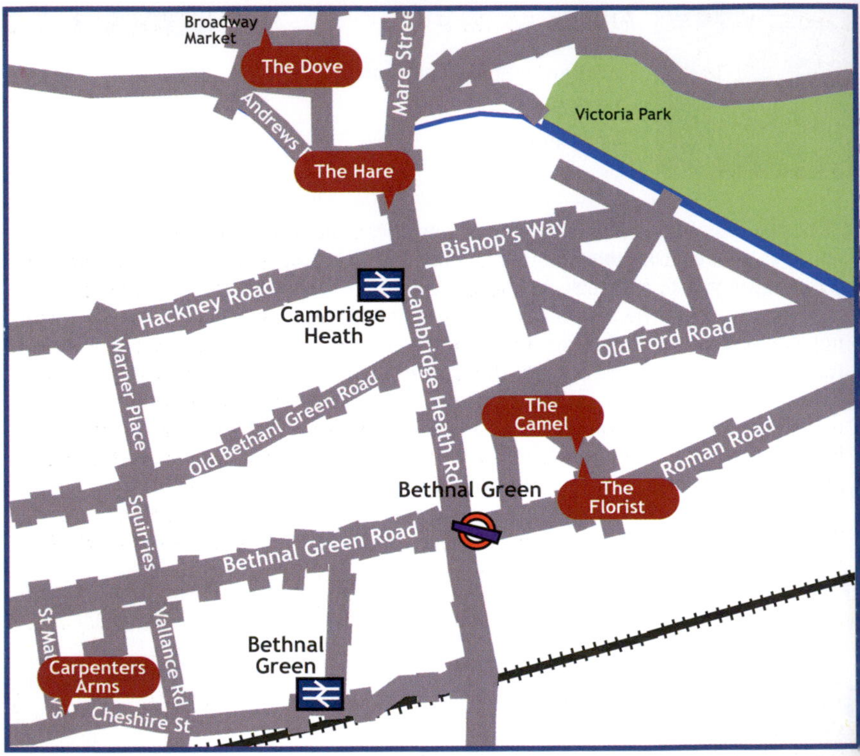

Broadway Market
The Dove
Andrews
Mare Street
Victoria Park
The Hare
Bishop's Way
Hackney Road
Cambridge Heath
Cambridge Heath Rd
Warner Place
Old Ford Road
Old Bethanl Green Road
The Camel
Roman Road
Bethnal Green
The Florist
Squirries
Bethnal Green Road
St Ma...s
Vallance Rd
Bethnal Green
Carpenters Arms
Cheshire St

The Camel

RATING: 3 pints

277 Globe Road
E2 0JD
020 8983 9888

If you like the nearby Florist, but find it getting a little too crowded and noisy for you, then your best bet is to try this pub. Run by the same people, it's a friendly, family affair. The great original tiling is intact but its been smartened up inside – the framed photos of the Camel from days gone by are a nice touch. The service is excellent, the food's good – really excellent pies – and there are a couple of decent ales from Adnam's on the hand pumps. It's understandably popular at Sunday lunchtime, but you'll usually find it comfortably busy most days of the week.

FEATURES: 

HANDY FOR: Museum of Childhood, York Hall

The Carpenters Arms

RATING:

73 Cheshire Street
E2 6EG
020 7739 6342

When the Carpenters Arms closed a couple of years ago, we naturally expected conversion into flats awaited it. So you can imagine our excitement to discover back in the autumn of 2007 that it had reopened. If nothing else, it's a little piece of East End pub history; many pubs in the area lay claim to associations with the Kray twins (some more tenuous than others), but the Carpenters was apparently owned by them and run by their dear old mum. So, what's it like now? In a word: 'nice' (or if you want two: 'very nice'). Not the largest of places, there's been a tasteful, comfortable pub refurb with an attractive bar area, photos of the local area dotted around and a pretty, small back garden. Our last Friday-night visit here found a pleasantly busy pub with a nice mix of customers and impeccable service. There's an excellent choice of drink, too – three ales on tap, an above-average selection of lager and some nice bottled choices. We have nothing but positive things to say about spending time here – we wonder if Mrs Kray would have agreed?

Reviewers' Award – Best Newcomer 2008

The Dove

RATING: 

24 Broadway Market
E8 4QJ
020 7275 7617

Well established here now, the Dove's Belgian theme is so well executed it doesn't seem to be anything out of the ordinary any more. If you're in the mood for a seemingly endless range of excellent Belgian beers and some pretty decent continental-style food that's not 21st-century gastropub fare, then this is the place for you. They also do real ales for the CAMRA purists and the wine list's not too shabby, either. The expansion of the premises a while ago means that it rarely suffers the overcrowding it used to and with so many nooks and crannies to accommodate the clientele, it shouldn't take long to find a table. We're pleased this one hasn't been 'improved' or updated and the same levels of service are being maintained. Still a great pub and an excellent reason to visit Hackney, the Dove is well worth the tramp up from Bethnal Green tube.

FEATURES:        **HANDY FOR:** Hackney Museum

The Florist

RATING:

225 Globe Road
E2 0JD
020 8981 1100

Numbering among its neighbours the London Buddhist Centre, a centre for Tibetan Art and a long-standing vegetarian cafe, it's no surprise that this old boozer was made over a while ago. Whilst not as painstakingly trendy as the bars a mile or so east, the Florist sticks to the standard bare floorboards and weathered-leather furniture look, interspersed with some original features. It's busier and noisier in the evening though, usually with someone having a go behind the DJ decks. Shame then that the choices behind the bar don't greatly inspire – it's the usual lager-y suspects plus Sharp's Doom Bar on a hand pump, though as the place makes a fuss about its cocktails we perhaps should have opted for one of them. As rejigged East End pubs go, despite the usually rather garrulous clientele, it's not a bad one at all.

FEATURES:   

HANDY FOR: Museum of Childhood, York Hall

The Hare

RATING: 

505 Cambridge Heath Rd
E2 9BU
020 7613 0519

This pub's unprepossessing exterior hides an excellent local. A popular, friendly place, it serves decent beers – Landlord, Speccy and Greene King IPA on the hand pumps, for instance – and jolly good sarnies too. And if you're feeling in a vino frame of mind there's a cheap, but decent wine list and possibly the cheapest champagne in any London pub. There's always a buzz of conversation going on and the sport on TV is not solely limited to the footy (although it will take precedence). In fact, more than one sort of sport can sometimes be viewed on different tellies simultaneously, catering for a range of tastes. There are also regular live jazz sessions on Sundays. The Hare's a thoroughly decent local boozer, we wish there were more like them.

FEATURES: 

HANDY FOR: Museum of Childhood, York Hall

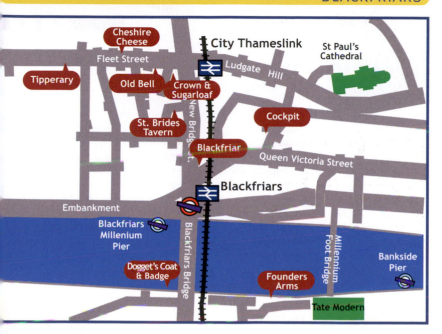

Cheshire Cheese
Fleet Street
City Thameslink
St Paul's Cathedral
Ludgate Hill
Tipperary
Old Bell
Crown & Sugarloaf
New Bridge St.
St. Brides Tavern
Cockpit
Blackfriar
Queen Victoria Street
Blackfriars
Embankment
Blackfriars Millenium Pier
Blackfriars Bridge
Millennium Foot Bridge
Bankside Pier
Dogget's Coat & Badge
Founders Arms
Tate Modern

The Blackfriar

174 Queen Victoria Street
EC4V 4EG
020 7236 5474

This is a cheat, but an honest cheat, as the almost mediaeval appearance is actually an early-20th-century Arts & Crafts extravaganza on the site of an ancient priory. Inside the pub, the eye delights at a thousand features and whether perching on a stool by the marbled bar or tucked into a semi-private booth you feel it's a special place. Braying City suits make it a bit of an ordeal on the earlier part of weeknight evenings – although happily in summer most of them are happy to cram shoulder-to-shoulder on the virtually table-and-chair-less pavement outside. Now that it's open on the weekends, you can visit it at a time when you can have a quiet pint and contemplate the wonderful interior. That, combined with very friendly service and a good range of beers, make this one you should go out of your way to experience.

FEATURES:    **HANDY FOR:** St Paul's Cathedral, Tate Modern, Globe Theatre

Cockpit

RATING:

7 Andrews Hill
EC4V 5BY
020 7248 7315

We usually avoid clichés like the plague, a cliché to us is like a red rag to a bull, but 'steeped in history' could have been minted for this hidden gem. Outside: it says established 1787, inside: it was rebuilt in 1842, but had been Shakespeare's house in the 16th century. It's an odd-looking little place in a tangle of alleys. Count every bar stool and narrow bench – built for smaller backsides than the 21st-century model – and you'll never reach 30. Then look up and ponder why the ceiling is 18 feet high. The Cockpit is what it says: you are sitting where razor-spurred fighting cocks tore blood, feathers and the very life from one another. Look up again and notice the narrow, balustraded galleries where the mob once roared. Appreciate the strutting, stuffed fighting bird over one door, the models, prints and paintings wherever the eye roams. Feel London's sometimes unpalatable history wash over you. For the record, it's quite homely. Working men mix with City workers and it gets busy at the usual times. Hand-pulled beers and basic food, the landlord friendly and helpful.

FEATURES: 

HANDY FOR: St Paul's Cathedral, Tate Modern, Globe Theatre

Crown & Sugarloaf

RATING:

26 Bride Lane
EC4Y 8DT
020 7353 3693

The Punch Tavern on Fleet Street was originally called The Crown & Sugarloaf but was renamed in honour of the founders of *Punch* magazine who met here. Back in the 90s The Punch was relaunched but, due to a falling out, the bar at the side was walled off. This Crown & Sugarloaf is that bar, reopened in all its high Victorian grandeur. Sam Smith's brewery – the Marmite of pub chains – is in charge here so you're either going to love the fact that only their brews are available or you're not. Even if you're not a fan, it's worthwhile sticking your head around the door to marvel at the cut glass, mosaic floor and period furniture. It's often less busy than other places nearby, but still busy enough for there to be no seats available – like most places in the area, though, it empties out considerably around 9pm. Perhaps one day the original Crown & Sugarloaf will be reformed, but given how the Punch Tavern is doing its best to transform itself into an 'informal gastropub' (translation: buffet), perhaps it's going to be a while yet.

HANDY FOR: St Paul's Cathedral, Tate Modern, Globe Theatre

Doggett's Coat & Badge

RATING:

Blackfriars Bridge
SE1 9UD
020 7633 9081

Run by Nicholson's, Doggett's Riverside Bar and Terraces (to give it its full name) is the least Nicholson's-like of all their properties, being a modern (well 1980s) building rather than an ornate Victorian gin palace. Nevertheless, in keeping with the rest of the pubs in the chain, the full range of Nicholson's beer, wine, spirits and food is on offer here. As is only to be expected, this pub exploits its location to the full, with a variety of drinking and dining experiences arranged over four floors, all with views of the river, ranging from a roof terrace and restaurant, through to sports bar with pool tables and TV screens and a bar on the lowest floor, attracting Thames path walkers. Doggett's prominent location attracts a vast and varied clientele and for us that's this pub's downside – despite the excellent views, the overall experience is variable, it can be mobbed, it can be deathly quiet, sometimes the beer isn't up to scratch and the service patchy. We prefer a more reliable experience.

FEATURES:     **HANDY FOR:** Tate Modern, Globe Theatre

Founders Arms

RATING: 

52 Hopton Street
SE1 9JH
020 7928 1899

A modern Young's pub on the south side of the river very close to Blackfriars Bridge, it offers the usual Young's range of drinks and pretty decent food. Its location is what makes this place popular (and in summer it is very popular). It has a large terrace with seats and tables by the river, there are no major roads nearby (the heavy traffic on Blackfriars Bridge is shielded by the closer railway bridge) and there's a nice view of the dome of St Paul's rising above the squalid mass of buildings on the north bank, that is the Mermaid Theatre complex. The opening of Tate Modern has increased the clientele substantially, especially with the Millennium Bridge connecting across to the City, so sometimes service can be a little slow. The addition of a proper coffee bar in the corner suggests they know who their main clientele is and where they're coming from. It's still less crowded, has much better beer and is better value for money than the Tate café...

FEATURES:       **HANDY FOR:** Tate Modern, Globe Theatre

The Old Bell

RATING:

95 Fleet Street
EC4Y 1DH
020 7583 0216

The Old Bell is one of the legendary Fleet Street pubs from when this area was well and truly the Street of Shame. Sadly, those days are long gone and so have the marathon drinking sessions – printer and pundit alike. When you go in now, it's not easy to imagine what it was once like, when the front bar was the off-licence and the serious drinking went on (and on) in the tiny bar in the back. Nowadays, it's a jolly nice Nicholson's pub and it serves a very decent pint – plenty of hand pumps with plenty of well-kept guest beers. The beautiful St Bride's Church (Wren's prototype wedding cake) at the back of it makes a trip here all the more worthwhile (and make sure you visit the crypt). One of the best pubs in these parts – another fragment of London's history, with excellent beers to boot.

HANDY FOR: St Paul's Cathedral, Tate Modern, Globe Theatre

St Brides Tavern

RATING:

1 Bridewell Place
EC4V 6AP
020 7353 1614

No longer the cosy, traditional pub this, as it's been primped and tidied up and given the stripped-floor treatment. Gone is the wood panelling and in comes a modern bar. That's not necessarily a bad thing, as it did need modernisation, and, being Greene King, the beer is still kept to a high standard. Fortunately, this now means their standard IPA and a guest ale – Ridley's Witchfinder Porter when we were in last – they seem to have learned their lesson on promoting only their own beers. It's definitely gone more upmarket, and the local office workers don't seem to mind that. The menu's extensive, if a bit gastro, including wraps, decent-looking pies and fish and chips as well. The tiny front bar is deceptive, as it initially seems to be the whole place, but there's a large upstairs bar that provides more room to expand. While we miss the old place, this one's still worth a look and it's likely to be far less crowded than some of the more prominent pubs in the area.

FEATURES:    

HANDY FOR: St Paul's Cathedral, Globe Theatre

Tipperary

RATING:

66 Fleet Street
EC4Y 1HT
020 7583 6470

The Tipperary is a quaint, narrow, old (it celebrated its 400th birthday a short while ago) pub, with a rather welcoming wood-panelled interior, impressive mirrors and a groovy shamrock-design mosaic floor. If you're interested in the pub's provenance, there's a handy history of the pub on the wall outside. There's another room with a bar upstairs, but, even with this, the place is so narrow it's mostly standing room only – which actually adds to the charm and authenticity. Naturally, as you'd expect with a pub called the Tipperary, there's plenty of good Guinness on tap, unpretentious food is served all day and a jolly time is to be had by all. Here's to the next 400!

FEATURES:  

HANDY FOR: St Paul's Cathedral, Sir John Soane's Museum

Ye Olde Cheshire Cheese

RATING: 

145 Fleet Street
EC4A 2BU
020 7353 6170

This pub is something of an institution on Fleet Street. In the heyday of the Street of Shame, you could regularly find the great and (occasionally) the good gathering here to do the business of Fleet Street. Sadly (for some) those years are now over, but the history of Ye Olde Cheshire Cheese actually goes back much further than recent decades. As the sign in the passageway attests, the pub was rebuilt just after the Great Fire of London and there's been a pub on this site for much longer than that. Since Fleet Street's dispersal eastwards, tourists are now the pub's main customers, but that comes as no surprise – the pub oozes character and history: nooks and crannies abound, there are numerous large and small rooms (some with fireplaces) at different levels, dark wood on wall and ceiling, flagstone floors and there's not a right angle in the place. The past clientele reads like a roll-call of literature – Dr Johnson lived just around the corner, and scribes such as Voltaire, Dickens and Twain have all raised their drinking arms here. Sam Smith's excellent beers add their own touch of quirkiness to the offer, topped off with traditional pub grub. Ye Olde Cheshire Cheese neatly encapsulates the last few hundred years of London history in a single lunchtime – long may it last.

FEATURES: 

HANDY FOR: St Paul's Cathedral, Sir John Soane's Museum

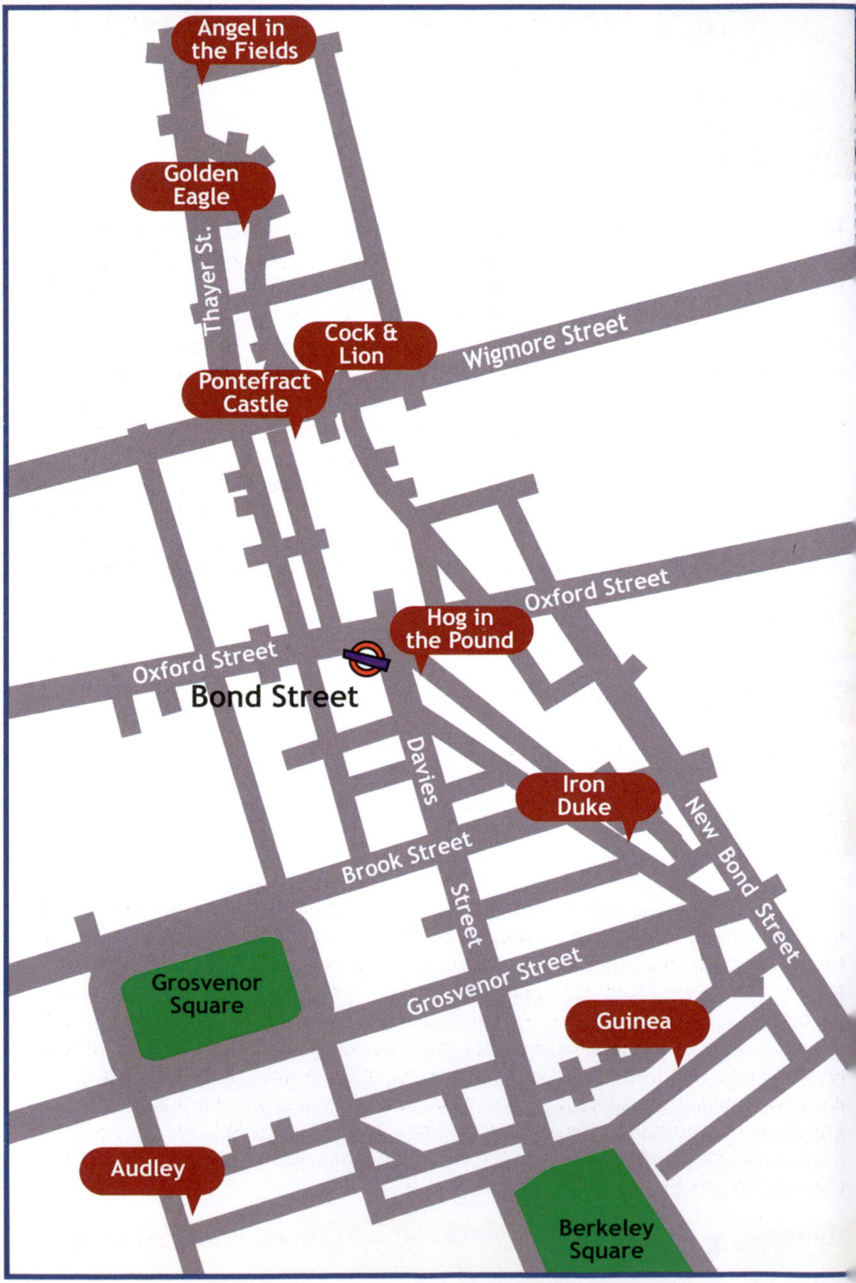

BOND STREET

Angel in the Fields
Golden Eagle
Thayer St.
Cock & Lion
Pontefract Castle
Wigmore Street
Oxford Street
Hog in the Pound
Oxford Street
Bond Street
Davies Street
Iron Duke
New Bond Street
Brook Street
Grosvenor Square
Grosvenor Street
Guinea
Audley
Berkeley Square

Angel in the Fields

RATING:

37 Thayer Street
W1U 2QU
020 7486 7763

Marylebone High Street is one of London's lesser-known upmarket shopping streets, with all sorts of expensive and fashionable boutiques and emporia lining both sides of the road. Guarding the southern entrance to this retail nirvana stands a trusty Yorkshire stalwart – Sam Smith's Angel in the Fields. If you're a fan of the brewery, then you'll know what to expect: solid, well-kept traditional bitters, ales and stouts supported by an esoteric assortment of own-brand wine, spirits and mixers all at a very reasonable price. We know the Sam Smith's offer is not everyone's cup-of-tea but it does the job for us. The pub's been recently refurbished, but if you weren't familiar with it before, you probably won't realise. It still has the same reassuring dark-oak panelling and cosy interior. The service is fast and friendly and the upstairs room can be a welcome relief if it's crowded downstairs – usually lunchtimes and just after work. Its cheapness has also been discovered by the local student population – there must be a college nearby – so be warned that the occasional visit can resemble a Student Union bar.

FEATURES:     **HANDY FOR:** Wallace Collection, Madame Tussauds

Audley

RATING: 

41–43 Mount Street
W1K 2RP
020 7499 1843

The grand building that houses this pub is a fine complement to its handsome interior. In a classy area such as Mayfair, you'd expect things to be grander than the norm and the Audley does not disappoint. Bedecked with chandeliers, fine decoration and topped with a magnificent mahogany clock, this pub provides an elegant setting for almost any social occasion. There's a good range of beers on the hand pumps and all the usual wines and spirits you'd expect of such a place. The atmosphere is civilised and friendly and there's a good range of traditional pub grub. The only downside, and it's a minor one, is this pub's a fixture on the tourist trail and you'll often encounter groups of uncomfortable, some-times unhappy-looking people in here, often around mealtimes, which makes for a less than relaxed atmosphere. At other times, though, this is a very fine place for a civilised pint or two.

FEATURES:    **HANDY FOR:** The Royal Academy, Wallace Collection

Cock & Lion

RATING:

62 Wigmore Street
W1U 2SB
020 7935 8727

Nestling parallel to Oxford Street, this pleasant little place offers refuge from the horrors of consumerism lurking just down the road, and a lovely pint to be getting on with. There are three beers on usually, with one of those a guest. The pub has regular sports coverage, though thankfully it never seems to be too packed. Of course, now that the smoking ban is biting hard, there are tables on the pavement which, unfortunately, are the only outside bits available to this pub, and not very nice in the rain. The former games room upstairs has gone, converted into a proper restaurant now, with no sign of the pool table. The menu is mostly proper pub food, not necessarily a bad thing. The staff are genial as always and still able to pull a pint, and happy to leave you be to finish your pint in peace. An oasis in a shopping desert.

FEATURES:    

HANDY FOR: Wallace Collection, Madame Tussauds

Golden Eagle

RATING: 

59 Marylebone Lane
W1U 2NW
020 7935 3228

An excellent little pub – and we do mean little, it's tiny – that was spruced up not so long ago, thankfully retaining its original character and brightening up the dingy route to the toilets. The beer is excellent, a good range – e.g. St. Austell's Tribute and Tinners – and well kept, which alone makes it worth a visit and the wine list has recently been updated. It's not always open (especially at the weekend), but it is one to seek out, if only to see what a traditional English boozer used to be like. The place is usually brimming with people who enjoy a sing song around the upright piano, when the pianist is in (Tuesday, Thursday and Friday), but it can be undeservedly quiet when he's not. It's straight out of an Ealing comedy. I say!

FEATURES:   

HANDY FOR: Wallace Collection, Madame Tussauds

Guinea

RATING:

30 Bruton Place
W1J 6NR
020 7409 1728

Although the term 'Pub & Dining Room' has recently been commandeered by reworked gastropubs, the time-honoured connotations of the term are fully evoked by this place. Located just off Berkeley Square on Bruton Place – on a site where a pub has stood since the 15th century – you'll find the Guinea Grill serving up award-winning pies (the steak and kidney was particularly spectacular, if a bit on the posh side, on our last visit) and other traditional fare and the separate Guinea Bar playing host to the local office staff. And it's good to see that Wells and Young's haven't decided to change a thing about this slice of pub history – after all, if it ain't broke don't fix it, and this definitely isn't broken. Due to the titchy size of the bar this one can get tremendously busy during the week. However, on Saturday nights the bar is often deserted, so, if you're after a quiet night out in secluded surroundings, this could be the one for you.

FEATURES:    **HANDY FOR:** The Royal Academy, Wallace Collection

Hog in the Pound

RATING: 

29 South Molton Street
W1K 5RF
020 7493 7720

This one should be familiar to any shopper on Oxford Street, right by Bond Street Station and at the head of South Molton Street – favoured by clothes shoppers – it's a hard pub to miss. It's not much of a place, actually, carrying a pretty standard range of beers, including real ales on the hand pumps, and it pushes the food heavily – which is why many people come into this place. But it's nothing special and comes at a premium price. The service is OK and keeps up well with the relentless waves of footsore, hungry and thirsty people coming and going with their large carrier bags (and probably larger credit-card bills). Its location means it doesn't have to try too hard to pull in the punters and in the evenings it packs in crowds meeting up for a drink or two before moving on to clubs in the West End. On Friday nights it has a late (1am) licence and hosts karaoke. It hasn't changed in years and, judging by the amounts they must be raking in, it probably doesn't need to.

FEATURES:    

Iron Duke

RATING:

11 Avery Row
W1K 4AL
020 7629 1643

No longer part of Fuller's Ale and Pie house scheme, this doesn't mean it's terrible or that the food's gone downhill – just that there's only one pie on the menu. The well-kept Fuller's beers and quick and friendly service have stayed pretty much the same, making it a reasonable drinking experience. The usual crowd of local workers still frequent it and the atmosphere is the same. It can still be a hard pub to find, hence the common site of chaps on mobiles outside the pub barking out directions to their chums. Maybe not one to go out of your way for, but in a rather exclusive part of town it's nice to stumble across a relatively down-to-earth pub that hasn't gone over to the gastro or stripped-out-bar side.

FEATURES:     **HANDY FOR:** The Royal Academy, Wallace Collection

Pontefract Castle

RATING: 

71 Wigmore Street
W1U 1QB
020 7935 8034

A large pub on several floors, it tends to get packed with office workers weekday evenings, shoppers during opening times at weekends and then shop workers relaxing after the day's mayhem. The layout is designed to get as many people in as possible (especially the ground floor) so it's not really a place for a relaxing pint. Though, as it's Nicholson's, it does serve a decent pint, with Tribute and Doom bar on when we were in last – they do know how to look after it. It's also quite a handy place to meet up in as it's easy to find and there is food to sustain you if all that shopping has worn you down. One thing that still perplexes us is the downstairs bar, which seems to be done in a Spanish stylie. Fernando's Hideaway is available for hire and can be much quieter when the rest of the pub is heaving.

FEATURES:      **HANDY FOR:** Wallace Collection

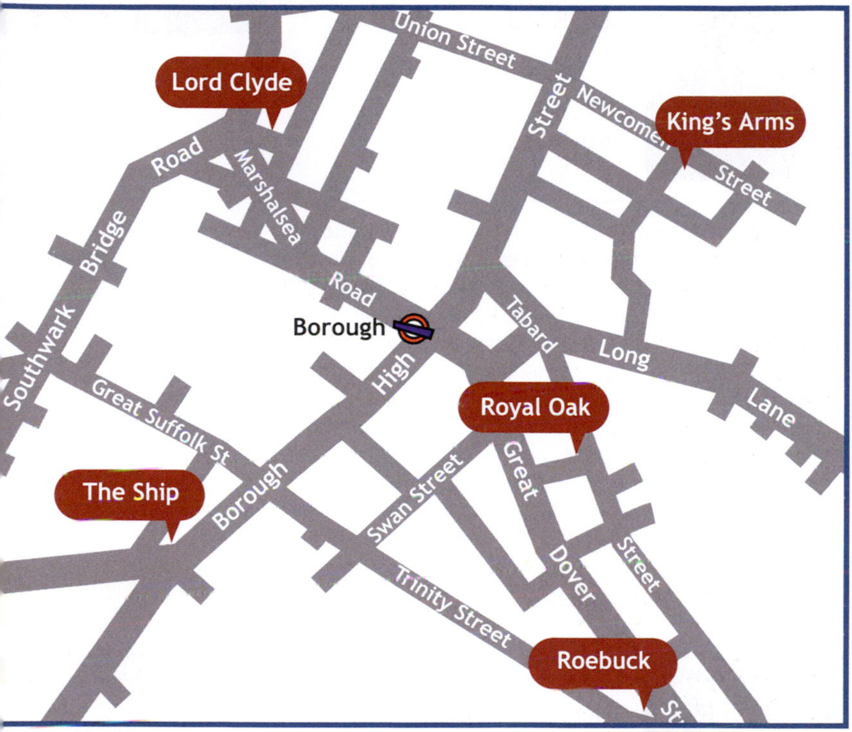

Lord Clyde
King's Arms
Royal Oak
The Ship
Roebuck
Borough
Union Street
Newcomen Street
Marshalsea Road
Southwark Bridge Road
Great Suffolk St
Borough High Street
Tabard
Long Lane
Swan Street
Great Dover Street
Trinity Street

King's Arms

RATING: 

65 Newcomen Street
SE1 1YT
020 7407 1132

A quiet, comfortable pub a short walk away from London Bridge and Borough stations. The King's Arms has Courage Best and Wadworth 6X on tap amongst the other usual lagers. The service is excellent and the clientele a good mixture of locals and people who work nearby. The big TV is there for big sporting occasions, but otherwise tucked well away. The old-fashioned decoration with large windows, pictures on the walls and amazing array of brasswork makes for surprisingly stylish and cosy interior and there's a fireplace for winter evenings. Food is typical pub grub and cheap with it (available 12-3pm). Give it a try.

FEATURES: 

HANDY FOR: London Dungeons, HMS Belfast

Lord Clyde

RATING:

27 Clennam Street
SE1 1ER
020 7407 3397

The Lord Clyde is a gem of a pub tucked away on what must be one of the tiniest streets in London. It's a welcoming place with friendly staff, a good atmosphere and a fine selection of real ales. An inn has stood on this site for almost 300 years and the current building is wonderfully preserved as rebuilt in 1913, featuring glazed tiles, wood panelling, brass fittings and long leather seats. The pub has been run by the Fitzpatrick family since 1956, and the landlady offers a menu of home-cooked English fare. If you need a literary incentive to come here, you might want to know that the Lord Clyde is located close to the original site of the Tabard Inn, where Chaucer's pilgrims started out towards Canterbury. The young Dickens also lodged nearby so that he could visit his father in the debtors prison at Marshalsea. At times this excellent boozer can a victim of its own success, with many more people flocking here, but in general we say: Get down here and see how things should be done.

FEATURES:   

HANDY FOR: London Dungeons, Tate Modern, HMS Belfast

Roebuck

RATING:

50 Great Dover Street
SE1 4YG
020 7357 7324

Regular readers of Fancyapint.com might undergo *déjà vu* whilst reading this review. Why? The Roebuck is another refurb in the predictable noughties pub style consisting of leather sofas, exposed floorboards, art on the walls and unobtrusive dance music, board games – hell, you know the routine by now. Gastro-ish main courses can be enjoyed for around £10, a range of Meantime and Purity ales on tap await, along with a range of lagers, Guinness, cider etc. The Roebuck is definitely a smart, relaxing pub aimed at a certain audience who clearly love it. After all, Bermondsey is hardly Clapham (yet) and there aren't many places of this kind nearby. For us, however, it is slightly predictable, but the lively atmosphere means it still receives a solid three pint rating.

FEATURES:            

The Royal Oak

RATING: 5

44 Tabard Street
SE1 4JU
020 7357 7173

A wonderful Victorian pub in the heart of Borough, the Royal Oak wins in every department. It serves a selection of excellent ales (including Mild, Pale, Best and Christmas Ale and Porter in winter) by Harvey's of Lewes and also offers a very good menu; on previous visits, we've enjoyed such delights as an excellent steak and ale pie, Lancashire Hotpot and rabbit casserole. The service is friendly and efficient, the shortish wine list is pretty decent and is mostly French (good) and now there's an extensive list of ciders should ale or wine not be to your taste. The pub has the feel of a vibrant local rather than just an after-office drinker, with a good mix of people in no hurry to leave. On this evidence, why would they? And now it's open at the weekends – great!

FEATURES:  

HANDY FOR: London Dungeons, Tate Modern

The Ship

RATING: 3

68 Borough Road
SE1 1DX
020 7403 7059

Home to some of our favourite drinkeries, Borough has an unusually high concentration of top-class boozers. The Ship, located a short walk from Borough tube, has some of the features that make other nearby pubs so great: a relaxed but lively atmosphere, a truly varied crowd of punters who live and work nearby, a decent range of beers (a good selection of Fuller's finest) and a healthy disrespect for pretension. Don't be put off by the somewhat 'estatey' exterior of this place, inside it's a good old-fashioned boozer. The décor's a little on the faded side, but this all adds to the atmosphere. There's pretty much something for everyone here: a dart board at the back, a quiet seating area at the top (with its own bar, although this wasn't in operation when we were last there) and the main bar, which, in addition to great beer, was serving up a pretty good selection of tunes (we didn't spot a jukebox anywhere). If there were international standards in 'decent' and 'solid', then this pub would be able to display its certification proudly.

FEATURES:    

HANDY FOR: Imperial War Museum, Tate Modern

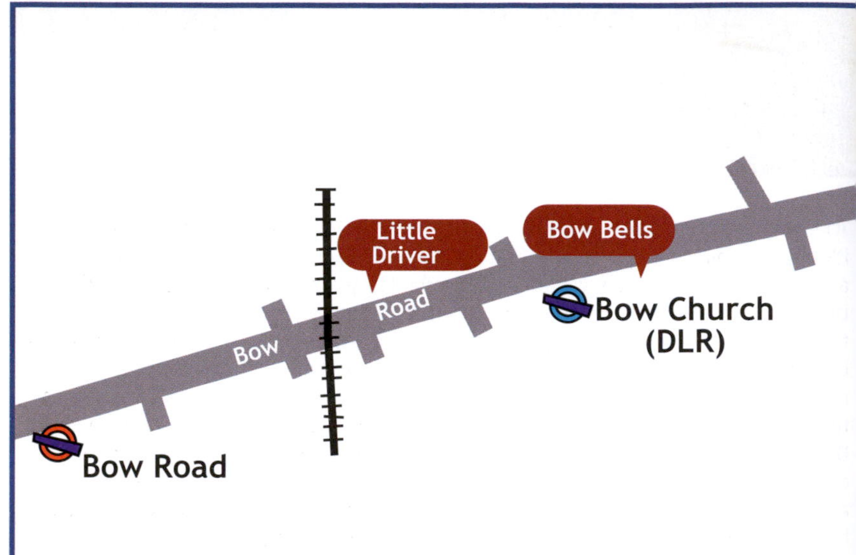

Bow Bells

RATING:

116 Bow Road
E3 3AA
020 8981 7317

It looks a bit dingy on the outside and the surrounding area is a bit off-putting, but don't let that worry you. This is an excellent local. It has an interesting range of beers on the hand pumps and an extensive, value-for-money food menu. It also offers big-screen TV, pool, a function room and, curiously, a jukebox which wasn't switched off even during the footy (surprisingly, it didn't spoil anything for anybody). An interesting mix of locals frequent the place and the service is prompt, friendly and attentive. Every so often a coachload of tourists pops into the place, we're not sure why, maybe it's something to do with Bow Bells (except they're in the Wren church in Cheapside in the City), nevertheless the tourists like it too. Anyway, they won't be disappointed, it's a top boozer.

FEATURES:    

Little Driver

RATING:

125 Bow Road
E3 2AN

The Little Driver has always been a pub for the locals in these parts and over the years it's served their needs pretty well. But things move on, the desires of the locals of yore are not the same as those of the apartment-dwelling locals of today and so the Little Driver has been updated to satisfy modern appetites. A lick of paint has cheered up the decor, both outside and in (it's no longer painted in the rather bright, but cheerless blue that once characterised it), and, thankfully, its Victorian character remains unmolested. The interior has been opened up to create a lighter, airier ambience and the beer garden has been transformed – you wouldn't believe you were on dreary old Bow Road. The drink is not much different from the older incarnation, there are a couple of hand pumps for real ale (unfortunately both were off on our last visit), although the wine list is somewhat improved and the service is cheerful, prompt and helpful. The big change is in the food, there's a much more ambitious menu, which seems reasonably priced. We've yet to try it, but we've heard quite complimentary remarks. All-in-all a sensible update to what has always been, in our opinion, a sensible pub.

FEATURES:  

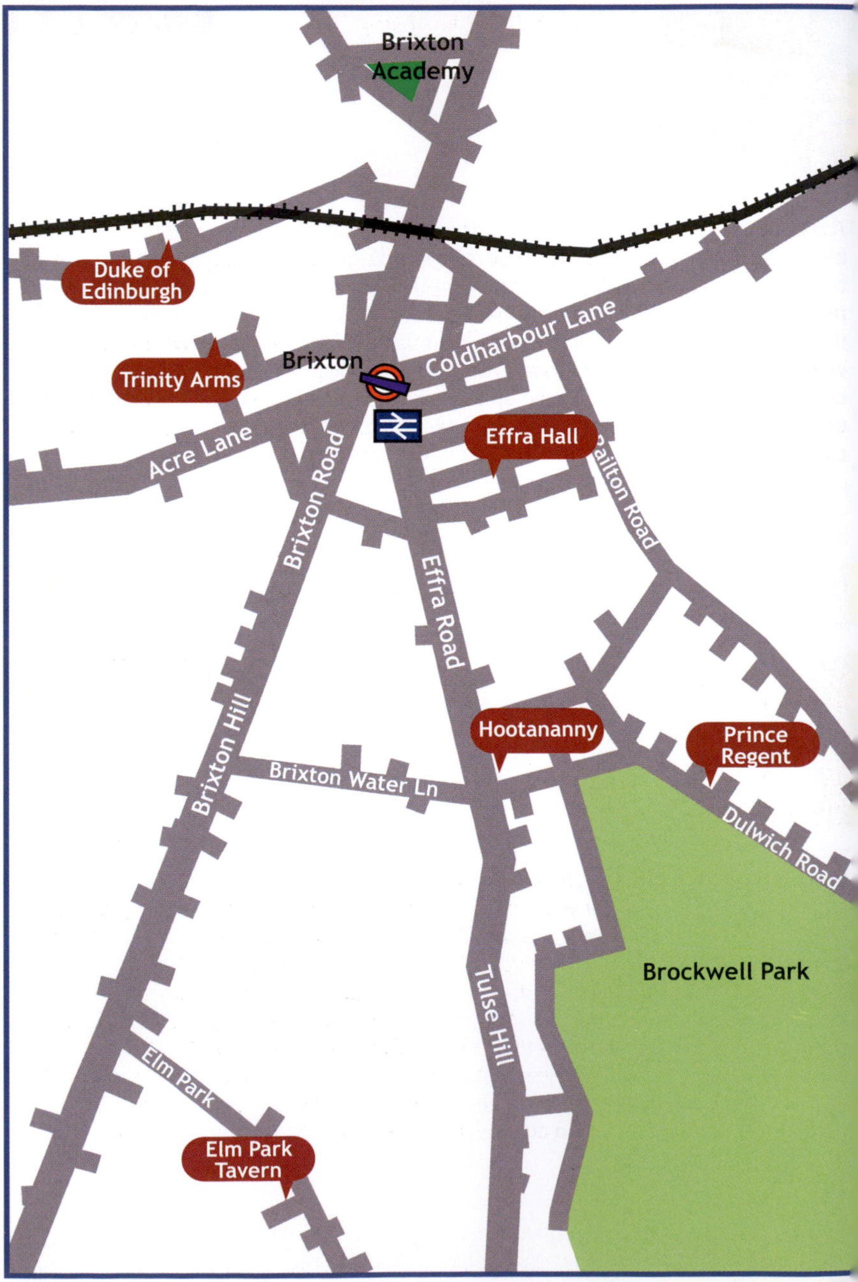

Brixton Academy
Duke of Edinburgh
Trinity Arms
Brixton
Coldharbour Lane
Acre Lane
Effra Hall
Brixton Road
ailton Road
Effra Road
Brixton Hill
Hootananny
Prince Regent
Brixton Water Ln
Dulwich Road
Brockwell Park
Tulse Hill
Elm Park
Elm Park Tavern

The Duke of Edinburgh

RATING: 

204 Ferndale Road
SW9 8AG
020 7326 0301

A couple of years back this one aimed for the pre-clubbing crowd (think full-on banging techno on a weekday afternoon); since then though, the Duke of Edinburgh has calmed down somewhat and is now one of the best pubs in Brixton. Despite the piss-lager-poor choice of beers, the service is friendly, with the classic 1930s decor of the pub equally charming. Add to that a beer garden which Rabelais's characters would have felt happy in – translation: it's very, very big – complete with giant barbecue in summer, and you end up with a boozer that's really not bad at all. And it offers accommodation, which is pretty rare for a pub in London. Oh, and it's pretty close to Brixton Academy, too.

FEATURES:         

The Effra

RATING: 

38a Kellet Road
SW2 1EB
020 7274 4180

Catering for a wide cross-section of Brixton society, this is the sort of constant, never-changing pub you could set your watch by. Well, hardly-ever changing – it's just had a lick of paint, but little else has changed. You can still expect Guinness and Red Stripe on tap, Jamaican home-cooking (except on Mondays) and regular live jazz in the evenings. It's not the largest of pubs, but the fact that it manages to cram so much into a small space adds to the Effra's air of bonhomie. Even with a lick of paint, you could quibble that the interior of this one has seen better days, but there's still enough remnants in the decor that hint at this one's rather grander past – particularly the nice wall and floor tiles on one side of the pub. The Effra is never going to be the trendiest pub in SW2, but, as a dependable local boozer in the area, it's hard to beat.

FEATURES:   

HANDY FOR: Brixton Academy

Elm Park Tavern

RATING: 

76 Elm Park
SW2 2UB

Despite its unprepossessing exterior, the Elm Park Tavern is a comfortably shabby local boozer with a welcoming atmosphere. Tucked away on a quiet corner among Brixton Hill's myriad Victorian terraces, the clientele is composed almost entirely of locals and it's rare that you won't find a seat, even during the raucous Thursday night quiz which is as close as this pub gets to being packed out. They show footy on the tellies scattered around the place. The bar has a small range of both lager and bitter on tap, and service is friendly and unhurried. No food is served, although having a takeaway delivered to your table seems to be a popular alternative. It's worth a visit just to check out the love seat settees in the main bar – fantastic!

FEATURES:    

The Hootananny

RATING:

95 Effra Road
SW2 1DF
020 7501 9671

A Ceilidh pub in the heart of Brixton may seem like the oddest idea since garlic-flavoured ice cream but – hold onto your sporran – it's actually rather good. The main bar (now boasting a massive projector screen) hasn't changed much since it was the Hobgoblin but the live music room is an entirely different kettle of haggis. Thankfully, they haven't gone overboard on the Scottishness; it would be all too easy to succumb to tartan overload, but the back room boasts surprisingly little in the way of twee Scots decoration – some Scottish newspapers used as wallpaper and the odd be-kilted barman are about as far as it goes. But coupled with a pleasingly dingy, candlelit atmosphere feels authentically Scottish. In terms of beer it has, fittingly, Caledonian Brewery's Deuchar's IPA on tap. It has what some have called the best beer garden in London, popular with the friendly locals (and their kids) on a sunny afternoon. Advertising live music every night 'from Ska to candlelit Celtic folk', you can get just about anything you fancy, assuming you get there on the right night – and any place that Chas and Dave play gets a recommendation in our book. With its extended opening hours this is always going to be a popular one past chucking-out time.

FEATURES:         

Prince Regent

RATING:

69 Dulwich Road
SE24 0NJ
020 7274 1567

The Prince Regent has recently undergone something of a transformation and is now (hurrah!) a jolly nice place to have a drink in what could be thought of as a less than salubrious area. While verging on middle-class gastropub territory, we were nonetheless impressed with the jugs of fresh flowers everywhere, swanky-looking dining area and tempting menu with a decent interior to boot. There are second-hand books for sale in aid of the local Green Party, and if all this is starting to sound a bit too right-on you can escape outside with a beer (they have quite a nice selection of real ales and Belgian lagers, if you like that sort of thing) and eavesdrop on the yummy mummies. All in all, a great place for a lazy Sunday lunch, and there's a good pub quiz too, we hear. We say: bravo! Well done that pub.

FEATURES:       

Trinity Arms

RATING: 

45 Trinity Gardens
SW9 8DR
020 7274 4544

If what you're after in Brixton is an unassuming pub rather than a style bar, this is probably your best bet. Off the main drag in a quiet Victorian square, it's a tad removed from the sights and smells of Brixton centralis. Despite the rather dated interior, it manages to attract a broad range of locals throughout the week, proving you don't need to make a pub trendy to attract customers. Well-kept Young's beer and a good beer garden as well as its distance from the main road make this one to recommend. A good local with a great atmosphere.

FEATURES:   

HANDY FOR: Brixton Academy

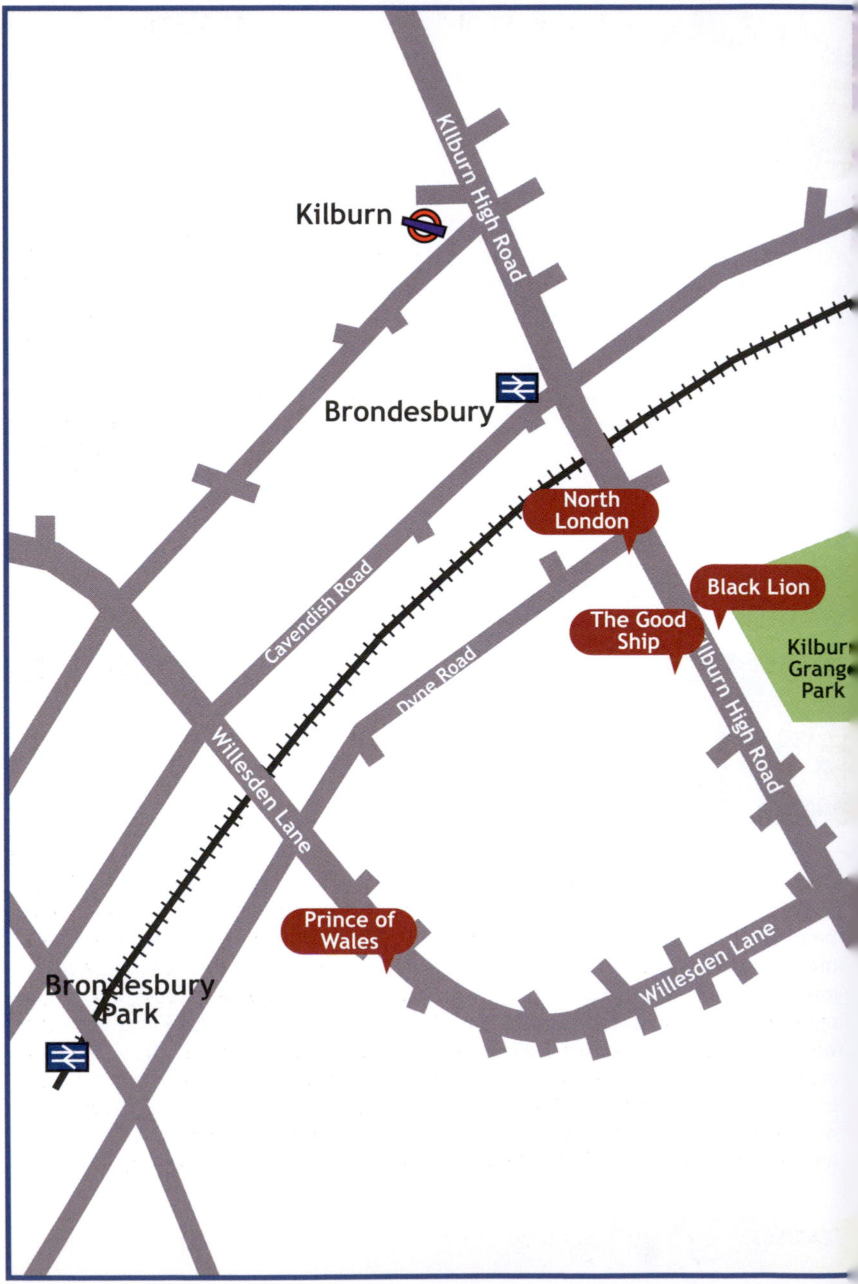

BRONDESBURY/BRONDESBURY PARK/KILBURN

The Black Lion

RATING: 4

274 Kilburn High Road
NW6 2BY
020 7624 1424

When last orders were called for the final time and the former Irish regulars wended their way over the road to the Kingdom, what they left behind was a spectacular Grade II listed Victorian interior, which had simply been ignored for years. During its transition into an upmarket gastropub, it was refurbished sympathetically, maintaining the interior – notably the very ornate ceiling – and a glorious separate dining room. Despite their commitment to attract the young, trendy crowd (who are only now discovering the delights of Kilburn) the main room still feels and looks like a pub rather than a loungers paradise. On the drinks front, after initially not serving ale, we're pleased to see two hand pumps have now made a belated appearance. We can't vouch for the quality of the food, and it is a bit pricey, but the surroundings ought to numb the pain. Previously one of the roughest pubs in Kilburn; now it's one of the best.

FEATURES:       

The Good Ship

RATING: 

289 Kilburn High Road
NW6 7JR
020 7372 2544

OK, maybe trendy DJ bars aren't actually aimed at anyone over the age of 25, so it's no surprise that we (well, some of us) often find them disappointing. Overpriced bottled beers and spirits, the young beautiful people full of disdain, nowhere to dance – but too loud to chat (OK, so now we really are sounding old). Well, The Good Ship is a trendy DJ bar on Kilburn High Road which seems to get it just right. It has a fair range of drinks, including London Pride on tap, Sky TV for your sports, a 100-CD jukebox that will astonish and amaze in its eclecticism and best of all a separate, stage/dance floor area. Looking through the listings of recent and upcoming events, it's clear that they're going out of their way to provide a range of entertainment with bands and quizzes as well as DJs. You'll have to pay for entry after 10.30, but three quid isn't going to break the bank. So, grab yourself a bottle of Asahi or a pint of Pride, relax and enjoy.

FEATURES:    

North London Tavern

RATING:

375 Kilburn High Road
NW6 7QB
020 7625 6634

Formerly as dependable as Jeeves in terms of Kilburn drinking, the North London Tavern reopened a while ago under new management, and started calling itself a 'pub and dining room'. The Irish flavour has gone, and been replaced by a much more cosmopolitan air. They kept the pub's nice original features (ceiling, pillars, stained-glass canopy) but replaced the furniture with new tables and lots of comfy chairs. The atmosphere has changed too, with jazz and Nancy Sinatra hits playing whilst you gaze at the gastro menu (typically £5 for snacks, £10 for mains) and sup your choice of ales or Belgian draught beer. They have an extensive wine list, too. It is an agreeable place for a drink, clearly aiming to draw in younger locals who didn't fancy its previous incarnation, but the crowd does tend to be fairly mixed. It's nothing like the auld tavern, but give it a go as it's still one of the better places to meet up in the area. And they do Sunday-night film nights for a fiver – worth a look.

FEATURES:     

The Prince of Wales

RATING: 

99-101 Willesden Lane
NW6 7SD
020 7624 9161

This fairly traditional, if a bit quirky, pub in the back streets of Kilburn has a lot going for it, though the smell of stale fag smoke does linger a bit – what must it have been like to last this long after the smoking ban? It's a massive pile with lots going on and what appears to be a dedicated following. Advertised when we were in last were karaoke, a disco, the regular quiz and a Sunday pool tourney. It does food, which is all prepared by the attached Malaysian/Thai restaurant (that appears to do karaoke as well – obviously a popular choice), including a few English dishes. Most of the regulars were eating Thai when we were in last, which is probably not a bad thing. The biggest complaint we had was the only bitter on the bar was John Smith's. It's nothing to go out of your way for, but you could do a lot worse. Besides, where else can you go to a karaoke/disco/quiz?

FEATURES:      

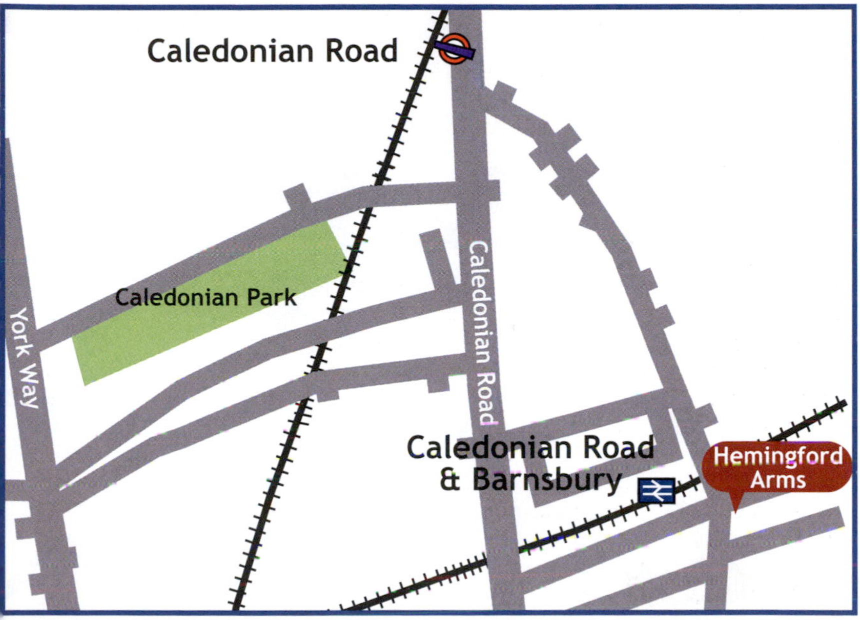

Caledonian Road

Caledonian Park

York Way

Caledonian Road

Caledonian Road
& Barnsbury

Hemingford
Arms

Hemingford Arms

RATING: 

158 Hemingford Road
N1 1DF
020 7607 3303

Tucked away in the affluent niche of Barnsbury, the Hemingford Arms can be a pleasant spot for a drink. Its cosy interior has a plethora of objects hanging from the ceiling and on the walls: these include a set of hickory golf clubs, film posters, trumpets and the odd Methodist church sign. These appear to be a genuine assortment of oddities rather than, as so often elsewhere, a cynical effort to give the place a forced quirkiness (though perhaps most disturbing was the male mannequin hanging over the gents loo with a sign between his legs pointing to said facilities). Five beers are available on the hand pumps in addition to the usual range of draught beer, and reasonable Thai food's on offer. The downside is the service, which can range from adequate to rude. You may also get the odd look from the regulars, but, once you're in, it's not a problem, although it can feel a bit intimidating to start with.

FEATURES:     

CAMDEN ROAD/CAMDEN TOWN

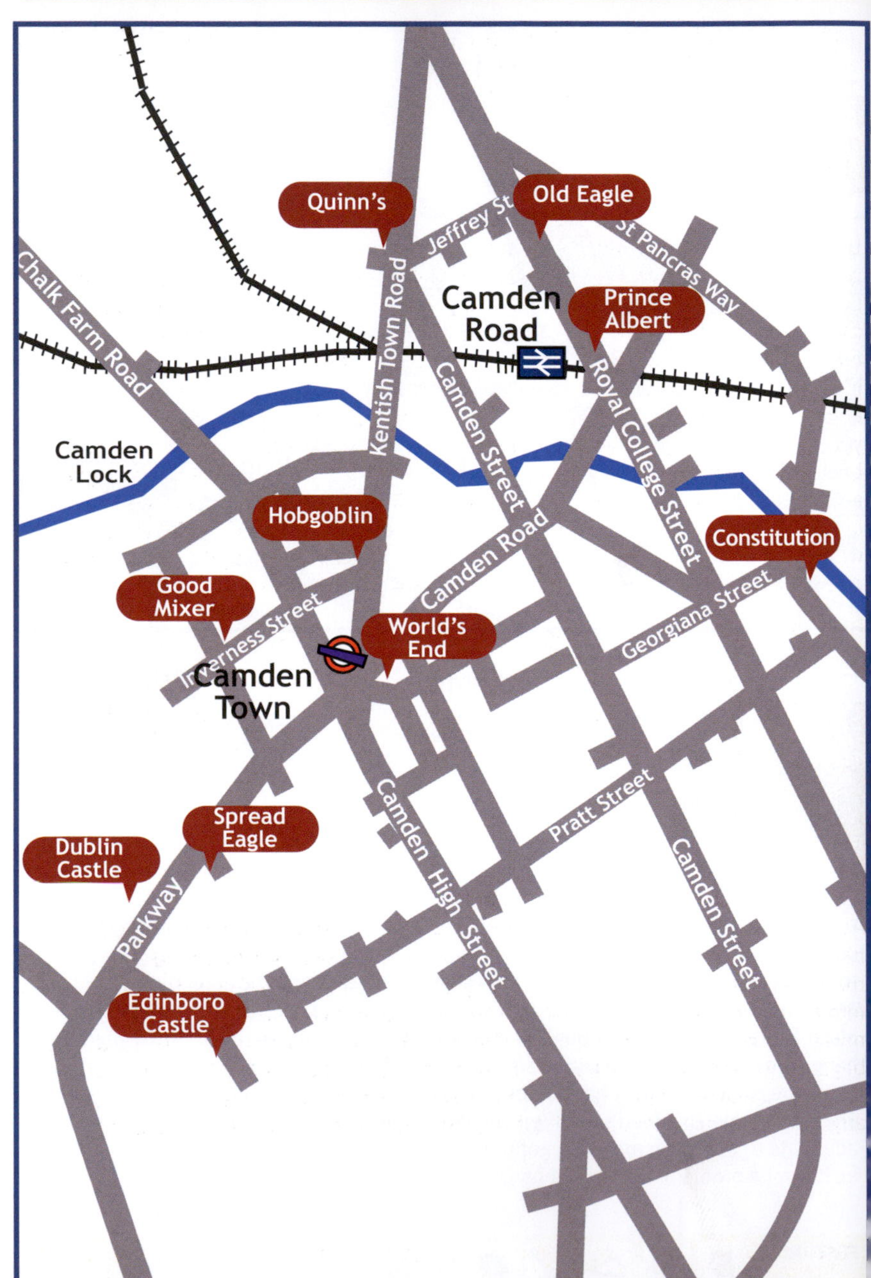

Quinn's
Old Eagle
Jeffrey St
St Pancras Way
Chalk Farm Road
Kentish Town Road
Camden Road
Prince Albert
Camden Street
Royal College Street
Camden Lock
Hobgoblin
Camden Road
Constitution
Good Mixer
Inverness Street
World's End
Georgiana Street
Camden Town
Pratt Street
Camden High Street
Spread Eagle
Dublin Castle
Parkway
Camden Street
Edinboro Castle

The Constitution

RATING:

42 St Pancras Way
NW1 0QT
020 7387 4805

Until comparatively recently the Constitution was predominantly a geezers' pub, in part due to being hidden away from the market-going throngs on the wrong side of Camden. While it's managed to avoid being molested by gastropubism and similar 21st-century afflictions, the crowd is however changing. Looking at how the Eagle around the corner – one of the last old-school pubs in the area – is frequently empty, it's both unsurprising and necessary. A smallish group of devoted but friendly enough blokey regulars still frequent the front, around the bar, but elsewhere younger regulars and newly located locals come here for a relaxing pint. The large beer garden overlooking the canal is understandably popular when the mercury goes anywhere above 15c (at least until the residents from the new flats opposite start moaning), while the diminutive basement bar offers up a variety of music nights, with DJs and live bands. The beer is well kept, with Adnams and regular guest beers offered on the hand pumps by friendly bar staff. A good, honest pub.

FEATURES:        

HANDY FOR: Camden Market

The Dublin Castle

RATING: 

94 Parkway
NW1 7AN
020 7485 1773

As other pubs move on, smarten up and strip down, the Dublin Castle remains. A hangover from the music scene of the 80s and 90s, this boozer attracts indie kids, rockers and tourists who come to convince themselves Camden isn't a shell of its former 'alternative' self. A definite weekend pub, the small back room has been a music venue for many a year and great shakes are made that Madness, among others, began their career here. We hasten to add that it also holds itself up as a good pub, too. Although not one for a quiet night, this is a busy, raucous place and is a must for anyone after an antidote to predictable gastropubs or the All Bar One-type scene.

FEATURES:  

HANDY FOR: Camden Market, London Zoo

Edinboro Castle

RATING:

57 Mornington Terrace
NW1 7RU
020 7255 9651

This large pub and larger beer garden probably benefit from not being too close to the hurly-burly of Camden Market. It's been modernised inside, with zebra-stripe wallpaper and curtains of hanging beads amongst the soft furnishings. It feels more designed, though, rather than just a bunch of furniture bought at a junk sale, and this helps give it a relaxed atmosphere. It's obviously working to appeal to a certain clientele, with fresh cut flowers scattered around and a decent mostly new-world wine list. You can still get a decent pint here, with a couple of ales on the hand pumps (kept to Cask Marque standards), and a selection of continental beers and lagers. There's a reasonably priced menu, unpretentious pub food, and the prices overall are pretty reasonable – this may be a conscious effort to provide good value in difficult times, but possibly just a sign of a well-run pub. If you fancy something more relaxed, this one never seems as manic as the pubs on Camden High Street, and it's probably right up your alley.

FEATURES:  

HANDY FOR: Camden Market, London Zoo

Good Mixer

RATING:  

30 Inverness Street
NW1 7HJ
020 7916 6176

If you remember Menswear, chances are you've had a few jars in the Good Mixer; in the early 1990s, it was the Brit-pop crowd's boozer of choice. Things have moved on since then, but the Good Mixer has hardly changed. It's a bare place with a pretty limited choice of beers – Old Speckled Hen was the only one on when we were in last – relying more on its reputation than anything tangible to attract the young indie punters (and their slightly older counterparts). The pool tables at the back are often occupied, but it might be worth dropping in if you fancy a game, or want to relive those heady days of Blur vs. Oasis.

FEATURES:   

HANDY FOR: Camden Market, London Zoo

The Hobgoblin

RATING:

33 Kentish Town Road
NW1 8NL
020 7284 0562

It's official: Goth is out, Rock is in ←sign of the horns→. Now a Hobgoblin pub owned by Wychwood Brewery, and with the name changed, it seems new life has been injected with a much-needed dose of ale into a pub previously best known for snakebite & blacks and dodgy Guinness. There are now three draught ales plus bottled beers to choose from, in addition to the usual standard fizzy yellow drinks. It is fair to say that, of all drinkers, Goths and Rockers should appreciate the darker side of beer the most. While there are probably some people who lament the passing of the old Dev, we were heartened by the more welcoming policies – though the 'no wankers' sign out front suggests not everyone's welcome. It's not just the drink that has broadened: the dress code has relaxed as well. It remains to be seen what impact this will have on the evening entertainment (which goes on until 1am on Fridays and Saturdays), but during the day there was still the same recognisable alternative crowd. Some of the more extreme decorations have gone, but it is by no means a redesign and the pub still feels as 'historic' as ever. And that is important in a world that increasingly swims in ready-made, flat-pack, false-fronted pubs; we must preserve the best in our traditional (and alternative) boozers.

FEATURES:   

HANDY FOR: Camden Market

Old Eagle

RATING: 

251 Royal College St
NW1 9LU
020 7482 6021

A warm and welcoming pub on any day but especially welcoming on a cold, wet, miserable day in November. Even though it's had the now traditional/obligatory/expected 'gastro' treatment (settees, stripped-down furniture, 'art' on the walls etc), it's only a nod to the genre and the pub is largely unblemished by it. It's a genuine, friendly, local boozer that serves decent, well-priced drink and food. The beer's pretty good and the service is excellent – all in all an offering that's rare in many locations, but especially welcome in Camden.

FEATURES:   

HANDY FOR: Camden Market

Prince Albert

RATING: 3 pints

163 Royal College Street
NW1 0SG
020 7485 1523

This is how to renovate a pub. It's no secret we like original features at Fancyapint?, but what was once a rather down-at-heel, back-street pub has been smartened up without ruining its charm. With great exterior tiling, original leaded glass, fireplaces and wood panelling all in place, it looks very nice indeed. The furniture complements the interior, there are three well-kept ales and a nice little front garden. Our last visit in 2007 found a distinctly unrelaxed hard-sell on food, but happily things seem to have calmed down since then. As for the food, that's improved too – upstairs is a proper restaurant, while downstairs is currently introducing a tapas bar menu. We were lucky enough to visit during a tasting session and it was uniformly good. Shame that they feel the need to add 12.5% service charge – it might make sense upstairs, but the downstairs pub should dispense with such things. Nevertheless, with a good atmosphere and charming service, a three-pint-rated pub this certainly is.

FEATURES:   

HANDY FOR: Camden Market

Quinn's

RATING: 4 pints

65 Kentish Town Road
NW1 8NY
020 7267 8240

Quinn's is a large, friendly pub boasting an amazing selection of beer on tap and in bottles. In particular, there is a very large selection of bottled German and Belgian beers, including some really high-quality and rare ones. So many varieties, in fact, that they are ordered by number, as in Chinese restaurants of yore. When we visited, a good atmosphere prevailed with some people watching football, some enjoying the food, and others just chatting; the pub is spacious enough to accommodate all of these without difficulty. There's also a cosy little yard out the back, if you fancy catching some sunshine (or rain) with your pint.

FEATURES:   

HANDY FOR: Camden Market

The Spread Eagle

RATING:

141 Albert Street
NW1 7NB
020 7267 1410

This is a very normal boozer for this area – not themed, not stripped out, not run down and, as a result, it can feel slightly out of place here in Camden. A decent pub, the premises are well looked after and up to Young's usual high standards – as are also the food and the drink – and the last refit has smartened things up a tad, though the changes aren't too wholesale and the pub still retains a great deal of its original character. There are some comfy-looking corners to hide away in or outdoor seating for when the sun comes out. Possibly the most un-Camden of all the pubs in NW1, the Spread Eagle is a safe bet for a couple of drinks. And, best of all, they do fish-finger sandwiches with tartar sauce!

FEATURES:   

HANDY FOR: Camden Market, London Zoo

World's End

174 Camden High Street
NW1 0NE
020 7482 1932

This rather large pub is really two pubs. The front is the original pub, with its cosy booths and fireplaces. The back is a later two-storey addition with a large central bar and balcony areas for sitting and watching the crowds. As it's directly over Camden's Underworld Club (they are both tied together), it can get very full if there's a band on, and consequently rowdy and rambunctious. Last time we were in was a Saturday night and it was a heaving mess. Six deep at the bar and so loud you can't hear yourself think – or order a drink. They do have bouncers on the door, but there was little sign of their turning anyone away – well, we got in. It's less uncomfortable during the day than at night, but there are better places nearby of an evening. Look upon it as Camden's answer to Disneyland and you're almost there.

FEATURES: 

HANDY FOR: Camden Market

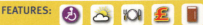

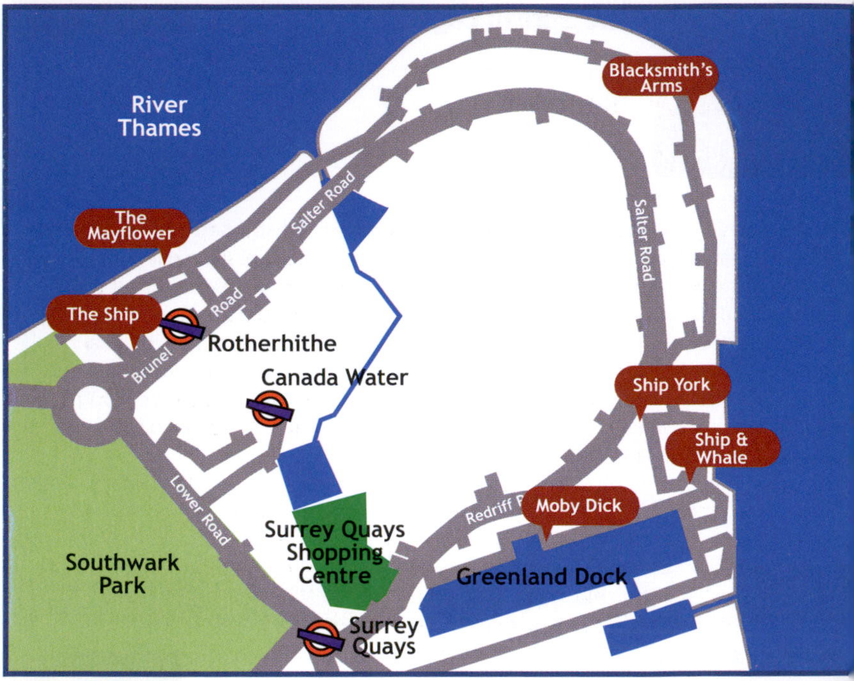

Blacksmith's Arms

RATING:

257 Rotherhithe Street
SE16 5EJ
020 7237 1349

The Blacksmith's Arms is a fine local that has served this area very well over the years. It hasn't been affected too much by the influx of people filling the many developments in the surrounding area in recent times, although the pub has edged a little more upmarket. This Tudorbethan pub has a nice oak-panelled, 1930s interior that hasn't been messed about with too much, simply spruced up, giving it a clubby, comfortable air. It's pretty relaxed during the week, though it does end up picking up refugees from the nearby Hilton; it does get busier at the weekend, although it can be pretty much a local affair. There's a good range of well-kept Fuller's ales on offer on the hand pumps, with a pretty reasonable wine list for those who aren't into pints. And all that's accompanied by an extensive Thai menu and some traditional pub grub.

FEATURES:     

The Mayflower

RATING:

117 Rotherhithe Street
SE16 4NF
020 7237 4088

This is probably the most famous pub on the river and rightly so, as it's named after the ship that set sail from a nearby quay in 1620, bearing the Pilgrim Fathers to America. At the time there was a pub on this site – the Shippe – which was rebuilt in the 18th century and renamed the Spread Eagle and Crown. The current name is much more recent (1957) when it was renamed in honour of its historic associations. Captain Christopher Jones, captain of the *Mayflower*, is buried in an unmarked grave in the church across the road – he died shortly after his return from America, little over a year after the *Mayflower* first sailed. And there's more: the Fighting Temeraire was broken up at the nearby Beatson's ship breaking yard and some of its timbers now constitute the communion table and chairs in the church. History aside, this should be on any pub aficionado's itinerary – it's a wonderful old place, exactly the image you conjure up when someone talks about a traditional English pub. With its oak beams, wood panelling, real fires, a jetty outside to enjoy views of the river, accompanied by Greene King ales and decent pub grub, the Mayflower fits the picture perfectly. Of course, it is so well known it's inevitably popular in high summer, but, at quieter times, it's a tranquil place to enjoy a pint or two and soak in the historic atmosphere of the area.

FEATURES:      

Moby Dick

RATING: 

6 Russell Place, Greenland Dock
SE16 7PL
020 7231 6719

The Moby Dick is a large pub on a dockside, just in from the river on the south bank of the Thames. It hasn't really changed much in recent history, maybe edged upmarket a little along with the surrounding area. The food looks good, the beer's more than palatable with a good range of Fuller's excellent ales on tap (including such delights as Festival Mild and Red Fox), and the wine list should cater for most tastes. Lovely place to spend a nice afternoon or evening, sitting outside and enjoying the sunshine reflecting off the water. It's the sort of pub that, if you're here, it's hard to leave, although that might be because everything else is so far away.

FEATURES:     

Ship

RATING:

39 St Marychurch Street
SE16 4JE
020 7237 4103

The Ship is a handsome boozer dating from around the 30s; it's a quiet, unassuming pub that serves the locals well. Young's bitter is the order of the day, in fact there's not a lot else to choose from, but that's OK. The service is friendly, the pint is good and there's a nice beer garden out the back for those warm days and (and occasional fags). It's a rare, honest, down-to-earth boozer and you're welcome even if you aren't a Millwall supporter.

FEATURES:    

The Ship & Whale

RATING: 

2 Gulliver Street
SE16 7LT
020 7237 7072

As the name suggests, once upon a time this part of London had strong ties to the whaling industry. Captain Ahabs are thin on the ground around Greenland Dock these days, and it's doubtful a trusty harpoon skewered the fish that featured on this one's menu. And that food choice gives an indication of what the pub is like: a (very) tidied-up affair which attracts the nearby flat-dwelling twenty-and thirty-somethings. Thankfully, it's not a gastropub: this is a pub first and foremost, and one which does feel of a certain age. Certainly one to pick off should you be attempting this stretch of the Thames Path, the Ship & Whale is also one of the better Shepherd Neame pubs we've come across of late: good beer, efficient staff.

FEATURES:   

Ship York

RATING: 4

Rotherhithe Street
SE16 5LJ

Ship York is a locals' pub that was here well before the latest redevelopments – it looks like a 30s building, but there's been a pub here for much longer than that. It's a big place providing good, honest food and drink and decent, friendly service for the local clientele. This pub is immaculate and the owners (and the clientele) are obviously (and justifiably) proud of the place. The locals are friendly, the landlord and lady are very welcoming, there are quizzes and other entertainments on offer and the beer's pretty decent too.

FEATURES:    

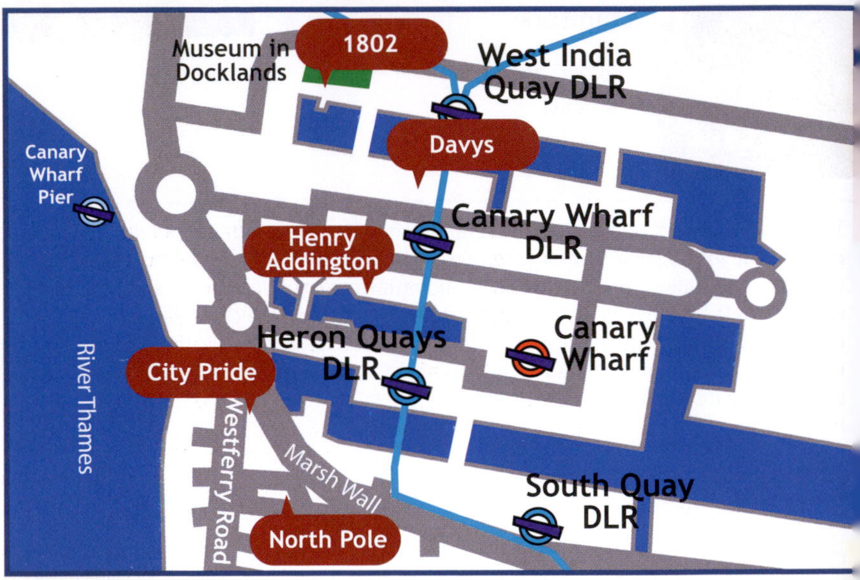

CANARY WHARF (DLR)/SOUTH QUAY (DLR)/WEST INDIA QUAY (DLR)

Museum in Docklands
1802
West India Quay DLR
Davys
Canary Wharf Pier
Canary Wharf DLR
Henry Addington
Heron Quays DLR
Canary Wharf
City Pride
River Thames
Westferry Road
Marsh Wall
South Quay DLR
North Pole

1802

RATING: 

Museum in Docklands No. 1 Warehouse
West India Quay
E14 4AL
0870 444 3886

It's not often that you'll decide to visit a museum for a pint, but, in the case of 1802, you might do just that. It is billed as *1802 Bar, Lounge and Dining* and 99% of the people who come are here for the good food. 1802's dockside location combined with decent weather can make a visit for liquid refreshment and pleasant conversation a worthwhile proposition. There are a few beers on tap and a range of bottled beers from about every continent: the Sleeman's Honey Brown Lager from Canada was particularly nice, slipping down easily on a hot afternoon. There's a decent wine list and if you do start to feel peckish you can always try the food. The prices are high, but all purchases go to the Museum in Docklands next door. You should be warned the aforementioned good weather can cause the quayside to be packed with punters, though at weekends it does tend to be quieter, although bank holidays can also see the crowds return. With its waterside location, broad, traffic-free pavements and terraces with table service, West India Quay is one of the few areas in London that truly emulates a continental-style ambience. And, if cultural curiosity should get the better of you, the museum is well worth a visit.

FEATURES:   

HANDY FOR: Museum in Docklands

CANARY WHARF (DLR)/SOUTH QUAY (DLR)/WEST INDIA QUAY (DLR)

City Pride

RATING:

15 West Ferry Road
E14 8JH
020 7987 3516

This pub will be familiar to the sadistic among you who enjoy the self-inflicted punishment of the participants in the London Marathon. The course of the marathon winds its way on both sides of the pub, putting it in a prime position, usually featuring in the TV broadcast. During this time, it's festooned and puts on live music and other entertainment. The rest of the year it provides refreshment to the ever-increasing number of office workers in Canary Wharf, a job it does competently enough. An extensive menu is partner to the unremarkable range of beers and wines on offer. It has a very large beer garden and terrace with views of Docklands and the river which provides a welcome respite from the hurly-burly of Canary Wharf and the other quays. It's been in the news lately: a property developer has bought the site for some £32 million – which probably spells the demise of yet another pub.

FEATURES:   **HANDY FOR:** Museum in Docklands

Davy's

RATING:

31–35 Fisherman's Walk
E14 4DH
020 7363 6630

Davy's may well have been established in 1870, but the current manifestations of Davy's outlets do no more than précis Identikit Britain. You well could be in a Davy's, All Bar One, Fine Line or Pitcher & Piano etc. and not know the difference (apart from a smattering of sawdust in the case of a Davy's), such is the predictability of the genre nowadays. Perhaps the only reason you would choose one over the other is geographical, but they're all located here anyway – so how to decide? For sure, Davy's has its Wallop, Lager and Bitter, but the quaint renaming of produce does not constitute a memorable drinking experience. Davy's is, indeed, a purveyor of fine wines and spirits and the service is universally good. But, when it comes to pub-going experiences, it's somewhat synthetic, a bit too olde worlde for its own good and especially ironic when it's in a location like Canary Wharf. In summer when you get the sun on the north side of Canary Wharf, the waterside tables are worthwhile, but for the rest of the time you'll probably be here because someone else decreed it.

FEATURES:    **HANDY FOR:** Museum in Docklands

Henry Addington

RATING: 2/5

Mackenzie Walk, 4 Canary Wharf
E14 4PH
020 7513 0921

This rather large Nicholson's pub ticks a lot of boxes without being a brilliant pub, but it probably meets the demands of the local workers in Canary Wharf. It's still got all the tellies it had before, decent beer with regular guests – and, if you haven't tried the 'sup before you tup' scheme, it's a great way to try a beer you've never come across before. It's also near the water for a pleasant place to sit on a sunny day. We're kind of disappointed that the disco floor has gone, but it obviously wasn't working. Like a lot of places in and around the City, it's now open for 'breakfast' from 10 and, even more intriguingly, offers 'sausage and ale tasting' every Wednesday. And, as it's Nicholson's, you can at least expect the standard of food and drink to be pretty good. Worth popping in for one if you're in the area, or just want a sunny place to sit.

FEATURES:      

HANDY FOR: Museum in Docklands

North Pole

RATING: 4/5

74 Manilla Street
E14 8LG
020 7987 5443

Quite simply, this is a top local a little off the beaten track on the Isle of Dogs in an area that's probably more than due for a massive redevelopment and expansion (fingers crossed, it won't happen any time soon). We've known this pub for a few years now and the service is still polite, fast and friendly. It offers some fairly standard, but well-kept beers on the hand pumps – Pride, Pedigree etc. And everyone in the pub seems to know everyone else, but somehow they never seem to make you feel left out. An excellent preference to the unimaginative bardom in the dockside areas. Sadly, it's not open all the time – especially at weekends and, when we were in on a Saturday night, it was woefully empty. This one's definitely worth going out of your way for – go on, give it a go, you know you want to.

HANDY FOR: Museum in Docklands

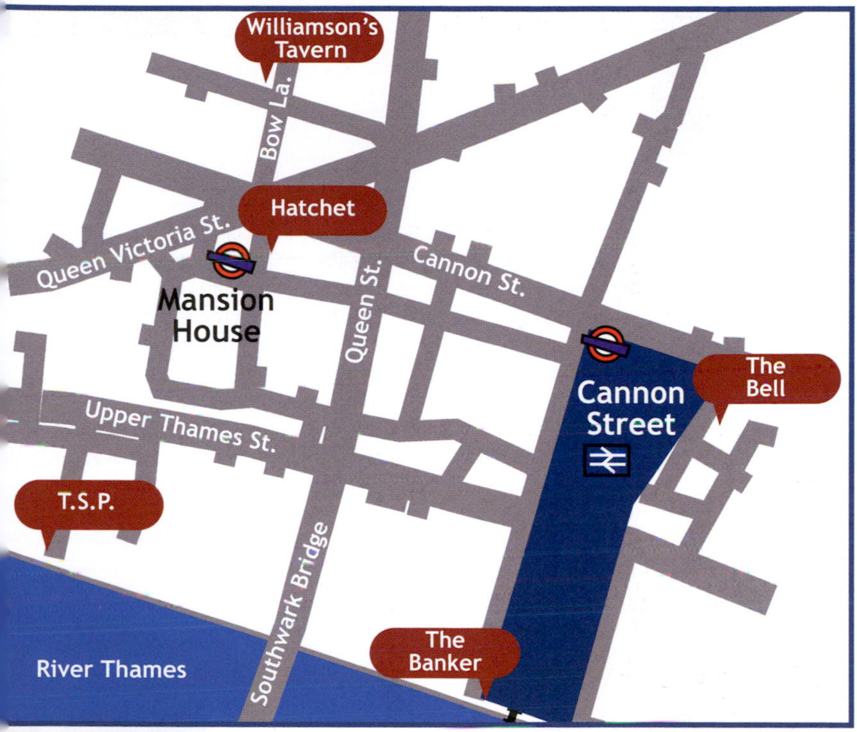

Williamson's Tavern
Bow La.
Hatchet
Queen Victoria St.
Mansion House
Queen St.
Cannon St.
Cannon Street
The Bell
Upper Thames St.
T.S.P.
Southwark Bridge
The Banker
River Thames

The Banker

RATING: 

2 Cousin Lane
EC4R 3TE
020 7283 5206

Tucked down a side street under the shadow of Cannon Street Station, we weren't expecting this to be much of a revelation. We were wrong. Spacious pub, well lit, cracking conservatory area overlooking the river. And reasonable outside seating also with river views. OK, if you look too closely you have a loading bay (actually containers of refuse) in your eye-line but, hey, river views of London whilst having a few beers are not to be sniffed at. On a sunny day, the terrace is usually crowded if you don't get your beach towel out first thing – but the well-trained staff cope well with crowds. Recommend you sneak off to get there early if it's a nice day.

FEATURES:        **HANDY FOR:** St Paul's Cathedral

The Bell

RATING:

29 Bush Lane
EC4R 0AN
020 7929 7772

Not so long ago, this was one of many old-style, untouched, City pubs, but now the Bell's something of an endangered species. Its tiny size means it gets packed to the gunwales at commuting times, but the service is prompt and polite and the range of real ale on the hand pumps is pretty well looked after. Claiming to be one of the few houses that survived the Great Fire of London in 1666, much of the original structure of the building survives (back then this one would actually have been on the banks of the Thames). Still half-timbered throughout, the time-warp interior décor is in keeping with the old-fashioned service and we don't want it to change a thing. Devotees of style bars and gastropubs won't be battering down the doors to get in, but if you want a pub that harks back to times past you should give it a go. The recent introduction of two TV screens has changed things somewhat, but not so much as you might expect. See it while you can and before the interior ends up in the Museum of London as an example of 20th-century social history.

FEATURES:  

HANDY FOR: Bank of England, Globe Theatre, HMS Belfast

Hatchet

28 Garlick Hill
EC4V 2BA
020 7236 0720

A classic City pub this. It's made up of two rooms: a bar and a small room at the back, both of which have been the scene of many a Square Mile liquid lunch. Although it can get very crowded at the customary lunch and pre-commute times, outside of these hours, the traditional feel of this one provides a welcome break from the hurly-burly of the City. As iconic, old-fashioned – and rare – as a City gent in a bowler hat, make sure you give this one a look whilst you still can.

HANDY FOR: St Paul's Cathedral, Bank of England, Globe Theatre

T.S.P. (The Samuel Pepys)

RATING: 2 pints

Stew Lane, High Timber Street
EC4V 3PT
020 7489 1871

There used to be a Samuel Pepys here years ago, a typical bare floorboards and oak beams place in a Victorian warehouse. It was a dark place spread over a couple of floors, where the only view of the river was from a small balcony, which got laughably crowded in summer. Now the warehouse has been redeveloped, retaining the original shell, and the Pepys has been reinstated in more or less the same place with a number of improvements. The spit and sawdust has been replaced with a brighter, more contemporary interior, although there still is just the one balcony – and that's in the section that's diners only. It's decent enough, there are a couple of (Cask Marque) real ales on the pumps and a range of bottled beers including a few Belgians. There's a strong emphasis on food, wine and cocktails now, catering for lunchtime punters from the City and this is probably what you'd come here for. Yes, you can come here just for a pint, but really this place is geared for the hungry City types.

FEATURES:  

HANDY FOR: St Paul's Cathedral, Tate Modern, Globe Theatre

Williamson's Tavern

RATING: 3 pints

1 Groveland Court, Bow Lane
EC4M 9EH
020 7248 6280

Whatever the hocus-pocus about this being London's oldest excise licence and a watering hole since the Great Fire of London, the reality is most of the structure dates from the 1930s. But it's kept the magic. The location is superb, tucked in a courtyard off an alley from Bow Lane through the magnificent wrought-iron gates presented by William III after he'd enjoyed a particularly fine pint. It has two inter-linked bars: the smaller front bar boasts probably the most uncomfortable benches ever designed, the larger back bar includes a range of hard and soft seating and separate dining area. Charming staff dispense great beers from a fine range. It can get busy – and nowhere round here is safe from the braying yahoo-in-a-suit brigade – but seats and a quiet(ish) corner can usually be found. Oh and did we mention the ghosts? At least one barmaid refuses to do evening shifts after one experience too many. And it's said police dog patrols can't persuade their canine chums to venture anywhere near the place.

FEATURES:  

HANDY FOR: St Paul's Cathedral, Bank of England

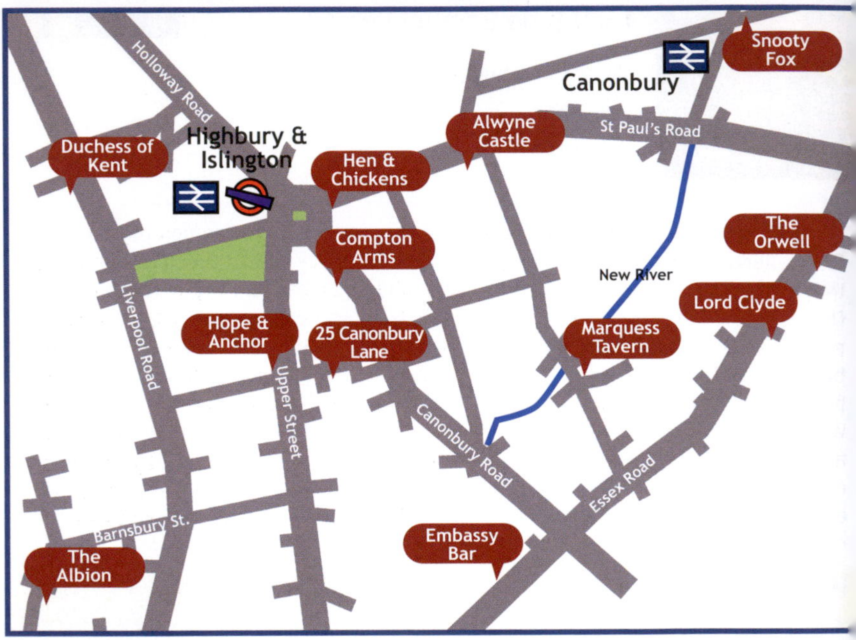

Holloway Road
Highbury & Islington
Canonbury
St Paul's Road
Liverpool Road
Upper Street
Canonbury Road
Essex Road
Barnsbury St.
New River
Snooty Fox
Duchess of Kent
Hen & Chickens
Alwyne Castle
Compton Arms
The Orwell
Lord Clyde
Hope & Anchor
25 Canonbury Lane
Marquess Tavern
Embassy Bar
The Albion

25 Canonbury Lane

RATING:

25 Canonbury Lane
N1 2AS
020 7226 0955

A makeover and more upmarket direction – if that's possible – for this tiny style bar just off Upper Street. It's opulently decorated, with gilt mirrors, fresh flowers, funky lampshades and stencilled walls and beautiful people to match. In compensation for a selection of average beer with no bitters to speak of, there's an extensive cocktail list and reasonably priced (and pretty fab-smelling) Thai food available to keep the hunger pangs at bay. Importantly for a place like this, the clientele are pleasantly mixed, albeit in a decidedly upmarket sort of way, which, when mixed with attentive, friendly and capable staff, make it a great place to go. So, if you're after a more genteel experience at the northern end of Upper Street, '25' is certainly worth a look.

HANDY FOR: Business Design Centre

The Albion

RATING:

10 Thornhill Road
N1 1HW
020 7607 7450

This gastrofied pub in Barnsbury has obviously done something right, judging by the full-to-capacity crowd on the Saturday afternoon we were in last. Well, almost full, but they were obviously well on their way with two huge tables reserved for large parties. Don't get us wrong, there's not a lot wrong with the Albion, and the families and other punters that go here obviously like it the way it is. We were a little disappointed in the beer selection, with only two on the hand pumps, Black Sheep and IPA, but then they probably sell more wine here. The food looks good, and we were tempted to stop, but we couldn't actually find a table. Overall it's pretty much par for the gastropub course and the scene is pretty familiar, by now – safe and comfortable, but it really depends on when you visit. The Albion is a pub of two halves – on a sunny spring afternoon it's a pleasant place to relax and converse; on a Friday night it can be completely the opposite: crowded, noisy and uncomfortable.

FEATURES:     

Alwyne Castle

St Paul's Road
N1 2LY
020 7288 9861

Having been an average boozer a few years back, The Alwyne has been gastrofied for a while now. You'll recognise it as a fairly typical 21st-century conversion: polished wood floor, comfy sofas, gastropub menu. But, that said, it has kept the great fireplace and mercifully decided against polished chrome fittings. It's probably a sign of the times that what we'd have thought was paying over the odds for a meal a few years ago now seems a bargain. How things change. The service is friendly enough, albeit sometimes pitifully slow, and there are a couple of ales on tap, along with a good choice of lager. It's a rangy place, with three large rooms including a conservatory, but the uncomfortably laid-out furniture can make it feel slightly less cohesive than it should be. It's more relaxed earlier in the week, while Saturday night can find it verging on uncomfortably full; and on match days you'll find the pub absolutely heaving and your drink will come in a plastic, not a glass.

FEATURES:    

Compton Arms

RATING:

4 Compton Avenue
N1 2XD
020 7359 6883

We've always had the impression that this pub likes to think it's somewhere out in the wilds of Surrey or Sussex and, come to that, so do the locals. But that's OK and it certainly does look after its beer really well, with an extensive and ever-changing range of bitters on the hand pumps ready for your delectation. It's a tiny place that fills up very, very easily, though the street outside and the compact beer garden at the back do their best to cope with the overflow. Decent grub, a wide range of punters and the sort of traditional pub atmosphere you won't find on the nearby Upper Street – which is probably why it's so popular. A very fine place.

FEATURES:    

Duchess of Kent

RATING:

141 Liverpool Road
N7 8PR
020 7609 7104

This Geronimo Inn's pub has obviously found its place in the hearts of the locals, as it shows no sign of waning. It attracts all sorts, from families to younger trendies and lads in to watch the footy. It is a little schizophrenic, in that it's half restaurant, half pub, but the clientele don't seem to mind too much, even with tables with reserved signs on them. The beer's excellent, with Cornish Coaster and Harvey's bitter amongst the selection on the pumps last time we were in, and the offer of a pie and a pint for £5 was pretty tempting – a meat pie on its own was just £2.50. That said, the food on the menu looked and smelled pretty good, too. They do have a selection of continental beers, with Budvar and Edelweiss fairly representative. It's good to see a pub doing as well as this one appears to be when it is so local. If you're in the Highbury area, it's well worth a look. We were also quite intrigued by an advertised 'conker fight' – novel and probably one to bring the kids to. Oh, and the typeface on the exterior is reminiscent of a Double Diamond label, though that's probably unintentional.

FEATURES:      

Embassy Bar

RATING:

119 Essex Road
N1 2SN
020 7226 7901

Along with the nearby (now defunct) Social, Embassy was one of the original Islington bars to give the kids an alternative to the nearby scary boozers and insipid chain pubs. Whilst others have taken their time to catch up – with mixed results – Embassy remains popular. With its stylish, darkly illuminated interior and red velveteen flock wallpaper (which made an appearance when flock wallpaper was still uncool), it's easy to forget you're actually sat in grey Essex Road. Surprisingly, drinks aren't extortionate, while DJs feature Thursday to Sunday, playing tunes invariably from the more predicable soul, hip-hop and funk end of the spectrum. On weekdays it's a satisfying and lively place to have a drink, if you arrive early enough to get seats. However, on weekends, it gets very busy and with the allure of a dance floor in the basement it essentially becomes a club, complete with an entry fee after 9pm. Not to everyone's taste, this is nonetheless a reasonable example of the kind of bar that's often done rather badly.

FEATURES:   

HANDY FOR: Business Design Centre

Hen & Chickens

RATING: 

109 St Paul's Road
N1 2NA
020 7704 2001

This small pub on the northeast corner of Highbury roundabout looks a fairly unremarkable pub which serves moderately good beer in pleasing enough surroundings. However, it does open later than many nearby places and has a great comedy theatre upstairs, which has witnessed the birth of many a famous comedian's career. The seating has been marginally improved from our last visit, but is predominantly high level, in no small part to accommodate the pre-and post-theatre crowds. As such, the place feels a little transitory, but at least attempts to gain repeat custom with an eclectic jukebox and frequent live music acts in the main bar. There are certainly far worse places to visit this close to Highbury & Islington tube, but it's probably only worth a major detour if you're coming to see some comedy, or it's after 11pm and you're thirsty for a couple more...

FEATURES:    

Hope & Anchor

RATING:

207 Upper Street

N1 1RL

020 7354 1312

The Hope & Anchor attracts the crowd not catered to in the numerous All Bar One-type bars further up the road towards Angel. It proffers live music in a tiny basement, and the imbibing of liquids while sweating to said tunes. Upstairs, there's a cracking jukebox and it's all very cool and skinny jeans-esque, apart from the local old geezer who sits and people-watches all night. It may appear a bit tidier than in its punk heyday, but it's (still) a music pub, it's a bit sticky and it sells beer. Nuff said.

FEATURES:  

HANDY FOR: Business Design Centre

Lord Clyde

RATING: 

342 Essex Road

N1 3PB

020 7226 5907

When we discovered that Irish boozer Kendrick's Bar had remodelled itself as a 'food-led pub', a collective groan went around Fancyapint Towers. As the penultimate vestige of old Islington's public-house legacy bit the dust, did we really need another pub turned restaurant? As it happens, repeated visits have indicated you shouldn't always believe the hype; there's no cutlery pre-emptively laid out on tables as we half-expected and, overall, this is simply a good pub which happens to sell pretty fantastic food. Service is consistently great: friendly, chatty and polite, while a couple of well-kept real ales whetted our whistles nicely. The music is always spot on, going from Pink Floyd to The Roots via Primal Scream. In addition to a fortnightly quiz, they've also started themed food nights on Wednesdays which look like they're popular and an added bonus, too. It's a big pub, still complete with its lovely original Charringtons wood panelling and parquet flooring, but they need to bring some warmth and light to the rather dull back room. There's a few issues to iron out and they need more customers, but we feel it could become great here.

FEATURES:      

Marquess Tavern

RATING:

32 Canonbury Street
N1 2TB
020 7354 2975

Off the beaten track, but surprisingly near Essex Road's mob of bars, lies the Marquess Tavern. A magnificent unspoilt Victorian building, it boasts a comfortable front bar with original wood panelling and a back room (probably once a games room) which claims an impressively high ceiling. A recent change of management (it's now run by a gaggle of former regulars) hasn't changed the gastro emphasis dramatically and the aforementioned back room remains the dining room. An expensive dining room at that: £10 for the veggie dish, £18 for the venison. Still, lounging in the front bar continues to be a pleasure – there's still plenty of beer here with an excellent selection of (mainly bottled) ales and a highly impressive selection of lagers from the continent and beyond. Service too remains down-to-earth and friendly. The place gets very busy but it does feel more of a locals' place than other gastropubs we know – due to its back-street location, Islington's weekend visitors simply don't see it.

FEATURES:    

The Orwell

RATING: 

382 Essex Road
N1 3PF
020 7359 4651

While Angel teems with life every weekend, the crowds ebb away the further down Essex Road you travel – a problem several previous versions of the Orwell have struggled to cope with. The new owners have come in with a different approach, operating it as a music venue to draw crowds from further afield, instead of only looking for locals after a pint. There is sometimes a small cover charge (mostly at weekends), while the music on offer varies so checking ahead may be recommended, with metal, new wave, post-punk and Brit-pop among the current offerings. The stage area also plays host to bands and occasionally comedy. Whereas some music venues don't deliver on the drinks front, here ale and lager drinkers are looked after, while Franziskaner also makes an appearance. The Orwell stays open until 2am on Friday and Saturday, while it doesn't open at all on Monday or Tuesday. This welcome addition to the area will hopefully last longer than its predecessors.

FEATURES:    

Snooty Fox

RATING:

75 Grosvenor Avenue
N5 2NN
020 7354 0094

This loungey pub has just got better as time has gone on and it's obviously a hit with the locals. When we were last in, on a lazy Saturday afternoon, there were people dotted all over the place reading the papers with a quiet pint or indulging in a late lunch. As we've said before, it's easy to lump this one in with a lot of other places trying too hard nearby, but there is something about the Fox – a freshness and originality to the place. Perhaps it stems from the pub's old-fashioned vinyl jukebox: there're not many of them left in London, probably as relying on A and B sides of singles can result in a rather odd selection of tracks (if you have a burning desire to hear the Instrumental Dub Mix B-side of Bowie's 'Absolute Beginners' be sure to stop by). There's also the promise of regular DJ nights to be had here, and we're not too surprised at that. The food's changed a bit, as they've opted for spit-roasted chicken for the majority of the mains – don't worry, there are vegetarian options. But to be honest, the pork pie, pickles and piccalilli for under a fiver sounded pretty good, too. Stylish is probably the best way to describe this place, with some nice touches on the décor front – the wooden cabinet for the spirit bottles was a particular favourite, and it's hard to be critical of a bar where posters of Debbie Harry and Marianne Faithfull adorn the walls. And it's one we'll be coming back to.

FEATURES:     

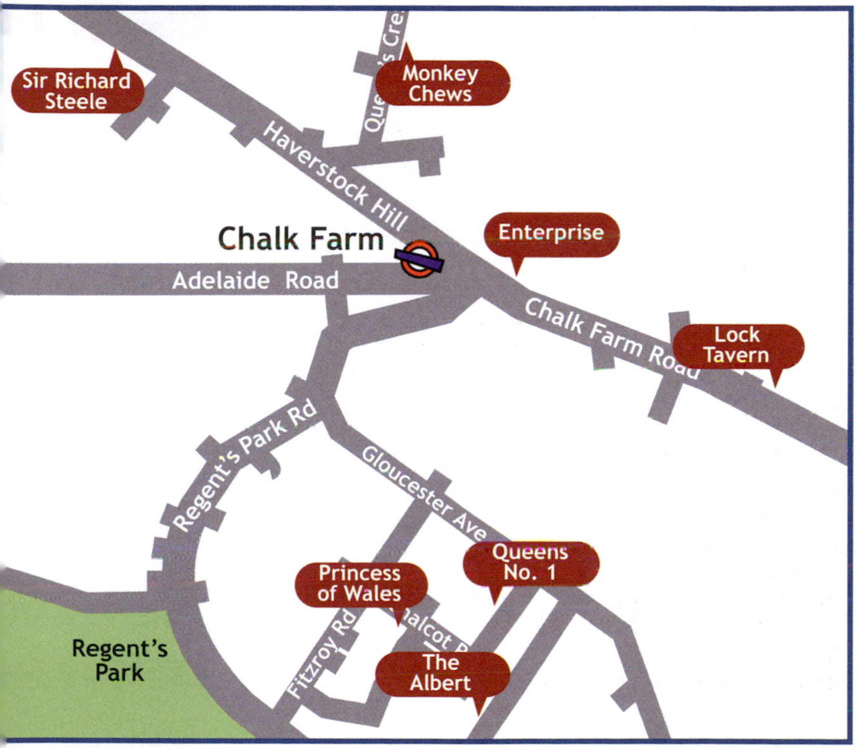

Sir Richard Steele
Monkey Chews
Haverstock Hill
Chalk Farm
Enterprise
Adelaide Road
Chalk Farm Road
Lock Tavern
Regent's Park Rd
Gloucester Ave
Queens No. 1
Princess of Wales
Regent's Park
Fitzroy Rd
The Albert

The Albert

RATING: 

11 Princess Road
NW1 8JR
020 7722 1886

Not surprising for the area, The Albert is an old pub that had an upgrade a few years ago now. With good, fresh food being served at inflated Primrose Hill prices, it would be easy to argue that this is a pub bordering on gastro territory. However, it's still distinctively a pub, even if the stripped interior and country kitchen tables simply mean a slightly more modern version. Plenty of old-school locals still pop by and the atmosphere is unpretentious and welcoming. A great beer garden, complete with an apple tree in the middle, only adds to The Albert's charms. Relaxed and pleasant – a very good one for this neck of the woods.

FEATURES:    

HANDY FOR: London Zoo, Camden Market

The Enterprise

RATING:

2 Haverstock Hill
NW3 2BL
020 7485 2659

An honest pub with none of the pub theme park style of décor you seem to get in this area. There's a strong Irish literary theme to the décor – pictures of numerous notables adorn the walls and there are poetry evenings continuing the literary tradition. There's a large band of regulars, supplemented by visitors to the upstairs events, but depending on the time of day, it's a place where you could sit alone and read a paper, or have a full-on night out with your mates – it takes it all in its stride (which is lucky as our Friday-night visit found it full to bursting with young trendy Camdenites). A decent range of drink is on offer, including stuff ranging from real ale to Belgian and other continental beers, and the service is OK too.

FEATURES:   

HANDY FOR: London Zoo, Camden Market

Lock Tavern

RATING: 

35 Chalk Farm Road
NW1 8AJ
020 7482 7163

Once an old spit and sawdust affair, it's now owned by DJ Jon Carter and chums and is more in keeping with the trend-setters of Camden. With its designer black interior, ever-changing DJ sets and a mix and match menu the place could easily have ended up its own back garden. It hasn't though. The bar staff know what they're doing and, even if there's an air of studied cool about some of the punters, they're not the sort of crowd who'll stare at you if you're not sporting an old-skool Adidas top. Plenty of room inside and outside (including a garden and roof terrace) but come early, as it gets filled to capacity on the weekend. All in all, a fine advert for the rejuvenation of old pubs. If only they kept hold of that MP3 jukebox... Oh, and the beer's good too.

FEATURES:   

HANDY FOR: London Zoo, Camden Market

Monkey Chews

RATING:

2 Queens Crescent
NW5 4EP
020 7267 6406

It would be a travesty to describe Monkey Chews as anything less than a really great place to spend an evening – the sort of place you can go, intending to have just a drink or two, and end up staying until closing time. It's a clever and modern take on the British pub, with friendly service, a decent array of drinks (cocktails a speciality), while the food served, both in the main bar area and a more meal-orientated back room, surpasses in quality the offerings of many a gastropub. The lighting is understated, with reddish tones, and there's a wide array of knickknacks all around. The seating is proper seating, and comfortable too. The soundtrack was eclectic, with everything from Motown to Morricone, Marley to Morcheeba. The relative discretion in the way Monkey Chews presents itself counts heavily in its favour, as does its slightly hidden-away location on the boundaries between sleb-ville and ASBO-central. Regulars seem to love it, and so do we. All very impressive, it must be said.

FEATURES:   

Princess of Wales

RATING:

22 Chalcot Road
NW1 8LL
020 7722 0354

Somehow, thankfully, the Princess of Wales was missed in the trendification of Primrose Hill and is definitely the better for it. This pub has it all: large windows at the front (which fold back for summer) and cosy nooks and crannies towards the back and in the basement. There is even a (sadly, under-utilised) garden. The central bar creates a good focal point and the numerous pot plants are a nice touch. A fair selection of real ales can be found and the food is both the cheapest in the area as well as superb. It can attract the older locals, witnessed by the popularity of the Sunday-evening live jazz sessions, but also a younger crowd who have grown tired of the post-modern affairs that are all too common in the area. So for people whose idea of going to the pub is all about style over substance, the Princess of Wales won't suit them. However, for those who want a warm, genuine pub and are trapped in the wilds of NW1, it's thoroughly recommended.

FEATURES:      *Reviewers' Award – Overall Winner 2008*

Queens No. 1

RATING:

1 Edis Street
NW1 8LG
020 7786 3049

Apparently, way back when, this used to be a cosy, traditional local. We never saw it then, because at some point it was deemed better to gut the place and start again. Outside is a studiously cool and minimalist black, which made us wonder what the tiles underneath look like, while inside finds a warm but contemporary feel. Leather, wood and candles – the staples of many a modern pub – feature heavily, but it's been done with a degree of individuality, as illustrated by the unusual and ornate fireplace. The lager choice is fine and they pride themselves on their jugs of Pimms and Sangria, but they need to improve the below-average ale selection. Food wise, lunchtime offers reasonably priced British pub fare, while evening sees the reins handed over to a Thai chef. There's a few seats out front, which is perfectly agreeable in this genteel part of London and the front windows open out for the warm weather. All in all, Queens No1 might not stun you into amazement, but it's considerably nicer than some of the area's more pretentious gastropubs.

HANDY FOR: London Zoo, Camden Market

The Sir Richard Steele

RATING:

97 Haverstock Hill
NW3 4RL
020 7483 1261

This pub is a big old rangy place that is very possibly the template for all those London pubs furnished with curios and knickknacks. Even without the toy carts and fruit bat display looming down over you, there's also a large old-master-style fresco on the ceiling to take in, with some of the notable regulars forever immortalised in paint. Aside from the decoration this is still a noteworthy pub with Thai food on offer, a beer garden for the summer and hardened winter smokers, four real ales and a piano in the corner for any impromptu sing-a-longs. This pub offers up a more traditional pub experience than the more loungey bars nearby, and its temperament, clientele and furnishings add up to one of North London's more idiosyncratic boozers.

FEATURES:   

Reviewers' Award – Winner 2008

ington St
King's Arms
Clerkenwell Road
Clock House
Farringdon Road
Leather Lane
Hatton
Bleeding Heart
Greville Street
Garden
Grays Inn Road
Cittie of York
Ye Olde Mitre
Holborn
Chancery Lane
Furnival
Fetter Lane
New Fetter Lane
Shoe Lane
Castle
Chancery Lane
Cursitor St
Bream's Buildings
Knights Templar
Carey St

Bleeding Heart Tavern

RATING:

Bleeding Heart Yard
EC1N 8SJ
020 7242 8238

This Adnam's house has kept its standards high over the years, and is a great place to try their range of beers. If you're looking for lager though, they only do Bitburger in smaller continental glasses – they won't pour you a pint due to its strength (4.8%!) – or bottles of Beck's and the like. The wine list is pretty good, and potentially more of their customers are drinking wine or bubbly. It's a reasonable place to go if some of your friends want a wine bar and some of them want a pub. The all-French staff perform as if they've been running the place for years and they're always polite and efficient – it's no surprise it feels quite a lot like a continental establishment and the menu reflects that, too. We can heartily recommend the lamb burger, and the chips are superb! There's also breakfast, from 7.30 until 10.30 – and we'll be back to check this out. It does get busy of an evening, with punters spilling out onto the pavement, but it quietens once most of the customers have commuted their weary way home.

FEATURES:  

HANDY FOR: Sir John Soane's Museum

The Castle

26 Furnival Street
EC4A 1JS
020 7405 5470

Once upon a time, even though it's in the heart of hectic Holborn, this quiet, smallish pub was far enough off the beaten track for it to be a refuge for those looking for an undisturbed drink. Now, it's in the hands of the same people who look after The Bell (on Cannon Street), and the relaunched Castle is much improved. The main draw now is the real ale selection, with the pub offering up to eight, regularly rotating, guest beers and, on the basis of our visit, they'll be in for a treat with a good range of unusual and well-kept ales on offer. The food is, thankfully, simple pub grub (which goes well with the beers on offer, though, surprisingly, there was no fish and chips on the menu when we were in last) and the quality's pretty decent too, sourced locally from Smithfield and Borough Markets and priced pretty cheaply. As it's not the largest of pubs, it's popularity is only likely to increase, and become busier and more crowded as a result, as it does when the landlord gets it right. You should definitely give this one a look.

FEATURES:   

HANDY FOR: Sir John Soane's Museum

Cittie of Yorke

RATING:

22 High Holborn
WC1V 6BS
020 7242 7670

A well-known, large, magnificent pub with a host of unusual architectural features, especially in the back bar, with its cubicle-like nooks and crannies and giant vats above the bar. Of particular interest is the triangular fireplace in the centre of the room with its chimney and flue diverted under the floor and up the wall. It's inevitably packed lunchtime and evenings with people associated with the nearby Inns of Court, but don't let that put you off, it's worth a visit and it's much quieter at the weekends. The beer is just what you'd expect – this is a Sam Smith's pub of course – and if you're a fan of Sam Smith's produce you won't be disappointed. The cellar bar is available for hire and often as not as full as the upstairs bars. There's food at lunchtimes, but it's not likely to set gastropub fans' pulses racing; you come here for the beer, the company and the surroundings.

FEATURES:  

HANDY FOR: Sir John Soane's Museum

Clock House

RATING: 

82 Leather lane
EC1N 7TR
020 7430 1123

A decent, well-looked-after, Greene King pub. All the old favourites are there, Abbot and IPA among them. Its proximity to Leather Lane Market means that it does a booming business when the market's on. At lunchtimes it's pretty packed, but in the evening it's a much more modest affair. Being mostly regular locals, as the trendies go off to their favourite bars in the area. The service is friendly and there's a games room upstairs with a pool table and a TV, and TVs are dotted around the place downstairs for the footy. A reasonable choice if you're in the area.

FEATURES:   

HANDY FOR: Sir John Soane's Museum

King's Arms

RATING:

11a Northington Street
WC1N 2JF
020 7405 9107

This is essentially a friendly, traditional, boozer, with cheery crowds spilling out onto the street in the early evenings in summer. The main bar is sparsely furnished, with wooden floors, tables and chairs. There are also two rooms upstairs: a quieter, more sumptuous front room, popular with couples and small groups of friends, drinking or dining, which is adorned with photographs by Frank Meadow Sutcliffe depicting scenes in and around Victorian Whitby. This room also has a fine view of one of the smartest Georgian streets in London. The back room is a games room that packs an awful lot in without quite feeling cramped. There are two pool tables, a dart board (with darts provided) and table football, all of which can be reserved if necessary on weekdays; for weekends a guaranteed minimum spend is required for a booking. Thai food is served most of the day and it usually has a decent selection of beer on tap.

FEATURES:       

Knights Templar

RATING:

95 Chancery Lane
WC2A 1DT
020 7831 2660

Popular Wetherspoon pub in Chancery Lane, next to the Law Society. This used to be the Union Bank and the main banking hall forms a very large, high-ceilinged, public bar that is choc-a-bloc at lunchtime with hungry lawyers and a few students from Kings College. Lovely old Georgian building but JDW haven't been as sympathetic with this as with others, such as the Crosse Keys. It's not at all subtle – nasty fruit-pattern carpet has been put over the original monochrome tiling, original plaster ceiling painted orange, poor murals of medieval scenes made to look like charcoal drawings and the odd bit of charcoal-coloured marble dotted about. What it does have going for it is a little mezzanine that feels like a comfy middle-class Surrey anteroom. Food is tasty, though not as cheap as other Wetherspoons, but these punters can afford it. Most of the tables have high stools so it's not that comfortable to eat here. And it's a freehouse, of course, with well-kept guest ales and staff are helpful and friendly. However, there are better pubs in the area, and better bank conversions in the Square Mile.

FEATURES:   

HANDY FOR: Sir John Soane's Museum

Ye Olde Mitre Tavern

RATING:

1 Ely Court
EC1N 6SJ
020 7405 4751

This well-concealed pub (in a little yard just off Hatton Garden) can often be an oasis in a somewhat manic area. Of course, like any pub in the City, it gets overrun at the usual times – lunch and immediately after work – but outside of those hours it's a haven. The beers are well kept, usually a couple of decent real ales with regular guests on the hand pumps. The food is honest pub grub and the service is old-fashioned and excellent – many newer pubs should take note. There are a lot of rumours about this pub, particularly that it's not actually in London. The origins of the pub can account for some of the confusion. The original pub was built in 1547 for the servants of the Bishop of Ely from Cambridgeshire, whose London palace was just next door in Ely Place. And, as such, the palace and its environs (including the pub) were his domain. The pub was demolished in 1772 and quickly rebuilt. From what we can ascertain, it stayed (officially) under Cambridgshire's aegis until sometime in the 20th century – the City of London police, apparently, had no jurisdiction there. There's also a legend that the tree trunk preserved in the corner of the small bar was the original boundary marker for the diocese and that Queen Elizabeth I danced the maypole around it – but, as we say, that's the legend. Nonetheless, this pub is historic, quirky and atmospheric, replete with the panelling and odd little nooks and crannies you'd expect in such a place – and we hope it stays this way for ever. By the way, if you don't spot the sign on the lamp post in Hatton Garden pointing into the alleyway, you will walk straight past it. Not one to miss.

FEATURES:   

HANDY FOR: Sir John Soane's Museum

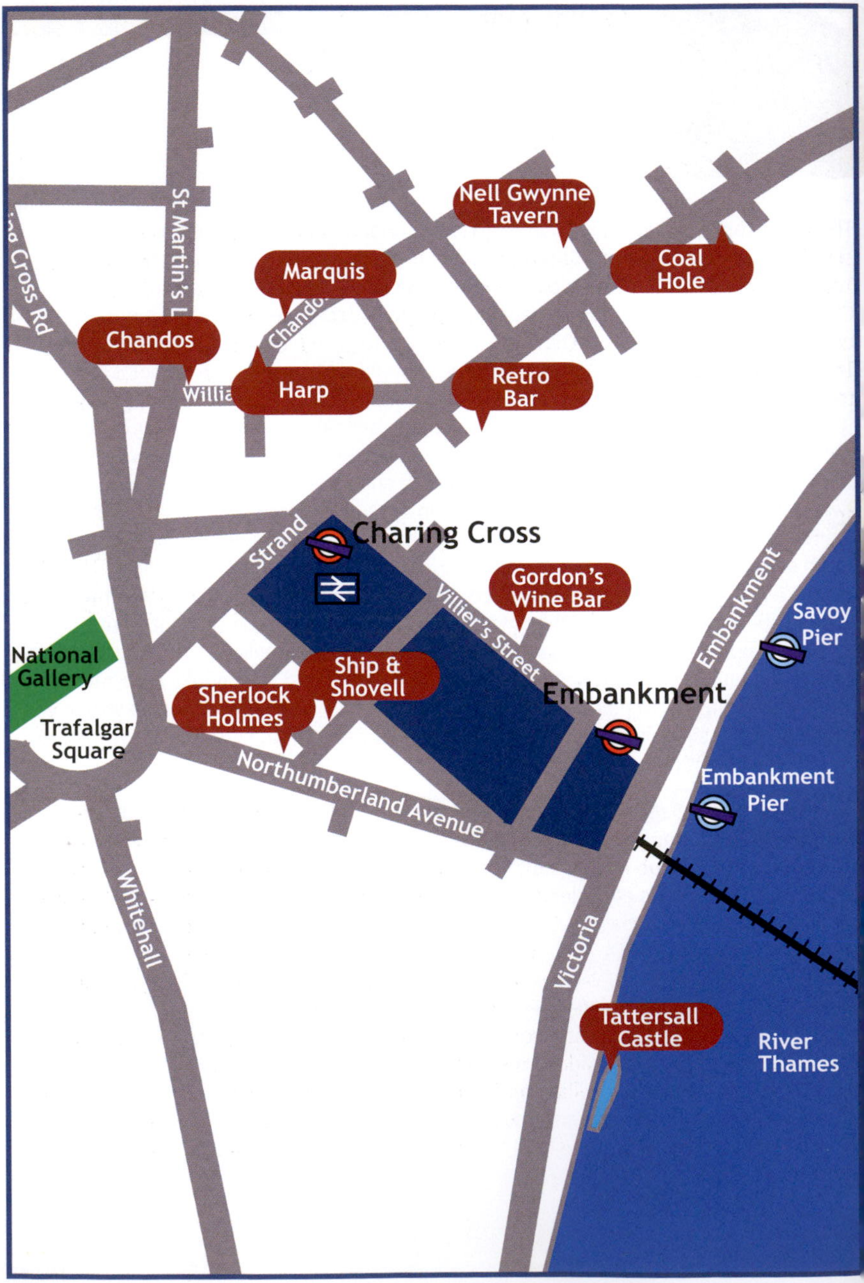

CHARING CROSS/EMBANKMENT

The Chandos

RATING: 

29 St Martin's Lane
WC2N 4ER
020 7836 1401

The Chandos is an attractive pub: the beer is Sam Smith's and is up to their usual standard, there is lots of room and an upstairs bar/restaurant with nice window seats. The pub suffers from its location, though. Perfectly placed to draw people from Charing Cross, St Martin's Lane and Trafalgar Square, consequently it's often uncomfortably packed. They do, however, surprisingly find room for a dart board. There are few pubs around here which could be described as being away from the tourist hustle and bustle, so either brave the crowds here or visit out of peak times.

FEATURES:  

HANDY FOR: National Gallery, Trafalgar Square

Coal Hole

RATING: 

91 Strand
WC2R 0DW
020 7379 9883

Probably the most famous pub in the area, the Coal Hole is pretty much unchanged over the years, although it has had its ups and downs. Built in a corner of the Savoy Hotel complex, the pub has a medieval (*circa* 1904) style décor – dark beams, leaded lights, stone flag floors etc. – lending it a theatrical air, which not only fits with the fact it's next door to the Savoy Theatre, but is doubly apt given the past clientele. Being a Nicholson's pub, along with the splendid interior, you get a good range of well-kept beers (with regular guests) on the hand pumps – which you can try before you buy and the service is good. As the pub is easy to find, expect it to be crowded at the usual times, with tourists, office workers and Covent Garden shoppers, who spill out into the alleyway down the side of the pub. There is some, but not much, relief on the pressure in the downstairs cellar bar. The crowd factor and the perennially over-amped PA upstairs – quiet conversation is not feasible – means this pub gets a solid three pints, rather than the four it might otherwise merit. It's open till midnight, now, too.

FEATURES:  

HANDY FOR: National Gallery, Trafalgar Square

Gordon's Wine Bar

RATING:

47 Villiers Street
WC2N 6NE
020 7930 1408

Not a pub, we know, but a wine bar with more charm and atmosphere than many of London's boozers (particularly those nearby); Gordon's is one of the most idiosyncratic drinking holes in town, its darkened alcoves a world away from your average pub interior. Yellowing newspapers from yesteryear adorn the walls, and candles plugged into dusty wine bottles provide the illumination. If Miss Haversham was in the licensing trade, this could have been the result. As for the choice of drinks, a wide range of both old-and new-world wines are available, though port or sherry (decanted from barrels above the bar) often feels the most appropriate tipple. Given the proximity to Trafalgar Square, it's no wonder the place is sometimes standing room only (hence only a three pint rating). So it's worth visiting at a quieter hour at the weekend to get a bit more space. Either that or get off work early and nab a table. Though take care entering from the side entrance – one false step and you'll be head first into the salad bar.

FEATURES: 

HANDY FOR: National Gallery, Trafalgar Square

Harp

Chandos Place
WC2N 4HS
020 7836 0291

Given that drinking real ale in the middle of London can often result in a Wetherspoon experience, this little freehouse so close to Trafalgar Square comes as something of a surprise. The regular ales are Timothy Taylor Landlord, Harvey's and Black Sheep, with two guest beers – and some powerful ciders – also on offer. The pub's tasty sausage (there are several varieties to choose from) sandwiches do the business too. This one fills up most evenings but if you can find a seat, or catch it at a quieter time, we recommend a visit. Keep an eye out for the oil paintings – the one of a young James Mason is especially fine.

FEATURES: 

HANDY FOR: National Gallery, Trafalgar Square

The Marquis

RATING:

51–52 Chandos Place
WC2N 4HS
020 7836 7657

Closed since late 2006, this one's back with a new name and a new look resulting in a watering hole which encapsulates a good deal of the London pub experience in 2008. On the plus side, that means a good array of drinks (noteworthy are the bottled beers from across the world and a couple of brews from the Low Countries on the pumps) and a menu that's competitively priced for the middle of town. On the other hand, there's something characterless and formulaic to the new pub; noticeable in both the refitted décor of soft woods and walls painted gastro green and the relentlessly AOR music being played on our visit. Perhaps its no surprise this one plays it safe – it is situated on a prime tourist route through London – but we'd still like to think there could be something distinctive about a building with a bit of history attached to it. As it stands though, this new incarnation feels less pub, more Starbucks with a drinks licence. Which to some people, probably sounds idyllic.

HANDY FOR: National Gallery, Trafalgar Square

Nell Gwynne Tavern

RATING: 

1–2 Bull Inn Court
WC2R 0NP
020 7240 5579

On the face of things, it's *Ye Olde Worlde Pubbe*, but the Nell Gwynne is not as touristy as its location and cosy size would make you think. Sure, it's dimly lit and makes the most of its historical associations, but it still has the feel of a locals' pub. Friendly bar staff and decent fare add up to an honest, busy boozer. Even though it's about the size of a phone box inside, it's usually a better bet than some of the other tourist traps nearby (beware the hellish stairs to the toilets though). The Nell Gwynne is one of the more characterful boozers in Central London and, what with it now under threat of closure, a visit here is strongly recommended.

FEATURES:  

HANDY FOR: National Gallery, Trafalgar Square

Retro Bar

RATING:

2 George Court, Strand
WC2N 6HH
020 7321 2811

With a preponderance of standy-uppy stripped-pine bars and corporate pseudo olde-worlde places nearby, Retro Bar stands out by being just a little bit different. Tucked down a little alleyway, it's certainly more Camden than Charing Cross. An intimate arrangements of seats, a smattering of neon-lit nicknacks, photos of rock stars and a great jukebox all add up to a place suited for a both a swift weekday pint or a longer Saturday night. There was a gay-friendly crowd but it was still pretty mixed, interspersed with only a smattering of suited office workers. Certainly, Retro Bar is worth seeking out if you're in the area and tired of the usual drinking places.

FEATURES:  

HANDY FOR: National Gallery, Trafalgar Square

Sherlock Holmes

RATING: 

10–11 Northumberland Avenue
WC2N 5DA
020 7930 2644

You have to be a bit of a Sherlock Holmes to find this pub, as Baker Street is a good Hansom Cab's ride away from Northumberland Avenue. Nevertheless, the pub has plunged wholeheartedly into its chosen theme to please pub-going Conan Doyle fans with an entertaining divertissement. The walls are adorned with innumerable Holmesian memorabilia, there's the 221B restaurant upstairs and the TV shows non-stop Sherlock Holmes movies and TV programmes – the colour on the TV being turned down to render even the newest TV prog in nostalgic black and white. The news is pretty good on the beer front with the likes of Speckled Hen and the pub's own Sherlock Holmes bitter on the hand pumps with plenty of wine and pub grub (albeit a little pricey) to round off the victuals – all competently and pleasantly served. However, this pub's unique selling point appears to be of interest to only about half the clientele, as the other half are civil servants and other officerati from workplaces roundabout. There are few pubs in these parts and this is one of the better ones – an achievement even more impressive for a themed, tourist pub.

FEATURES:   

HANDY FOR: National Gallery, Trafalgar Square

The Ship & Shovell

RATING: 

1–3 Craven Passage
WC2N 5PH
020 7839 1311

Claiming to be 'the only London pub in two halves', the Ship & Shovell is a good pub in an area short of them. Its pleasant red and black facade, adorned with street lanterns, presents a mirror image across the narrow passage. Each half of the pub has its own bar serving an interesting range of draughts including Badger Best and IPA, Tanglefoot, Sussex, JB Pilsner and Stinger. Due to its proximity to the railway and tube stations, the pub tends to be busy in the evenings but it's also possible to enjoy a standing drink outside in the passageway. Either way, no matter how crowded it gets, this pub always has a good atmosphere.

FEATURES:  **HANDY FOR:** National Gallery, Trafalgar Square

Tattersall Castle

RATING:

Kings Reach, Victoria Embankment
SW1A 2HR
020 7839 6548

Resplendent in its new livery, the ex-paddle steamer the Tattersall Castle is a fitting tourist attraction for the area, located in an ideal spot almost opposite the London Eye and County Hall and close to Westminster. The refurbishment didn't end with a coat of paint to the outside either, the interior has been extensively revised. Once you're off the deck, it looks more like a modern hotel bar (albeit with a curved floor and low ceilings) rather than the ex-British Rail rust-bucket it once was. The drink is also pretty much on par with an average modern hotel, there's nothing remarkable about it apart from the price – it's not cheap and the clientele is also pretty much the kind you'll find in a hotel too. It's a vast place with plenty of seats on the upper deck (when the weather's fine and dry) and there's a lot more space downstairs inside the boat. If you fancy a drink on the river, you might well give it a try, but don't expect to recreate a nautical experience – once you're inside you might as well be in a Portakabin on a barge, rather than a piece of British maritime history.

FEATURES:   **HANDY FOR:** Banqueting House, London Eye, Downing Street/Whitehall

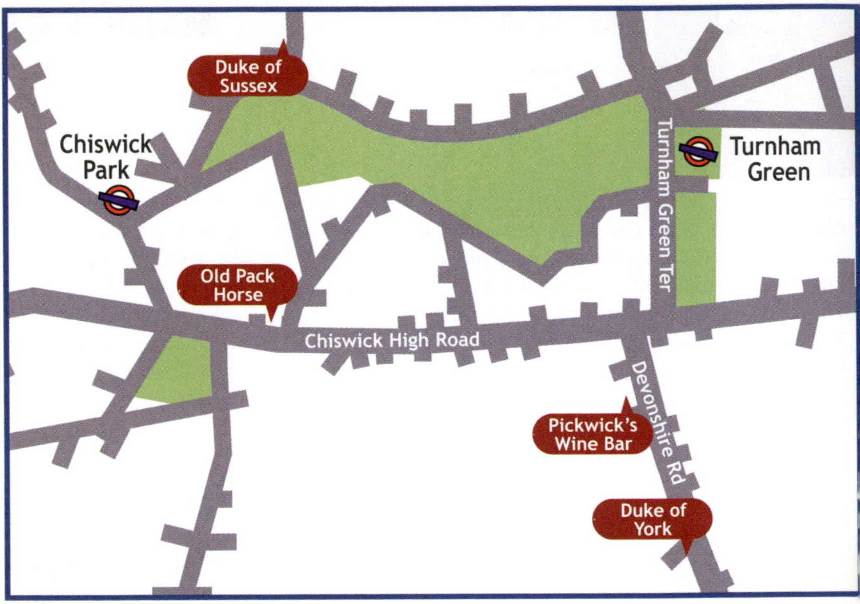

Duke of Sussex
Chiswick Park
Turnham Green
Turnham Green Ter
Old Pack Horse
Chiswick High Road
Devonshire Rd
Pickwick's Wine Bar
Duke of York

Duke of Sussex

RATING: 3/3

75 South Parade
W4 5LF
020 8742 8801

When the Duke of Sussex was revamped in late 2007 from a yoof-orientated and rather raucous place, it signalled the almost complete blanketing of Chiswick in upmarket gastropubs. Of course, like anything else, no two are identical – even if they are aiming for roughly the same demographic – and what can differentiate them is what remains of the old boozer they replaced. In the case of the Sussex, this was clearly once a grand Victorian pub and happily some of this grandeur remains – ornate bar, acid-etched glass and high ceilings are the order of the day. The rear dining room, which was probably the billiard room, benefits from stunning triple-height ceilings and intricate decoration. After years languishing, it's been sympathetically restored and for that we must be grateful. The menu has British and Spanish influences, but we weren't in the mood to fork out the mid-teen prices to sample it. Drinks wise, there's a good wine list (served in carafes, if that's your predilection) and three ales on, well kept. It's proving popular and was pleasantly busy on our visit – a good pub for the residents.

FEATURES:   

HANDY FOR: Tabard Theatre

Duke of York

RATING: 

107 Devonshire Road
W4 2HU
020 8994 2118

Although Cafe Rouge and All Bar One are probably the most representative of the Chiswick High Road's drinking opportunities, dip down Devonshire Road and you'll find a solid old pub still plying its trade. A fine local in a residential area, the Duke of York serves up Fuller's ales to its regulars and has a rather untouched feel about it. There's no indication it's due for a gastro relaunch any time soon – long may that be the case.

FEATURES:    

HANDY FOR: Tabard Theatre

The Old Pack Horse

RATING:

434 Chiswick High Road
W4 5TF
020 8994 2872

The Old Pack Horse is a good, solid pub. It has a sleepy feel out of hours, but picks up in the evening when a mixed bunch of locals fill the place up. It's a Fuller's pub and the beer's brewed just down the road so a decent pint is assured. Standing prominently at a busy junction, the Old Pack Horse's splendid Edwardian exterior is matched by a welcoming interior, with leather settees dotted about. There's a cosy fire in winter and a courtyard garden out the back for the summer – all seasons, it seems, are covered. It's been smartened up a little recently, but this hasn't affected the character. The Thai Café at the back is popular and comes recommended and it does takeaways, so, if you really can only stop for a swift one, you can at least take the food out with you. A jolly decent pub and easily one of the best in the area.

FEATURES: 

HANDY FOR: Tabard Theatre

Pickwick's Wine Bar

RATING:

13 Devonshire Road
W4 2EU
020 8747 1824

Sometimes, just sometimes, a place comes along which restores your faith in the art of running a pub. Pickwick's – one of Chiswick's last independent bars – was apparently saved some years ago from being turned into a restaurant by a rather wealthy philanthropic regular who has kept it pretty much the same since. Inside the place is vaguely reminiscent in ambience of an understated German or Dutch bar from 1975, complete with wooden-beamed walls and ceilings. There doesn't appear to be any food on offer and the beer selection isn't amazing, but these things didn't matter. Some of the 'stack' em high, sell 'em cheap' chains should take some lessons from the welcome people receive here – warm and genuine, not just reserved for the regulars, but to greet new faces too. On our first visit, the owner even cleared space by the (real) open fire for us to warm up after arriving soaked from the cold winter rain; it was so cosy, it almost felt like we were in someone's front room in the country. This one certainly stands out from the rather Identikit pubs and bars in W4.

FEATURES: 

HANDY FOR: Tabard Theatre

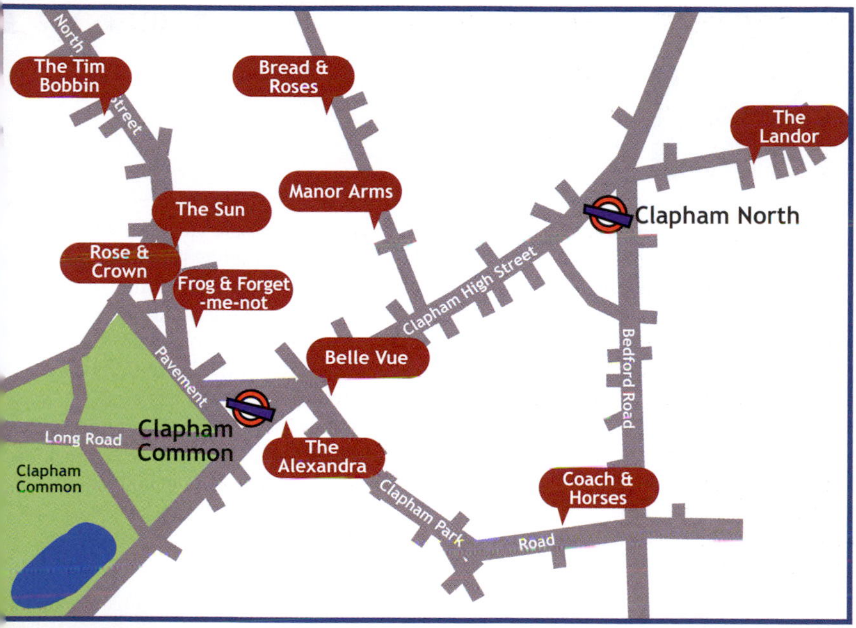

The Tim Bobbin
Bread & Roses
The Landor
Manor Arms
The Sun
Clapham North
Rose & Crown
Frog & Forget-me-not
Belle Vue
Clapham Common
The Alexandra
Coach & Horses
North Street
Clapham High Street
Pavement
Bedford Road
Long Road
Clapham Common
Clapham Park Road

The Alexandra

RATING: 

14 Clapham Common South Side
SW4 7AA
020 7627 5102

Not a bad place, this one, it's a large pub with some rather eccentric (but appealing) décor. Outside it's an unpretentious Victorian pub, but inside it's crammed with various old pieces of farm kit, nautical items, shop tills, printing presses and ancient pub games – highly entertaining to look at or tinker with after you've had a few. The upstairs 'Balcony Bar' sports big screens, for, er, sports and indeed the pub promotes sporting events up here, but, if your legs aren't up to it, there are loads of smaller screens downstairs too. Overall the clientele are mostly younger locals, but, thankfully, you won't be assailed by the braying of the stereotypical Clapham dweller. Especially popular for big footy matches, it's a very welcome presence amongst the wine bars in this locale. Oh, and it does Thai food as well.

FEATURES:  

CLAPHAM COMMON/CLAPHAM NORTH

The Belle Vue

RATING:

1 Clapham Common South Side
SW4 7AA
020 7498 9473

A few years of steady evolution have slowly transformed the Belle Vue from a fairly decent swanky pub into arguably one of the best all-round watering holes in Clapham. The changes have been gradual and piecemeal, with a steady erosion of the mismatched pictures, gimmicky drapes and cumbersome furniture that once gave the interior a high-class junk-shop feeling. Now the focus is very much on comfortable, not eye-catching, replacing all the tat and boot-sale furniture with simple tables and chairs, possibly down to the ownership by the Capital Pub Company. The best elements of the Belle Vue have also been maintained, with the bar continuing to serve a wide range of lagers and cask ales, and decent food. Equally, for those who like a bit of glitz with their bottle of Leffe, the Belle Vue does retain its basic polished wooden fittings and smooth decor, its just that this nod to swankville is not as false nor in your face as in the past. If anything, it owes much more to trendy bars than pubs, but that isn't necessarily a bad thing.

FEATURES:      

Bread & Roses

RATING: 

68 Clapham Manor Street
SW4 6DZ
020 7498 1779

As its name signifies, the Bread & Roses has strong links with socialism, and it's owned by the trade union-backed Workers Beer Company. But working class style it isn't; if images of flat caps and northern club comics come to mind, you're in for a disappointment. This place is very 21st century and cool – and upmarket. There may be three hand pumps offering traditional ales, but there's also a good wine list and an impressive array of spirits if you're in a cocktail mood. The food is pretty swish and reasonably priced and the music's decent. There's usually something on here – a regular pub quiz, burlesque nights (gasp) – if you need something more than drink, food and a relaxed vibe. If pubs were newspapers, you feel this one might be the *Observer* – a bit Sunday supplement to look at, but sincere.

FEATURES:          

Coach & Horses

RATING:

173–175 Clapham Park Road
SW4 7EX
020 7622 3815

A fair while ago The Coach & Horses cleaned itself up and became a successful and popular tastefully modernised pub. At the tail end of 2007 it was taken over and the new owners have built on the positives of this pub. If anything, they've improved matters here. A decent, unpretentious and reasonably priced menu has been installed, which promises to be entirely home cooked, right down to the sauces. The choice of ale is also pretty good, with four available at any one time. Outside seats give the smokers and their pals a space for summer drinking and traffic watching. On our visit, a smart midweek crowd was in situ, but, for those into football, there's a couple of big screens downstairs and a couple more plasma screens upstairs to keep you entertained. As it's just far enough from Clapham Common to avoid the worst of the maddening SW4 crowd, this has to be rated as one of the better pubs in the area.

FEATURES:       

Frog & Forget-Me-Not

RATING:

32 The Pavement, Clapham Old Town
SW4 0JE
020 7622 5230

Popular Clapham pub that manages to border into loungey bar territory, but without succumbing to the pretensions of the area. The sofas are old and knackered, but have more charm to them than your usual bar furnishings. The food is Thai during the week, but it's worth a look on Sunday if you're after a huge roast, but make sure you get here early to get a table – oh, and the paper napkins are ideal for post blowout doodling. If the weather's nice there's a roof terrace, where, for a change, you can rise above the pavement. Not as trendy as some of Clapham's bars, though more appealing than some of its pubs. We like it.

FEATURES:     

The Landor

RATING:

70 Landor Road
SW9 9PH
020 7274 4386

Just what you want when wandering the wastelands where Brixton and Clapham merge. This welcoming place offers eccentric decoration – well a full-size boat and other assorted knickknacks hanging from the rafters – a theatre upstairs with regular comedy nights, a good range of drinks, including decent real ales, and a genial atmosphere. It's starting to look a bit down at heel (which probably means it's due for a refurb), down to the old Truman, Hanbury and Buxton brewery name outside, but that just adds to its charm in our opinion. Be sure to give a look to the rather large beer garden: it's a welcoming spot, with a mural and an overgrown street lamp to keep you company. If that wasn't enough Sunday nights have an intelligent-looking pub quiz too. Hard to fault really. So we won't.

FEATURES:       **HANDY FOR:** Brixton Academy

Manor Arms

RATING: 

128 Clapham Manor Street
SW4 6ED
020 7622 8856

A traditional pub just off the High Street and just off the radar of the younger crowd that throng the main street of a weekend. Its a friendly place and offers a pretty decent range of beer on the hand pumps. It's small size (even with the tent out the back in the beer garden) means that the tellies tend to dominate when there's a sporting event on, but the atmosphere is jovial and the beer is good and you can't say fairer than that. It's had a tidy up, but it hasn't really changed the pub. Decent beer, sport on the telly, beer garden out the back to enjoy good weather, what more do you want?

FEATURES:     

Rose & Crown

RATING:

2 The Polygon
SW4 0JG
020 7720 8265

We had our fears for this one. The long-standing landlord and landlady had waved farewell and we thought they would take all the charm of their idiosyncratic real ale mecca with them. However, despite the changes in décor (out go the privacy of the old booths, in come some more tables and chairs and some enlarged photos of Ye Olde Clapham) there's still the essence of the old pub here. The beers still have the regularly rotating guests of old (as well as Greene King and decently kept) to entice any passing ale fans in, but devotees to fizzy beer will find themselves well catered for. The pub grub still seems good value, whilst an eye cast at the wine list was a temptation hard to resist. As far as we can see the old claim of the Rose & Crown being 'Clapham's only traditional pub' still has a certain truth in it.

FEATURES:    

The Sun

RATING:  

47 Old Town
SW4 0JL
020 7622 4980

Like Marmite, you'll love or hate this one. The crowds that gather to enjoy sun and lager here (in the beer garden and the side-road) testify to its popularity with the young of Clapham and beyond. Inside and out, it's a pleasant spot to while away an afternoon, with a large bright main bar. The yard bar only opens occasionally, whilst the upstairs bar is usually open evenings – also bright and airy, and sports real (gas) fires in winter. There's a pleasant artiness about the place and a curious fresco upstairs. The Thai food is recommended, and lunch for a fiver is a decent promise too. Well, that's the good bit. A limited range of beers at hefty prices, with Guinness and Staropramen on offer. In our experience, towards the end of the week the place is often so rammed you'll make slow progress at the bar which soon spoils your night. The staff may not wear blinkers, but, they might as well. This pub has entertained Clapham's young for years, but, until they sort out watering them reliably too, it'll be staying a two pinter for us. Shame, but we doubt it'll stop the summer crowds.

FEATURES:  

The Tim Bobbin

RATING: 3 pints

1–3 Lillieshall Road
SW4 0LN
020 7738 8953

Renovated a few years back now, this pub has settled down to a life somewhere between aspirational gastropub and local boozer. Given its location in a residential side street in middle-class Clapham, this is probably the only way it could survive, but it seems to work quite well. The beer's not bad at all, with guest ales, and, though the food's pretty dear, it's of a good quality and the service is good too. The range of spirits is excellent and the décor is pleasant, if a bit of a mixture. The clientele consists of locals by daytime, with the more stereotypical Cla'am dweller of an evening and at weekends. And on one visit the locals would have made Roger Melly blush, but they're amiable enough and the atmosphere is generally quieter than the rowdier bars in the area. If you're keen, you might even get a game of darts in. Oh, if you are wondering who Tim Bobbin was, he was an 18th-century Lancastrian poet and illustrator. A satirist of both working-and upper-class life, copies of his drawings adorn the walls here.

FEATURES:      

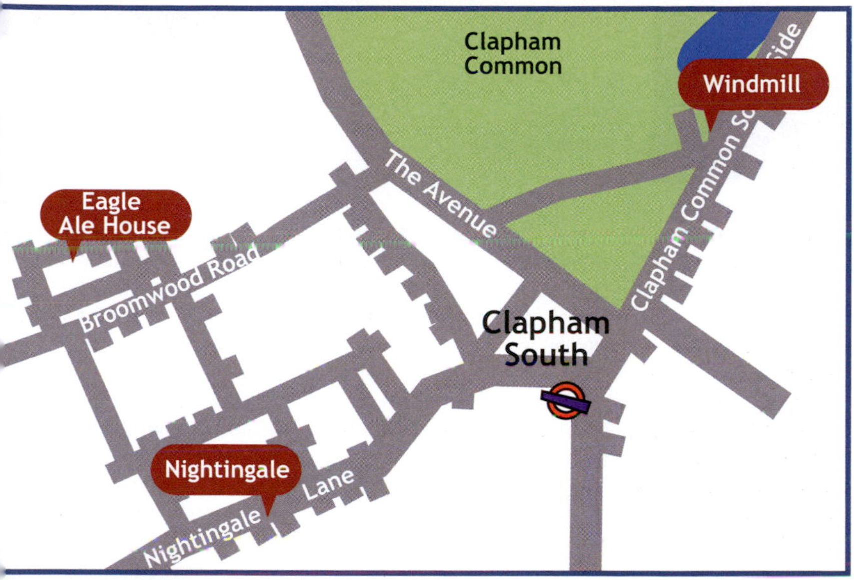

Clapham Common
Windmill
The Avenue
Clapham Common S…
Eagle Ale House
Broomwood Road
Clapham South
Nightingale
Nightingale Lane

The Eagle Ale House

RATING: 

104 Chatham Road
SW11 6HG
020 7228 2328

A pleasing discovery between Wandsworth Common and Clapham Junction, here's a local pub with an independent spirit to it. The beers are great, with regular guest ales on offer at the pumps. Added to this, with a stack of board games available, and some tables inbuilt with chess and backgammon tops, the place is ideal for an afternoon of slothful drinking. Saying that, the empty champagne bottles on the bookshelves suggest it's pretty handy for a night of excess too – maybe in the marquee you can hire out the back. Said marquee manages to pack in some leather sofas and a giant screen (a great space, particularly if you're a smoker). Though located very much in the heart of the Nappy Valley, this is the sort of pub parents go to escape the rigours of parenthood, not a place where they take the pram along with them. It's also a rugby pub and can get very busy when there's a big match on. The Eagle may take a while to track down, but it's well worth the walk – and it also gives you a chance to work up a thirst.

FEATURES:       

Nightingale

RATING:

97 Nightingale Lane
SW12 8NX
020 8673 1637

When an area gentrifies there's usually an impact on the local pubs. Round these parts the rise in house prices has seen pubs remodelling themselves with lounge-style interiors, or, as in the case of the Surrey Tavern, being shut down to make way for luxury flats. For remaining true to its boozer roots then, this Nightingale is indeed a rare bird. Devotees of gastropubs won't be stepping foot over the threshold until there's at least one lunchtime option featuring balsamic vinegar; the rest of us will make do with a pub that plays to the traditional pleasures of good beer, bantering locals and an atmosphere conducive to knocking a few back. And given the pub is big on collecting for charity (photos of all the Guide Dogs the pub has raised money for take up a whole wall) the punters seem a decent lot as well. All in all, a fine little pub.

FEATURES:     

Windmill on the Common

RATING:

Clapham Common South Side
SW4 9DE
020 8673 4578

What with a bar, lounge, restaurant, conservatory and plenty of tables outside, there's enough room here for anyone who ambles in from Clapham Common – though you might be forgiven for thinking that you have to have at least two children to live in the area, particularly on a sunny Sunday afternoon. It can feel a bit dead inside when everyone's out on the terrace or on the Common. That said, all the bars were five deep last time we were in on a warm day and the staff didn't seem able to cope with the demand. The car park right next to the beer garden can give the place the feel of a Midlands travel tavern. Those criticisms aside, usual Young's fare and regular guest beers (Tribute and Doom Bar were on when we were in last) are on offer and it can be a handy meeting place before heading elsewhere. The menu is extensive and in line with prices in the area – slightly pricey, if you must ask. If you're dying of thirst, we wouldn't recommend it on a hot day, but, if you catch it on a quieter day, it's a good place to soak up the sun with a pint.

FEATURES:           

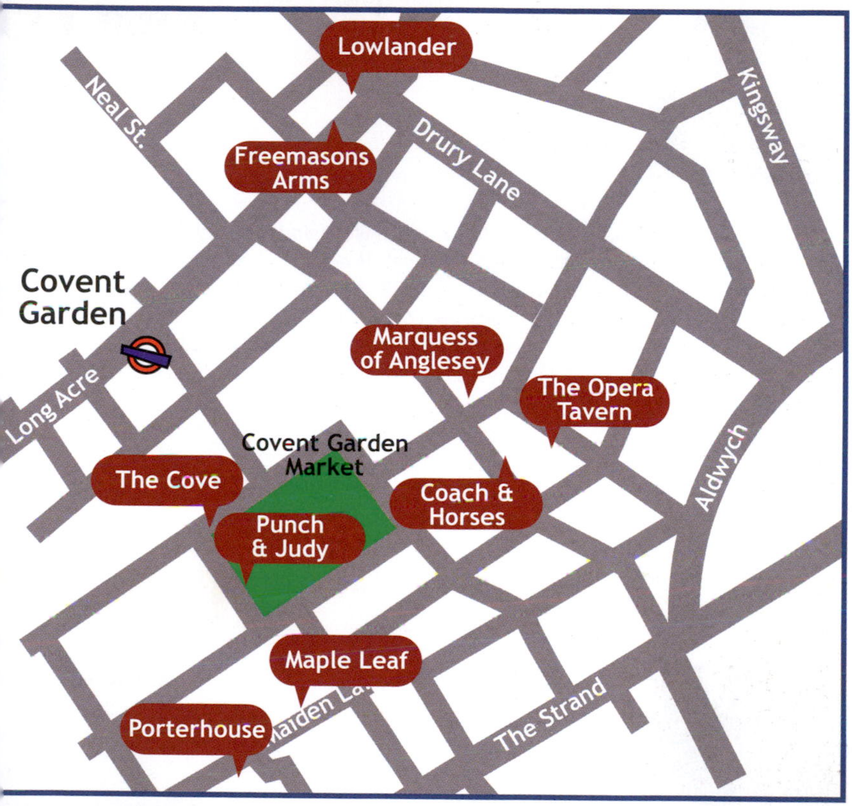

Lowlander
Neal St.
Freemasons Arms
Drury Lane
Kingsway
Covent Garden
Marquess of Anglesey
Long Acre
The Opera Tavern
Covent Garden Market
Aldwych
The Cove
Coach & Horses
Punch & Judy
Maple Leaf
Maiden La
Porterhouse
The Strand

Coach & Horses

RATING: 3 pints

42 Wellington Street
WC2E 7BD
020 7240 0553

The Coach & Horses is a fine traditional pub, a cut above most of the tourist-oriented offerings in these parts. There are a couple of ales on the hand pumps and, as there's an Irish theme here, a good drop of the black stuff. In addition to the booze, jolly good beef, salt beef and sausage sandwiches are available should you feel peckish. It's a friendly, welcoming place, but it's also rather small, so it fills up pretty quickly, especially immediately after work.

FEATURES:  

The Cove

RATING:

The Piazza
WC2E 8RB
020 7836 7880

Once upon a time this was probably the world's (well London's, anyway) only Cornish theme pub, now it has a sister pub on the King's Road. Like that one, this pub sells Cornish ale from the St Austell Brewery and delicious (and good-value) pasties from an impressively large menu. The chairs are comfortable and the balcony is great to watch the 'entertainers' below. It is, however, a little let down by cramped toilets and Europop on the jukebox, but it's still 10,000 times better than the Punch & Judy opposite.

FEATURES:  

Freemasons Arms

RATING:

81–82 Long Acre
WC2E 9NG
020 7836 3115

This is one of the better Covent Garden pubs; it bears up to the strain of office worker and tourist crowds quite well. A recent lick of paint has brightened the place up, but not affected it in any other way. It's not worth making a special journey to visit it, but it's a useful meeting place if you're in the area. Standard Shepherd Neame fare served pleasantly and promptly. If you sit in the back you'll notice a good few historic footy photos around the wall and a sign proclaiming 'The Football Association was founded here in 1863'. Given this heritage, no surprises to find this pub has many a screen to follow the match on.

FEATURES:   

Lowlander

RATING:

36 Drury Lane
WC2B 5RR
020 7379 7446

The Lowlander is a top-notch establishment for those of us who like to sample different beers, especially continental beers – 15 different beers on tap and over 70 in bottles albeit at a thoroughly Covent Garden price. The Lowlander likes to bill itself as a grand café of the Low Countries – meaning Belgium and Holland – hence it does wines, coffee and European food. It can get more than a bit busy here, so, if you are coming along in the evening time, try to get here early or phone in advance to reserve a table. And when it is busy, it gets bloody noisy.

FEATURES:  

Maple Leaf

RATING: 

41 Maiden Lane
WC2E 7LJ
020 7240 2843

No prizes for guessing the theme of this pub – sacre bleu! C'est Canada! You don't have to drink Molson, watch the ice hockey or wear a checked shirt to come here, but, if you haven't got an interest in things Canadian, you'll naturally find yourself in the minority here. The staff are attentive (if not necessarily Canadian), though service can be a little slow when it's crowded – which is quite often. There are untypical beers on offer – particularly the Sleeman's Honey Brown Lager on tap and now IPA; wines and spirits are also on offer. It's one of those Covent Garden fixtures that's pretty much unchanged over the years.

FEATURES: 

Marquess of Anglesey

RATING:

39 Bow Street
WC2E 7AU
020 7240 3216

The worst time to visit this pub is at 6:30 on Friday night in summer. It will be absolutely packed with tourists, office workers celebrating the end of another week and people on their way out for the night. The rest of the time it's just full. It's an easy place to find (hence it's a useful rendezvous) and it's not too bad a pub in itself – despite the All Bar One look. It's a Young's pub after all – but the endless tides of people coming in and out throughout the day don't make this the place for a relaxing pint. it's no surprise to see all of Young's beers on tap here, though we weren't expecting the extra pump dispensing Pimm's... Must be a sign of the times.

FEATURES: 

Opera Tavern

RATING: 

23 Catherine Street
WC2B 5JS
020 7379 9832

This has been a jolly little pub for ages and continues to be so. It does get crowded with tourists and theatregoers, but when the bell goes in the theatres for the next performance the place empties like it has just received a bomb threat, so don't be alarmed if you're suddenly the only people left in the place. It's a Nicholson's pub, so expect decent beer on the hand pumps and an opportunity to try the beer, before you buy a pint. The upstairs room gives some relief from the crowds when it's not being used for food or a private function. This is one of the better pubs in the area.

FEATURES: 

Porterhouse

RATING:

21 Maiden Lane
WC2E 7NA
020 7379 7917

Very often we like to bring you a choice little hideaway, an undiscovered gem with a few enchanting flaws. But we also have to concede, if a place is really popular, chances are they're doing something right. Porterhouse is a brewing company in Dublin who opened their own select chain of pubs. There aren't many in the chain – quality is the watchword rather than quantity. The one in Maiden Lane is a huge boozer and expensively decorated in brewery copper and antique doodads and yet is designed full of cosy nooks for you to hide away in. The house beers are brewed in Dublin to their own recipes – three stouts (including a miraculous oyster stout), real ales and lagers. Responsible pub reviewers would, of course, never suggest that you try a pint of each one in one night – but they're all good (ahem). One lift entrance and toilets offer some disabled access. Live music, decent food, a patio and a location in the heart of London's theatre and eating district mean it's very busy. But they've done their research, they know what the 'craic' is – it's another word for a niche.

FEATURES:     

Punch & Judy

RATING: 

The Market Piazza
WC2E 8RF
020 7379 0923

We've known the Punch & Judy for a long, time and for most of that time we've considered it pretty dire and best avoided. But it seems things have moved on and it's not quite as awful as it once was. It's not as aggressive on Friday and Saturday nights as it used to be, but it still gets crowded and it still offers expensive, but not particularly high-quality, food and drink – the place often smells of vinegar from the abundance of chips consumed here. However, there's still a dreary, depressing air to the place. Smack bang in the centre of one of the biggest tourist attractions in the capital and, rather than providing something befitting this unique and handsome location, we have a pastiche of a not very good provincial pub. Maybe it's revenge for the Venetians charging tourists £5 for an espresso when they visit the Piazza San Marco, but we do wish someone would turn this pub into something we could recommend.

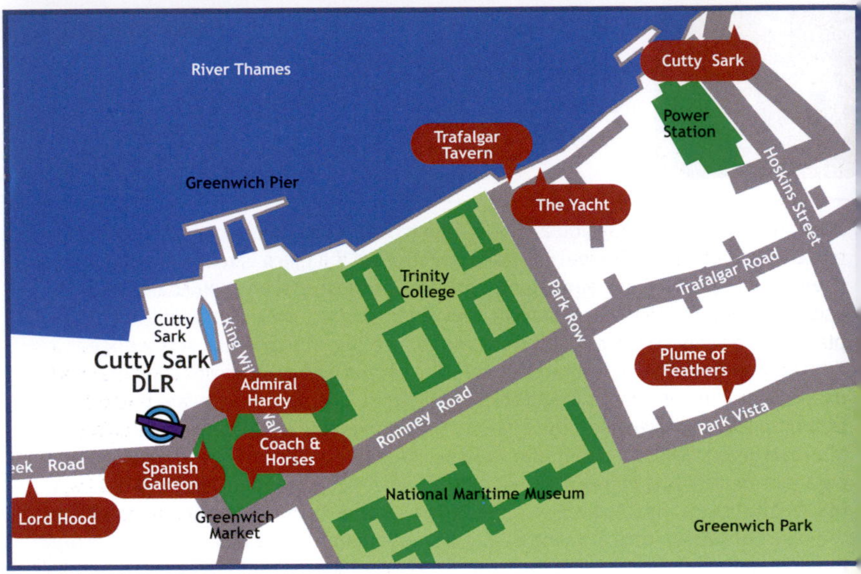

Admiral Hardy

RATING: 

7 College Approach
SE10 9HY
020 8858 6452

This place has two things going for it – its location and a better-than-usual range of booze on offer. It also has two major things working against it – clientele and its location. Situated in the heart of Greenwich market, this pub will inevitably be popular, it's easy to find and it's a handy refuelling stop after a day spent inspecting the pricey tat on offer all around it. And in the evenings, especially towards the weekend, it's popular with kids, especially students, out on the town (well Greenwich anyway) with their mates. The Hardy once tried to be different, with a food shop and foodie menu, but in the end it bowed to the pressure – out went the shop and the menu and in came the 'lounge bar' features with its pretty standard menu – and sure enough the crowds followed. So, despite the drink – there's a good range of real ales on offer, with regular guest beers – it's not really a pub enthusiast's sort of place. However, if you're a student or young local out on the razz, you're probably going to be a big fan.

FEATURES:  

HANDY FOR: Cutty Sark, National Maritime Museum

The Coach & Horses

RATING:

13 Greenwich Market
SE10 9HZ
020 8293 0880

Not so very long ago, the old Coach & Horses in the market was given the inevitable stripped-out gastropub treatment and we feel it probably deserved it – the old pub was never up to much. Now, the beer and food is good – e.g. real ale on the hand pumps, accompanied by a range of continentals such as Amstel, Paulaner. It's quite a comfy place with its settees, easy chairs and newspapers, the music is decent and there's a relaxed vibe – when it's not crowded, although if it's warm enough you can always sit outside (now helped by heaters). Prices are tourist high, which some may find off-putting but there are enough well-off locals to fill the place on a Saturday evening. Market days will see it packed with tourists and shoppers and on Friday and Saturday nights younger locals having a few pre-club drinks. Smokers, however, may find the place unappealing as it's strictly no-smoking even in the external bit in the market.

FEATURES:  **HANDY FOR:** Cutty Sark, National Maritime Museum, Old Royal Observatory

Cutty Sark Tavern

RATING:

Ballast Quay
SE10 9PD
020 8858 3146

Confusingly, the Cutty Sark Tavern is not as near to the Cutty Sark (well, what's left of it) as you'd imagine. There are quite a few pubs a lot nearer that would probably better qualify for the name. Still, once you find it (it's a five-minute walk down river) it's a jolly decent place. The Georgian building and the riverside terrace are what make it worthwhile visiting here. And there are fine beers on to be enjoyed here too – such as Tribute, Broadside and Tiger. The service is polite and prompt and copes admirably with the crowds as they flock down here on a warm summer's evening (on the rare occasions we get them). The food's decent as well. Off season, it's a very nice place for a pint or two with its excellent views and relaxed atmosphere, but the freneticism of the summer months removes some of the shine – but such is the way with many tourist pubs. Well worth a visit though, any time of the year.

FEATURES:    **HANDY FOR:** Cutty Sark, National Maritime Museum

Lord Hood

RATING:

300 Creek Road
SE10 9SW
020 8858 1836

Despite its proximity to central Greenwich, the Lord Hood is firmly a locals' pub. Although a little scruffy around the edges, it has a genuineness lacking in many of the tourist-oriented places nearby. There's nothing unusual in the way of drink here – although it's decent enough – and only pub grub in terms of food, but if it's just a pint you want, the Hood is usually worth a go. Every so often, the Hood gets threatened with demolition and, with the demise of the Cricketers in 2005, the Hood is now the last locals' pub in central Greenwich and it would be a shame to see it disappear. Update – the Lord Hood has dodged the wrecking ball again and all is set fair (at least until after the recession).

FEATURES:    **HANDY FOR:** Cutty Sark, National Maritime Museum

Plume of Feathers

RATING:

19 Park Vista
SE10 9LZ
020 8858 1661

Established in 1691, the Plume of Feathers has a lovely tiled exterior and outdoor seating to the front and rear. Inside, the walls are packed with pictures and nautical ephemera, and the fireplace adds to the cosy atmosphere. Attracting locals, walkers and some tourists, the place gets packed and buzzes with a lively, congenial atmosphere. The Plume serves good pub grub, with a decent Sunday roast, which you can have in the restaurant area at the back or in the bar area. Adnam's and Fuller's ales are amongst the beers behind the bar and the service is excellent. Turnover is pretty brisk at lunchtimes, so if you can't get a table immediately, wait a short while, it's worth it. There's also a children's play area where the kids can disappear, leaving you to sup your pint in peace, although occasionally customers don't avail themselves of this facility, to the annoyance of the people around them. We like this pub – it's the best in the area.

FEATURES:       

Spanish Galleon

RATING:

48 Greenwich Church Street
SE10 9BL
020 8858 3664

Even the most unobservant will find this place, bang opposite one of the exits to the DLR, yet, curiously, until relatively recently, this place was largely ignored by the people who throng the area day and night. However, the Spanish Galleon's apparent unpopularity now seems to be a thing of the past. Where once it used to be the place for a spot of quietish refreshment, it's now elbow to elbow with people yelling at each other and the bar staff, especially on Friday and Saturday night. The beer and food has not changed much, it's Shepherd Neame after all, but, alas, the food's not really of the quality we've come to expect of their pubs. We suppose nowadays it doesn't really need to try, the competition in these parts certainly doesn't seem to – the name of the game is to bang it out as quickly as possible to the punters. Par for the course around here.

FEATURES:  

HANDY FOR: Cutty Sark, National Maritime Museum

Trafalgar Tavern

RATING: 

Park Row
SE10 9NW
020 8858 2909

Anybody who's ever been to Greenwich should know the Trafalgar Tavern. It's a huge, handsome pub, well in keeping with its grand and historic surroundings. Situated right on the river, next to Wren's grand edifices, with views to the north it is, as a result, incredibly popular. We usually visit this pub when we're meeting people who are new to the area and then we have to move on. It's not the pub's fault, but the boisterous tourist crowds, seemingly packed floor to ceiling, cause us to repair to other establishments, should we require quiet conversation – you'd do the same in any tourist haunt in any city. The restaurant has a reputation for good food, although we haven't eaten here, blame the crowds again and the beers are pretty well kept. But it's all a little too pricey, although that's hardly a surprise given where it is. Its overwhelming popularity is such that it's had to expand into the street and onto the riverside to provide more tables and seating.

FEATURES:     

HANDY FOR: Cutty Sark

The Yacht

RATING:

5 Crane Street
SE10 9NP
020 8858 0175

The Yacht is often a better choice for a tipple along this stretch of the river, as, usually, it tends to be less crowded. The beer is good – usually four beers on the hand pumps – and there's a reasonable wine list of mostly new-world varieties, to support a range of reasonably priced food, with main courses for less than £10. The pub has a welcoming atmosphere, but it can get crowded here at weekends when families come for lunch. If you're lucky enough to get a window table, a view from Borthwick Wharf in Deptford around to the Millennium Dome awaits. The Yacht may not be the ultimate pub in Greenwich, but it's a jolly decent boozer all the same.

FEATURES:   

HANDY FOR: Cutty Sark, National Maritime Museum

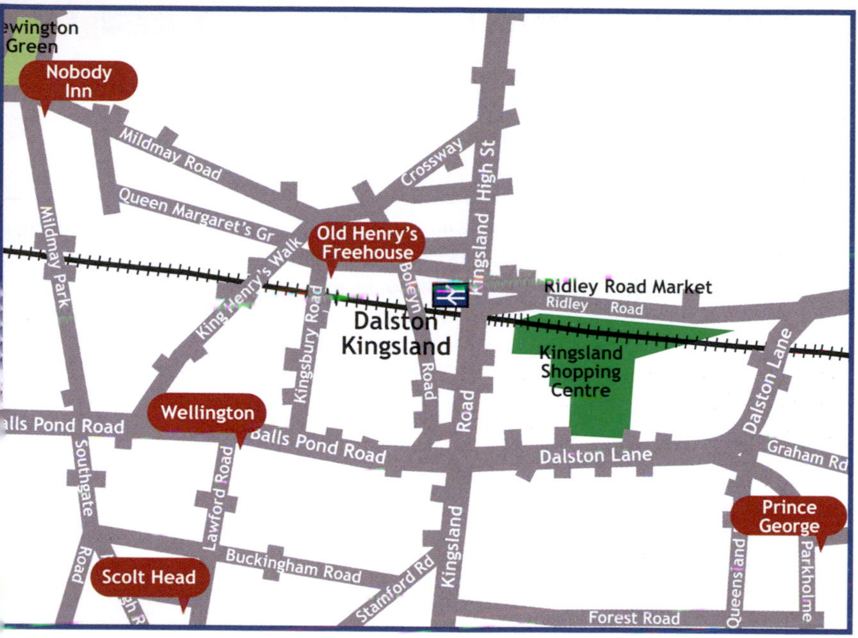

The Nobody Inn

RATING:

92 Mildmay Park
N1 4PR
020 7249 6430

Spruced up and rejuvenated in the not too distant past, the Nobody Inn is a transformed pub, going from a solid, unremarkable place to a lively venue with plenty going on for one and all. The booze is decent with regular guest beers on the hand pumps, a reasonable selection of wine, if you're that way inclined, and all the other liquid refreshments demanded of a 21st-century pub. The Thai food is good, reasonably priced and plentiful and there's a whole range of other pub things to do from watching sport on the various screens to the twice-weekly quiz. The atmosphere is buzzy and friendly (especially on quiz nights/afternoons) and the service prompt and affable. We particularly like the old red phonebox in the corner. Well done all round, we say.

FEATURES:     

Old Henry's Free House

RATING:

2 St Jude Street
N16 8JT
020 7254 5696

We thought we knew Dalston's pubs pretty well and as such it was certainly a surprise to discover Old Henry's Free House, on the back streets not far from Dalston train station. It's a traditional-style boozer, with décor identifiable from the 70s, 80s and 90s but overall quite homely, if a bit quirky – suit of armour anyone? There's a couple of ales on the pumps, some basic food and a pretty mixed clientele. If you're in the area it's worth popping in for a refresher, but probably isn't one to make a special journey for.

FEATURES:     

Prince George

RATING: 

40 Parkholme Road
E8 3AG
020 7254 6060

We feel that some of the pubs in the Remarkable Restaurants group go a little overboard on the décor and food front, but this one, thankfully, focuses firmly on the basics. The main bar leads away to darkened alcoves with some original furnishings still intact. The whole prospect is ideal for ale-fuelled conversation and, if a modicum of exertion is needed, a neatly tucked away pool table is on hand. Food only appears to be a going concern on a Sunday, but the rest of the week you're left with the usual Remarkable Restaurants mix of Belgian beers, Czech lagers and traditional ales to work your way through – hardly a chore. Add on one of this chain's archetypal excellent jukeboxes and a quiz on a Monday night and it's no wonder such a wide cross-section of locals stop by.

FEATURES:      

HANDY FOR: Hackney Museum

Scolt Head

RATING:

107a Culford Road
N1 4HT
020 7254 3965

Until relatively recently an unreconstructed locals' pub called the Sussex, this grand property with a good-looking front garden got a makeover. As is the norm now, the new look errs towards trendy. The once-daunting frosted glass has gone; the leaded windows remain, but you can see inside now, which certainly helps attract new locals. Inside it's the usual distressed floorboards and shabby furniture, with a couple of retro couches thrown in. There's some nice touches however: rows of old penguin classics to flick through, some great industrial salvage flanking the entrance and alphabet fridge magnets used to create the various notices dotted about (we resisted the temptation to rearrange them into rude words). One area looked suspiciously like it was reserved for eating, a tiny but interesting menu is on offer. But unlike full-on gastropubs there's also a 'sports room', with pool table and big-screen footy. Overall, it looks like they're onto a winner here – there's usually a good crowd, although it can get somewhat boisterous late on a Sunday afternoon. It must be said, we prefer it to some other nearby places.

FEATURES:          

Wellington

RATING: 

119 Balls Pond Road
N1 4BL
020 7249 3729

Part of the gentrification of the Hackney/Kingsland High Road area, this is a pleasant enough pub catering to a predominantly local, young upmarket crowd, though it's become a focal point for the local community (apparently the local Labour party meets in the back room). The main room, painted creamy-white, still retains many of the original features and etched glass, now punctuated with art and plants. We also spied the mosaic floor in the entrance showing its old name 'The Duke of Wellington', which made us wonder why pubs so often remove half their name when they refurbish – usually the royal bit. Due to the large central bar, some of the tables are too close together and rather cramped, but even on a Saturday night it wasn't busy enough to cause problems. There's a decent menu available, including Sunday roast, and a couple of good ales on tap, as well as a back bar, which also doubles as a theatre and function room.

FEATURES:     

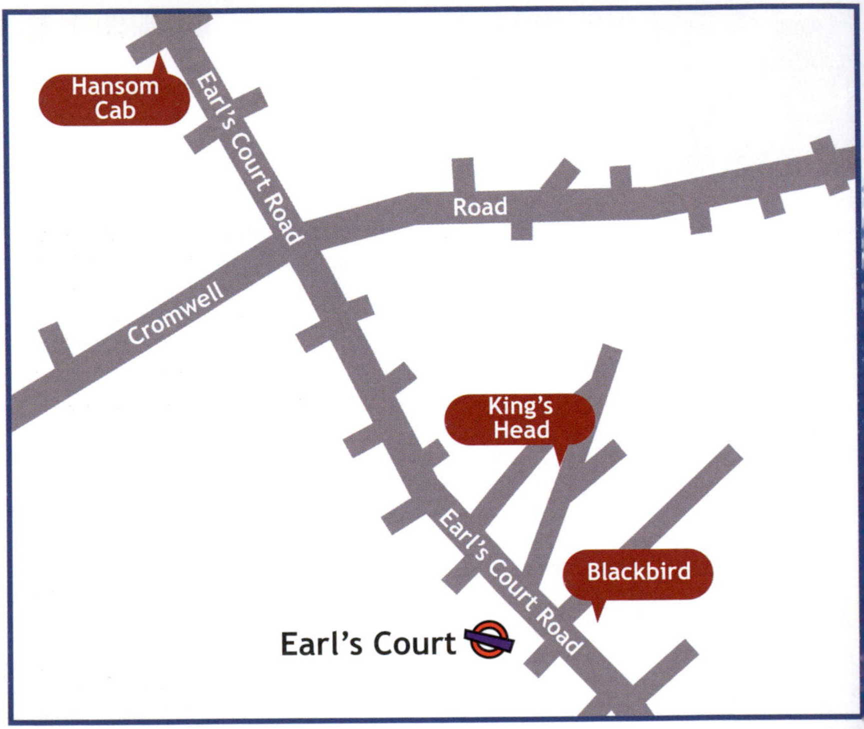

Hansom Cab
Earl's Court Road
Road
Cromwell
King's Head
Blackbird
Earl's Court Road
Earl's Court

Blackbird

RATING: 3/3

209 Earls Court Road
SW5 9AN
020 7835 1855

Not an outstanding pub by any means, but this one's probably your safest bet on Earl's Court Road. Being a Fuller's Ale and Pie House, it's no surprise that the food, drink and decor are of a reasonable quality. That's really the pub's strength and what pulls in the customers. As this is Earl's Court, the sound of tourists trundling suitcases along pavements is never far away, but this is the sort of safe, middle-of-the-road pub that you'd probably give a look to if you're new in town.

FEATURES: 

HANDY FOR: Earl's Court

The Hansom Cab

RATING:

86 Earl's Court Road
W8 6EG
020 7938 3700

Following another refurb, we're not entirely sure what they changed beyond the colour of the outside, to be honest. From what the barmaid said, they only keep a couple of beers on tap now, London Pride and a guest as well as Erdinger wheat beer and the usual suspects. It's still got some excellent features around the bar, combined with smart furniture and a gastro-ish menu. The clientele of mostly locals is quite varied and it's not a bad place for the area. As previously noted, just keep an eye out for the rather too boisterous groups taking advantage of the late licence and you won't go far wrong here.

FEATURES:     **HANDY FOR:** Earl's Court, Olympia

King's Head

RATING: 

17 Hogarth Place
SW5 0QT
020 7244 5931

Hidden away on a street which serves as a charming oasis away from Earl's Court High Street, the King's Head is a revamped pub with lounge and gastro touches. Taken on its own merits it's not bad at all: there's decent beer on the hand pumps, Belgian bottles in the fridge and a competent-looking menu, all topped off with first-class service. Couches, retro flock wallpaper and a tabletop Pacman would indicate aiming for a younger crowd, but we found people of all ages happily sharing the pub on our afternoon visit, with the section around the ornate fireplace particularly popular. We also spied a plasma screen off to one side, indicating some sort of sports action, but it was switched off on our visit. It gets pretty busy here later on, with seats hard to come by, but, considering it's the best pub in the area, that's hardly surprising.

FEATURES:      **HANDY FOR:** Earl's Court

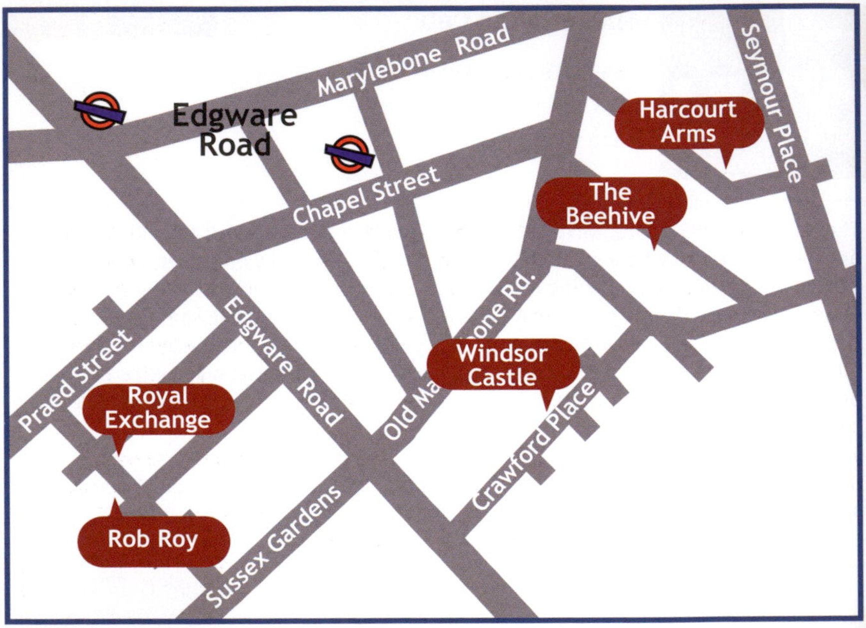

The Beehive

7 Homer Street
W1H 4NJ
020 7262 6581

Marylebone is home to some of the friendliest pubs in London and this little bar is a prime example. Perhaps conversation is induced by the small interior – it's hard to avoid speaking to your fellow drinkers and the staff when there's so little space. Like a few other pubs in the area (the other Beehive for instance) this one's had its *Changing Rooms* makeover and is now aiming at a more upmarket crowd. This doesn't mean you can no longer get a decent pint, as they still offer Pride and Timothy Taylor's Landlord for those discerning fans of real ale. And, while the rest of the beer offerings are all fairly average, it's definitely the cheery atmosphere and friendly staff that make it worth coming along.

FEATURES:  

HANDY FOR: Madame Tussauds, Wallace Collection

Harcourt Arms

RATING:

32 Harcourt Street
W1H 4HX
020 7723 6634

The Harcourt Arms belongs to a nexus of great pubs in the Marylebone Baker Street area, and has pretty much everything you could ask for in such a place. It's very welcoming, clean and well maintained, serves a decent selection of beers, including Pride, Adnam's as well as a monthly guest ale, and has a good beer garden. Many of the pubs in this area have their own little eccentricities or things that make them that little bit different. Whilst lacking in strange memorabilia or acting as a meeting place of odd societies, the Harcourt proudly boasts a link with the area's Swedish community – its proximity to the Swedish Church down the street no coincidence. If you don't fancy sitting in the main bar, what about the Svenska Salongen situated at the back? You can also be served Swedish ciders by the Swedish bar staff. They also show Swedish sport, if that's your thing – and that's when the place can get really crowded. When the ice hockey's on the box, if Forlunda or HV 71 means nothing to you, forget it. But, overall, a pub that goes from strength to strength.

FEATURES:     

Rob Roy

RATING: 

8 Sale Place
W2 1PH
020 7262 6403

The name (and the Aberdeen FC shirt on the wall) mark this one out as something different from your average London pub. Very much a Scottish bar, it's the venue of choice for exiled members of the Tartan Army when there's a big match on. Perhaps not for the fainthearted on such occasions – especially if Scotland are tackling one of football's 'lesser nations' – but if you pop by at a quieter time you'll find a decent enough little boozer.

FEATURES:  

Royal Exchange

RATING:

26 Sale Place
W2 1PU
020 7930 5826

A long time ago, when we didn't know any better, we would often arrive at Paddington after a long journey and wonder where on earth we could go for a decent pint before the pubs closed. And we'd end up in a pretty dismal sort of place, only because it was the only pub sign we could see, beckoning us from the station. If only we'd known about the Royal Exchange. A five-minute walk away from Paddington Station gets you to a fine, traditional boozer of the old school. Serving real ales, hot and cold Guinness, Murphy's and a bunch of other traditional tipples, this place is a real down-to-earth, honest pub. The atmosphere is friendly, as is the service, the food is proper pub grub and the pub hasn't been renovated to within an inch of its former life. If you want to visit an example of a pub as they used to be (and as some of us remember them), you'd better get here, before someone decides it's worth 'improving'.

FEATURES:   

Windsor Castle

RATING: 

27–29 Crawford Place
W1H 4LQ
020 7723 4371

This is certainly one of the oddest pubs you'll ever drink in and it's a real treat. Once inside, you encounter an Aladdin's cave of royal/celebrity photos (including a signed photo of Pélé), glass cabinets and generally enough gee-gaws to fill every gift shop in Blackpool, Brighton and Bournemouth. Even the ceiling is covered in plates in display cases. As for the beers, there's not a huge selection – just as well as the pub is intoxicating enough in itself – but there's a selection of decent, hand-pumped ales and a couple of ciders. It's a friendly place too and its quirky reputation means it's on the itinerary of many a tourist, but an influx of newcomers does nothing to upset the ambience (unlike a few places we can think of). There's also offers pretty decent Thai food, with food served in the bar or the separate restaurant upstairs (where you can also get good old fish 'n' chips). And, if all that isn't enough for you, the pub is also home to the Handlebar Club. Excellent.

FEATURES:    *Reviewers' Award – Winner 2008*

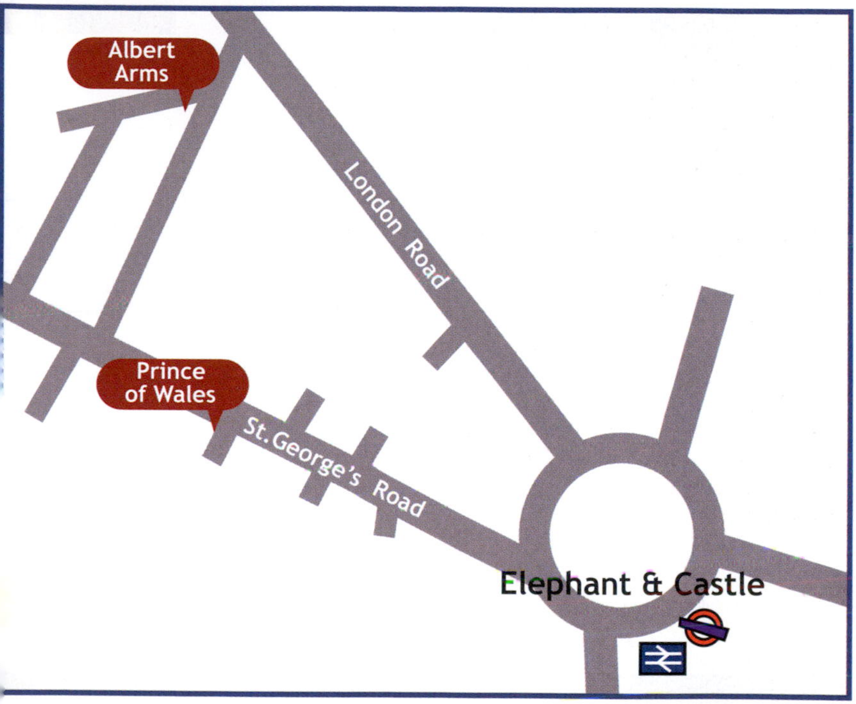

Albert Arms
London Road
Prince of Wales
St. George's Road
Elephant & Castle

Albert Arms

RATING: 

1 Gladstone Street
SE1 6EY
020 7928 6517

Off the main roads which dominate the area, the Albert Arms is a neat two-room pub with a bit of character. Beer mats, brass kettles and other ephemera decorate the walls of the two bars. Reasonably priced pub grub is on offer and a few wines, with three hand pumps sporting beers such as Greene King IPA and the usual suspects on the tap. Its proximity to South Bank University means some student clientele, but it's got a regular local crowd who are genial enough. Still, this pub has got things going for it and is one of the better bets for drinking in these parts.

FEATURES:    

HANDY FOR: Imperial War Museum

ELEPHANT & CASTLE

Prince of Wales

RATING:

51 St George's Road
SE1 6ER
020 7582 9696

This is a traditional boozer and very much a locals' pub, which looks more like a working man's club than anything else. And, despite the England flags everywhere, it has more than a hint of Irishness about it – and the Gaelic football on the telly last time we were in did nothing to dispel this feeling. Even so, everyone seemed quite content and fairly friendly when we were there. If you don't live nearby, there is probably no reason you would go here, but, if you stumble out of the Imperial War Museum in the wrong direction, it's all right for a pint. With two fairly large rooms and a large outside area at the back, there is plenty of space, especially in summer. It does pub food, and everything costs a fiver. What we're most intrigued by is the offer of 'Sunday Roast to take away' – beef, pork or lamb. No mucking about, it knows exactly what it's there for.

FEATURES:     

HANDY FOR: Imperial War Museum

EMBANKMENT – *see Charing Cross, page 104*

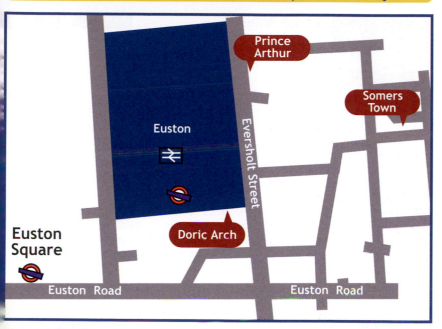

Prince Arthur
Somers Town
Euston
Eversholt Street
Doric Arch
Euston Square
Euston Road
Euston Road

Doric Arch

RATING: 

1 Eversholt Street
NW1 1DN
020 7388 2221

Once called the Head of Steam, the Doric Arch has settled down over the last year or so to be as solid a pub as its predecessor ever was. The refit was on the benign side of things, and even though the owners changed (this one's now run by Fuller's) the reliance on guest beers remained. Also, the old pub's railway memorabilia remains (even if it does appear to have been slightly rearranged). Always a beery, blokey sort of place, the Doric Arch is still a safe bet should thirst get the better of you whilst you're waiting at Euston Station.

FEATURES:  

HANDY FOR: British Library

Prince Arthur

RATING:

80–82 Eversholt Street
NW1 1BX
020 7387 2165

The Prince Arthur has long been a favourite of ours, but things are starting to change on Eversholt Street. Gone is the cheap and cheerful Thai food menu, to be replaced by a much more upmarket nod to gastro fare. They have terrine. They have butternut squash and parsley risotto. They have kidneys and shallots on toast. Oh my. What's more intriguing is the catering is done by some outfit by the name of Tovey. Now the only Tovey we're familiar with is potential Doctor Who and current star of *Little Dorrit* Russell Tovey, but we reckon that might not be the case. He might be a bit busy just now. The beer is still kept beautifully and the table service is still up to scratch, but we can't help but feel it's moving on to pastures new. Whether they'll be taking the loyal customers with them or seeking out new regulars remains to be seen. It's still way above anything else in the area though, so don't despair too much.

FEATURES:   

HANDY FOR: British Library

Somers Town Coffee House

RATING:

60 Chalton Street
NW1 1HS
020 7691 9136

An establishment with a bit of history, apparently once a favoured meeting place for Huguenot intellectuals to catch up on events and drink coffee. More recently, however, the fortunes of the Coffee House (caffeine-related sales more or less sidelined) have tracked the misfortunes of the surrounding neighbourhood, caught as it is between three main railway lines out of London and located on the more unfavoured side of Euston Road. However, the Coffee House has undergone a refurbishment to become a rather smart gastropub. Lots of polished wood and subtle lighting, and a few of the cosy-looking, high-backed, cushioned seats are reminiscent of those formerly found in the single-compartment portions of trains running out of London. It's quite spacious, with a central island bar, and retains the feel of a proper pub. One side is given over to dining, with the other for both drinking and eating. There are a few real ales, as well as some other interesting beers. The food was pretty good too, although relatively expensive. The bar staff were friendly, and the music was funky but unobtrusive.

FEATURES:  

HANDY FOR: British Library

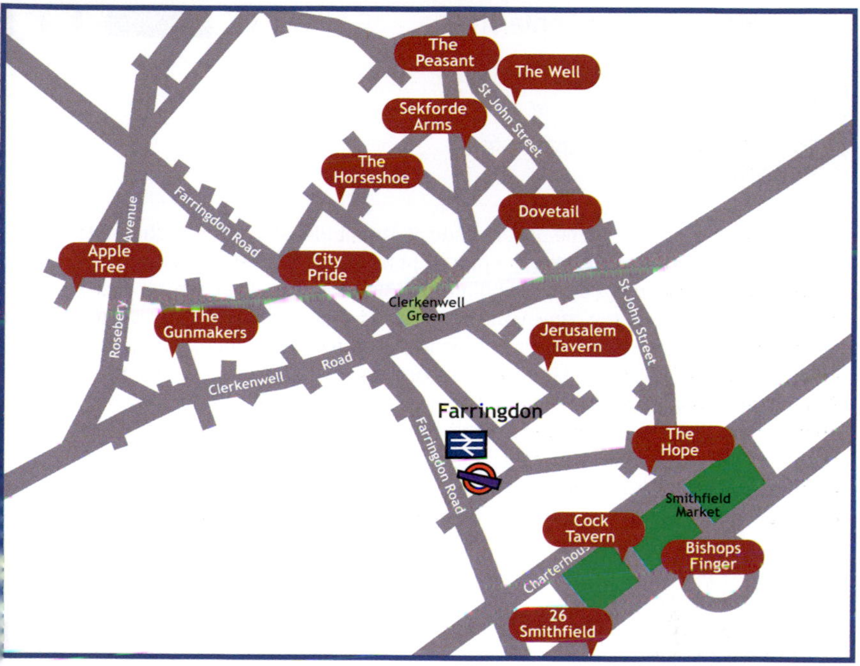

The Peasant
The Well
Sekforde Arms
St John Street
The Horseshoe
Dovetail
Farringdon Road
Rosebery Avenue
Apple Tree
City Pride
Clerkenwell Green
The Gunmakers
Jerusalem Tavern
St John Street
Clerkenwell Road
Farringdon
Farringdon Road
The Hope
Smithfield Market
Cock Tavern
Bishops Finger
Charterhouse
26 Smithfield

26 Smithfield

RATING: 

26 Smithfield Street
EC1A 9LB
020 7248 2464

A few years ago this pub was host to Smithfield meat workers, amongst others. It reopened early 2007 with a new name and direction, aiming for a more upmarket crowd. Putting in a good menu and hardworking, genial staff means things have got much better. There's a reasonable wine list, and numerous lagers on tap to choose from – the only ale on when we were in last was Adnam's, which was well kept and went down a treat. It also plays host to live music events and opens occasionally at the weekends as a music venue (most of the pubs in these parts shut for the weekends). One other attraction is the Roof Terrace – an unusual thing in this part of London – though it's no surprise it's become a smoker's paradise. Having worked hard to muscle in on the Smithfield drinking market, the pub has its adherents, mostly nearby office workers. And in light of recent closures nearby, that's a pretty good achievement.

FEATURES:     **HANDY FOR:** Museum of London, St Paul's Cathedral

The Apple Tree

RATING:

45 Mount Pleasant
WC1X 0AE
020 7837 2365

It's been a while now since the posties' pub at Mount Pleasant got a gastro-style makeover, in an attempt to move the place upmarket. By and large it succeeded, with the Apple Tree now largely being populated by media types – the creators of crap having taken over from the conveyors. But who can blame them? It's a pretty decent place, you can usually rely on Greene King to put on a decent range of drink and food, which they certainly do here (although one of the two hand pumps seems to be permanently dry nowadays). If you're not familiar with the pub, there's the usual range of mismatched chairs, tables and settees, the odd chandelier, artwork on the walls and piped music (usually an eclectic but reasonable quality mix). The service is fast and friendly – it needs to be on a Thursday and Friday night when the place can get pretty packed. There are regular Country music sessions (alternate Sundays) and weekly poker nights to keep you entertained, should conversation be found wanting. A deservedly popular place, one wonders where the poor posties go to, now that even the old Penny Black is a restaurant.

FEATURES:    

HANDY FOR: Sadler's Wells Theatre

Bishops Finger

RATING: 

9 West Smithfield
EC1A 9JR
020 7248 2341

An old favourite in Smithfield, this one has stayed pretty constant for the last few years. Located practically next to St Bartholomew's Hospital and St Bartholomew the Grand (one of the churches from *Four Weddings and a Funeral*), it's also near the place William Wallace was executed, way back when – it's in a pretty historic area all in all. It's got a good range of Shepherd Neame ales to work your way through and a decent range of pub food to fill up on while drinking (though with the famous Smithfield meat market across the road you'd expect little else). Some fine old cartoons and drawings decorate the walls and add to the pleasant air of the place. It can get pretty crowded at lunchtimes and after work, but it's still worth a look if you're in the area or need a break from sightseeing.

FEATURES:      

HANDY FOR: Museum of London

City Pride

RATING:

28 Farringdon Lane
EC1R 3AU
020 7608 0615

A very pleasant Fuller's pub in the heart of Clerkenwell. It serves a good pint (Pride, Adnam's, ESB), decent honest pub food and the clientele are usually a jolly crowd. It also has the added advantage of being able to open up most of the front of the pub, which is nice in hot weather. It usually doesn't get too crowded, even when all around are packed to the gunwales and there's a room upstairs to expand into if it does. Sport's a bit deal here, with TVs scattered all over the place showing Sky Sports and Setanta, and it definitely gets the punters in for the games. In addition to the usual range of Fuller's fine beers, it also serves decent guest beers too. If you're in these parts looking for a proper pub, you won't go wrong coming here.

FEATURES:  

HANDY FOR: Sadler's Wells Theatre, Museum of London

Cock Tavern

RATING:

East Poultry Avenue
EC1A 9LH
020 7248 2918

Given this pub used to shut up shop of an afternoon, signs advertising 'Live Jazz' took us by surprise; that it was even open at night – let alone showcasing live music – unheard of. We knew Smithfield's future was far from secure but had this bastion of bloodied butchers been homogenised for local loft dwellers? Well, give it a look some early morning and you won't see many changes. In the bowels of the Smithfield Market, The Cock is a comfortable cross between pub and greasy spoon, with a bar on one side, a dining space on the other and a café-style area separating them. The fact it's underground adds a nefarious edge to your drinking; that it's in Smithfield means you can start on the sauce at a very early hour – although, with the new licensing laws, that frisson has now disappeared. The Cock used to close in the early afternoon, but now it stays open: there's a hand-over in the kitchen and an upmarket lunchtime menu offered. Make the trip here before the area becomes just like any other – there's already a Starbucks and Pizza Express around the corner. To see it at its best though, grit your teeth, set the alarm and visit before 9am. Your vegetarian friends might not approve but this irreplaceable bit of London is worth making the effort to see before it goes.

FEATURES:  

HANDY FOR: Museum of London, St Paul's Cathedral

The Dovetail Bar

RATING:

9 Jerusalem Passage
EC1V 4JP
020 7490 7321

This place specialises in things Belgian, mainly beer, moules etc., but also more esoteric continental stuff such as Genevers and the like. While typical English pub fare (burgers and lagers) are available, the more curious pub explorer will revel in the huge range of Belgian beers found on the pumps and in the menu – there will almost certainly be something for everyone. The place does a pretty good impression of being Antwerp rather than London and is a refreshing change from the identikit bars and gastropubs in the area. The food and service are decent and priced for the area – i.e. not cheap, but not too expensive either. And, as it's continental, they take your drink orders at your table (when it's not too busy). It gets pretty popular towards the end of the week with people who work in the area, and they often spill out onto the pavement. Nevertheless, well worth seeking out if you want something different and don't want to cross the channel to get it.

FEATURES:  

HANDY FOR: Sadler's Wells Theatre, Museum of London

Gunmakers

RATING: 

13 Eyre Street Hill
EC1R 5ET
020 7278 1022

Clerkenwell is underrated as a place to go pubbing – being predominately a designer's paradise of bars and clubs, but there are a good few pubs that reward you for following up on that instinct that says 'I wonder what's down that side road'. The Gunmakers was always one of those that hit the spot and continues to do so. It's a small front-room bar with two tables, followed by a parlour decorated in Student Union green with attendant red PVC benches, and a back room full of tables for two. It's patronised by one or two local firms possibly at the expense of the curious explorer. And the loos let them down a bit (we needn't go into details, right?). The good news is it's still very good for food – pub grub certainly – try the slow-roasted pork belly – but with genuine flair, well presented and reasonably priced. They do decent grog too (Summer Lightning and Landlord were both well kept) and it still feels like a local with a friendly greeting.

FEATURES:    

The Hope

RATING: 

94 Cowcross Street
EC1M 6BH
020 7250 1442

This old early-opening pub in the heart of Smithfield meat market has serviced the traders here for many a year. Still retaining a few of its original features, the well-kept beer and genial bar staff make this a good place to meet and have a couple of drinks. It also has a critically acclaimed restaurant on the first floor and serves excellent roast meat sandwiches at lunchtime. Quiet enough of an evening, be warned that it often closes early (8:30–9:00ish most nights – well, you would too if you opened at 6:00 in the morning). However, if you like a place with a bit of activity and a comfortable atmosphere, or like the idea of a Guinness with your breakfast, the early-opening Hope is a sound bet.

FEATURES:  

HANDY FOR: Museum of London, St Paul's Cathedral

The Horseshoe

RATING: 

24 Clerkenwell Close
EC1R 0AG
020 7253 6068

That London term 'village' for often apparently undifferentiated bits of the capital suddenly makes sense when you slip away from the trendies cluttering up Clerkenwell Green and find yourself a hundred yards – and possibly – a hundred years away. The Horseshoe could sit happily in any true village, jostling with the church and duck pond. Externally it's 16th century-quaint and tiny – but inside it runs back further than you would expect to give quite a long bar area and a separate eating section. Décor is pretty basic and it's got no airs and graces – rather you have Greene King IPA or Sharps Cornish Coaster and reasonably priced pie and mash. And the two dart boards are obviously well used; a lunchtime group seemed regularly to get their exit doubles at the first time of asking – and when was the last time you saw a treble top scored in a local boozer? The little beer garden is probably a great sun-trap – well at least for an hour or so either side of noon as the towering buildings around make it feel rather like sitting inside a cooling tower.

FEATURES:        

Jerusalem Tavern

RATING:

Britton Street
EC1M 5NA
020 7490 4281

No stranger to those who have an interest in good beer and good public houses, The Jerusalem Tavern is a serious contender for best pubs in London. Converted from a fabulous-looking 18th-century clockmaker's shop, it's the only pub in London owned by the Suffolk-based St Peter's brewery. As such, you will see their complete year-round range of excellent award-winning ales, both in bottles and on tap. Other drinks available tick the right boxes (lager, wine, cider) but will rarely be the usual high-street names. Food is served at lunchtime (12–3pm), and we recommend 'sausage Tuesday' in particular. The place is tiny and the only negative is that it gets seriously busy quite often. Lunchtimes and after work are predictably crowded, both inside and out on the pavement, but regulars will share a table if there are just a couple of you – overall there is a very genial atmosphere. You can also book a table in advance for a largish group. Overall, if you're lucky enough to find some free seats, the Dickensian feel of the place is perfect for a cosy winter's evening of tasty ale, warming fires and good conversation. Highly recommended.

FEATURES:  

The Peasant

RATING:

240 St John Street
EC1V 9PH
020 7336 7726

The Peasant is a grand former gin palace turned upmarket gastropub languishing in the middle of Clerkenwell, surrounded by an uneasy mix of Victorian townhouses and council estates. Like many gastropubs, it's unsure of how to strike an even pub/restaurant balance, indicated by the wine glasses and cutlery on a scattering of ground-floor tables, in addition to the upstairs restaurant. Still, its aim in life appears to err towards minimising pretension and due to the pub's size there's plenty of space to sit and have a well-kept pint from a good selection, whilst possibly enjoying one of the (expensive) bar snacks. And for the Frasier Cranes of the world, there's even a sherry selection. With a relaxed atmosphere, friendly service and a tastefully refurbished interior (which retains many wonderful original features), The Peasant is a more traditional and comfortable alternative to nearby bar 'The Well'.

FEATURES:   

Sekforde Arms

RATING:

34 Sekforde Street
EC1R 0HA
020 7253 3251

This is a very pleasant Young's pub in an old residential area just off Clerkenwell Road. Of course, it's all residential round here nowadays, with all the warehouse conversions and new apartment blocks going up, but the Sekforde Arms is no mere arriviste – we'd hazard a guess that it's been like this round here from very early in the 19th century. The service is friendly, the beer very well kept and the food unpretentious (and without the pretentious price tag). This pub fits very comfortably with its surroundings, it's a genuine local and outside the immediate area hardly anyone seems to know about it. It can get busy, with local workers and regulars, but they tend to be an easy-going lot, so we can't say it really detracts from the experience. Definitely one we'd recommend looking out for. Let's just hope it doesn't get the shortened name and gutted interior that a lot of other Young's pubs – excuse us – 'lifestyle bars' – are getting.

FEATURES:     

The Well

RATING:  

180 St John's Street
EC1V 4JY
020 7251 9363

This place really needs no introduction, it's one of the earlier trendy bars in the area and has appeared in countless pub and bar guides before. It gets pretty crowded at the end of the week, especially in summer and that's when it can often be better to go elsewhere. But if the crowds are thinner and your wallet's up to it, it's not a bad place at all. The drink's interesting – continental beers on the pumps such as Hoegaarden, Leffe Blonde and Paulaner Weiss bier – the wine list is OK, the gastro-type food is decent and the service is good. Look out for the fish tanks in the basement bar, too.

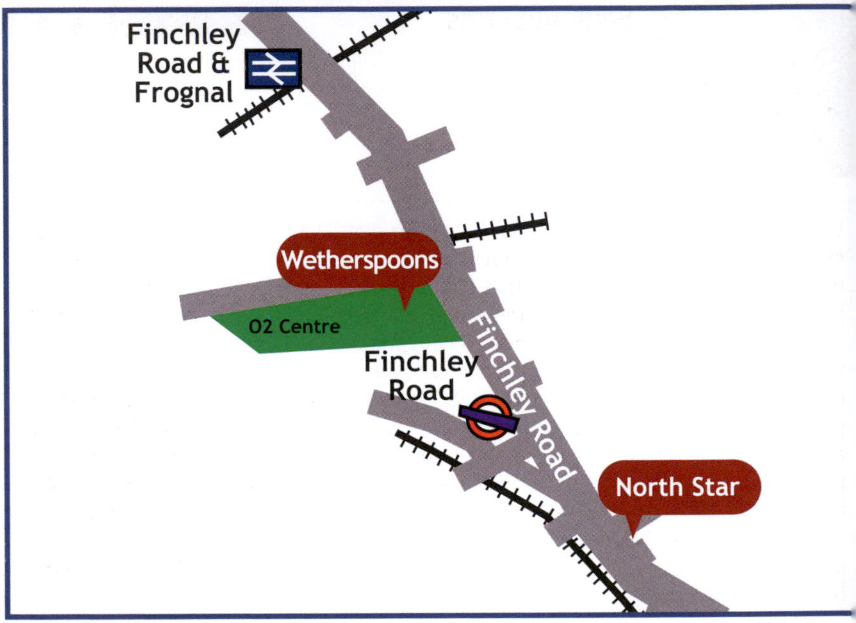

North Star

RATING:

104 Finchley Road
NW3 5JJ
020 7435 6287

An otherwise unremarkable pub can suddenly take on a new appearance when it, by default, becomes the best place to drink in an otherwise barren area. Ultimately doing nothing wrong, it's a large open pub, with a raised seating area to one side. It's never totally full, nor empty, serves average but perfectly edible food, has a reasonable beer selection, and a large screen showing the usual football fixtures. Basically, it's a comfortable place for the locals, or those who have come down to visit the wonders of, er, Finchley Road.

FEATURES:    

Wetherspoons

RATING:

O2 Centre, 255 Finchley Road
NW3 6LU
020 7433 0920

Given that this is a Wetherspoon pub located in a late-1990s shopping/entertainment centre, this really isn't so bad. Although it is to damn with faint praise to say so, this is the better of the two pubs in the O2 centre (given that the other is a Walkabout, this is perhaps to damn with very faint praise indeed). The old pedantic Wetherspoon rule of 'no music' is ignored here, and, while you are unlikely to hear any outstanding or breathtaking tunes as a matter of course, it does liven up the atmosphere considerably, as do the floor-to-ceiling windows along one whole, curved side of the pub. It's a pity, then, that the view, of Finchley Road and the Midland Main Line, is not all that. The clientele are young and old, perhaps reflecting the strange lack of decent pubs nearby, and the place seems well run, efficient and friendly enough, albeit a bit, inevitably, corporate. There were an astonishing number of real ales – was it eight in all? Or ten? – generally good ones on the hand pumps on our last visit. Not sure it's a place you'd go far out of your way to visit, necessarily, but we think this Wetherspoon is good for more than just a pre- or post-cinema pint.

FEATURES:      

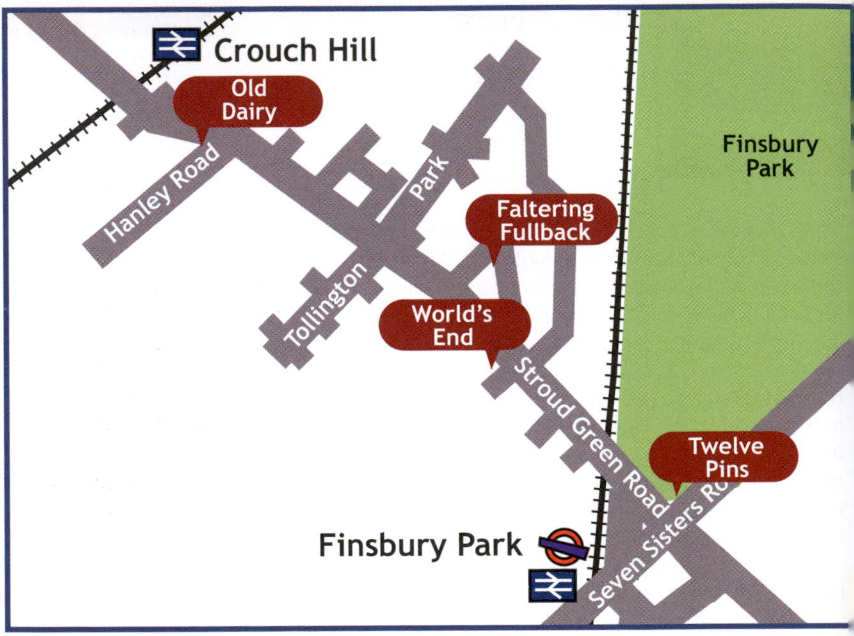

Crouch Hill
Old Dairy
Hanley Road
Park
Tollington
Faltering Fullback
World's End
Stroud Green Road
Finsbury Park
Twelve Pins
Seven Sisters Ro
Finsbury Park

Faltering Fullback

RATING:

19 Perth Road
N4 3HB
020 7272 5834

Hidden away on a back street just north of Finsbury Park, the Faltering Fullback is a distinctly better alternative than any other pub within the vicinity of the station. It stocks an impressive range of draught and bottled beers, and has a friendly, laid back local atmosphere. There's also an impressively cavernous back room full of picnic tables and a pool table, that appears to attract a younger crowd than the front area. In keeping with its name the pub regularly screens football and rugby, though it's pretty unobtrusive and quite possible to enjoy your drink if you're not interested in the game. Recommended.

FEATURES:      

The Old Dairy

RATING:

1–3 Crouch Hill
N4 4AP
020 7263 3337

The people responsible for a small gaggle of upmarket gastroesque pubs in North London have turned their hand to the impressive space occupied by the popular Old Dairy. They've stuck to their tried and tested formula – sympathetic refurbishment, dark, moody lighting and a large restaurant area. In some of their smaller pubs this latter feature has been frustrating, as it leads to unpleasant overcrowding in the drinking section, whilst the eating bit remains stubbornly underpopulated. At the Old Dairy, the pub's size saves the day, as there was enough seating on our weekday visit for everyone. We can't vouch for the weekend though, but it looks like becoming very busy. There's a laidback atmosphere, a good selection of ales and a good British menu. As elegant as their ambitions are, they're also apparently prepared to bow to popular culture and were showing the football on our visit. We liked the Old Dairy before, but its new incarnation isn't too shoddy either.

FEATURES:       

The Twelve Pins

RATING: 

263 Seven Sisters Road
N4 2DE
020 8809 0192

The sheer size of The Twelve Pins and its proximity to Finsbury Park station limit its appeal a little, but it's not really so bad. The interior is quite magnificent, if a little careworn, a good example of a Victorian pub interior. The varied mix of punters seem oblivious to its charms, content to drink quietly and keep themselves to themselves, and, as it's an Irish pub, there's a decent drop of Guinness to be had here. The pub shows all kinds of sport, and has regular appearances by Irish bands – it can get lively when they're on.

FEATURES:     

The World's End

RATING: 3 pints

21-23 Stroud Green Road
N4 3EF
020 7281 8679

Until a refit in late 2007, a visit here was almost enough to make you wish the world would end. But now, although the interior designers have hardly broken the mould for recent pub refurbishments, there are plenty of reasons to visit. The biggest change has been the revival of live music, with a regular night for bands on Thursdays and jazz on a Sunday night. It still caters for football fans with several TVs and a 10-foot projector screen, and being two minutes from Finsbury Park station is a decent stop-off on the way to the Emirates. Both ale and lager drinkers are well catered for, with Adnam's and Bombardier joined by regular guest choices, and Bitburger and Heineken also available. There is seating on all sides of the central bar, with the back area providing the most relaxed atmosphere. All in all a welcome improvement.

FEATURES:     

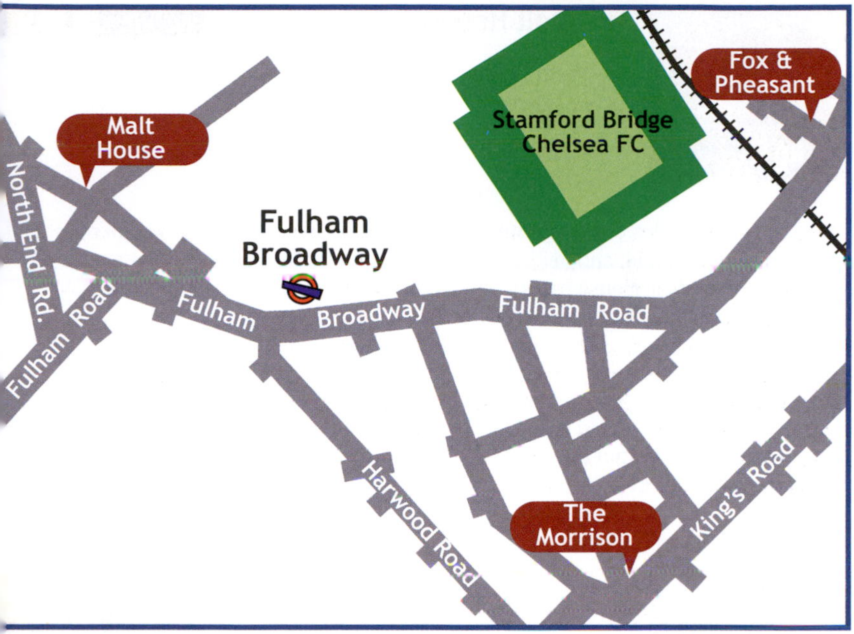

Malt House
Fox & Pheasant
Stamford Bridge Chelsea FC
Fulham Broadway
North End Rd.
Fulham Road
Fulham Broadway
Fulham Road
Harwood Road
The Morrison
King's Road

Fox & Pheasant

RATING: 

1 Billing Road
SW10 9UJ
020 7352 2943

Unless you're of the Chelsea persuasion, you'll probably stay clear of this one when there's a game on at Stamford Bridge. At any other time, though, it's worth a look if you like your pubs cut from the same traditional cloth as Knightsbridge's Nag's Head or Barons Court's Colton Arms. Like those two, the Fox & Pheasant is a small affair, managing to fit a dart board and a TV screen into its classic low-ceilinged pub interior. There are some seats out the back and there's a small lunchtime menu (weekdays only) to nosh whilst you sample their Greene King ales. An untouched gem in an area where most of the pubs chase after the latest trends, it's the sort of old boozer where it's no great surprise to find a signed Britt Ekland picture behind the bar.

FEATURES:   

HANDY FOR: Chelsea Football Club

The Malt House

RATING:

17 Vanston Place
SW6 1AY
020 7385 3593

Not too long ago, this one was noted for two things: Chelsea fans and karaoke nights. A name change, a refit, and neither appear to be part of this pub's apparel any more. It's not as if the Malt House has gone that upmarket, but it just goes to show how much a pub's atmosphere can change once it cancels its Sky subscription. Oddly, the smartening up of the pub has also brought about the addition of famous quotations concerning drinking: something we thought had gone out of fashion in pub design about five years ago. Nevertheless, both food and drink are straightforward and the layout – with a fine covered space out the back – and the music played added to the experience. All good stuff and any place that mixes up a cocktail called a Des Lynam surely has its heart in the right place.

FEATURES: 

HANDY FOR: Chelsea Football Club

The Morrison

RATING: 

648 King's Road
SW6 2DU
020 7610 9859

This one impressed us when it opened a few years back, clearly marking itself apart from the predictable pubs and bars of the area. On revisiting it recently it appears to have toned down its Irishness and gone even more towards catering for sports fans. So much so, that plasma screens – at least eight of them – seem to adorn almost every available wall space of this not overly large pub. It's quite an imposing sight, and in between the action the pub does give off the impression of being trapped in a hall of mirrors with Richard Keys. And in the unlikely event there's no sport to show and you need to put your twiddling thumbs to use, there's a PlayStation available. As for the food and drink on offer, this place makes great play of its cocktails, but there isn't the greatest selection on the pumps. As for the food, the ostrich burger on the menu looked an intriguing choice... There are a lot of good aspects to The Morrison but unfortunately the pub is starting to look slightly frayed around the edges and some TLC could come in handy. It detracts a bit from the overall feel, but, hey, if you're in this part of town and need a pub to watch the football in, then this is the one.

FEATURES:    

HANDY FOR: Chelsea Football Club

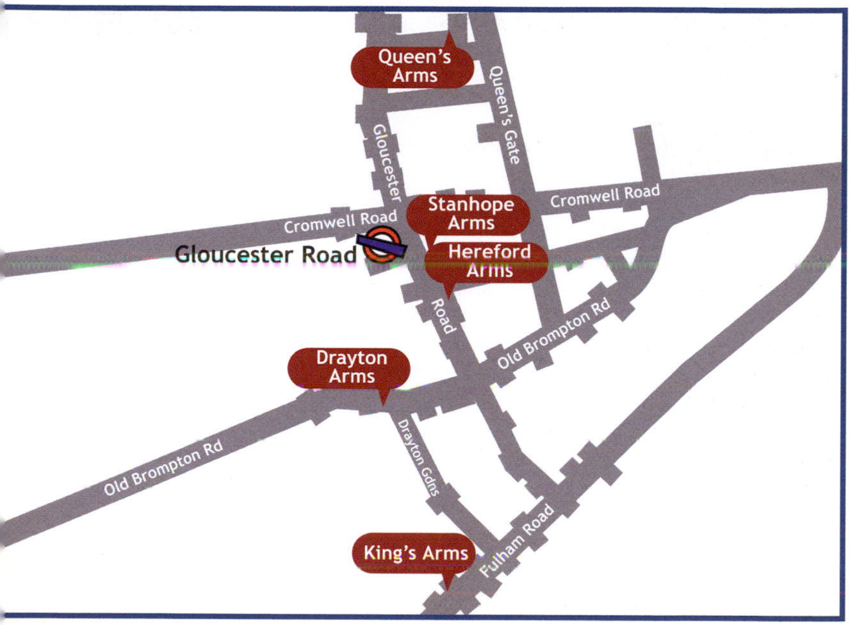

Drayton Arms

RATING: 

153 Old Brompton Road
SW5 0LJ
020 7835 2301

The Drayton Arms is a Victorian pub with some nice touches of interior detail, it was one of the first M&B unbranded pubs and it still sticks to the mission statement of a bar stocked with a range of continental beers and wines and a pub interior packed with as many contrasting forms of furniture as possible. Upon them you'll find a mostly young clientele (who've been on our visits here rather laidback and relaxed rather than achingly stylish trend-setters). There are enough goodies behind the bar to cover all tastes and, if you're after entertainment, it comes in the form of DJs on Friday nights. Not a bad pub for the area, this one.

FEATURES:  

Hereford Arms

RATING: 

127 Gloucester Road
SW7 4TE
020 7370 4988

Not surprisingly for the area, this is very much a pub for the tourists. It's been given the old rustic pub interior décor treatment, which is a bit of a shame as the old place was OK – a normal boozer, but a bit shabby. It's also a pretty big place, serves decent enough food and drink and is not too badly priced (at least for London) given the area. Whilst the committed pub-goer might spend more effort looking for something a little less formulaic, if you're thirsty and/or hungry and in the neighbourhood, it's a safe enough bet.

FEATURES:   

King's Arms

RATING: 

190 Fulham Road
SW10 9PN
020 7351 5043

A change of name for this pub and, in line with Young's current programme of refurbishing their pubs, the TV and the fruit machine have made way for rather more plush furnishings. Added to the original tilework on the wall of the pub, the redecoration makes for a smart and decorous one-roomed pub. The problem, alas, is the upgrade has slightly taken away the character of this one: the pub's promotional literature waxes lyrical on how it once attracted rakes of the quality of Richard Harris and Oliver Reed; but now we get the impression that the rather formal feel of this one isn't aimed at too many modern-day hellraisers. If the music played in a pub suggests its personality, then the fact that the moderate tinklings of Jamie Cullum were being aired on our visit gives you a fair indication of how this pub is pitching itself.

FEATURES:  

HANDY FOR: Chelsea Football Club

Queen's Arms

RATING:

30 Queens Gate Mews
SW7 5QL
020 7581 7741

A former Fancyapint? award winner, this pub is tucked out of site in a small mews not far from Hyde Park. The surrounding colleges explain the high student numbers, but that's not the whole story. It's also a good place to meet before going to see something at the Albert Hall and often shows the effects of major events like the Proms, spilling out into the hapless mews. It's been refreshed, but it's still kept the high standards that have made this a perennial favourite, including decent beer on the four hand pumps, a selection of Belgian beers, friendly staff and a reasonably priced (if slightly gastro) menu. And we're always pleased to see Sunday roasts – advertised as available all day Sunday. A lively place, the harried staff even manage to stay pleasant after a long evening. It's less busy during the day and on weekends, which makes it a good spot to meet in Kensington, if a little off the beaten track.

FEATURES:     

HANDY FOR: Royal Albert Hall

Stanhope Arms

RATING: 

97 Gloucester Road
SW7 4SS
020 7373 4192

The Stanhope Arms is a handy pub for a quick pint or as a place to meet before going to the Albert Hall or one of the other nearby attractions (just remember to leave enough time to get there). It offers pretty standard pub fare (both beer and food) served up by attentive staff, so there are no real surprises, pleasant or otherwise. As it's located in the heart of London hotel-land, this pub usually quickly fills up with tourists and, after work, a few TVs encourage locals and office workers in for the sport.

FEATURES:   

HANDY FOR: Royal Albert Hall

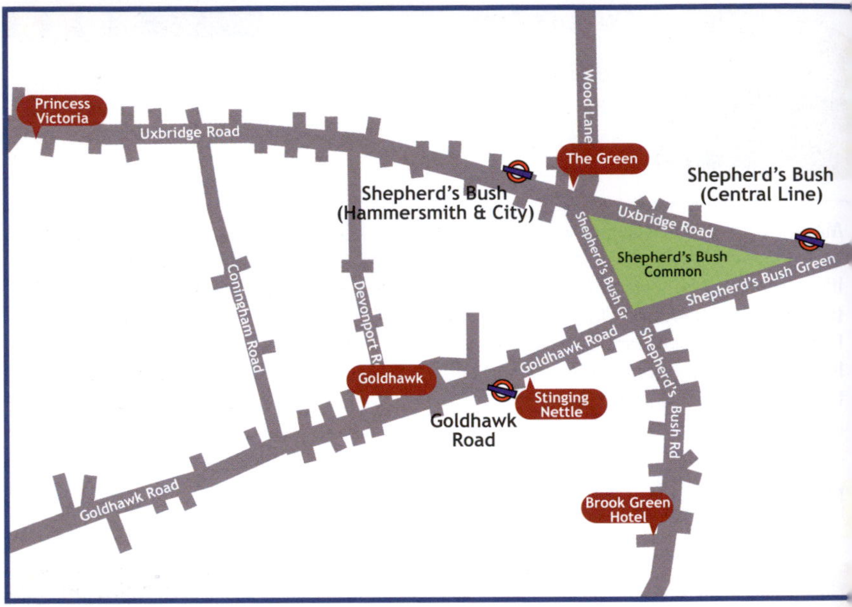

Brook Green Hotel

RATING:

170 Shepherd's Bush Road
W6 7PB
020 7603 2516

This one's proved to be a safe bet over the years, managing to exist as a popular Young's house whilst the nearby pubs in Brook Green evolved into gastropubs. However, this one's now received its Young's upgrade and the result is akin to many of the other Young's refits we've had over the last few years. In have come more chandeliers, a softer tone to the walls and more squishy sofas. This one always had a lounge feel to it, but there's now a more respectable, cleansed air to proceedings. It's still of use as a pit stop on the way to the Shepherd's Bush Empire from Hammersmith tube, but we feel there's something been lost in the upgrade – a shame.

FEATURES:    

The Goldhawk

RATING:

122 Goldhawk Road
W12 8HH
020 8576 6921

Making a deliberate attempt to appeal to a clientele different from all the Irish boozers round these parts is this loungey pub. All squishy furnishings and laid-back sounds, it's hardly one to make a beeline for if you want a big party, but it does serve a need in this neck of the woods if you need a drink but don't fancy watching the Racing from Fairyhouse. With decent ales on the hand pumps, continental beers on tap, a fair wine list, cocktails, modern pub food (and Sunday roast) and arguably the cleanest pub toilets on the Goldhawk Road, this pub's a pleasant place to while away an afternoon.

FEATURES:   

The Green

RATING:  

172–174 Uxbridge Road
W12 7JP
020 8749 5709

Arguably the best place to meet up for gigs at the nearby Shepherd's Bush Empire – though the O'Neill's beside the Empire may disagree – this one has decent beer on tap, friendly enough regulars and genial staff who seem more than happy to pour a pint of decent beer in short order, regardless of how busy it is. The big tellies spread around the place show the sport when it's on, and the locals seem pretty happy with the place, all in all. There's a downstairs bar which takes overflow from the main bar. This is one worth remembering, particularly if you've had little or no luck getting served at one of the trendier places nearby.

FEATURES:   

HANDY FOR: Shepherd's Bush Empire

Princess Victoria

RATING:

217 Uxbridge Road
W12 9DT
020 8749 5886

There's been enough hoo-ha about the new-look Princess Victoria that it almost seems as if this were the first gastropub to open in West London. The imposing nature of the property makes some of the fuss understandable. Up the Uxbridge Road, the pub's juxtaposition to surrounding council blocks means you can't fail to be impressed by its grandeur. Once a splendid gin palace, it's been a rough Irish pub for as long as memory serves. Interestingly, this helped it retain some original features. Punters didn't care about the decor, so no one bothered to rip out the old bar or strip the Victorian mouldings: a salutary lesson to anyone thinking of butchering interesting fittings in the name of progress. There's an imposing circular bar, leather bench seating, a nice parquet floor, wood panelling and lovely skylights throughout. Speaking of which, the dining room was considerably busier than the bar during our last visit, but we resisted the interesting bar menu (Butchers brawn terrine!) and stuck to the well-kept ales. There's also an unnecessarily long wine list which would keep any budding vintner happy for months. Overall, it stills feel like a pub and we thoroughly enjoyed the relaxed atmosphere.

FEATURES:   

Stinging Nettle

RATING:

55 Goldhawk Road
W12 8QP
020 8743 3016

Formerly the Bushranger, this one's now been relaunched by Young's with one of the more intriguing London pub names of recent years. It's very much in the mould of the other pubs Young's have remodelled over the last few years: a plush refit where gilt-framed mirrors adorn flock-wallpapered walls. It looks a sizeable pub from the outside, but the ground floor is quite a narrow space, dominated by high stools and tables. Upstairs has more comfortable seats but not a great deal more space, though there is the benefit of a roof terrace if you fancy an eyrie above the Goldhawk Road. The Stinging Nettle is a prime example of Young's rebranding: it's the sort of place where the big screen isn't for the watching of sport but for the playing of Wii games (if you hire out the upstairs room). The Stinging Nettle won't appeal to all the local residents, but if you want a safe pub in this area, then this one comfortably fits the bill.

FEATURES:  

HANDY FOR: Shepherd's Bush Empire

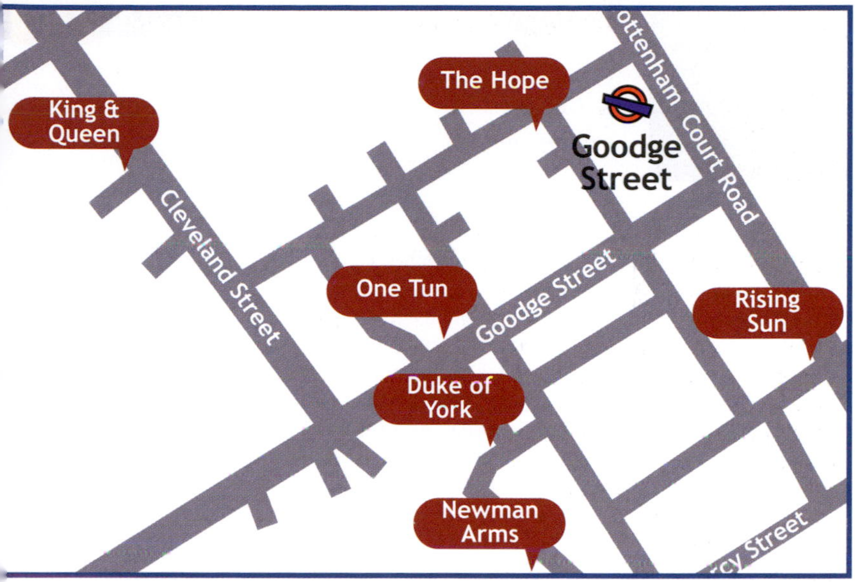

The Hope
King & Queen
Goodge Street
Tottenham Court Road
Cleveland Street
One Tun
Goodge Street
Rising Sun
Duke of York
Newman Arms
Percy Street

Duke of York

RATING:

47 Rathbone Street
W1T 1NQ
020 7636 7065

This old favourite, tiny though it is, has had a bit of work done. That's a good thing, as it's now got a pleasant upstairs bar that can be hired or just enjoyed. Happily, the changes have actually improved the drinking experience all round. With four beers on the hand pumps, this one caters quite happily for the ale drinkers, complemented by an assortment of lagers and a reasonable wine list. There's a single screen in the pub now, so the former emphasis on sport seems to have been watered down a bit. A new standing ledge outside the pub for the smokers is about the only concession they've made to providing an outdoor drinking experience, and as the pub lacks any real estate other than what it's sitting on, that's probably all they can manage. Frankly, we're glad to see that it's not been gutted and made into a trendy bar.

FEATURES:   

The Hope

RATING:

15 Tottenham Street
W1T 2AW
020 7637 0896

The Hope is a small, popular, traditional pub located just off Tottenham Court Road. It's a bare-boards sort of pub and a bit grubby with it, but its heart's in the right place. Serving real ales – six pumps, but only three working, with Landlord and the rare Cornish Buccaneer on when we were last in – it's a handy spot for people who work in the area (mostly media types) who want good, honest beer and unpretentious pub grub (we like the sausage of the week). There are a couple of flat-screen TVs for the big matches, free WiFi and a bar/function room upstairs that does stand-up comedy on Tuesdays. It's a friendly place – everyone seems to know the bar staff – and it's very popular, so arrive early if you plan to meet here, especially towards the end of the week. The Hope's scruffiness might not be everyone's cup of tea (especially the loos), but it's a welcome antidote to the antiseptic refurbishments that abound in the West End.

FEATURES:     

King & Queen

RATING: 

1 Foley Street
W1W 6DL
020 7636 5619

A lot of the pubs between Warren Street and Goodge Street are moderate drinking holes, but this one sticks out. It's a bit off the main drag, but a Friday-night visit found it to be one of the most popular pubs in the area. It attracts a fair mix of punters, the beers (especially Adnam's and now the excellent St Austell Tribute) are well kept and a jovial atmosphere pervades. The bar staff are prompt and friendly and aren't overawed by big crowds at the bar. It's perhaps one worth sampling on a quieter night – a winter's evening drinking next to the fire is something we're looking forward to. Fine brass till too.

FEATURES:    

Newman Arms

RATING:

23 Rathbone Street
W1T 1NQ
020 7636 1127

The Newman Arms is another old favourite of ours. It's had a lick of paint and lost some of the eccentricity that used to define it – the upstairs Pie Room is no longer the haven from the heaving masses downstairs that it used to be – nevertheless it's still a good pub. And, whilst we'll miss the old version, we guess the owners decided some things should move with the times. You can usually find Adnam's bitter and London Pride on the hand pumps, along with Stowford Press Cider. The pies served upstairs are probably some of the best in London, with organic and free-range ingredients wherever possible – apparently they can tell you which farm the meat came from. On the people front, the veteran bar staff continue to pour a decent pint, and are generally convivial and seem pleased to see punters coming in. Just be aware that it gets tremendously busy at office-quitting time, but wait a while and you'll probably get a seat. A sometime sanctuary in Fitzrovia.

FEATURES:   

One Tun

RATING:  

58–60 Goodge Street
W1T 4LZ
020 7209 4105

Despite receiving a bit of a makeover, including the addition of some squishy chairs this is still a traditional, decent Young's pub. You'll find all the usual Young's & Wells ales along with a regular crowd of locals and local workers that, combined with the easygoing staff, keep the atmosphere pretty friendly. It has two attributes worth mentioning: it's heavily into sport so all the big sporting events are catered for and it hosts a quiz every Tuesday evening, with drink prizes (which must be consumed on the evening). Jolly good fun it is too.

FEATURES:     

GOODGE STREET

Rising Sun

RATING:

46 Tottenham Court Road
W1T 2ED
020 7636 6530

With its impressive Victorian exterior, this easy-to-find place is a popular pub on Tottenham Court Road and a safer bet for a drink than some of the other pubs in the area. The interior is equally impressive and is probably why so many tourists find it – it looks like a pub. With five beers on the hand pumps, a reasonable wine list and an updated menu, you'll find it to be a reliable place for a pint and a bit of grub. Its high profile also makes it a good place to meet, even if you're going on to somewhere else. One obvious sign of their main clientele is the sign on the bar that says '4 pint jugs available' which, when combined with the beer prices, makes it prime student territory. It's not that bad during the day, just try to be out by about 3 if you have an aversion to students.

FEATURES:   

GOSPEL OAK/TUFNELL PARK

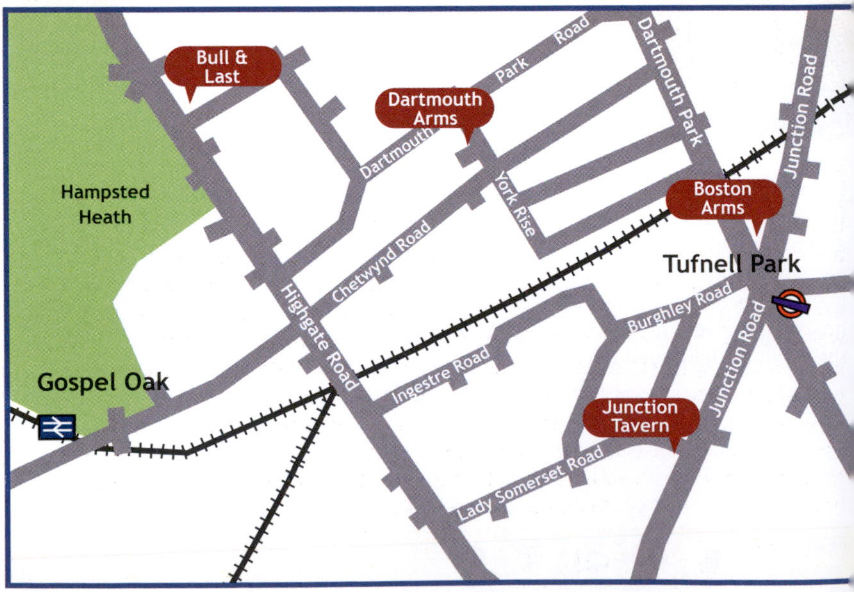

Bull & Last
Dartmouth Park Road
Dartmouth Arms
Dartmouth Park
Junction Road
Hampsted Heath
York Rise
Boston Arms
Chetwynd Road
Tufnell Park
Highgate Road
Burghley Road
Ingestre Road
Gospel Oak
Junction Road
Junction Tavern
Lady Somerset Road

Boston Arms

RATING:

178 Junction Road
N19 5QQ
020 7272 8153

What with the stately exterior and its position next door to the former Dirty Water Club, we've always expected more from the Boston Arms. Perhaps that tower on the outside promised too much, but we thought there would be an inkling of that grandeur inside. Alas, much of the décor seems to have been stripped away, leaving an interior not unlike that of a large social club – the cry of the bingo caller never seems too far away. Still, the punters seem happy enough with the entertainment on offer: giant TV screens fill the perspective but a pool table and two tucked-away dart boards suggest a pub that takes its games seriously (and one look at the packed trophy cabinet proves it). Like most Irish bars, the closest it gets to real ale is Guinness and John Smith's behind the bar but the cheap and filling food really hits the spot.

FEATURES:    

Bull & Last

RATING: 

168 Highgate Road
NW5 1QS
020 7267 3641

The Bull and Last is situated in a bit of a quietly prosperous no-man's land, north of Kentish Town, south of Highgate. Still, its proximity to Parliament Hill means it's worth popping in for a post-stroll pint. Although, if given the choice, we'd rather walk a little further to the Dartmouth Arms. Our visit was typified by a general lack of good grace and manners – from the barman who just about managed to greet us with a 'yeah?', to the group of scrabble players who blocked the pathway to the toilets, being just two examples. The décor is fine; it was once an ornate Victorian boozer, but we know it was eviscerated a fair few years ago now and nowadays is pretty stripped out. This isn't necessarily a problem, but the homogeneous mass of flatsharers in their mid-twenties were so loud and the wooden furniture so unable to absorb their din that staying indoors verged on stressful. It's a shame because we might have otherwise been tempted by the wood pigeon (priced at £13.50) while we enjoyed our Hook Norton ale. Still it's a very popular pub so they must be doing something right; however, it's just not our favourite place in NW5.

FEATURES:    

HANDY FOR: The Forum

Dartmouth Arms

RATING: 4

35 York Rise
NW5 1SP
020 7485 3267

Set in a quiet back street, this is a bustling, lively and (more often than not) full pub. With a foot in both the traditional pub and gastro camps, it manages to keep its punters happy by providing not only a very good choice of real ale and excellent food but also a selection of cider which rates as one of the widest in London. There's a singular touch at work here, most clearly manifested in the witty menus and the range of second-hand books for sale. The Dartmouth Arms offers a good medium between the full-on gastro of the Lord Palmerston and the more hardcore boozers of Junction Road, and is easily the best pub in the neighbourhood.

FEATURES:    

The Junction Tavern

RATING: 

101 Fortess Rd
NW5 1AG
020 7485 9400

On the surface this seemed like another gastropub done by the book, with the book in question being 'How to Make a Gastropub in 10 Easy Lessons'. A wine list more expensive than local restaurants? Check. Large 'eating-only' area? Check. Trendy young things trying to lounge nonchalantly? Check. This one does, however, fare better than some other North London casualties. The exterior and wood-panelled drinking area have been left more or less intact – so there's a dark, luxurious feeling to the place. A large back garden promises a pleasant alfresco experience for the summer and a heated conservatory a compromise for the other 49 weeks of the year. Unusually for a gastropub, not only has the Junction Tavern resisted the temptation to remove one of the nouns from the name and start calling itself a bar, it even has three real ales on tap (and fairly regular mini beer festivals). Certainly worth a visit if you're in the area, although you might need to book for the restaurant section at busy times.

FEATURES:    

HANDY FOR: The Forum

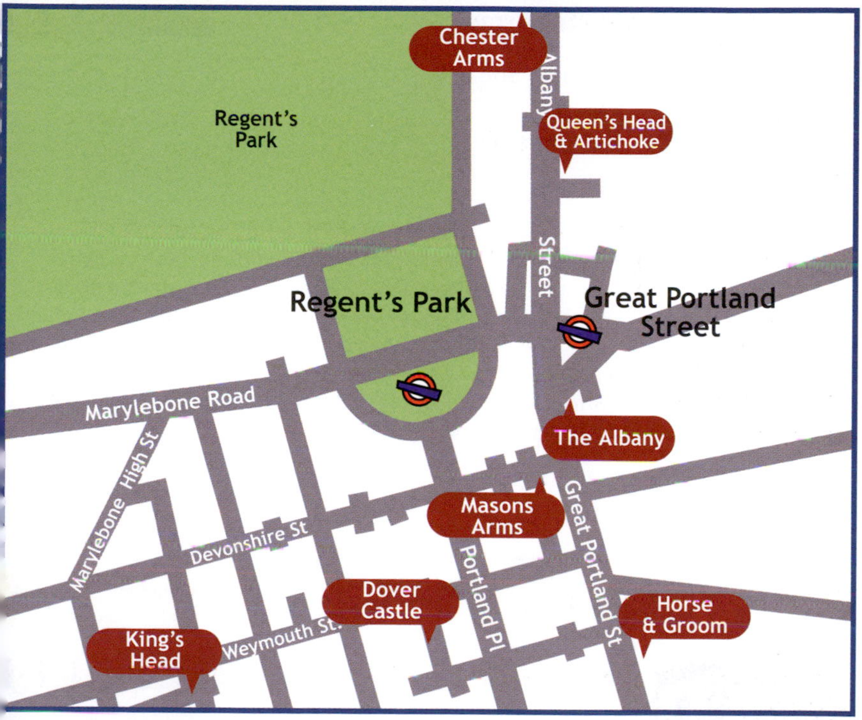

Chester Arms
Regent's Park
Albany Street
Queen's Head & Artichoke
Regent's Park
Great Portland Street
Marylebone Road
The Albany
Marylebone High St
Devonshire St
Masons Arms
Portland Pl
Great Portland St
Dover Castle
Horse & Groom
King's Head
Weymouth St.

The Albany

RATING: 

240 Great Portland Street
W1W 5QU
020 7387 0221

The Albany is a pretty decent pub. The beer is fine – up to Cask Marque standard, no less – with a selection of guest ales on the hand pumps as well as Leffe and Hoegaarden for those in a continental mood. The service is good and there's a stronger emphasis on food with an improved menu, including lunch and evening snacks. It's got a fairly traditional interior, but was done up a few years ago when pubs went for 70s and 80s furniture and butcher's block tables, so it's probably due for a refurb (even though it's not changed in years). We've done Post Modern, we've done Post Ironic, let's hope they think of something new. Also well established, the basement is known as Low-down and has comedy on every night, interspersed with regular club nights.

FEATURES:  

HANDY FOR: Madame Tussauds, Wallace Collection

Chester Arms

RATING:

87 Albany Street
NW1 4BT
020 7681 6017

Perhaps not as stately as the Regency architecture which surrounds it, this is still quite a cosy little boozer with a pleasant air. Having just been refurbished, it's a lot lighter and brighter inside than one initially expects and, to be honest, there aren't a lot of original features left. It attracts strong support from the local rugby club and there's an emphasis on sports coverage. The menu's now basic and reasonably priced Thai food. The only real ale on tap was Bombardier when we were last in, with a selection of continental lagers to go with it. If the sight of too many joggers in Regent's Park is driving you to drink, this one is a handy port of call.

FEATURES:  

HANDY FOR: Regent's Park Zoo, Madame Tussauds

Dover Castle

RATING:

43 Weymouth Mews
W1G 7EH
020 7580 4412

This is a fine old Sam Smith's pub tucked away in a mews, just a short distance away from the hustle and bustle of Marylebone Road and Portland Place. And, as it's a Sam Smith's pub, the well-kept beer is what you'd expect – excellent if you like Sam's, not so good if you don't. There's decent enough pub grub (filling a hole, rather than tickling the taste buds) and there are no 21st-century distractions such as piped music, TV or gaming machines – another Sam Smith's thing. The pub rarely gets crowded, although it picks up after work for a couple of hours. It is on the tourist map and, every so often, you'll find a few in here, but it's in such an obscure location that only a few manage to find it. If you're a fan of Sam's produce, the Dover Castle is just the place to put your feet up and read a good book or ponder eternity. And it's open for Sunday lunch too.

FEATURES: 

HANDY FOR: Madame Tussauds, Wallace Collection

Horse & Groom

RATING:

128 Great Portland Street
W1W 6PX
020 7580 4726

The Horse & Groom is an oft overlooked but beautiful Victorian pub a few minutes from Oxford Street. Along with plenty of original tiling and woodwork, the pub has four distinct sections: the front is predominantly standing room, the middle area has a rare-to-see dart board and the back room is the most cosy, with bench seating and a fireplace. There's also a very civilised upstairs bar. Our numerous visits have given the impression that, although busy, it's probably the only pub in Fitzrovia which doesn't become packed like a rush-hour tube train – it's usually possible to get a seat, even on a Friday night. Definitely an advantage for after-work drinks, it points to possibly being frighteningly quiet at other times. It's possible the pub's position – most other nearby pubs occupy imposing corner plots – means it somewhat blends in with the anonymous shops on Great Portland Street. Still, if it means we can have a seat with our pint, we're not going to complain too much.

FEATURES:    **HANDY FOR:** Madame Tussauds, Wallace Collection

King's Head

RATING: 

13 Westmoreland Street
W1G 8PJ
020 7835 2201

A tiny, quiet, traditional local pub in the posh West End dormitory bit between Marylebone Road and Oxford Street. It's a Greene King pub so the beer is decent, there's champers by the glass (we did say it's in a posh area) and Sunday lunch too. The pleasant staff, genial locals and local workers make this an oasis away from the burly of Marylebone High Street. You wouldn't make a special journey to get here, but it's handy for a quiet pint if you're in the area. Give it a look.

FEATURES:     **HANDY FOR:** Madame Tussauds, Wallace Collection

The Masons Arms

RATING:

8 Devonshire Street
W1W 5EA
020 7580 6501

Tucked away near Great Portland Street tube, the Masons Arms is a solid well-kept pub worthy of a visit. The beer on the three hand pumps is excellent – Deuchar's, Pride and Spitfire, the service polite and friendly and the Thai food's pretty decent too. A variety of masonic (in an architectural sense) paraphernalia adorns the walls, and subdued orange lights create a pleasant, relaxing atmosphere. And, as it's off the main street, it can be a bit quieter than pubs nearby, particularly in the afternoon, although it gets its share of commuters from the local offices at quitting time.

FEATURES:   **HANDY FOR:** Madame Tussauds, Wallace Collection

The Queen's Head & Artichoke

RATING:

30–32 Albany Street
NW1 4EA
020 7916 6206

Nestled behind the back of the Royal College of Physicians, this place is reasonably handy for the Indian food nirvana of Drummond Street. The wood-panelled bar gets pretty packed with local workers and some locals during lunchtime and in the evenings, with the upstairs restaurant doing a booming business as well. The bar also serves an extensive tapas menu and daily specials, though we wouldn't necessarily classify them as cheap. There's some good ales on the pumps which are well kept. The place looks like a continental café – albeit one with a large selection of religious icons in a case at one end of the main bar. If you can bag one of the capacious sofas you may well feel tempted to stay a while and hold forth on questions of existence and philosophy.

FEATURES:     **HANDY FOR:** Regent's Park Zoo, Madame Tussauds

The Chequers Tavern

RATING: 

16 Duke Street
SW1Y 6DB
020 7930 4007

Another small St James's pub. Usually the quietest pub in this neck of the woods, it means there's more chance to get a seat. It gets the basics right, with good real ales, and a simple but cheap food menu. The service is also very good and they clearly take pride in running their pub, regularly cleaning the brass at closing time. It's an old place, apparently dating back to 1666, and the pub gained its name from the coachmen who whiled away their time drinking ale and playing chequers on the steps of the pub, waiting for their masters to finish enjoying their evenings elsewhere. History aside, although interior doesn't look that old, this is still a good, solid boozer.

FEATURES:   

Coach & Horses

RATING:

5 Hill Street
W1J 5LD
020 7355 0300

A very nice little pub indeed, set in in rather posh surroundings, it has a well-looked-after interior, with enough old bits remaining to give it a genteel sort of feel without it looking like a museum. As it's a Shepherd Neame place, the beer is pretty good and so is the rest of the booze and the prices aren't bad given where it is. There's a pretty extensive food menu, with vegetarians well catered for, again at decent prices and the service is excellent. Everybody seems to know everybody in this pub (including the bar people) and it doesn't take an Einstein to work out why they keep coming back. It can get rather crowded after work, towards the end of the week, understandable, but inconvenient if you're looking for a quiet pint. It's a pity it's not open on Saturday and Sunday – but then it's pretty quiet around here at the weekends and it probably wouldn't have as much atmosphere, although you can hire the pub at the weekend, so you could create your own.

FEATURES:   

HANDY FOR: The Royal Academy

Golden Lion

RATING: 

25 King Street
SW1Y 6QY
020 7925 0007

Whilst its interior may not quite match its exuberant exterior, this one's worth a pop should you find yourself idle in St James's with no club membership to fall back on. The Nicholson's chain pride themselves on their traditional food and drink selection, though the local office clientele keep this one from being too much of a touristy 'ye olde pubbe'. It does get pretty crowded straight after work, but quietens down as the commuters wend their weary ways home and the place relaxes somewhat. There's also an upstairs room with a balcony where, if it's not packed with smokers, you can get a unique bird's eye perspective on the local life.

FEATURES:   

HANDY FOR: The Royal Academy

King's Arms

RATING: 2

2 Shepherd Market
W1J 7QB
020 7629 0416

Another popular establishment in the pub-heavy Shepherd Market. Nowadays, this is one of the better ones – a recent refurbishment has improved the menu and brought the pub up to date. There's decent beer on the hand pumps, but the other beers and wines are pretty standard – especially now there are plenty of interesting continental beers (particularly Belgian) more generally available. Like most of the other pubs in the locality, on summer evenings it often gets crowded with people spilling outside, as non-smokers join the smokers to catch the last rays of sun. It's probably one for a quick pint rather than a long evening's session, but with the steady demise of the pub just up the way it's probably the best one in the market to meet up in.

FEATURES:    

HANDY FOR: The Royal Academy

Market Tavern

RATING: 3

7 Shepherd Street
W1J 7HR
020 7408 9281

With its parent company systematically rebranding them, one by one, it's time to say goodbye to another branch of the O'Neill's chain. As is usually the case, it's updated itself by appearing more traditional and individual, as well as moving slightly upmarket compared to its predecessor. Flock wallpaper and low lighting give a subtle retro feel and the overall effect is quite appealing. An excellent choice of ales and lager give other local pubs a run for their money, but the service is little more than perfunctory. As with most places in Shepherd Market, it's popular with the after-work crowd – and not being the largest of places makes this even more apparent. But it's still worth considering if you're meeting people in the area.

HANDY FOR: The Royal Academy

The Only Running Footman

RATING:

5 Charles Street
W1J 5DE
020 7499 2988

It's perhaps surprising that there aren't more places in Mayfair like this one. How best to describe it? Gastropub? Pub and Dining Room? What's easier to define is how much of it is actually a pub. In floor space, it's half of the (small) ground floor: a couple of tables, tall stools around the windows – the rest is table-clothed dining space. So, even with a decent drink selection including three real ales and friendly enough staff, there's just not that much room to enjoy it in, though the large windows opening onto the side are a boon on nice days. Upstairs is a first-floor restaurant, there's a function room on the second floor and a chef's table on the third. If that wasn't enough stress on this one's foodie credentials, there's even a cookery school in the basement (honest). The food here may well be a knockout but as a pub, as somewhere to relax over a couple of drinks (even if the loudish music allowed it) we're not convinced.

FEATURES:    

HANDY FOR: The Royal Academy

Punch Bowl

RATING: 

41 Farm Street
W1J 5RP
020 7493 6841

The Punch Bowl has been a long-standing favourite of ours, so we were a little dismayed by the celebrity hoo-ha surrounding the pub's ownership in recent months and even more alarmed to hear the pub was to be refurbished. It turned out we needn't have worried – it's a pretty sympathetic revamp and many regulars won't notice a difference. If anything, it looks a little darker and more distressed, which actually suits it – the previous version was too manufactured looking with modern old-style furniture and unsympathetic lighting. We guess it was too much to expect the old wooden partition between the public and saloon bars to be reinstated, but the overall effect of the work is pretty much in keeping with this old building. The beers are much the same too, although prices are somewhat elevated, especially the wines, but it's not as if the locals around here can't afford it. The live music – a banjo and guitar duo playing old (cliché) Irish numbers on the night we were in – is probably an affectation too far, in our opinion, but it doesn't spoil the mood. Now the Red Lion round the corner is closed, expect the place to be pretty crowded towards the end of the week.

FEATURES:  

HANDY FOR: The Royal Academy

The Red Lion

RATING:

23 Crown Passage, King Street
SW1Y 6PP
020 7930 4141

Tucked away down a side street in St James's, this is a charming boozer. Its age and location may suggest a soulless dive aimed purely at tourists, but by and large this is as genuine and a genial a pub as you'll find. The TV is muted on and there's no music, but what you do get is well-kept beer (Adnam's), a cracking selection of whiskies and excellent sandwiches, all served up by some of the politest bar staff in town. It also helps that many of the punters – from businessmen to builders – are up for a natter. Granted, it can get very busy on weeknights (try for a seat upstairs if so) but it's a handy hideaway of a Saturday. If you're after a warm and comfortable pub, give it a look. (Closed Sunday.)

FEATURES: 

Shepherds Tavern

RATING:  

50 Hertford Street
W1J 7ST
020 7499 3017

Not a bad little pub – built in 1735 and still going strong. Does food during the day and there is a separate dining room upstairs for a more comprehensive menu. The steak baguette is quite tasty, and the ale was equally good – a nice spot for a few afternoon pints if you are in the area. Quite a cosy atmosphere and not usually as crowded as other pubs in the area.

FEATURES:   

HANDY FOR: The Royal Academy

GREEN PARK

Ye Grapes

RATING:

16 Shepherd Market
W1J 7QQ
020 7499 1563

Ye Grapes is a handsome old building set in a corner of Shepherd Market, containing an eccentric collection of olde worlde knickknacks creating a cosy sort of feel to the interior. It's been a favourite of the people who work and live around here for a good while now, but, until recently, it seemed to have been experiencing something of a decline. Now that negative trend appears to have been reversed. The interior has been repainted and the seats reupholstered, the plentiful staff are attentive and, most importantly, there's decent ale all on all six hand pumps, pretty much all of the time. (Previously, there had been times where there was no beer at all.) The beer is pretty good with a few interesting guests mixed with predictable regulars such as Pride and Doom Bar. For the hungry, there's Thai food available seven days a week and there are a couple of TVs for the sport. We're happy to report the Ye Grapes is pretty much back to how it used to be: a popular, loquacious, vibrant pub – it's what the market needs.

HANDY FOR: The Royal Academy

GREENWICH & GREENWICH (DLR)

Ashburnham Arms

RATING:

25 Ashburnham Grove
SE10 8UH
020 8692 2007

Hidden just a few minutes away from the bustle of central Greenwich, the Ashburnham Arms is an excellent place to draw breath over a pint or two of top-quality ale. The pub is situated on a quiet street in a very pleasant part of Greenwich and has a fine beer garden if you fancy a drink outside. It was given a makeover a good while ago – farewell bar billiards table, hello arty prints and loungey deco, but the style and standard of the refit is questionable and, apart from the fact that we preferred its previous look, we think the Ashburnham deserves better. Nonetheless, the usual range of excellent Shepherd Neame beers on tap remains, the service is friendly and the clientele amiable – the Ashburnham is still a good pub.

FEATURES:      

HANDY FOR: National Maritime Museum

The Greenwich Union

RATING: 

56 Royal Hill
SE10 8RT
020 8692 6258

Opening up next door to a fine pub like the Richard I can't have been easy, but the Greenwich Union pulled it off. It's a smart, spacious place that's modern and has a relaxed vibe. The bar offers a unique range of superb beer from the nearby Meantime Brewery, including raspberry beer, blonde ale and chocolate stout. When unable to make up our minds, a friendly barmaid gave us some free samples of different beers – excellent service matched by the enthusiasm of the staff for their wares. If the draught beers don't tempt you, there's a good selection of bottled beer in the fridge. A varied gastro-esque menu has main courses for around £8. Greenwich Union is somewhere that you could happily bring friends who aren't really into pubs. The only negative can be the abundance of parents and pushchairs around at the weekends, so, if kids don't induce a warm sentimental glow, then you might choose to do your boozing elsewhere at these times. This is really nit-picking, though, as the Greenwich Union is a top place.

FEATURES:    

HANDY FOR: National Maritime Museum, Cutty Sark

Prince Albert

RATING:

72 Royal Hill
SE10 8RT
020 8333 6512

The Prince Albert's walls are covered in nautical pictures and ephemera, yet you won't find too many tourists or museum-goers here; the pub has a down-to-earth feel that we like for its honesty and hospitality. The big-screen TV is handy for sports events and there always seems to be a good atmosphere. When other Royal Hill pubs are crowded, we often end up here, drinking with the friendly, older local crowd.

FEATURES:  

HANDY FOR: National Maritime Museum

Richard I

RATING: 

52 Royal Hill
SE10 8RT
020 8692 2996

As long as we've known it – and it's been a long time – this place has been a great pub. The Richard I is everything a good local should be. Of course, it does excellent Young's beer, the service is polite, friendly and prompt and the food comes recommended. As it is a popular place, seats inside can often be hard to come by, but, on warmer days, the large beer garden draws the punters outside, consequently leaving a little more space within (though the place is never empty) should you need to rest your feet. The regulars come in all shapes and sizes and are a friendly lot. It's just up the hill enough to deter all but the most determined of Greenwich tourists, but, when they get there, they'll find their efforts are rewarded. There are plenty of pubs in this little area of Greenwich, but this one's still amongst the pick of them for us.

FEATURES:     

HANDY FOR: Old Royal Observatory

The Royal George

RATING: 3 pints

2 Blissett Street
SE10 8UP
020 8692 1949

The Royal George is an excellent little local, next to one of the biggest fire stations we've seen. The colleagues of Captain Flack, Barney McGrew, Dibble et al were not in evidence when we last visited, but what we did get was a warm and friendly welcome. It's a Shepherd Neame pub so fine pints of Master Brew and Spitfire are available. Attractive stained-glass windows at the front, ship models and tankards give the pub's interior character too. Recommended.

FEATURES:    

HANDY FOR: National Maritime Museum

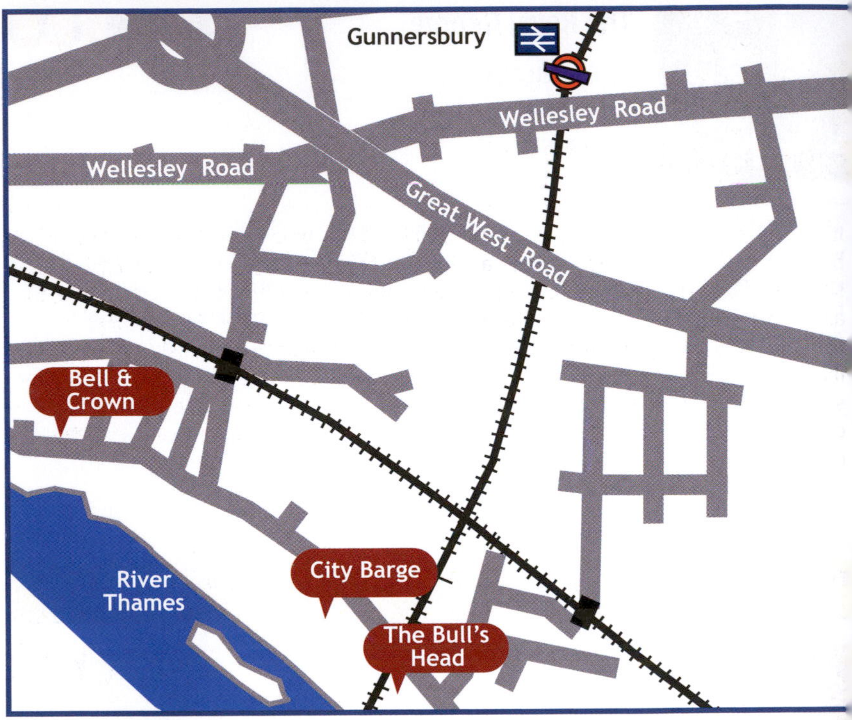

Gunnersbury
Wellesley Road
Wellesley Road
Great West Road
Bell & Crown
River Thames
City Barge
The Bull's Head

Bell & Crown

RATING:

11–13 Thames Road, Strand on the Green
W4 3PL
020 8994 4164

If you fancy a riverside stroll and a couple of drinks, the three pubs on Strand on the Green certainly fit the bill. Start at Kew Bridge and the Bell & Crown will be the first one you come to. Probably the biggest and busiest of the three, it's a safe, dependable Fuller's pub. The beer tastes good, the food looks fine and there's a comfortable air of repose to the place (added to the classical music CD playing when we visited). It's the sort of place you take your folks to when they visit London – nothing flash, just a decent pub.

FEATURES:   

HANDY FOR: Kew Gardens/Kew Palac

The Bull's Head

RATING:

15 Strand on the Green
W4 3PQ
020 8994 1204

It's been gone a few years now, but we still have fond memories of the sticky-floored boozer this once was. Probably such a thing was thought uncouth for such a prime site and after a sprucing up it became a Chef & Brewer pub. And so it remains, and, try as we like, we just can't warm to the place. The wide range of real ales certainly appeals but a good pub needs more than that. It's olde worlde but overly so: like many other Chef & Brewer pubs, it's a slight air of artificiality that takes hold. This one seems geared more for punters after food rather than stopping in for a drink and a chat. It's a perfectly pleasant enough pub, but we've tried and we just can't find this one's heart and soul.

FEATURES:  

HANDY FOR: Kew Gardens/Kew Palace

City Barge

RATING:

27 Strand on the Green
W4 3PH
020 8994 2148

Different in feel to the other two pubs on Strand on the Green, the City Barge does the job for a local clientele who want something a bit more energising than the rather sedate atmosphere of the Bull's Head and the Bell & Crown. It's hardly a raucous affair, but it is the only pub of the three to have Sky Sports available. Kudos too to the chatty barman, doing his best on our last visit to have a word with all of his customers. It's a fairly straightforward pub and, when all's told, could perhaps do with a gentle refurb. But we'd hate to see this one change too much, offering as it does a counterbalance to the other pubs it shares this stretch of the Thames with.

FEATURES:  

HANDY FOR: Kew Gardens/Kew Palace

HACKNEY CENTRAL

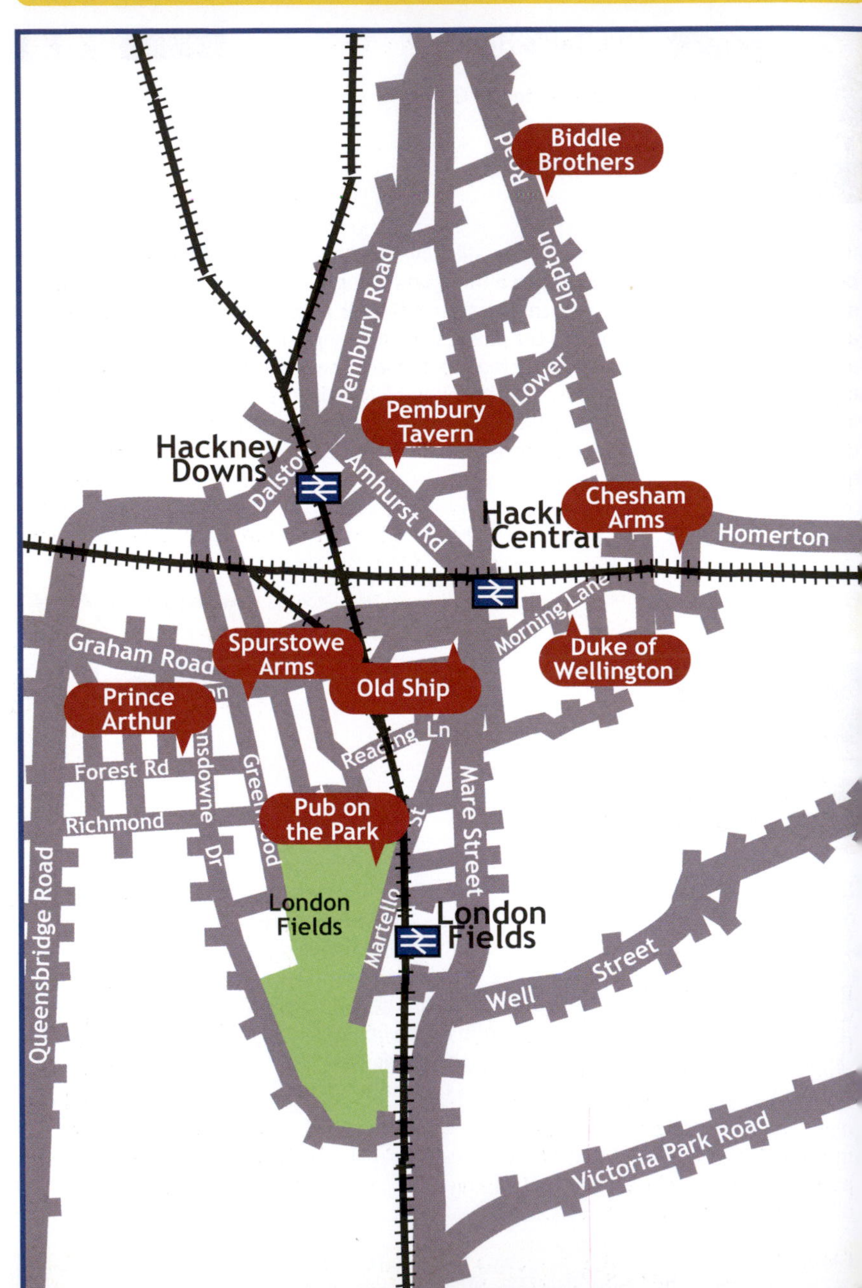

Biddle Bros Builders Ltd

RATING:

88 Lower Clapton Road
E5 0QR

One of the more interesting names for a bar, Biddle Bros is one of those (few) establishments which chose to retain the signage of the property's former life. As in this case it used to be a hardware shop, we were rather sad not to see the builders theme carried on inside, although a bar filled with claw hammers and Nitromors perhaps wouldn't have been the best of ideas. Still, what there is instead is a bright and comfortable space decked out with distressed furniture and which does a good turn in live music. With events such as a Tuesday songwriters showcase and with indie, folk and reggae artists, the focus seems to be on acoustic performers. DJs playing some good tunes also make regular appearances. The range of customers reflects the music policy and it seems popular with the younger locals who live on the nearby Victorian back streets. Clapton lost its 'murder mile' notoriety a while back now and for us Biddle Bros is a good place to spend an evening.

FEATURES: 

Chesham Arms

RATING: 

5 Mehetabel Road
E9 6DU
020 8985 2919

The Chesham Arms is the epitome of a friendly back-street local. Although it's recently changed ownership, the fundamentals which make this a great pub still remain. Although overshadowed by a 1960s council estate, it's actually hidden away on a pretty little Victorian terrace off Homerton High Street and our visit found a clean, warm and inviting pub. A good mix of regulars of all ages and backgrounds call this their local and service is cheery and welcoming. We were also impressed to find a good choice of ale – around three or four at any one point, including a choice from smaller breweries. A good-looking back garden, some good food and a popular quiz night add to the charm. The only obvious negatives come from the TV, as the choice of music isn't always great and it's hard to escape the football's presence in such a small pub. Even so, with places like this becoming increasingly rare in London, it's therefore all the more deserving of your custom.

FEATURES:     

HANDY FOR: Hackney Museum

Duke of Wellington

RATING:

90 Morning Lane
E9 6NA
020 8985 9735

Once you go beyond the Tesco on Morning Lane in Hackney, you don't have high hopes for anything particularly appealing, which probably helps make The Duke of Wellington a pleasant surprise. From the exterior it looks well maintained, painted in a relaxing shade of dark green, while the garden, with its neat lawn and trio of apple trees, is bettered only by the nearby Chesham Arms. Once inside you'll find a simple but attractive enough pub. There's a functional metal gantried bar, while off to the left is a nice alcove with leather armchairs. Round the corner's a pool table, while the presence of two dart boards and a darts team indicate local enthusiasm for the game. Service from the girl behind the bar was superb and, while we could only find generic lagers on tap, we did spy a rather good array of bottled ales. Our Sunday afternoon found it fairly quiet, but hopefully it picks up in the evenings; from our visit, this would appear to be one of the best pubs in Hackney Central and we'll definitely be returning again.

FEATURES:   

HANDY FOR: Hackney Museum

The Old Ship

RATING:

2 Sylvester Path, Mare Street
E8 1EN
020 8986 1641

From the High Street you'd be forgiven for missing the Old Ship, down a long passageway leading off who-knows-where. On closer inspection, old Courage tiling offering luncheons gives a small glimpse of days gone by. After a refurb, a sign with the words, 'hotel, bar, grill' lets you know things have changed – described at launch as an 'Urban Inn'. This apparently is an excuse for a refurb-by-numbers; leather couches, light pine and heavily patterned wallpaper abound, while half the space was set with cutlery for the benefit of non-existent eaters. The young Hackney residents were outside or in the drinking section, where the inclusion of a plasma screen showing BBC News (with the sound off) was an unnecessary distraction. Service was pleasant and there was a reasonable selection of ale, though lager drinkers fared less well, with San Miguel being the best option. The pub grub was also reasonably priced and the bar snack menu more interesting than most. Overall, though, it didn't set our juices flowing.

FEATURES: 

HANDY FOR: Hackney Museum

Pembury Tavern

RATING:

90 Amhurst Road
E8 1JH
020 8986 8597

The Pembury Tavern – a grand-looking pub in deepest Hackney – has been owned by the excellent Milton Brewery since 2006 (their second pub in London, after the Oakdale Arms in Haringey). It's a real ale enthusiast's favourite with a great selection of Milton produce, plus ciders and continental bottled beers. Inside, it's a big space with lots of hard-wood surfaces and could be described as slightly bland. Personal touches are appearing though and beer mats festoon the walls from the guest ales which have featured in their worthwhile mini-festivals. Still, some soft furnishings or perhaps a few plants would be nice to see. Our last Sunday-afternoon visit found it nicely busy and it seems like groups of younger locals have now discovered it. Bar billiards and pool are also good to see and the kitchen serves up some hearty pub grub. A good one for the area.

FEATURES:     **HANDY FOR:** Hackney Museum

Prince Arthur

RATING:

95 Forest Road
E8 3BH
020 7249 9996

Anyone in the know is buying property in this part of Hackney right now. Hot on the heels of these new residents are amenities to support them, including a smattering of newly revamped pubs. Most recent is the Prince Arthur, not far from the soon-to-be-reinstated Dalston Junction station. This newcomer – the latest offering from those responsible for the gastro-tastic Gun and The Well – is a handsome pub. We weren't sure what to expect coming here on a Friday – it is, after all, hidden in the Hackney hinterland. But lo! the place was very busy indeed; with every seat taken, it appears success was assured within only a few weeks of opening. Inside, a mix of the original features and clean lines create a bright, relaxing air. The pumps offer reasonable ales alongside a decent wine list and a full-blown gastromenu. It's certainly nice to see an old pub spring back into life – a wander around nearby streets offers a ready supply of recently closed-down pubs – and the crowds at the nearby Prince George indicate there's a demand. Unfortunately it's already standing room only towards the weekend (if you can get in), which is good news for the owners, less so if you're looking for a relaxed pint to finish your working week. Which is a pity, because when it is quieter it's a rather nice pub.

FEATURES:  **HANDY FOR:** Hackney Museum

Pub on the Park

RATING:

19 Martello Street
E8 3PE
020 7275 9586

London Fields is steadily becoming an oh-so-trendy sort of place, with even the lido getting a makeover. A lot of pubs in these parts have been gastrofied and trendified, but the Pub on the Park was ahead of the game and was revamped well in advance of the current onslaught and is beginning to look a little worse-for-wear in comparison. A bit of a novelty when it first opened, the extensive range of continental beers and laid-back atmosphere seem to be too old hat for the fashion-conscious locals and it no longer seems to pull them in like it used to. Call us stick-in-the-muds, anachronisms, fuddy-duddies, whatever, but we still quite like the place – the beer is decent (and a good choice is to be had, though the Grolsch Weissbier is somewhat pricey). The atmosphere's laidback and the service polite and friendly. The decking overlooking the park is a nice place to be in summer – if there aren't too many screaming kids and parents around – and, with a bit of a spruce up, this pub could easily hold its own with the surrounding arrivistes.

FEATURES:   

Spurstowe Arms

RATING:

68 Greenwood Road
E8 1AB
020 7254 4316

Thankfully there are a lot of nice Victorian houses in parts of Hackney, missed by both developers and the Luftwaffe. Interspersed in these domiciles are some fine pubs and the Spurstowe Arms is one of them. The pub has been done up in a kind of 'bare brick living room' style – complete with standard and table lamps – but the overall effect is not at all displeasing and it has quite a homely atmosphere. The beer garden is very nicely done and provides a pleasant place for an evening's quaffing and conversation (and smoking, nowadays), helped in unseasonal times by outdoor heating. The beer is good – Black Sheep, Flowers and Pedigree on the hand pumps and a reasonable range on the other pumps – including the now ubiquitous Leffe and Hoegaarden. The food is OK too, maybe a little pricey, but some of the items are particularly nice. As each day passes, Hackney seems to move further upmarket and the Spurstowe only adds to the impression that, more and more, West (London) is moving East.

FEATURES: 

Blue Anchor

RATING: 

13 Lower Mall
W6 9DJ
020 7383 2681

The Blue Anchor – licensed since 1722 – is the first in a succession of Thames-side pubs which stretch from Hammersmith to Chiswick and is arguably one of the better ones. Having undergone a refurbishment earlier this year we were grateful to see that it's still primarily a pub. With an exterior bedecked in an appropriately nautical blue and white, the interior seems to have been left with plenty of original features, including some lovely wooden panelling. We found it odd that a fair few people wandering along the Thames during our lunchtime visit took a look at the menu, but rejected it in favour of the multinational chain pub next door – we could see nothing wrong with either the price or the choice. If you're lucky you might be able to bag the limited number of outside seats on the upstairs terrace in the restaurant area, which might prove a handy vantage point once the locals and after-work crowds descend to pack it out on sunnier days.

FEATURES:   

The Chancellors

RATING: 

25 Crisp Road
W6 9RL
020 8748 2600

The Chancellors is directly opposite the Riverside Studios yet it's a world away from media-land. It's a fine little boozer, a warm and friendly place that attracts a large mix of punters who are all looked after by a wonderfully attentive landlady. An unpretentious pub with a good atmosphere, good beer and great toasties, this is a real gem, a pub that eschews fashion in favour of atmosphere and service. Snacks on the bar at Sunday lunchtimes, too.

FEATURES:    

HANDY FOR: Riverside Studios

The Queen's Head

RATING: 

13 Brook Green
W6 7BL
020 7603 3174

This pub looks tiny from the outside but appearances are deceiving – it's enormous on the inside. This is another old coaching inn, so there's a long history of the pub on the menu and plenty of copper stuff. Chef & Brewer, the company that owns the Queen's Head, specialises in big local pubs that do food and are aimed at non-teenaged drinkers and families. They haven't strayed from the formula here and so, rather weirdly, this does not feel like a London pub but like a successful country boozer. The result isn't too bad. The food looks fine, though a little frilly, and, because the old bits are actually old and the pub is made up of what were once adjoining smaller rooms, there is a genuine cosiness to the place. Worth a look on a warm day too, as the beer garden is one of the largest in town.

FEATURES: 

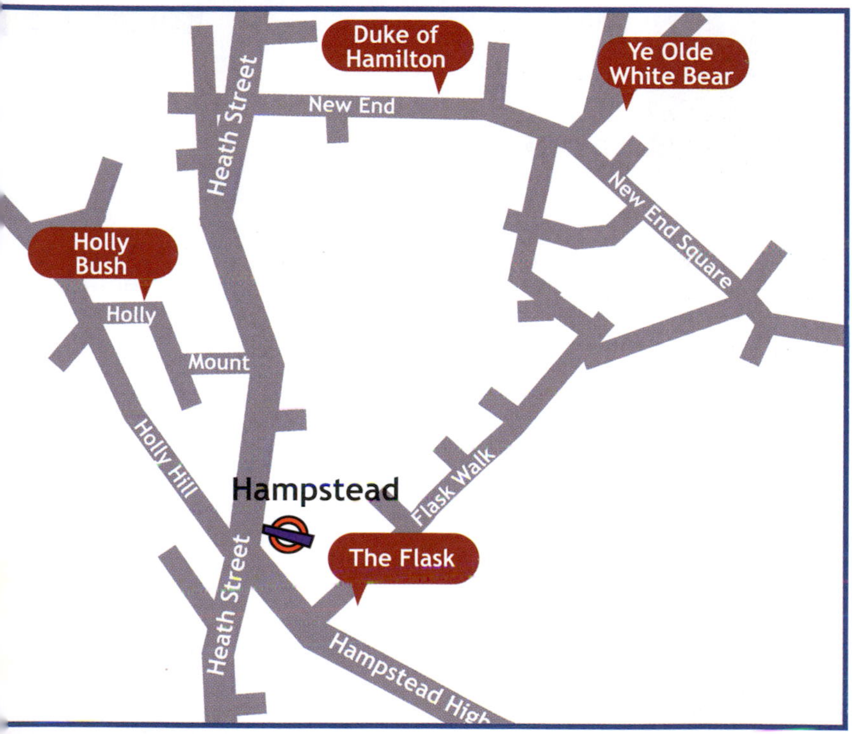

Duke of Hamilton
Ye Olde White Bear
New End
Heath Street
New End Square
Holly Bush
Holly
Mount
Holly Hill
Hampstead
Flask Walk
The Flask
Heath Street
Hampstead High

Duke of Hamilton

RATING:

23–25 New End
NW3 1JD
020 7794 0258

Not the most famous pub in Hampstead but arguably one of the friendliest, the Duke of Hamilton is an amiable local which you soon warm to. It has an excellent barman and one or two regulars who are always up for a chat. They pride themselves on their wide selection of real ales, which usually include some well-kept seasonal choices. With a relaxed unpretentious atmosphere, it's the sort of pub you wish was your local. It's next to a local community theatre, the New End, so invariably you get some of the theatre crowd in. Go see.

FEATURES:   

The Flask

RATING:

14 Flask Walk
NW3 1HE
020 7435 4580

One pub trend we're seeing a lot more of is the continuing rollout of refits of pubs owned by the Wells & Young's brewery. So, prepare yourselves for more carpets to be taken up and photographs of the Queen Mother pulling a pint to be packed away, all to be replaced by more modern interiors and soft lighting. The changes here actually haven't been as dramatic as in other old Young's pubs, mostly due to the elegant partition which separates the pub into two distinct bars remaining in place. The smaller 'public' bar to the left of the partition was always more of a traditional drinking area to the 'saloon' to the right, and this feel has definitely been maintained along with the lovingly preserved interior (and that's not always the case). Whilst more emphasis is now placed on the quality of the food served here, there hasn't been any discernible drop in the quality of the beers served. This one will still prove a popular spot for locals and visitors to Hampstead alike, and when we last looked in was proving popular with local parents with their prams (a delight to some, a hindrance to others).

FEATURES:          

Holly Bush

RATING:

22 Holly Mount
NW3 6SG
020 7435 2892

Beauty is a rare and precious thing in this world and it is even rarer and more precious in a public house. The Holly Bush is one of the older pubs in London dating from the time when Hampstead was a country town. Inside this listed building, its stripped-wooden interior and slightly ramshackle atmosphere lend it the charming aspect of a 19-century coaching inn. That said, it can get a little crowded at times (although we have spent many a Saturday afternoon and evening here without suffering unduly) and some of the punters do seem like parodies of *Guardian*-readers. But there is something deeply fine about this place – maybe the history, maybe the wooden booths and log fire, or maybe the good beers – which engenders wit and conviviality. Just avoid the rather bland renovation in the back room.

FEATURES:   

Ye Olde White Bear

RATING:

Well Road
NW3 1LJ
020 7435 3758

Considering the history, character and heritage of Hampstead, it's surprising that there aren't more classic pubs in the area. Of course, many have now smartened themselves up and moved into gastropub status, or simply closed down. Nevertheless, Ye Olde White Bear certainly has a good claim on being the best pub for a drink in Hampstead. It's comfortable and friendly, has board games and an impressive selection of six real ales which on our last visit included no fewer than four guest beers. Food wise, there's a relatively unpretentious pub menu which – especially considering the neighbourhood – is well priced. We've heard that there's been a decline in recent months regarding the food's quality, but we didn't have any problems on our last visit. Overall, the least pretentious and most homely pub in the area: a splendid establishment.

FEATURES:     

HAMPSTEAD HEATH – *see Belsize Park, page 42*

HERON QUAY – *see Canary Wharf, page 82*

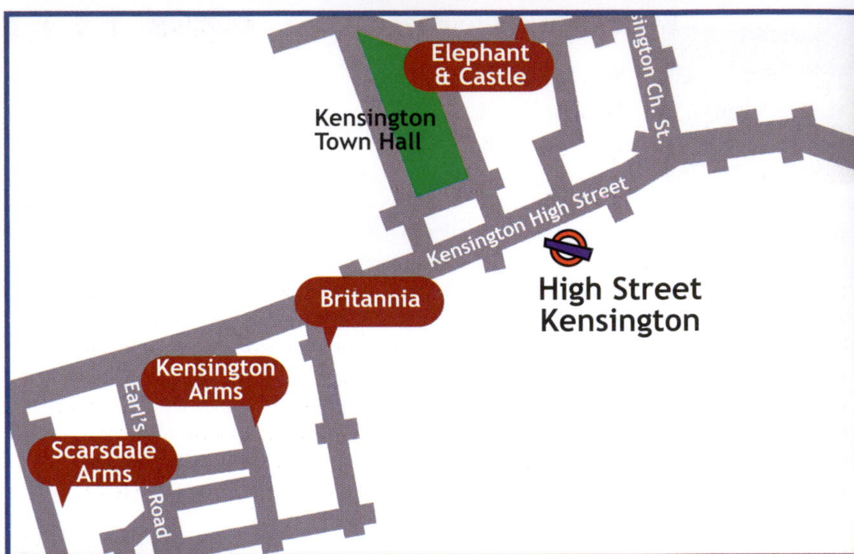

The Britannia

RATING: 

1 Allen Street
W8 6UX
020 7937 6905

Back in 2006, this was one of the first Young's pubs to be refurbished and relaunched and, since then, many more of their pubs have followed in its footsteps. In our opinion there was nothing much wrong with the old place, it might have needed a lick of paint here and there, but it was a warm and inviting pub – the atmosphere of which was helped enormously by the three real fires. Even though the refit kept the fires, this one – like many of the other Young's refits which followed – has the air of a pub that favours dining over brewing: drinkers are clustered around the entrance of the pub, leaving most of the rest of the space to those patrons sampling offerings from the gastro menu. Whilst this one remains a professional enough establishment, there's a certain part of its charm that's gone, and we won't be coming back anytime soon.

FEATURES: 

HANDY FOR: Kensington Palace

Elephant & Castle

RATING: 4

Holland St
W8 4LT
020 7368 0901

A welcome refuge in the quiet back streets two minutes from Kensington High Street, the Elephant and Castle's multi-award-winning flower-festooned facade almost hides this small and homely pub. Though taken over by Nicholson's, it's not the normal routine for their pubs. The beer and service are good and the atmosphere is usually pretty lively. The food is very good, and not Nicholson's usual menu, with daily menu choices and specials, and not too expensive either. It used to be that whenever there's a hint of sunshine the locals deserted the bar for the tiny front garden – now turned into a smoker's paradise – spilling out onto the street. But there must have been complaints from the neighbours, as the signs make it clear that drinking on the pavements isn't allowed or past a certain time in the evening as a courtesy to the aforementioned. Still, it's got a lot going for it and it's worth a look in.

FEATURES:  

HANDY FOR: Kensington Palace

Kensington Arms

RATING: 

41 Abingdon Road
W8 6AH
020 7938 3841

We always had a soft spot for this one. It wasn't flash, it wasn't foodie and it certainly wasn't what you'd expect off the side of Kensington High Street. We thought such a regular boozer wouldn't be long for this world and so it proved, as this one – just like its near neighbour the Britannia – was remodelled and upgraded. The makeover produced a stark and bright interior, reminiscent of style bars from the turn of the (21st) century. The one aspect that remained the same was the multi-screens for the sport, though the refit clustered them above the bar leaving the back of the pub free to operate as a dining space. The pub has strong Cornish connections now, with landscape photos on the wall, Cornish beers behind the bar and and some Cornish selections on the menu. Those beers are from Sharp's Brewery (IPA and Doom Bar) and this was one of the first pubs in London where we saw them stocked. All in all, an intriguing mix but one that's gradually won us over. And you can fairly say – unlike many pubs which claim the accolade – there's nothing quite like this one around. Though did we really see the Cornish Pasty (with chips and gravy) on the menu priced at nearly £8?

FEATURES:  

HANDY FOR: Kensington Palace

HIGH STREET, KENSINGTON

Scarsdale Arms

RATING:

23a Edwardes Square
W8 6HE
020 7937 1811

Offering the sort of old-world experience you'd expect in this neck of the woods, the Scarsdale Arms is a cut above most of the nearby pubs. The darkened interior evokes a genuine atmosphere as does the intriguing history of the place (it was reputedly built as living quarters for the officers of Napoleon's conquering army). Rather than being a full-on gastropub it's first and foremost a pub, yet one with very good food. It also sports a restaurant space at the back if you're after a grander dining experience. And, if the empty champagne bottles that ring the walls of the pub are anything to go by, then over the years plenty of punters have done so. Rather similar in style and clientele to the Grenadier in Knightsbridge (though this pub is a tad larger), its refined feel is upmarket yet not ostentatious. Busy all days of the week, but definitely worth a look.

FEATURES:   

HANDY FOR: Olympia

HIGHBURY & ISLINGTON – *see Canonbury, page 88*

Queens Wood

Muswell Hill Rd

Archway Road

Wood Ln

The Woodman

Highgate

North Hill Ave

The Park

Southwood Lane

Jackson's Lane

The Boogaloo

Southwood Ave

Wrestlers

Winchester Hotel

North Road

Southwood Lane

Archway Road

ampstead Ln

Prince of Wales

Flask

South Grove

Highgate High Street

Hornsey

est Hill

The Boogaloo

RATING:

312 Archway Road
N6 5AT
020 8340 2928

From the people who brought you Filthy McNasty's, so no surprise on our first visit to see a selection of the CDs on the jukebox had been picked by Shane McGowan (often to be spotted sitting at the bar) and Spider Stacey. And what a jukebox it is: if you've waited for a pub where you can select Captain Beefheart or Pere Ubu instead of picking your way through Now! 5,000,000 you should pay it a visit. There's a fairly limited (by modern standards) range of drinks available, and the food on offer doesn't stretch past nuts and crisps (not always a sticking point but if you have the word 'kitchen' etched on your front window you're leading hungry passers-by rather far up the garden path). The regular quiz nights (Tuesday – music, Wednesday – film) will test the grey matter and, just like Filthy's, expect literary nights and 'secret' gigs every so often. It's not far off a cool record shop with a bar in the corner – not a bad thing in our book. Oh, and just so you know, it's only open in the evenings during the week, and from 2pm on weekends.

FEATURES:   

The Flask

RATING:

77 Highgate West Hill
N6 6BU
020 8348 7346

For a long time the Flask has been a great traditional boozer – a rambling olde worlde experience in the olde world village of Highgate. Stories of ghosts and Dick Turpin only add to a sense of its being a bit special. Sadly the only ghost you're likely to encounter these days is that of a once excellent pub. Being an M&B's unbranded pub, it does the usual good range of ales and continental lagers. Some of the obligatory loungey furnishings sit at odds with the aged interior and the view from the front is now filled with an ugly permanent gazebo. Its also odd for a pub which is frequently incredibly busy to have closed the larger of the two bars, leading to frustrated customers and long queues. Ultimately, to get the best out of The Flask, visit out of peak times and avoid the food, but it really should be performing better than this.

FEATURES:  

Prince of Wales

RATING:

53 Highgate High Street
N6 5JX
020 8340 0445

The Flask seems to get all the attention round these parts, though we're not complaining as it usually means more space in this one. The olde worlde interior may not be as rambling as The Flask's, but it's certainly on the right side of cosy. Plenty of beers on tap and the menu is of Thai and Laos origin – it promises a good Sunday roast as well. The sort of villagey pub you'd expect in this villagey part of London, it's a fine local with a well-loved feel to the place. The Tuesday quiz night, which had been a regular feature for twenty years, is so popular there it warranted the publication of a book a couple of years back. To top it off, a small terrace at the back opens out onto where the old ponds used to be: shame they're not still there, though if they were the pub would be almost too good to be true.

FEATURES:    

The Winchester Hotel

RATING:

206 Archway Road
N6 5BA
020 8374 1690

The first thing that hits you when you enter this pub (and it's not a pint glass, thankfully) is the verdant nature of the place. It's home to an array of soothing plants, comfy leather sofas and unobtrusive blinds shielding you from both the hot sun and the traffic throttling past on the Archway Road outside. But it's not that sort of place. Unlike many pubs of late, it's been done up, but not done over. No, the Winchester remains very much a Proper Pub. It's got plenty of tables for you to spread out and get comfy, a nicely sized bar where it should be (not stuck in the corner like other pubs), and a bit of a games area where the puggy and the dart board live. Even better, it's got a lovely little 'quiet corner' for those looking for a more intimate pub experience, and its got a beer garden too. What more could you ask for? Food. Of course. It does big white plates of food, but, for a nice change, the plates are laden with some right good grub, very much of the lamb shank, fresh fish and huge pastas variety. It's not cheap, but you're not spending a tenner on some pine nuts and spaghetti. The clientele are a good mix of locals, reflecting the cosmopolitan mix of the area with fashionistas and fitters happily taking up the same floor space.

FEATURES:     

The Woodman

RATING:

414 Archway Road
N6 5UA
020 8340 3016

Since coming under new ownership, the Woodman has been a consistently pleasant place to spend a couple of hours. It helps that they were successful in removing the ne'er-do-wells who once occupied this pub and there's now a healthy mix of punters. Service from the bar staff is extremely friendly, but, if a pub offers table service, they'd do well to memorise what drinks they serve. Speaking of drinks, it's a bit of a missed opportunity to offer four ales, but be so predictable in the selection; Greene King doesn't exactly get the pulse racing. Food wise, it's pretty good and an excellent Sunday lunch proves they're taking things seriously. Sadly, the two pool tables have been removed to make way for a massive function-room table and while improvements to the garden have been promised they haven't made progress yet. Finally, we're rather concerned about the bizarre CCTV link providing a video feed of the men's toilets into the ladies – it was unplugged on our latest visit and we hope it stays that way.

FEATURES:   

The Wrestlers

RATING: 

98 North Road
N6 4AA
020 8340 4297

The sort of pub that always seems dark, even on the sunniest days, The Wrestlers is a bit of a find in Highgate. Decked out in dark wood, with minimal modern lighting on the walls and a stunning Inglenook fireplace, The Wrestlers offers punters the opportunity to step up to a set of mounted antlers and participate in its biannual Swearing on the Horns, a silly tradition allegedly dating back to 1635 (the pub itself started life in 1547). Ceremonials aside, this remains a fine boozer, with plenty to tempt the palate on the drinks front, along with a small upmarket but reasonably priced food menu. There's plenty of space available, with some comfy sofas to the front, and proper pub furniture in the back and a couple of huge tables providing plenty of space to spread your newspaper. There's also ample outdoor seating which seemed to be metamorphosing into a conservatory on our visit. Even though we've known it to close on weekday afternoons, The Wrestlers is a fine place to enjoy a pint.

FEATURES:   

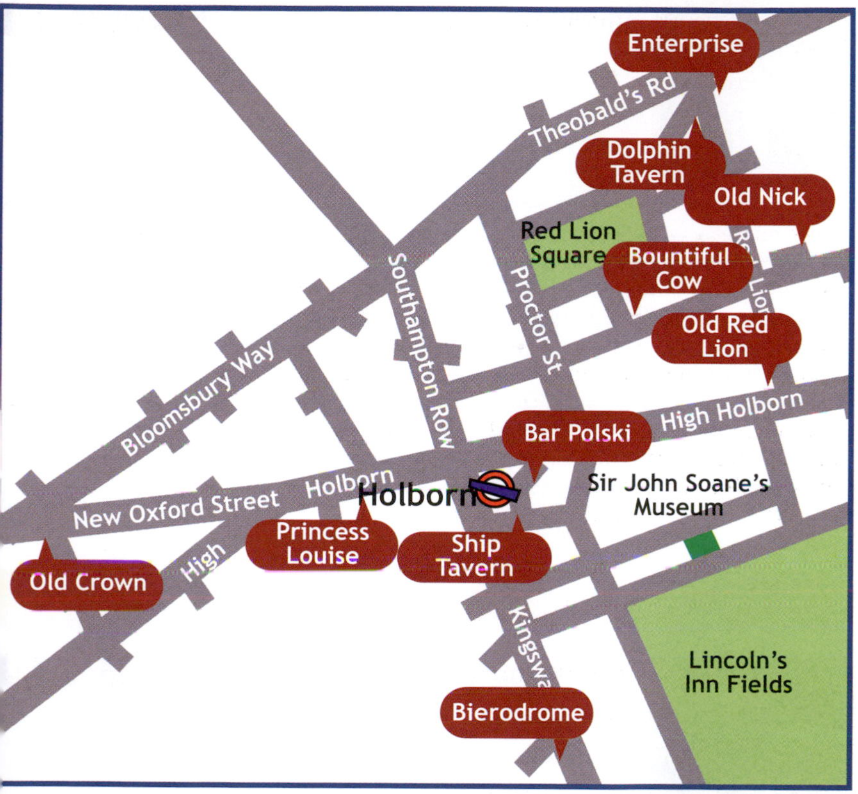

Bar Polski

RATING: 3/5

11 Little Turnstile
WC1V 7DX
020 7831 9679

That's Polish as in 'coming from Poland' not that stuff you clean a table with. This place is great – a selection of Polish beers and vodkas are served by friendly, interested staff who will laugh at your pronunciation of the Polish names. The food is cheap and filling too. The décor's not up to much and the music (bland Europop) was a bit loud on our last visit but that's more than made up for by the friendly atmosphere, tasty beer and sheer randomness of the place.

FEATURES: 

HANDY FOR: Sir John Soane's Museum, British Museum

Bierodrome

RATING:

67 Kingsway
WC2B 6TD
020 7242 7469

Anyone familiar with the Belgo concept will find few surprises here. As with the other bars in the chain, a vast array of beers can be found: white beers, dark beers, Trappist ales and the fashionable fruit beers are all in evidence. The food is reasonable, especially considering the alcohol prices and the long-running 6–8pm food offer is deservedly popular. It is a shame, then, that the ambience leaves something to be desired. When quiet, the design makes the place feel soulless, but once the after-work crowd from the nearby legal offices descends, it becomes incredibly busy, noisy and gains an unfortunate air of pretension. The window of enjoyability is small. The idea of selling a large selection of Belgian beers is no longer the novelty it was in 1999 and there are now plenty of places to experience the beer in a better atmosphere.

FEATURES:   

HANDY FOR: Sir John Soane's Museum, British Museum

The Bountiful Cow

RATING: 

51 Eagle Street
WC1R 4AP
020 7404 0200

Just like its sister pub the Seven Stars, this one shares both an owner and a devotion to the Suffolk beers of Adnam's. The interior, too, takes its cue from the aforementioned pub, being both small and having walls decorated with old movie posters. That the Bountiful Cow's are for cowboy films illustrates the emphasis here on burgers, steaks and all things bovine-related (vegetarians look away now). So, perhaps more steakhouse than boozer then, but at least we're not talking one of those touristy Aberdeen Angus abominations. We haven't tried the downstairs dining room yet, but the ground-floor bar was pleasant enough. Still, this one offers something different from the other eateries and drinkeries of the area and, given its slightly secluded location, you can usually bag a seat here.

FEATURES:  

HANDY FOR: Sir John Soane's Museum, British Museum

The Dolphin Tavern

RATING:

Red Lion Street
WC1R 4PF
020 7831 6298

A decent small place tucked slightly out of the way in Holborn, the Dolphin Tavern is but a step from the far more wholesome – and thoroughly wonderful and wonderfully unique – Conway Hall, home of the Ethical Society in Red Lion Square since 1929. It's a nice contrast in a way: you can be assured while the Socialist Workers Party are discussing rising working-class militancy in Conway Hall, the working class are actually enjoying a well-earned pint in the Dolphin. Gets packed at times, but it's only a little place, so that's to be expected. The beer is well kept, and there's usually a couple of real ales on (Pride and Young's when we were last there). The service was very prompt and friendly too. Not a bad little place by any means.

FEATURES:  **HANDY FOR:** Sir John Soane's Museum, British Museum

The Enterprise

RATING: 

38 Red Lion Street
WC1R 4PN
020 7404 8461

A lick of paint (gastro green, naturally) and a bit of care and attention and the Enterprise is a revived pub. Cask Marque ales are on offer, there's plenty of choice for those who don't fancy something pumped by hand, there's a beer garden out the back and comfy settees for those who prefer not to perch on bar stools. The grub is refreshingly unpretentious but only served lunchtimes and early evening. The new look certainly seems to have brought in the punters: the disco ball may not go with the old Victorian tiling but this one works all the same. It also now opens on Saturdays, the classical music on the CD player creating a pleasant atmosphere for an afternoon pint or three.

FEATURES:    **HANDY FOR:** Sir John Soane's Museum, British Museum

Old Crown

RATING:

33 New Oxford Street
WC1A 1BH
020 7836 9121

The Old Crown is a dark and serious-looking bar, situated away from the throng of Soho and Covent Garden. Outside lacks an obvious name, save for a wrought-iron crown and a small '33', presumably to help the postman, but we were assured it is indeed still the Old Crown. Assuming they didn't have problems finding a sign writer, it certainly gives the place an edge of minimalist cool. Inside, dark flock wallpaper lines panels of the bar, behind which distressed brickwork is highlighted by subtle lighting and bottles sit on shelves made from what appear to be old railway sleepers. The attractive curved leather bench seating is unfortunately better to look at than sit on, but both the staff and crowd make up for it by creating a relaxed atmosphere. Drinks wise, prices are at the upper end of average, but it was good to find a couple of well-kept ales along with a good spirit and cocktail list. The Old Crown may not be in an area short of pubs, but, if you're hankering for something slightly more trendy (but still elegant), this might just be the place to go.

FEATURES:    **HANDY FOR:** Sir John Soane's Museum, British Museum

Old Nick

RATING: 

21–22 Sandland Street
WC1R 4PZ
020 7430 9503

A few years ago when the Old Nick reopened after a period of closure, we breathed a sigh of relief. The place obviously had money lavished on it and happily the décor and ethos were of a good traditional British pub. Sure enough, it gained an award from our good selves. Sadly, since this inaugural high point, the shine has rather dulled for us. For a start, it's overly bright inside and, save for the cosy back section, it feels more like a vertical drinking establishment. It does serve a decent selection of Hall & Woodhouse's Badger Ales, but service can be very slow, sometimes simply due to the weight of custom, other times due to being understaffed. If you hadn't guessed, it gets very, very busy after work, but it can be practically deserted at the weekend; a previous Saturday-evening visit offered a typically lacklustre atmosphere, with disinterested staff who closed up early when they decided they wanted to go home.

FEATURES:    **HANDY FOR:** Sir John Soane's Museum, British Museum

Old Red Lion

RATING:

72 High Holborn
WC1V 6LS
020 7405 1748

A pretty decent place, with a good, well-kept range of Greene King beers. The service is prompt and friendly and there's an upstairs bar you can escape to if it gets crowded downstairs. The building itself is a fine old Victorian pub that's been well looked after and worth popping into, if you're in the area.

FEATURES:   

HANDY FOR: Sir John Soane's Museum, British Museum

Princess Louise

RATING: 

208–209 High Holborn
WC1V 7BW
020 7405 8816

Closed for most of 2007, the Princess Louise is back open again. Its classic Victorian interior is still gloriously intact; indeed, it's come back with extra period additions, with partitions now running down the sides of the island bar, creating the sort of subdivided drinking spaces common to 19th-century gin palaces. Whilst in keeping with the rest of the pub's design, the partitions, however, bring their own problems, with the reduction in floor space being the most obvious. Minor quibbles aside, the Princess Louise is still an enticing pub, arguably the most beautiful in London. Given this, it's also an extremely popular one so a visit out of peak hours is recommended to fully experience its wonders (including the ornate gents' toilets). Definitely give it a look though; any serious list of London's must-see pubs has this one close to the top. A last point to remember: as a pub owned by the Samuel Smith's brewery, the Princess Louise only sells Sam's branded drinks.

FEATURES:  

Reviewers' Award – Best Renovation 2008

Ship Tavern

RATING: 

12 Gate Street
WC2A 3HP
020 7405 1992

Small pub frequented by those who know the shortcut that misses out the corner where Holborn station is. Amazingly it's been refurbished relatively recently but the designers have eschewed the tired 'battered furniture and bare boards' look and redecorated it to look... just like a proper pub! For this alone it's worth visiting; when you add in well-kept draft beers, friendly service, a relaxed atmosphere and the fact you can usually find a seat in here, it comes high up on the list if you're in this area.

FEATURES:    

HANDY FOR: Sir John Soane's Museum

HOLLAND PARK

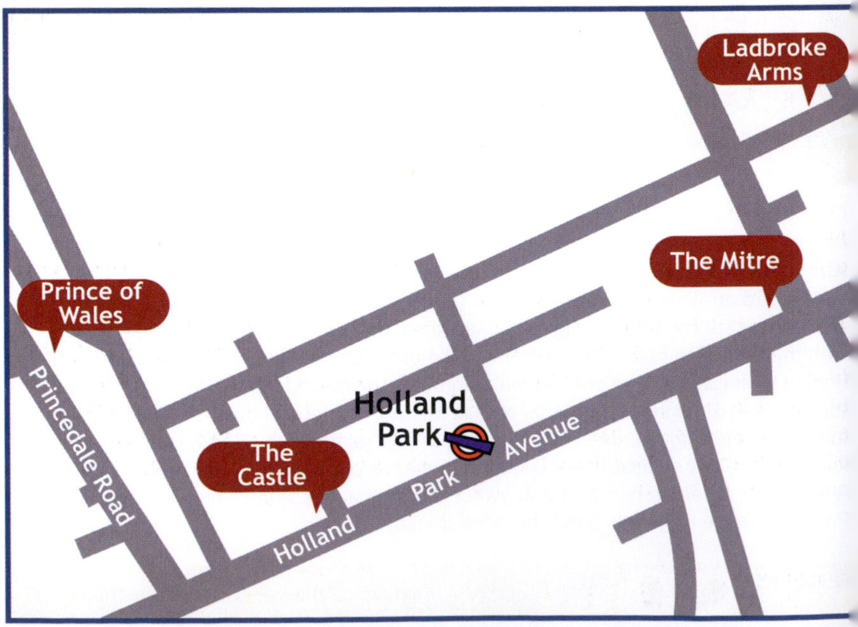

Ladbroke Arms
The Mitre
Prince of Wales
Princedale Road
Holland Park
The Castle
Holland Park Avenue

The Castle

RATING:

100 Holland Park Ave
W11 4UA
020 7313 9301

This one's settled in nicely, becoming that slightly bohemian local so many long for, and so few actually get for their troubles. Saying it's got an eccentric interior's a bit like saying the Royal Albert Hall's a bit big. There's just about every type of furniture imaginable (and we can imagine a lot), from comfy sofas to chaise longues and red velvet-covered loveseats. There's also a fish tank with a solitary fish in it in the corner. The locals don't seem to mind the quirkiness, and frankly it suits the place. There's a decent menu – we're mourning the loss of the fish-finger sandwich, always one of our favourites – and decent beers on the three hand pumps, as well as a selection of continental lagers and beers. The locals are pretty tolerant, and the service prompt and friendly. It's also not as pricey as many of the places around, either. It can get crowded towards the weekend, especially as it's on the main drag, but, if you can find a seat, it's not a bad place for a pint or two.

FEATURES: 

Ladbroke Arms

RATING:

54 Ladbroke Road
W11 3NW
020 7727 6648

Although a pretty good pub, it's gone the gastro route and the emphasis now is definitely on the dining. However, it's still possible to pop in for a pint where you'll find the service to be pretty good and decent, well-kept beer on the four hand pumps. There's also an extensive range of wines and spirits on offer – including a bunch of decent single malts – so the accompaniment and digestif are nicely taken care of. The food is pretty good too. On a warm summer's day, it should be nice to sit out the front of this place and sip your pint with a good book or a couple of mates, but everyone else in the area usually has the same idea – so you'll soon find yourself elbow-to-elbow with the braying hordes from these parts. When it's quiet, it's great, when it's not, it's not. C'est la vie.

FEATURES:   

The Mitre

RATING:

40 Holland Park Avenue
W11 3QY
020 7727 6332

Well, this cavernous pub, a little bit further out of Notting Hill than most, has gone through a number of changes over the years. But now it's nailed its gastro colours to the mast, describing itself as a 'Bar and Dining Room', and pulls no punches, aiming to out-gastro any competition in the neighbourhood. The menu looks fine, but it's not cheap. And, while it's got a couple of beers on the bar, the focus is more on its lagers. The changed focus from pub to eaterie has made the drinking side of things suffer a little – you really get the impression that people are coming here for a meal rather than a drink.

FEATURES:  

Prince of Wales

RATING: 

14 Princedale Road
W11 4NJ
020 7313 9321

This pub's refit a few years ago was not much of a surprise to us, nor was the style of refurb: a M&B makeover, with 70s light fittings, colour scheme and mixed furniture, a look that has grown to be very familiar to the contemporary pub-goer. It is, however, a very decent boozer, with an imaginative range of beers on the hand pumps, continentals on the ornate pumps and the usual keg stuff discreetly hidden away. The wine list is decent if you favour the new world and there are plenty of spirits if you're thinking of fuelling up for a night out. The tiny TV won't set sports fans' pulses racing, but we'd hazard a guess they're not the P.o.W.'s main market. The rather splendid beer garden makes a pleasant place for an alfresco pint (though it does close rather early to appease the neighbours) and this one also makes great claims for its Sunday roast (followed by a quiz). All in all, this one's a pricey, posh local, and one that we've found to be the most relaxed of all the pubs in the area.

FEATURES:   

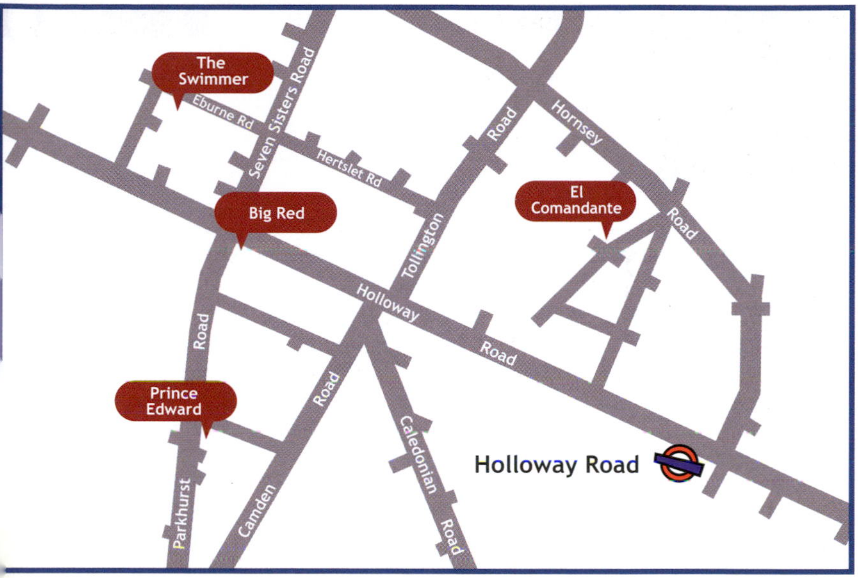

The Swimmer
Big Red
El Comandante
Prince Edward
Eburne Rd
Seven Sisters Road
Hertslet Rd
Tollington Road
Hornsey Road
Holloway Road
Parkhurst Road
Camden Road
Caledonian Road
Holloway Road

Big Red

RATING:

385 Holloway Road
N7 0RY
020 7609 6662

This pub, now resplendent on the outside with flames painted on the walls, is a favourite haunt of students from the nearby university and those seeking a more alternative experience on Holloway Road. The subtly lit interior is dominated by a large rectangular bar, which is surrounded on three sides by seating, including several cosy booths and a number of sofas. At the far end stand four pool tables and a pinball machine. Previously Big Red hosted live bands but now the stage has gone to be replaced by more sofas, while a giant projector screen hangs above them ready to show football. This doesn't seem to have affected their clientele and it's as busy as ever on a weekend. Without entertainment from the stage the jukebox becomes the centre of attention and it doesn't disappoint, especially for fans of rock. Previously we found the bar staff tended to look aggrieved when you interrupted them by doing something audacious like ordering a pint, but this seems to have improved. They can get plenty of practice as Big Red has a late licence.

FEATURES:     

El Comandante

RATING: 3 pints

10 Annette Road
N7 6ET
020 7697 0895

Holloway is a surprisingly decent area for pubs, but it was still nice to discover the El Comandante a few years ago. Formerly the Lord Palmerston, with its original name still visible, clues to its reinvention are subtle: a small poster in the window and the glass in the old Watney's lantern replaced with something a little more, well, revolutionary. Essentially, this is a South American bar in an old pub. Not much has been done to renovate the interior – a fresh lick of paint and some huge Che Guevara posters is about the sum of it – the usual huge palms were sadly missing on our last visit. The lager on tap is unexceptional but the Latin music from the jukebox definitely adds to the ambience, although unless you like R&B it's best to avoid Saturday nights. At other times, however, with a warm welcome from the Bolivian landlord, it's easy to forget you're on the grey back streets of N7. If nothing else, it puts most other – more popular – South American bars to shame. Viva la Revolucion!

FEATURES:   

Prince Edward

RATING: 2 pints

38 Parkhurst Road
N7 0SF
020 7607 2369

We didn't have many nice things to say about the Prince Edward on our last visit – with an intimidating atmosphere, it was an unpleasant time. The emails we subsequently received didn't help. We recently undertook a return visit and had a much better time. Up the road from the infamous women's prison, it wasn't – as you might expect – full of prison officers. Instead, there was good service and a broad mix of customers, young and old – even if a couple of the regulars around the bar didn't exactly make it easy to order our drinks. Apart from plenty of interesting features to admire, there are also Watney Coombe & Reid brewery lanterns hanging outside – an indicator of a bar in the traditional mould. A gantried bar, comfy bench seating and a wonderful-looking jukebox add to its charm. There is also a pretty, well-maintained beer garden. The Holloway Road area has its fair share of older-style pubs and whilst not outstanding – there's no real ale for instance – the Prince Edward is a good pub for the nearby residents.

FEATURES:    

Swimmer at the Grafton Arms

RATING:

13 Eburne Road
N7 6AR
020 7281 4632

Whilst it can be easy to criticise gastropubs, when the emphasis is still on the pub rather than the gastro they're often hard to fault – and the Swimmer is a prime example of when it does work. A smart and professional establishment, it's still first and foremost a pub – and a good one at that. There's usually a range of Fullers and a few guest beers on tap, plus Czech lager Litovel and Erdinger, a fair wine list and excellent service. It must be said though that, considering the area, the prices of the food might be a bit high – but hardly in terms of London and they've obviously got a regular clientele. But, putting this to one side, once you add on a jukebox for which the word 'eclectic' was devised, and a friendly atmosphere, you have the sort of watering hole that, even if you're not ordering swordfish steak off the menu, you can still feel at home in, and it's pretty comfortable at that. It's also pretty handy for the Odeon round the corner.

FEATURES:   

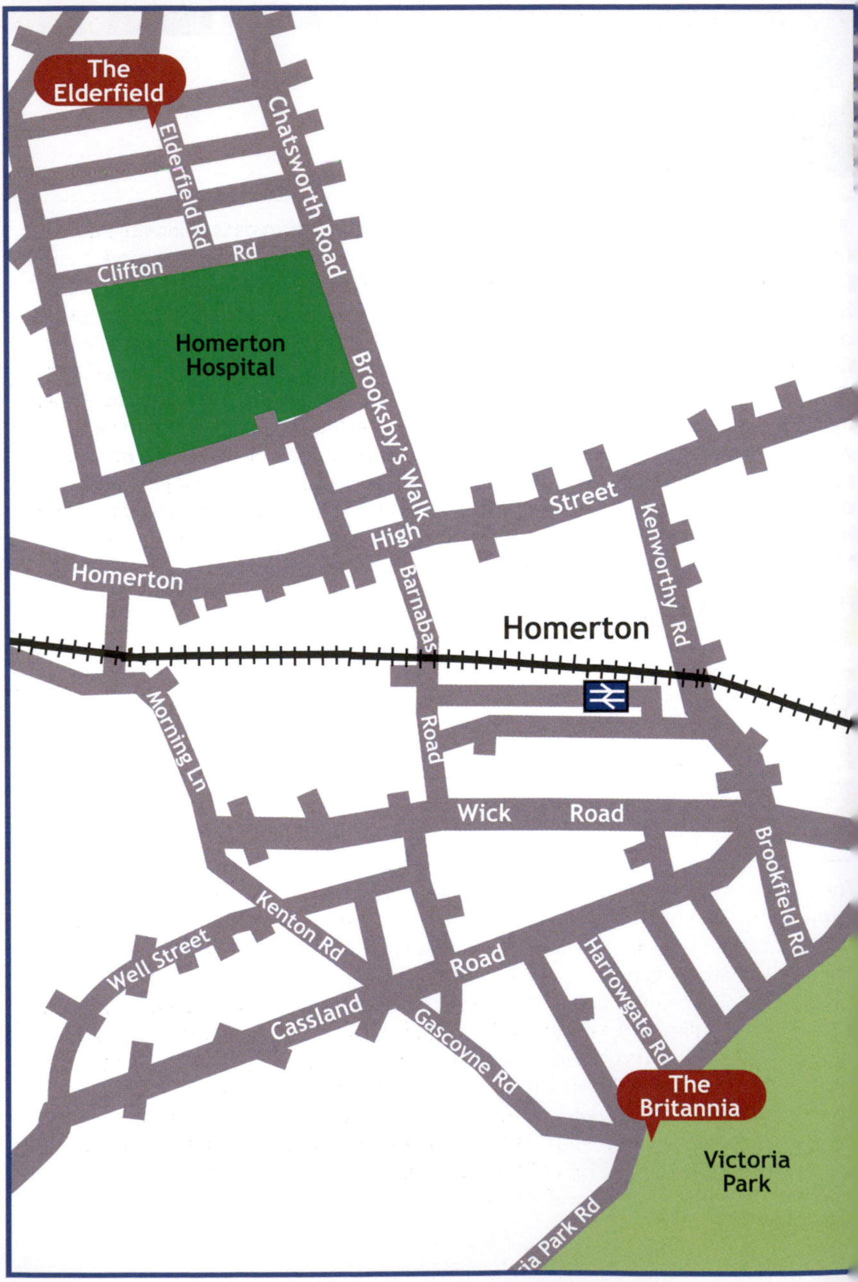

The Elderfield
Elderfield Rd
Chatsworth Road
Clifton Rd
Homerton Hospital
Brooksby's Walk
High Street
Homerton
Kenworthy Rd
Barnabas Road
Homerton
Morning Ln
Wick Road
Brookfield Rd
Kenton Rd
Well Street
Road
Cassland
Gascoyne Rd
Harrowgate Rd
The Britannia
Victoria Park
ia Park Rd

The Britannia

RATING: 2 pints

360 Victoria Park Road
E9 7BT
020 8533 0040

The tawdry Victoria Park has been replaced by a more sombre pub. Gone are the pool tables, video screens and bright colour scheme, to be replaced by a smarter, sober, paint job and furniture of the now customary (or is it mandatory?) mix and match second-hand style. The bright lights and garish pre-mixers are gone and there's decent booze on the pumps. It's early days but the overall impression doesn't seem much different from before. The clientele is much as it was, and the pub still seems to be aimed at the Friday/Saturday-night crowd. There's a lot of empty floor space, with decks, mixer, PA, lights, hinting at club ambitions. This didn't really work before and we're not sure it will now. During the day and evenings early in the week, there's hardly anyone around and the club gear just looks incongruous. It seems aiming for one demographic doesn't make financial sense in these parsimonious times. The Britannia's a huge pub in a prime site, it could become a destination for all who live around here. Maybe things will pick up, but right now we feel it's a sadly under-exploited opportunity.

FEATURES:   

The Elderfield

57 Elderfield Road
E5 0LF
020 8986 1591

The signs of the smartened-up pub are in attendance, yet this one still stands out from your usual done-up boozer. For a start, the stripped-out look actually helps to accentuate the lovely original thirties wood panelling of the back bar, while the scattering of plants softens the corners nicely. Beers? A pretty good selection of Timothy Taylor Landlord, Harvey's Best, London Pride and Adnam's is usually in place. If that doesn't suffice, a small list of wines and cocktails will probably do the job. Our latest Saturday-night visit found it pleasantly busy, filled with a good cross-section of locals. Some were partaking in the selection of board games available – four sets of Scrabble at the last count – while others were enjoying the bar snacks offered (paninis and pizza are the mainstay here). Despite being a bit of a trek to find the Elderfield, it's a worthwhile place to spend your time, especially as this part of Clapton is rather lacking in quality drinking establishments.

FEATURES:   

Hyde Park
Hyde Park Corner
Hyde Park Corner
Knightsbridge
Crescent
Grenadier
Buckingham Palace Gardens
Grosvenor
Grosvenor Place
Headfort Place
Halkin St
Montrose Place
Chapel St
Horse & Groom
The Talbot
Belgrave Square
Chester Street

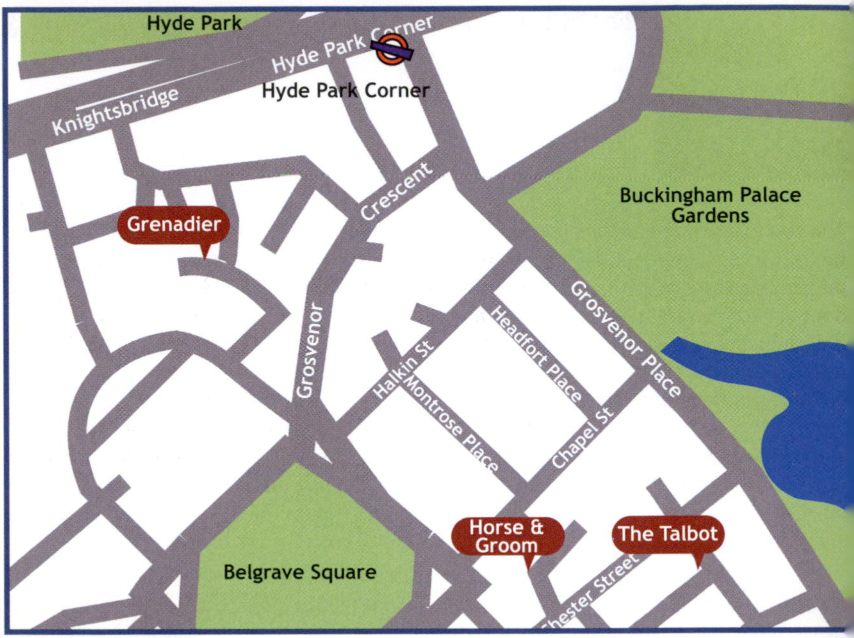

The Grenadier

RATING:

18 Wilton Row
SW1X 7NR
020 7235 3074

Before their split, the Ritchies used to pop in here every now and again apparently (Guy and Madonna, not Shane). This is another one of those small Knightsbridge pubs you would expect to find in the middle of Suffolk, but maybe not the middle of London. As you'd surmise from the name, military memorabilia hangs from the walls of both the bar and the small dining area at the back, and there is an air of old-fashioned gentility about the place. There's usually a good range of well-kept beers on the hand pumps – Spitfire, Bombardier, Pride and 6X when we were last there – and there's plenty of decent pub grub – we especially like the fish-finger baguettes and the pie, pint, chips and salad deal for a tenner. Occasionally, the stuck-up nature of some of the clientele can be a bit off-putting, but the professional staff and the general ambience of the pub make up for it. It's a small place, so a visit out of peak times is recommended if you want to get a seat.

FEATURES:  **HANDY FOR:** Buckingham Palac

Horse & Groom

RATING:

7 Groom Place
SW1X 7BA
020 7235 6980

Another Belgravia pub in another mews, this small Shepherd Neame pub is everything you might wish for in a local – if you're lucky enough to live in SW1. This small wood-panelled bar might be described by some as scruffy, but 'well worn' is a better description. The beers are well kept, wine list interesting, the service friendly and (although possibly out of character for its location) a rather tempting cocktail list is also available. It's very easy to just sit back and enjoy your well-kept pint here, perhaps with a packet of dried Elk sausages or one of the sarnies from the bar. The mix of clientele means neither feeling like you're invading a sacrosanct local – like some other nearby pubs – nor being swept along in the throng of the after-work and tourist crowd all too common in nearby Victoria. Recommended.

FEATURES:    

HANDY FOR: Buckingham Palace

The Talbot

RATING:  

1 Little Chester Street, Belgravia
SW1X 7AL
020 7235 1639

Tucked away off a blink-and-you-miss-it mews, The Talbot is one of the less traditional pubs in the area. It's a big place, with plenty of standing room and seating both inside and out, but its character clearly suffers from the lack of imagination put into its hotel-lobby-carpet and magnolia-wall refit. Of course, things like carpet patterns don't matter to the less fussy after-work crowd they're aiming at. Nevertheless, the food menu was extensive and there was the bonus of probably the only cash machine within a 10-minute radius. Although not bad by any means, with a number of rather excellent pubs within walking distance, the incentive to stay for more than a couple is limited.

FEATURES:   

HANDY FOR: Buckingham Palace

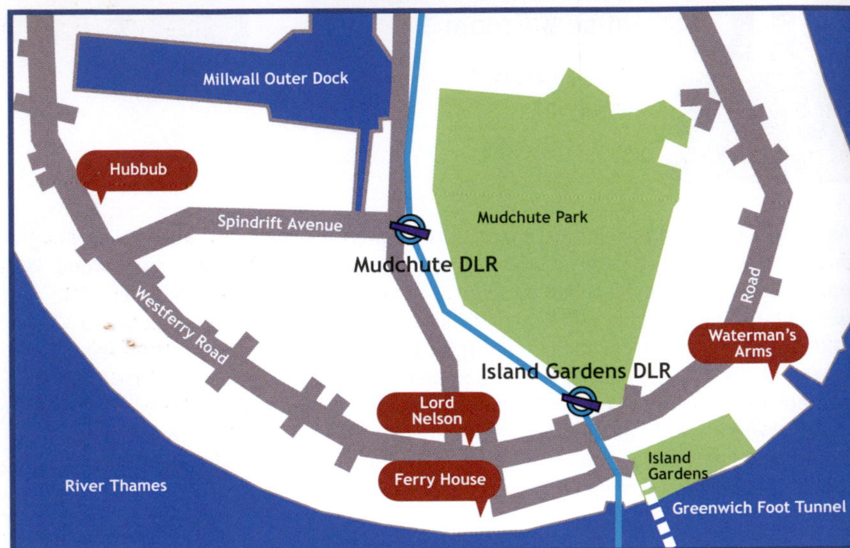

Ferry House

RATING:

26 Ferry Street
E14 3DT
020 7537 9587

The ferry to Greenwich has gone but the Ferry House still stands. It may appear a rather rough-hewn locals' pub from the outside, but it still offers a touch more colour and atmosphere than the modern bars around Canary Wharf. Here you sense 'redesigning the bar' means getting in a few new CDs for the jukebox. Apart from a new TV, the pub appears unchanged from the days when cargo ships were offloading at Millwall dock. It also sports a pub rarity – an old 'London Fives' dart board. A genial barman is on hand to pull the pints and banter with the regulars.

FEATURES:     **HANDY FOR:** Cutty Sark, National Maritime Museum

Hubbub

RATING:

269 Westferry Road
E14 3RS
020 7515 5577

A former Victorian chapel built for the shipworkers who came down from Scotland to work on the Great Eastern, this one's now an arts centre (The Space) and Hubbub – a small bar located upstairs at the back of the building. It's a cosy, gas-lit place with decent food and a good range of drinks – wines, spirits, cocktails and coffees, although there are no real ales on the pumps (only Guinness, Kronenbourg and Fosters, but there are bottled ales). On previous visits, we've seen young and older Docklanders in comfy chairs, wining and dining to a Coltrane jazz odyssey. In an otherwise dull – and dry – location, you can see why they come here.

FEATURES:    

Lord Nelson

RATING: 

1 Manchester Road
E14 3BD
020 7987 1970

A great local pub, it's got a pool table, quiz nights, darts and almost anything else you'd care to mention. They do a good range of food, the beer's decent and the staff are very friendly and helpful. This is one of the places that goes out of its way to make everyone welcome, putting events on for the regulars all the time. Children are welcome before 7pm and quiz nights are great fun and very popular. Showing how a local should be run, the Lord Nelson is definitely worth looking out for if you're in the area.

FEATURES:    

HANDY FOR: Cutty Sark, National Maritime Museum

ISLAND GARDENS (DLR)/MUDCHUTE (DLR)

Waterman's Arms

RATING:

1 Glenaffric Avenue
E14 3BW
020 7093 2883

Despite the relentless move upmarket as the City spreads eastwards, there are still a few old boozers left in these parts and the Waterman's Arms is one of the best of them. Solid in all departments, it's a popular one with both locals and any visitors who've stumbled across it whilst looking for that famous view of Greenwich. It's a rangy old place, made famous by a previous landlord – Dan Farson – and whilst there's a fair-size restaurant section at the side don't expect gastro fare. Oh, they use an old-style 'London Fives' dart board (just in case you've got your arrows handy). Well-kept beers, Irish malts and a pool table are some of the other features. Add on the mandatory 'solid gold 60s' compilation airing from the CD player and a huge beer garden and you have a steady three pinter.

FEATURES:       

KENNINGTON

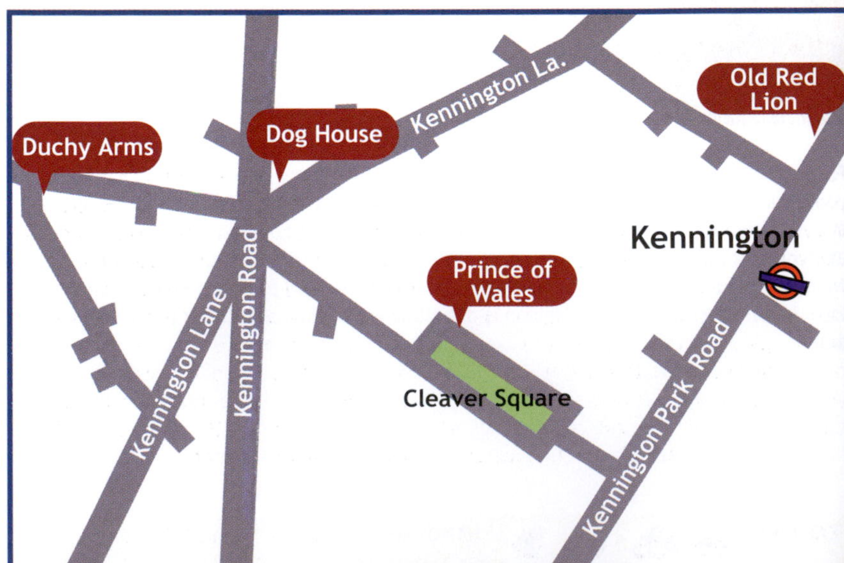

Dog House

RATING:

Kennington Cross, 293 Kennington Road
SE11 6BY
020 7820 9310

Despite the odd name, the Dog House affords a more traditional pub-like experience than one would initially expect. That's not to say there aren't some alternative touches – with carpet lining the sides of the bar, we couldn't claim otherwise – but compared to the nearby gastropubs and fading boozers it feels refreshingly normal here. Its positioning on Kennington Cross, coupled with the large windows and a fair amount of outside seating, offers a fine vantage point for a spot of people watching. Inside it's not too bad either, with two separate bars, a couple of ales and decent, reasonably priced pub grub. Overall, this is a pub that feels comfortable in its skin and is just the thing if you fancy a couple of lazy drinks in pleasant surroundings.

FEATURES:    

HANDY FOR: The Oval

Duchy Arms

RATING: 

63 Sancroft Street
SE11 5UG
020 7735 6340

Forgive the estate agent speak, but Sancroft Street contains some highly desirable properties, both period and modern. We're not sure if the boys and girls of Foxtons, Winkworth, Keatons et al make much of the street's pub, but this is the sort of amenity we wouldn't mind at the bottom of our road. A friendly and old-fashioned local, the Duchy Arms doesn't do too much out of the ordinary: Sky Sports dominates in one bar; darts and pool in the other. Its range of drinks is conventional enough – and we like the pie and mash specials (double pie and mash £4.20, excellent) – but what raises this one out of the ordinary is the merry atmosphere on display. We won't kid you on that newcomers are greeted with a warm handshake and a free go on the pool table; rather that the locals are having such a good time enjoying themselves they'll hardly notice any newbies on their patch. Seems a decent arrangement to us.

FEATURES:    

HANDY FOR: The Oval

Old Red Lion

RATING:

42 Kennington Park Road
SE11 4RS
020 7735 3529

A mock-Tudor pub from the 1930s, the rarity value of this one rises by the year. Well serviced by its regulars, it's well worth the jaunt south if you want to check out a pub style slowly being realised as something worth preserving. Unlike many Red Lion pubs, this one plays the (Lion Rampant) Scottish card through its decor. Misty-eyed Jacobites should note the large-scale picture on the wall of Bonnie Prince Charlie arriving at Arisaig in 1745 – ideal if a spot of drinking the King o'er the water is your thing. It's certainly a locals' local, but one whose interior raises it above the average.

FEATURES: 

HANDY FOR: The Oval, Imperial War Museum

Prince of Wales

RATING: 

48 Cleaver Square
SE11 4EA
020 7735 9916

Cleaver Square is a beautifully preserved Victorian square which, in Kennington, stands out 'like a tarantula on a slice of angel cake' (thank you, Raymond Chandler). The Prince of Wales lives up to the location too. It's a relaxed place with some good beer (Spitfire, Oranjeboom and others) to quench thirsts, a decent wine list, great service and excellent food. We've enjoyed a selection of their ciabattas on previous visits and the beef pie comes recommended; we suspect the other daily specials also make the grade, too. The excellent music on the stereo is just a bonus. An unspoilt pub and the best in Kennington.

FEATURES:  

HANDY FOR: The Oval, Imperial War Museum

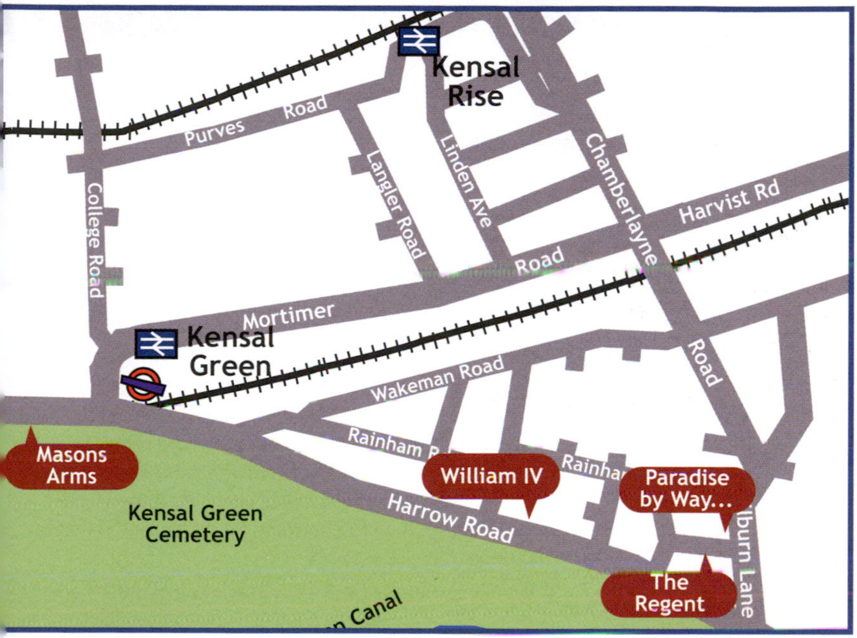

Masons Arms

RATING: 

665 Harrow Road
NW10 5NU
020 8960 2278

Now owned by the Real Pub Company, behind the North London Tavern in Kilburn and The Oxford in Kentish Town, and it's happily their equal. Some of the old flavour of the place has gone, but the last refit has enhanced the Victorian interior and the new pub still plays host to some of the old punters. It's still a pub and the beer's decent along with a decent array of drinks, but the menu's gone more upmarket and a bit gastro. As pub refits go, this one gets the thumbs up – though if only they had kept the old place's jukebox: we were itching to choose something from 'Classic Irish Colleens' to blank out the noodly jazz-funk heard on our last visit...

FEATURES:      

HANDY FOR: Kensal Green Cemetery

Paradise by Way of Kensal Green

RATING:

19 Kilburn Lane
W10 4AE
020 8969 0098

Befitting a pub that takes its name from a line in a G. K. Chesterton poem, there's a deliberately idiosyncratic feel to this place. A rather ramshackle pile with sanded floorboards and Louis XIV-style furniture, it's almost gastropub as envisaged by Laurence from *Changing Rooms*. If ever a hostelry was crying out for a chaise-longue it's this one. The restaurant at the back seems your standard gastro dining room so on previous visits we've tended to investigate upstairs where the alignment of floors and staircases brings the work of Escher to mind. Our daytime revelries here have been spoilt by one too many children running about the place: the offspring of the life-styling professionals of the area who make up most of the clientele. The overheard quote that sums up the clientele for us was one punter who on ordering Hoegaarden turned to his mate and said, 'Fancy a bit of fruit with that?' We stuck to the Spitfire on our visit, though a glass of absinthe might have been more in keeping with our environs. A bit too knowing for its own good maybe, but, if your local pub is proving too pedestrian, seek it out.

FEATURES:     

HANDY FOR: Kensal Green Cemetery

The Regent

RATING: 

5 Regent Street
NW10 5LG
020 8969 2184

It would be easy to miss this pub, as it's down an alley from its closest competitor the Paradise and away from the main drag. That would be a mistake. It's genial inside, with an attractive interior that feels well designed, coupled with decent beer, friendly staff and a loyal following from younger locals. It successfully pulls off the often tricky task of balancing its job as a modern bar while also giving a good nod to the past, with its elegant chandeliers and an attractive, ornate bar area. We can already see the fire being a draw when the weather turns a bit colder. The menu looks good – there's a heavy focus on burgers around the £10 mark. The large garden is a bit of a surprise, as it's practically an extension of the interior, complete with plenty of heaters, couches and covered areas. The only thing that put us off slightly was the burned-popcorn smell from the popcorn maker on the end of the bar: the smell you get at cinemas and shopping malls, it's not necessarily conducive to the otherwise relaxed atmosphere.

FEATURES:    

HANDY FOR: Kensal Green Cemetery

William IV

RATING:

786 Harrow Road
NW10 5JX
020 8969 5950

A Friday night at the William IV is quite often a busy, bustling, loud affair. There are happening tunes played at the usual Friday-night volume for the benefit of the young trendy local clientele, the lighting is suitably dimmed and the atmosphere is friendly and laidback. Drinks are average London prices, with a choice of beers on the hand pumps – the Dawlish Ale was very nice when we were in last. The food is Tapas and is original and tasty; however, eaters are urged to confine themselves to the brightly lit, quiet back room, making this a pub of two halves. It does have outdoor seating for the summer, and plenty of evening activities during the week. It's settled in now and obviously has a regular clientele, but it does seem that it's trying a bit too hard at times. Still, worth visiting if you're in the area.

FEATURES:

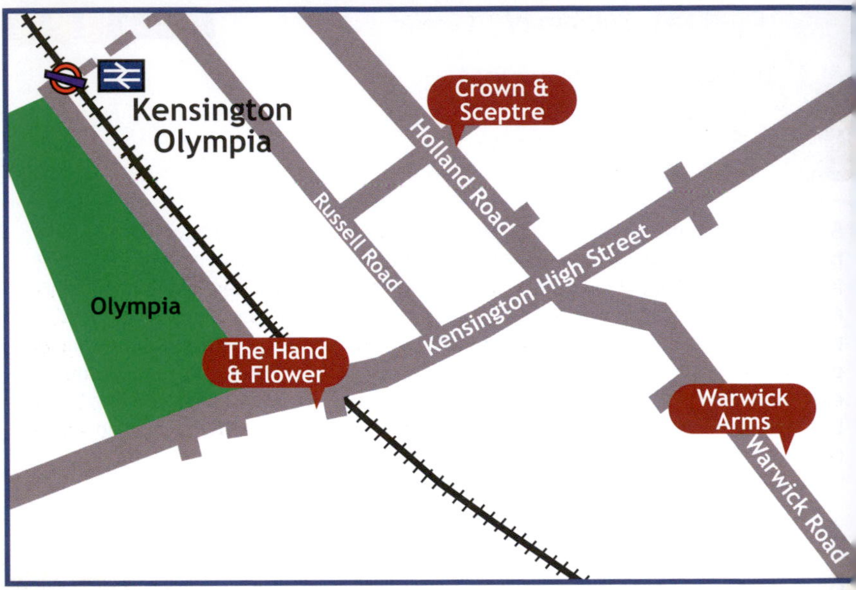

Kensington Olympia
Crown & Sceptre
Holland Road
Russell Road
Kensington High Street
Olympia
The Hand & Flower
Warwick Arms
Warwick Road

Crown & Sceptre

RATING: 

34 Holland Road
W14 8BA
020 7602 1866

Stuck on the busy Holland Road, the Crown & Sceptre looks like one of the earlier attempts at the 'stripped-out' look and it's beginning to show wear and tear. It has somehow been crossed with a Mexican restaurant, which manages to give it more personality and warmth. Inside, the front is a mishmash of couches and tables, not particularly well laid out, but the back section is more cosy. It's got a good selection of real ales (regular guests included) on tap and friendly service and genial locals, combined with the added bonus of good, reasonably priced Mexican food, plus a few British staples, on the menu. And, now that the Radnor Arms is no more, it's a bit of a haven if you're trying to escape the teeming masses from nearby Olympia. Give it a go.

FEATURES:      

HANDY FOR: Olympia

The Hand & Flower Hotel

RATING: 3

1 Hammersmith Road
W14 8XJ
020 7371 4105

Situated on prime pub territory opposite Olympia Exhibition Hall, it's safe to say this place will never be short of customers when there's a trade fair or conference on across the road. Owned by Marston's (makers of Pedigree, amongst other things), it's following their formula with a lot of success. Still more trendy bar than cosy pub, it's kept the big tellies which were showing football when we were in last. The food looks good in the Marston's pub vein too, with the promise of pie of the day catching our eye. To be honest, it's not changed much, and if anything has only got better as the beer's well kept and a nice change from the usual selection with their own ales and regular guests on most days.

FEATURES:      

HANDY FOR: Olympia

Warwick Arms

RATING: 

160 Warwick Road
W14 8PS
020 7603 3560

With choice memorabilia throughout the pub, including a brass ship's telegraph (which tells the engine room to stop or go), this pub does a lot of things right. The friendly staff, decent beer and genial locals make it a rather relaxed and easy going place. There are two menus: one traditional pub grub with all meat sourced from the same farm in Somerset, and one providing a decent range of Indian cuisine. We've heard good things about the Indian food on offer, but we've yet to sample it for ourselves – we like the fact that you get a choice between a sausage sandwich or chicken tikka masala. That said, the Friday all-you-can-eat Indian buffet sounds like something worth investigating. In our opinion, it's the sort of pub ideally suited to an afternoon of slothful drinking, which is hardly a chore with the range of Fuller's beers on tap.

FEATURES:   

HANDY FOR: Earl's Court, Olympia

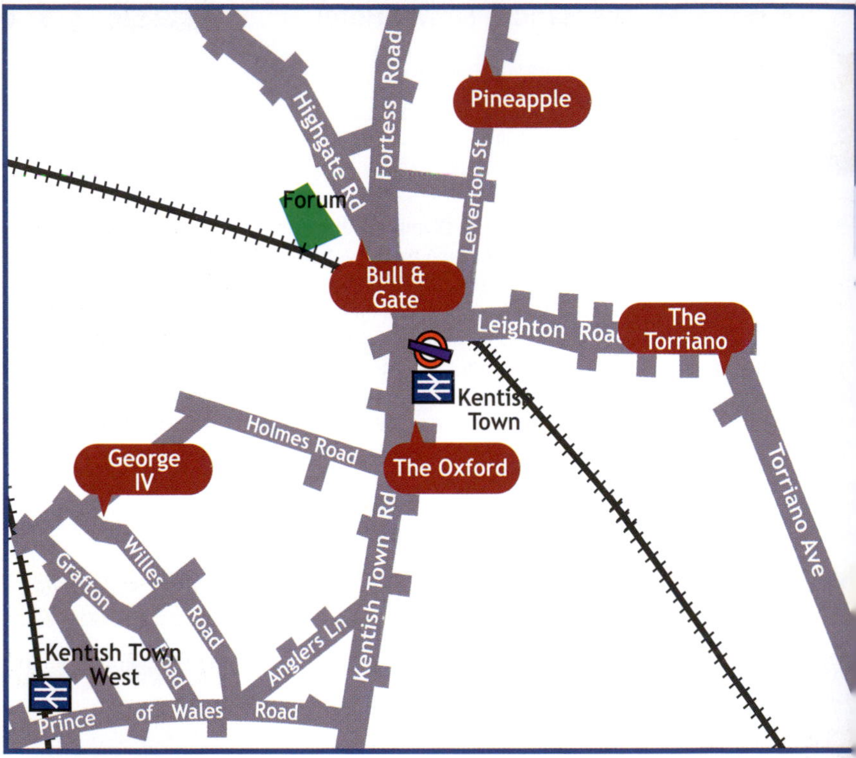

Bull & Gate

RATING: 

389 Kentish Town Road
NW5 2TJ
020 7485 5358

This is a traditional Irish boozer with no pretensions, no knickknacks, no gastro-fare – it's just an honest boozer in a fine old Victorian pub. Lovely interior, friendly staff and tolerant locals, and a nice drop of the black stuff – what more could you ask for? It does Bass as well as Guinness, which is a bit of a surprise, but a nice one. What more can we say? It's a refreshing place in these times and we're glad it hasn't changed in years.

FEATURES:    

HANDY FOR: The Forum

George IV

RATING: 

76 Willes Road
NW5 3DL

The George IV is a fantastic proper Victorian pub, just where you wouldn't expect one. Tucked off Kentish Town High Road on the edge of an industrial estate, the exterior is an ivy-covered wonder, complete with charming globe lamps inscribed with 'GR IV'. Inside is equally good, with pictures covering every inch of the wall space and perfect lighting, which included a lamp for every table. Nothing of note on the beer taps, sadly, and the food seems pretty minimal, but the service was as friendly as the locals who make up the clientele of this strong community-led pub. If they could find themselves some real ale and give the gents a sprucing up, we'd be regulars. Either way, the George IV proves that not every locals' pub is tired or unwelcoming.

FEATURES: 

HANDY FOR: The Forum 

The Oxford

RATING: 

256 Kentish Town Road
NW5 2AA
020 7485 3521

Owned by the same people who tarted up the North London Tavern in Kilburn. And, as a result, this one's very much in keeping with a standard gastropub arrangement: bar area at the front, open plan kitchen at the side, dining area at the back and the giant blackboard menu on the rear wall. It's probably not the market they're after, but this one does a decent enough job for a drink both before and after a gig at The Forum. With decent beer on the pumps and a good menu, it's definitely doing what it does best, and the friendly and prompt service is worth the effort. It's got lots of regular events going on, including live music, regular quiz night and DJ nights, and is obviously attracting a diverse clientele from families to gig-goers. Worth a look, even if you're just going to a gig.

FEATURES:       

HANDY FOR: The Forum

Pineapple

RATING:

51 Leverton Street
NW5 2NX
020 7284 4631

A comfy place that was saved from closure a while ago through the actions of its patrons. As a result, any criticism of the place could sound a little churlish. It's certainly one of the more charming pubs in the area: the lovely interior and a coal fire giving the place a warm feel, and the upright piano in the corner being almost a provocation to a sing-song. There's a touch of the lifestyle supplements to the place, but it's a fine pub. It's got lots of nooks and crannies, as well as a patio and outdoor area, which results in a Tardis-like effect. Under new management, it's gone back down the traditional-pub route, with decent beer on the hand pumps and an excellent Thai menu. At least it's not gone down the gastro route like some of the others in the area and it does a great job for the locals who go there.

FEATURES:    

HANDY FOR: The Forum

The Torriano

RATING: 

71–73 Torriano Avenue
NW5 2SG
020 7267 4305

Take a stroll around this residential patch of NW5 and what first strikes you are the friendly names of the local shops: Maria's Travel and Tours, Rita's Hair and Design and Susan's Mini-Market. As The Torriano is situated amidst such neighbourliness, expectations of a jolly local pub are raised high. After our most recent visit to the area, we're glad to say we encountered it – and its recent brush with closure and conversion into more flats appears to have been averted thanks to a local celebrity campaign, which is great news. There's a mix of chairs and couches, a decent range of drinks and a selection of toasted sandwiches to enjoy. Things are also helped along by the friendly staff and punters. The secluded sunken garden at the back is a nice little place for the summer (even if the generator occasionally whirrs into action), and a real fire means winter times are adequately covered too. A neighbourly little boozer then; worth the wander from Kentish Town to track down.

FEATURES:   

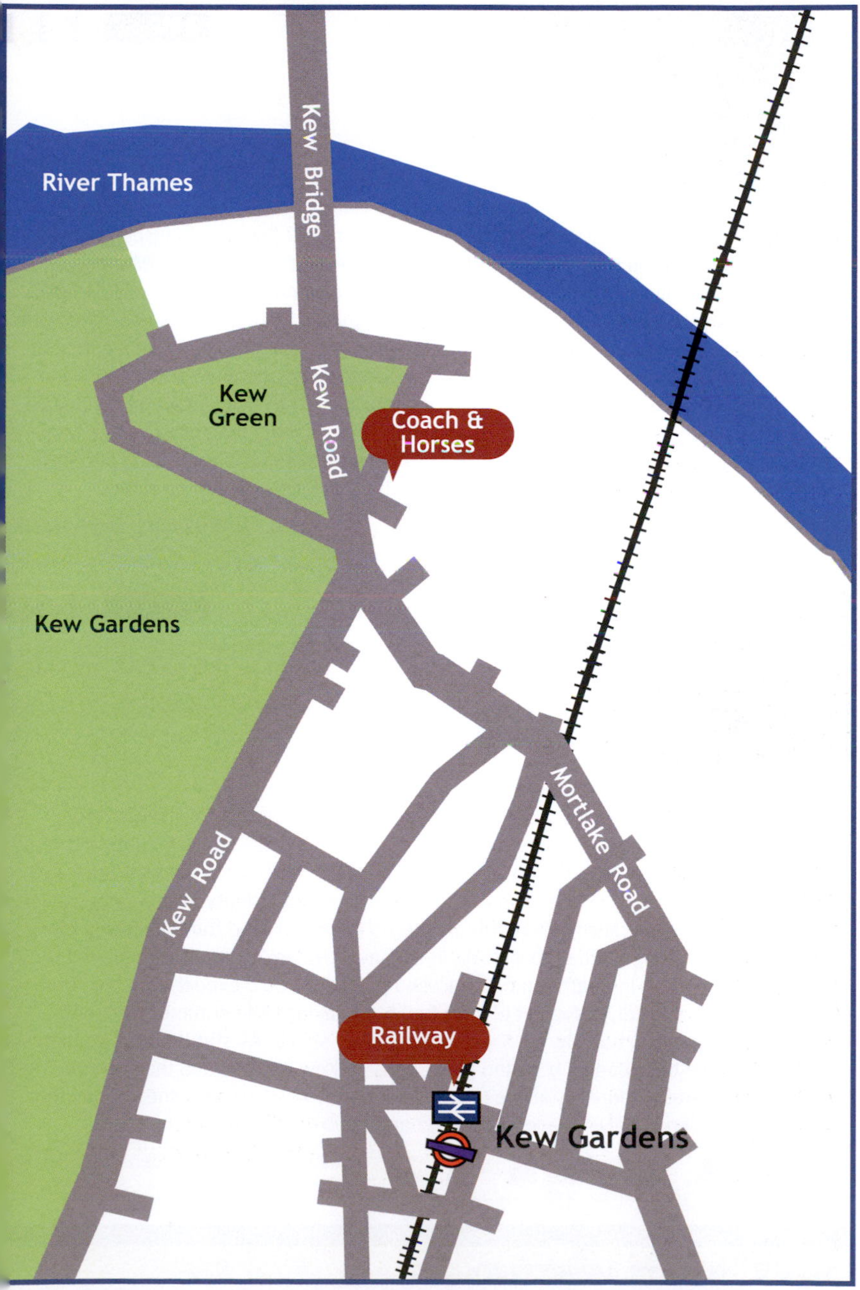

River Thames

Kew Bridge

Kew Green

Kew Road

Coach & Horses

Kew Gardens

Mortlake Road

Kew Road

Railway

Kew Gardens

KEW GARDENS

Coach & Horses Hotel

RATING: 3 pints

8 Kew Green
TW9 3BH
020 8940 1208

Despite being a fairly typical Wells and Young's refurbishment (loungey furnishings etc.), the Coach and Horses does a pretty good job of balancing its job as a hotel, dining room and local pub. Evenings find the pub populated by plenty of regulars, mainly middle-aged men, but sunny weekends will see the front terrace, which overlooks Kew Green, filled with people lunching and brunching, despite the always busy traffic. A large part of the front of the pub is set out as a dining room and the food prices are reasonable – between £8 and £13 for unpretentious, freshly prepared, modern pub grub. The choice of ale on the pumps is adequate (Young's Best, Special and Bombardier) and look out for a large bottled range behind the bar, along with a good wine list. The Coach & Horses is a good, solid pub that handles its multiple roles with measured calm and is a well-deserved three pinter.

FEATURES:          **HANDY FOR:** Kew Gardens

The Railway

RATING: 3 pints

Kew Gardens Station Parade
TW9 3PZ
020 8332 1162

With its lofty, stripped-out interior and prominent use of glass, the Railway's well placed to capture visitors en route to Kew Gardens – especially as it's actually in the station. It's not a bad place to stop for a breather either. With three Cask Marque ales on hand pumps – usually Pride, Adnam's, Bombardier – and plenty of other choices on tap, refreshment is usually not a problem. There's cheapish food too (especially for these parts) including Sunday roasts. We must say, however, the large tables and L-shaped design result in a rather more cramped pub than you'd expect from the exterior and, as a result, it doesn't always feel too relaxing. And summer weekends can see it fill up pretty quickly, even with the outdoor space. As station pubs go, it's easily one of the better ones, but then as stations go Kew station (and the surrounding area) is considerably more attractive than, say, King's Cross – despite the billions that have already been spent. A reasonable and handy pub for thirsty botanists.

FEATURES:      **HANDY FOR:** Kew Gardens/Kew Palace

KILBURN – *see Brondesbury, page 68*

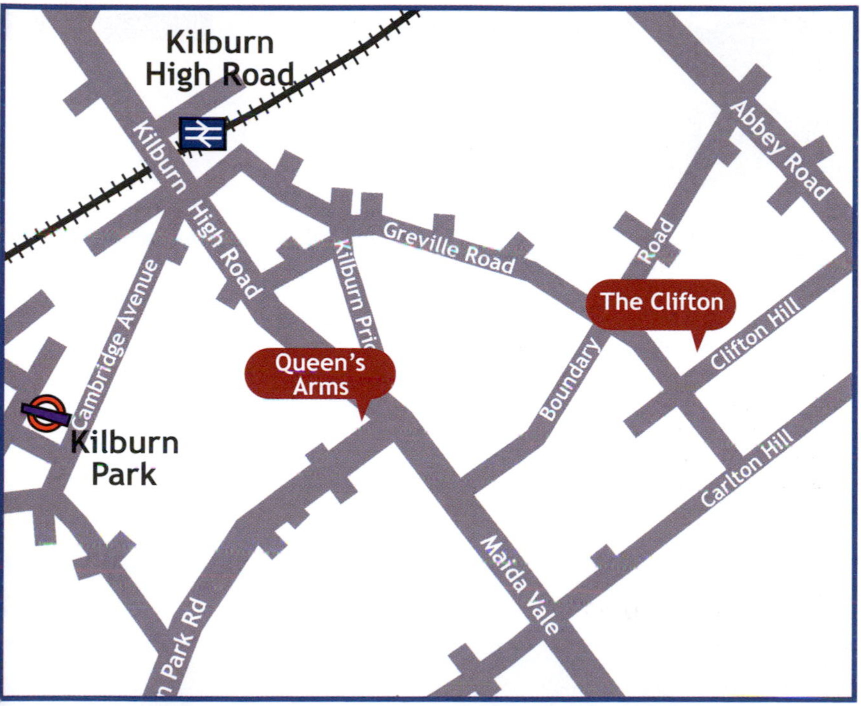

Kilburn High Road
Kilburn Park
Kilburn High Road
Cambridge Avenue
Kilburn Priory
Greville Road
Abbey Road
Boundary Road
Clifton Hill
Carlton Hill
Maida Vale
Park Rd
Queen's Arms
The Clifton

The Clifton

RATING:

96 Clifton Hill

NW8 0JT

020 7372 3427

An altogether charming villa establishment at which the future Edward VII was reputed to engage in trysts with Lillie Langtry. Located in a suitably elegant, peaceful and tree-lined back street, the best part of a century later the pub remains exquisitely charming, combining two wood-panelled rooms plus a couple of nooks with real fires as well as a conservatory-like area, and for good measure a few seats outside. The welcome is warm, a good selection of beers and board games are available at the bar (anyone for a lengthy session of Risk?), and food is also on offer. The Clifton is a very fine place indeed, and well worth the walk from whichever station you choose to reach it.

FEATURES:       

KILBURN HIGH ROAD/KILBURN PARK

Queen's Arms

RATING:

1 Kilburn High Road
NW6 5SE

The Queen's Arms is a large two-roomed locals' pub, with well-kept Young's beers on tap (a rarity on Kilburn High Road), real fireplaces and a genuinely mixed clientele. On our last visit, the youngest customer was barely 18 and the oldest well over 80. There's friendly service and a good atmosphere – it's the sort of pub where random people might come and chat to you about politics or football. Some may find it a rather dingy affair here, but others will infinitely prefer its down-to-earth nature compared to the anonymous stripped-pine sort of pub. It certainly serves the locals well enough and for that you can't complain.

FEATURES:   

KING'S CROSS ST PANCRAS

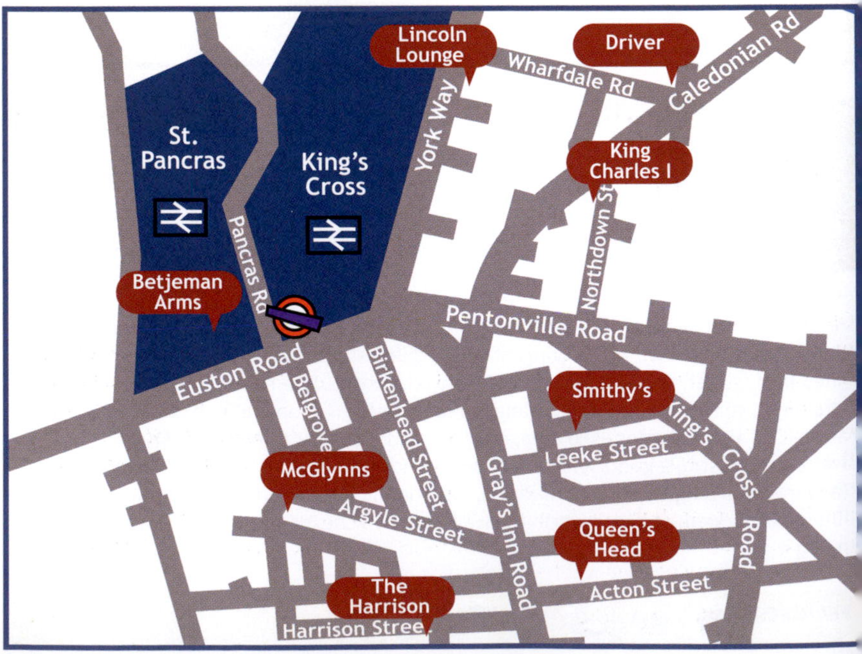

Lincoln Lounge
Driver
Wharfdale Rd
Caledonian Rd
York Way
St. Pancras
King's Cross
King Charles I
Northdown St
Pancras Rd
Betjeman Arms
Pentonville Road
Euston Road
Belgrove
Birkenhead Street
Smithy's
King's Cross Road
Leeke Street
McGlynns
Argyle Street
Gray's Inn Road
Queen's Head
Acton Street
The Harrison
Harrison Stree

The Betjeman Arms

RATING: 2 pints

Unit 53, St Pancras International Station
NW1 2QP
020 7923 5440

The wonderfully restored St Pancras Station had a very public opening at the end of last year but it was only very recently that the Betjeman Arms opened for business. And on the impression of our recent visit, they should perhaps have waited a little bit longer... Situated on the upper level of the station, the Betjeman Arms is a rather upmarket station pub and restaurant. It may aspire to be a gastropub, and it certainly looks like it's ready to be, but they're not there yet. Oh yes, the place looks great, three different areas, a few tables and sofas around the bar area, a lovely tiled space next to the 'scullery' and a fancy dining area with fireplace and chandelier. However, what it doesn't have are gents' loos and heating. In good weather it may not matter about the heating, but the gents are expected to leave the pub, take the lift down to the main concourse of the station and go and queue with the travelling public. This isn't on. The good points? A great selection of wines and beers, including a Betjeman Ale, specially brewed by Sharp's of Cornwall and tasty food – the main menu isn't in place yet so it's pies, burgers and pasta. Staff are attentive, maybe a little too attentive, but that'll wear off as it gets busier.

FEATURES:  

HANDY FOR: British Library

Driver

RATING: 

2–4 Wharfdale Road
N1 9RV
020 7278 8827

On our first visit, shortly after the pub reopened, we predicted this place would get pretty popular and, sure enough, it has. We can't claim any prescient talents, though, for prophesying this – a place as pleasant, smart and welcoming in a grubby area like King's Cross would be bound to attract people anxious to escape from the miserable environs and, in the last eighteen months or so, this has indeed happened. Apart from the increased clientele, the place is much as it was – a respectable array of wines and spirits accompanies a decent menu (including Sunday roast) and the service is fast and friendly. It hasn't got the beer selection it used to, the entire selection consisting of Pride and Landlord, but then the clientele aren't after that sort of thing. That said, it can be a welcome oasis in a still up-and-coming area.

FEATURES:   

HANDY FOR: British Library

The Harrison

RATING:

28 Harrison Street
WC1H 8JF
020 7278 3966

This back-street pub has had a lick of paint and a change of furnishings in recent years. Thankfully nothing too dramatic though. It helps that, even though the obligatory leather sofas have been installed, the period windows (with Watney's lettering) have been kept in place. Since opening, the drink options have improved, with Timothy Taylor's Landlord, Staropramen and Erdinger now being the most visible options. What this one does have in its favour is the eagerness of the staff and an amiable atmosphere. Best of all, even with the excellent food this one isn't a food-led gastro conversion: it's still a pub. You'll also hear some decent selections on the CD player (though the monthly psych-folk Sundays are a more acquired taste). Plenty of pubs have been remodelled in the area around King's Cross but this one's arguably the most compact and friendly.

FEATURES:    

HANDY FOR: British Library

King Charles I

RATING: 

55–57 Northdown Street
N1 9BL
020 7837 7758

A compact, one-roomed affair, this pub even manages to shoehorn in a bar billiards table into the clutter of knick knacks on display. This does provide a pleasing independent air to proceedings, with a decent range of beers on offer – Brain's SA and Adnam's Broadside were on when we were in last – as well as a few decent bottled ciders. Mix all that up and you have an atmosphere conducive to settling in for a couple of hours. As it's situated on a side-street off the King's Cross end of Caledonian Road, it's perhaps more convivial than you might expect, and it's a pleasant discovery should you (for some reason) be wandering round the back streets of King's Cross. Note that it doesn't offer food – though you can order your lunch at the cafe over the road and they'll bring it across to you. It's that sort of pub. Oh, and it seems to be vying for the award for smallest men's bog in London, too – don't go in with a friend.

FEATURES:    

HANDY FOR: British Library

Lincoln Lounge

RATING:

52 York Way, King's Cross
N1 9AB
020 7837 9339

From the exterior, this wasn't too promising. Stuck on barren York Way, outside it looked like a mercilessly renovated pub, reminiscent of a rundown 80s wine bar. Thankfully, then, inside was a pleasant surprise. The 'lounge' in the name is accurate, as armchairs and settees were the order of the day, even if it limits the seating somewhat. With walls covered in cow parsley patterns, along with a huge mural on the back wall and a giant world map, it makes for an eclectic and bohemian atmosphere. It's the kind of pub you could've found in Hoxton 15 years ago – tatty but vibrant, unpretentious and friendly. Regular live music, art exhibitions and even a book exchange all add to the impression that this is more than your usual bar. It's understandably popular (for those 'in the know', at least) and, in a pattern reminiscent of Shoreditch, another sign that King's Cross is becoming the place to be. Put simply this is a great bar and is wholly recommended.

FEATURES:  

HANDY FOR: British Library

McGlynns

RATING:

1–5 Whidborne St
WC1H 8ET
020 7916 9816

It's often the way that the more pleasant the exterior of the pub, the more attractive the interior. That's certainly the case here, where a colourfully painted frontage gives way to a well-cared-for boozer that has all the charms you'd expect of a hidden-away backstreet pub. Food at lunchtime for the experienced locals comes from a country-kitchen-style café at the back of the pub (china plates, Welsh dresser – all the works), whilst at night the workers and a few media types settle in for a pint or two, perhaps as a respite from the nearby Clerkenwell bars. It's the sort of place where you'd expect to find Neil Diamond and Chas and Dave on the jukebox (all present and correct) as well as some choice Irish balladeers (the work of Sean Wilson is especially favoured here). The south side of King's Cross isn't the most salubrious area of London to be walking around in but a few drinks here will see you right.

FEATURES:  

HANDY FOR: British Library

Queen's Head

RATING:

66 Acton Street
WC1X 9NB
020 77113 5772

An excellent, solid local. Generally good beers are on tap – though they only had Adnam's Bitter on last time we were in – and a decent mixed clientele but none too crowded. The music can be a bit loud, but it tends to add to the atmosphere. The menu is extensive and cheap and the portions huge – the home-made steak and Guinness pie sounds fantastic – and the service is excellent. It does get a little quiet during the day, which makes it a good place to meet people near King's Cross when you don't want a formal meeting. You wouldn't necessarily make a detour to admire the architecture – the pub is basically a hollowed-out Victorian shell with some of its original splendour still intact. That said, the façade is still in good nick and jolly handsome it is too and there is excellent tilework on the bits of the original pub that still remain inside. Good show.

FEATURES:      

HANDY FOR: British Library

Smithy's

RATING:

15–17 Leeke Street
WC1X 9HZ
020 7278 5949

A former blacksmiths, Smithy's proclaims itself to be a wine bar, but it's more than that. Laid out across two rooms, a smaller bar with cosy booths and the original cobbled floor and a larger area with tables. The food on offer is very good, with a bar menu and a full bistro-type menu offered. Brunch is available on the weekends, with rather fine roasts served on Sundays. The weekday lunch deals are excellent, and their chips are definitely some of the best we've tasted. But what you'll come here for is the drink. An extensive wine list is a given in a place like this, with plenty of fizz and no fewer than three rosés to choose from as well as a recent cocktail menu. But beers don't fall short of the mark either, with Sharp's Doom Bar hitting the spot on our last visit. The staff are friendly and attentive, which it has to be said is unusual around this area. The last few years' boom in the creative industries has seen a burst of new venues opening, many of which are really a triumph of style over substance. Smithy's is different. Try it: you're as welcome to come in for a pint and some crisps as you are for a bottle of vintage champagne and a three-course meal.

FEATURES:   

HANDY FOR: British Library

Bunch of Grapes

RATING:

207 Brompton Road
SW3 1LA
020 7589 4944

Architecturally, the Bunch of Grapes is excellent. Most of the features are 19th century and the pub still retains vestiges of the public bar and snug. Nice. The Bunch of Grapes offers an upstairs restaurant, a range of decent drinks, bar food and unobtrusive music for your enjoyment and the only downside is that it's located in a heavily touristy area (and shoppers), which, as ever, results in a very transient clientele and a constant tide of traffic in and out of the pub. Still, it's worth chancing a look if you're in need of refreshment.

FEATURES:  **HANDY FOR:** Victoria & Albert Museum, Natural History Museum

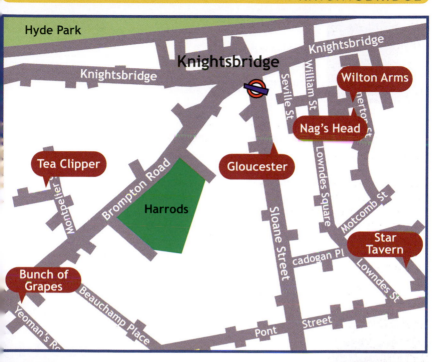

The Gloucester

RATING: 3

187 Sloane Street
SW1X 9QR
020 7235 0298

Surprisingly for its location, the Gloucester is still just a pub. We're sure the temptation was there just to gut the place and turn it into A. N. Other bar, but this has been resisted. There have been some small moves to modernise it and it now offers a more modern selection – Staropramen and Leffe are on the bar now alongside the real ales, including Bombardier, Greene King's IPA and Pride being on when we were in last. The menu's good, too, if a bit predictable, but then they're only meeting their customers' demands, no doubt. There are a few cosy corners and there's another whole bar upstairs (which is available for hire). The Gloucester is very close to all those upmarket boutiques, and is no doubt a haven for the husbands/boyfriends/sugar daddies, if not for the shoppers themselves. Amidst all the glitz and glamour it's a genuine oasis in a shopping desert.

FEATURES:  

Nag's Head

RATING: 4

53 Kinnerton Street
SW1X 8ED
020 7235 1135

Hidden away in a quiet Knightsbridge street, this is one well worth searching out. Wood panelled, low ceilinged and full of old penny arcade games, this pub has a character all of its own and is ideal for a leisurely afternoon of drinking. Unsurprisingly, there's not a TV or a jukebox in sight (but there is a 'What the Butler Saw' machine in the corner). In such a carefully realised environment playing CDs can seem a tad incongruous, but the choices from the bar are usually spot on (Nina Simone when we last looked in). The pub's independent nature comes from its landlord who, when not insisting that customers hang up their coats, is improvising quality pub food with whatever comes to hand (the shepherd's pie is especially recommended). None of this old-style quality comes cheap, however; even if we don't mind too much, be warned that the beer prices are surprisingly steep. We've also seen them kick out punters who persistently ignore the 'no mobile phones' signs. Top bloke, top pub.

FEATURES: 

The Star Tavern

RATING:

6 Belgrave Mews West
SW1X 8HT
020 7235 3019

Some would have you think (wrongly, we believe) that the Great Train Robbers supped here whilst pondering their cunning plan, but the Star Tavern doesn't need hackneyed gangster chic to attract the punters. Being on the small side and located in a mews at the back of a number of large embassies, it's not the place for a rowdy night out. But what you do get is a good selection of well-kept Fuller's ales and traditional pub food, served up by attentive staff who seem genuinely chuffed that you're frequenting their pub. The clientele is more mixed than many of the other boozers in the area – and the punters' accents hint at their work locations; it's also one of the few pubs in the area open at the weekend. Other attractions include a lovely upstairs bar and possibly the smallest gents' toilets in London. It can be a bit of a trek finding this place, and it can fill up rapidly, but it's definitely worth the effort.

FEATURES:  

Tea Clipper

RATING:  

19 Montpelier Street
SW7 1HF
020 7589 5251

From the outside the Tea Clipper promises a good, cosy, English pub experience. Inside, unfortunately, it falls a little short of the mark. It still has some Victorian stuff (mainly the windows) but most of the rest of the interior has been restored or faked. The nautical theme is there, but a little understated. However, following a recent relaunch, the beer on the three hand pumps is pretty good, particularly the Hogsback Brewery's T.E.A. beer and the food's also improved with a new menu and pretty prompt service, even when the pub's busy. It is easy to see why it's popular with the locals – particularly on a warm evening, as it's a nice place to sit outside and enjoy a little sun.

FEATURES:    

HANDY FOR: Victoria & Albert Museum

Wilton Arms

RATING:

71 Kinnerton Street
SW1X 8ED
020 7235 4854

Kinnerton Street is a quaint little street hidden away in the depths of Knightsbridge. It's the sort of street that wouldn't look out of place in the centre of a sleepy hamlet in the West Country or the Cotswolds. Naturally, in such a street you'd expect to find a pub or two and you'll be pleased to hear that there are indeed a couple of decent pubs and one of them is the Wilton Arms. Nowadays it's a Shepherd Neame pub so you can be pretty sure the beer is up to scratch and the food's not bad either – a wide variety of pub grub on the blackboard available most of the week (but not weekends). However, the downside is this is an affluent area, so things are pretty pricey (this is where the village analogy falls down) so an extended session is, unfortunately, only for the well-heeled. The service is prompt and friendly and there's usually a good mix of people – although most are visitors rather than locals. It's a decent enough pub and, because others in the area might attract a lot more attention, at busy times of the day you stand a good chance of getting a seat here.

FEATURES: 

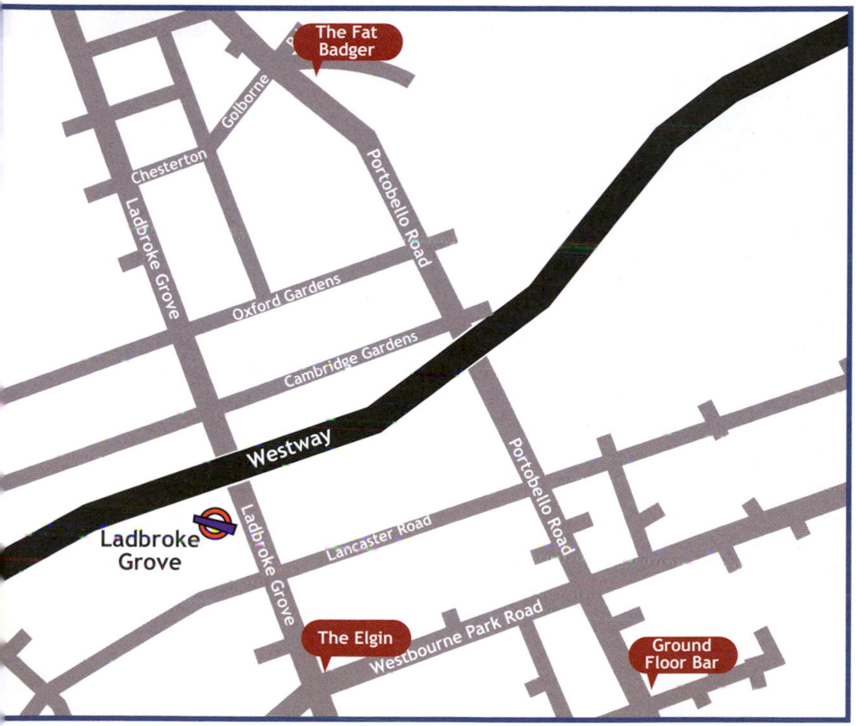

The Fat Badger
Golborne
Chesterton
Ladbroke Grove
Portobello Road
Oxford Gardens
Cambridge Gardens
Westway
Ladbroke Grove
Lancaster Road
Portobello Road
The Elgin
Westbourne Park Road
Ground Floor Bar

The Elgin

RATING: 

96 Ladbroke Grove
W11 1PY
020 7229 5663

We can remember when this was part of the old Firkin chain ('old' is a relative term, of course – about a decade ago they went out of business and sold all their pubs). It's retained a lot of the Victorian interior, with some modernisation in terms of furniture, but has kept a lot of the glass and tilework from its heyday. Despite attempts to make it more upmarket and gastro, it's still a solid, traditional local pub. It's a big place, with a reasonable selection of beers from the continent and real ales on the hand pumps. The pub grub is decently priced for this part of town and the overall impression is of a fine pub, whether for passing punters just after one or locals settling in for a longer session.

FEATURES:      

HANDY FOR: Portobello Road Market

The Fat Badger

RATING:

310 Portobello Road
W10 5TA
020 8969 4500

Having settled in over the last 18 months, this one is now firmly in the gastro zone which, while not always a success, seems to work well enough here. The locals like it and we have to admit that it doesn't have the pretentiousness (or should we say 'as much'?) of other places in the area. The menu looks good, if the prices are on a par with the neighbourhood. The interior isn't that huge, and is laid out with the familiar gastro furnishings of leather sofas and armchairs, chandeliers and exclusive wallpaper. As for the drink on offer, a lengthy wine list looked worthy of investigation, but Timothy Taylor Landlord is the only ale on tap for the real ale drinkers. While not necessarily one to cross London for, it's worth a look if you're in the area.

FEATURES:    

HANDY FOR: Portobello Road Market

Ground Floor Bar

RATING: 

186 Portobello Road
W11 1LA
020 7243 8701

Handy for the Electric Cinema, this place was one of the earlier pubs round here to get the bar treatment. Now decorated in bohemian chic, it attracts a certain clientele from the local community, but doesn't seem to cater for the market traders any longer. And, at these prices, it's not surprising. Over £5 a pint for a Weissbier is exorbitant in a hotel, much less in a bar on the Portobello Road – we had to check and see if we'd been mugged when we left, as our wallets were that much lighter. They have put a single real ale on, probably as a way to stop the whinging at the prices for everything else. The Ground Floor is typical of the genre – with its squashy settees, laidback tunes and smug clientele – so, if that's your scene, you'll be happy here; if you're into beer you'll need an alternative.

FEATURES:    

HANDY FOR: Electric Cinema, Portobello Road Market

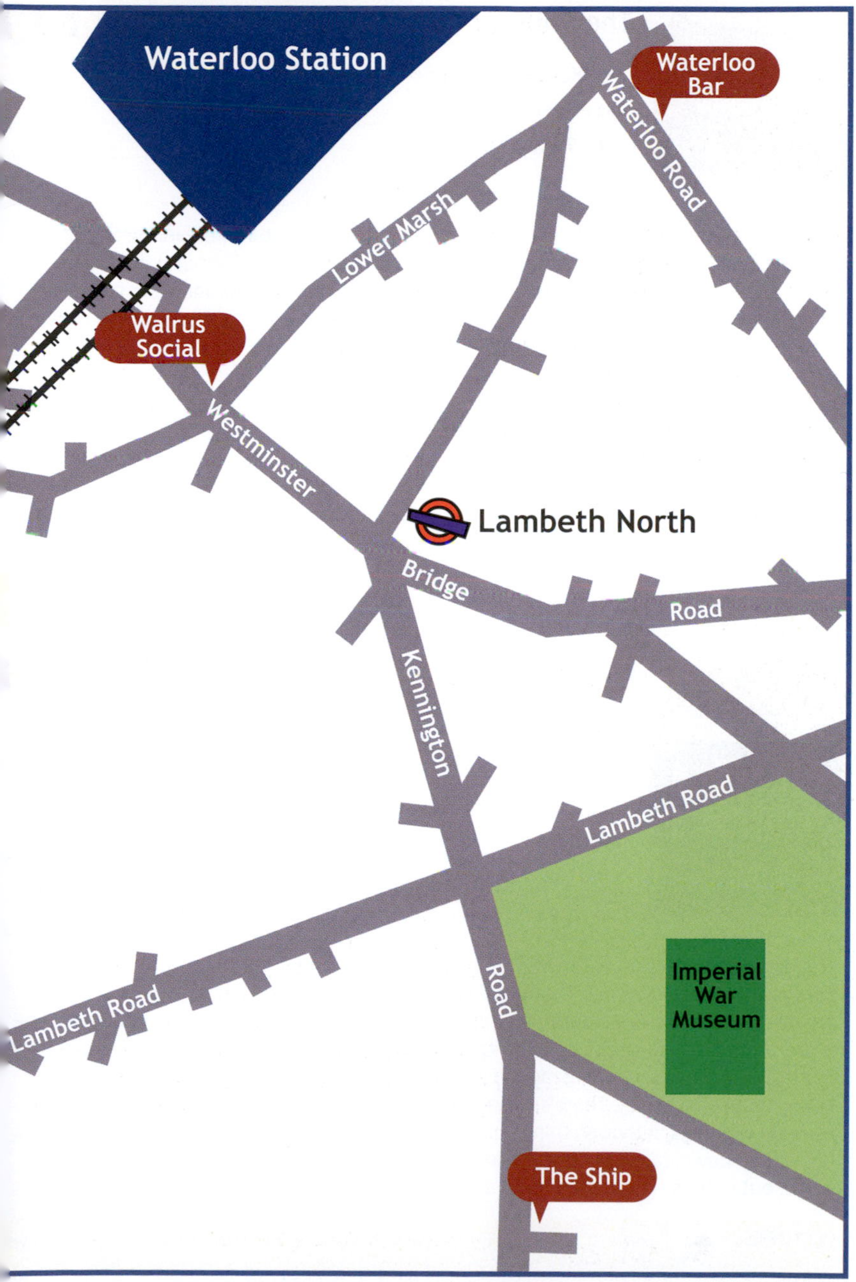

Waterloo Station
Waterloo Bar
Waterloo Road
Lower Marsh
Walrus Social
Westminster
Lambeth North
Bridge
Road
Kennington
Lambeth Road
Lambeth Road
Road
Imperial War Museum
The Ship

The Ship

RATING:

171 Kennington Road
SE11 6SF
020 7735 1371

The Ship is a handsome Victorian pub located in a bit of a no-man's land between Lambeth, Kennington and Elephant and Castle. Unless you lived around here, you probably wouldn't entertain the idea of a visit to the area and, in doing so, you'd be missing a top local. The pub sits on the busy Kennington Road, at the edge of a rather nice Victorian Square, that's just hidden away from view, from whence it predominantly draws its clientele. It's a friendly place, the staff are welcoming and everyone seems to know everyone else. There's a constant stream of people in and out of the place, even on a miserable Monday evening – creating a lively, but relaxed atmosphere. There are a couple of real ales on the hand pumps – Pride and Courage Best, and the usual gas-propelled brigade if you're not feeling the desire for ale. The closest you'll get to a gastro menu are the bar snacks and £2.50 toasties you can get all day. The interior of the pub is a cosy dark-wood affair, arranged as a few separate areas around a central bar, with a pool table in one of them – you can create your own space, or you can join in with the crowd, it's that kind of place. The Ship is friendly, comfortable and unpretentious and fits in well with its environment.

FEATURES:      **HANDY FOR:** Imperial War Museum, The Old Vic

The Walrus Social

RATING: 

172 Westminster Bridge Road
SE1 7RW
020 7928 4368

The Walrus Social is an old Lower Marsh boozer (once the Red Lion) that's been adapted for a bar clientele. There's still the air of a pub to the place; although there are no real ales, there's a pretty standard range of beers on tap and, as it aspires to be a bar, there are also spirits and cocktails. The word 'social' may appear in this place's name, but it ain't no working men's club – prices here are definitely in bar territory, being somewhat pricey. There's a function room upstairs that used to host music and comedy evenings, although things have been quiet on that front recently and there's a big screen downstairs for the the sport. It's quite lively here towards the end of the week, but in these parts there's not a great deal of competition.

FEATURES:  **HANDY FOR:** Imperial War Museum, London Eye

LAMBETH NORTH

Waterloo Bar and Kitchen

RATING: 3 pints

131 Waterloo Road
SE1 8UR
020 7928 5086

A gastropub (actually more of a restaurant), for sure, but one that is straightforwardly classy, rather than pretentious. The Waterloo Bar and Kitchen is popular in the early evenings with those en route to the nearby Old Vic, and the food is excellent. As far as the drinks go, there's a reasonable range of continental beers, including a German wheat beer that puts the stuff they sell in Sam Smith's pubs to shame. In many ways this is much more of a place to eat in, rather than just to drink, but we hear that those only popping in for liquid refreshment are made at home by the welcoming staff. All in all, the Waterloo Bar and Kitchen is a reassuringly civilised and enjoyable place to spend some time.

FEATURES:  

HANDY FOR: London Imax Cinema, The Old Vic

LANCASTER GATE

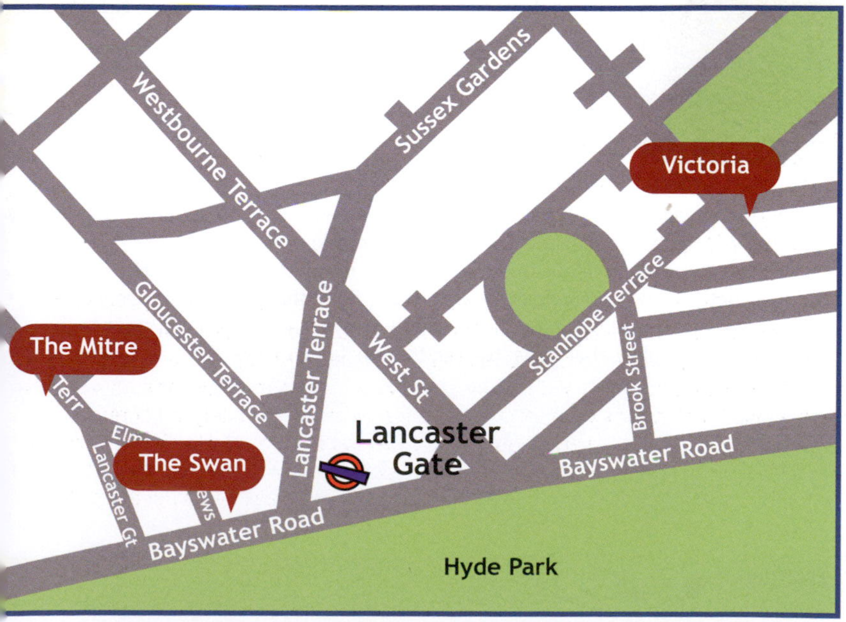

The Mitre

RATING:

24 Craven Terrace
W2 3QH
020 7262 5240

Given the rather drastic refits they've overseen in the last year or so, we were slightly concerned to see what Young's would do to the Mitre's Victorian interior. So, deep breaths were taken and thanks given when we discovered that very little has been altered here: the fittings are still intact and the back room still has the air of restful repose that seems almost custom built for pipe smoking. This one's hardly a museum piece though, and on our last visit a steady band of local regulars were in situ at the bar. We've long held this as one of the best pubs in the area, and the change of ownership hasn't altered our opinion: the food may be pricier than before and the upstairs now a diners-only space, but this one's very much a case of if it ain't broke, don't change it (much).

FEATURES:  

The Swan

RATING:

66 Bayswater Road
W2 3PH
020 7262 5204

This is a quintessential tourist pub: an old building which has been rather charmlessly updated and that sits opposite Hyde Park. Most of the punters head for the beer garden to escape the jukebox, but unfortunately any chances of a peaceful drink are roundly shattered by the traffic of the Bayswater Road thundering past. Only of note if you're meeting up with mates as there's plenty of room inside and it is close to the Tube. If you're actually after a real boozer, though, head elsewhere.

FEATURES:   

Victoria

RATING: 

10a Strathearn Place
W2 2NH
020 7724 1191

A very fine old-fashioned corner pub, inside a little smaller than it looks from the outside, but with a stunning Victorian interior – all etched mirrors, intricate tilework and two fires (the recently repainted exterior manages to even add to the grandeur). Thankfully the fare matches the setting – well-kept Fuller's ales, a large, well-priced menu and friendly service. Also of note are the rooms upstairs, a function room that resembles the library of a gentleman's club and a bar built from the décor of the demolished Gaiety Theatre's bar (allegedly). Sure, it's plush and opulent but there's still a local-pub feel to the place and everyone is made to feel welcome. This part of London has some quality pubs, but this one is the pick of them for us.

FEATURES:    

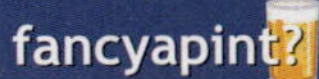

LEICESTER SQUARE

Soho Square
Charing Cross Road
Shaftesbury Avenue
Greek St
Frith St
Dean St
Cambridge
Three Greyhounds
Marquis of Granby
Moor St
Spice of Life
Old Compton Street
Tower St
West St
Upper St Martin's L
Admiral Duncan
Coach & Horses
Romilly St
Litchfield St
French House
Wardour St
De Hems
Gerrard Pl
Newport Pl
Salvador & Amanda
Long Acre
Gt Newport St
Lamb & Flag
Gerrard Street
Lt Newport St
Leicester Square
Cranbourn St
Garrick Street
Whitcomb St
Lisle Street
Leicester Pl
Cork & Bottle
Leicester St
Bear St
Salisbury
Roundhouse
Bear & Staff
Green Man
Leicester Square
Moon Under Water
Coventry St
Irving Street
St Martin's Lane
Charing Cross Road

Admiral Duncan

RATING:

54 Old Compton Street
W1D 4UD
020 7437 5300

There's been a pub on this site for quite a while – we can remember at least one previous incarnation, more traditional, but still one of London's premier gay pubs. It's always been a friendly and easy-going place, and the current version is just as welcoming, with the lurid chartreuse walls making it seem pretty intimate. Don't get us wrong, we're not always opponents of change, but it is somehow reassuring that places like this carry on and do the job they always have. Lager, cider and Guinness are the prime tipples, with numerous alcopops and varieties of shots available too. And to top it all off, there's a fab Top of the Pops jukebox in the corner, playing chart hits from the 70s, 80s and 90s. One word of warning, this place gets pretty packed on the weekends primarily because of where it's located in the heart of Soho. If it sounds like your sort of place, give it a go.

FEATURES:   

HANDY FOR: National Gallery, National Portrait Gallery

Bear & Staff

RATING:  

11 Bear Street
WC2H 7AS
020 7930 5260

A friendly enough pub on Charing Cross Road, which given its proximity to Leicester Square is seldom quiet. There's nothing that remarkable about it, other than it fits the image for many visitors to London of what a pub is – real ales, traditional pub grub – yet it also has a fair number of more regular punters, perhaps somewhat surprisingly. Its location does make it a great place to meet up near the National Gallery or theatreland all around it; it's fairly obvious on Charing Cross Road and hard to miss. And, as it's part of the Nicholson's chain, the beer is well kept and there's a good variety of it, as well – try their 'sup before you tup' scheme to taste the beer before you buy it, if you're uncertain what you're getting. Go on, give it a go – it's a touch above your usual West End pub – but that's enough.

FEATURES: 

HANDY FOR: National Gallery, National Portrait Gallery

The Cambridge

RATING:

93 Charing Cross Road
WC2H 0DP
020 7494 0338

Another easy-to-find pub in the West End, which seems to be doing pretty well since its move into the Nicholson's chain. These pubs make a play for the tourist market, with prominent signs for 'traditional fish and chips' and notices making as much mention as they can of the pubs' history. The overall effect is not unlike that of the Sam Smith's pubs in London: the chains sharing a lack of TVs and an attachment to recreating 'traditional' pub interiors. Whereas the Sam pubs offer a variety of interiors, the West End Nicholson's are rather more of a type, with their similar furnishings. On our most recent visit, the Cambridge was certainly pulling in a crowd of overseas visitors, though not too many seemed willing to try the four different ales on tap (and available on 'try before you buy'). This one fits the bill as a pub to meet up in and there's always the upstairs room – which everyone seems to miss, somehow.

FEATURES:  

HANDY FOR: National Gallery, National Portrait Gallery

Coach & Horses

RATING: 

29 Greek Street
W1D 5DH
020 7437 5920

Even though its long-standing landlord has retired, this one hasn't changed (yet). It's a dump, really. A famous dump, but still a dump. Famous for its clientele, you'll find the Coach crowded of an evening with punters looking for famous people and regaling each other with (often) second-hand stories of past times. If you need a pint and you're in the area, there are other, more accommodating places not far away – although we quite like it here weekday afternoons when it's quiet and the sarnies, unlike the beer, are cheap.

FEATURES: 

HANDY FOR: National Gallery, National Portrait Gallery

Cork and Bottle

RATING:

44–46 Cranbourn Street
WC2H 7AN
020 7734 7807

First up, an admission: you can't get a pint here. No Adnam's, no Young's, no Pride – not even a Guinness. Not a pub then, but a wine bar. But what a bar. This place has been setting the standards for wine bars since the early 1970s and the onus of the place is still on quality wines, lovely food and an agreeable atmosphere to enjoy them in. Even more remarkable is that this haven is located so close to the tacky horrors of Leicester Square. And whilst this place isn't a pub it shares the qualities of all good pubs: first-rate food and drink, staff that actually care about their customers (whether they be regulars or first-timers) and an overall atmosphere of cheery drink taking. The only downside is that, as the place has been so good for so long, the secret's out so turning up early (or phoning ahead) is sometimes necessary to guarantee a space. Otherwise, though, this one shares qualities with some of the wines behind the bar, being subtle, charming and damn near perfect.

HANDY FOR: National Gallery, National Portrait Gallery

De Hems

RATING: 

11 Macclesfield Street
W1D 5BW
020 7437 2494

This one wavered in our affections after a change of ownership diluted the unique Dutchness on offer here. Safe to say, the company in charge saw sense and this one quickly returned to a format of continental beers accompanied by a Low Countries menu (Bitterballen, Frikandel etc.). Always one of the most popular pubs in Soho – the ground-floor bar quickly becomes standing room only – we'd advise getting here early or giving a look upstairs, before giving up hope of a space.

FEATURES:  

HANDY FOR: National Gallery, National Portrait Gallery

French House

RATING: 2

49 Dean Street
W1D 5BE
020 7437 2799

This place hasn't really changed in decades (except for the landlord's retirement). Famous for being famous, small, crowded and one of the few exceptions to our rule that all pubs we include serve pints – they only serve halves and always have. It's got a strong history, French beer on tap alongside the usual suspects, and friendly staff that cope well with the crowds of customers. The atmosphere can sometimes be a bit unfriendly, and similar to that found in a lot of local pubs (for local people) and a clientele that could provide the dictionary definition of 'arrogant'. But when it's a little quieter – say in the afternoons – it's pretty good. The tiny interior's panelled walls are covered in photos of French film, stage and sport stars from the beginning of the last century, and it does have a bit of the flavour of a Tabac in darkest France. While we have to admire their Gallic resistance to change, this one really is better of an afternoon with the paper and a quiet half.

FEATURES:   **HANDY FOR:** National Gallery, National Portrait Gallery

Green Man & French Horn

RATING: 3

54 St Martin's Lane
WC2N 4EA
020 7836 7644

The Green Man & French Horn is a refreshingly ordinary pub in an area packed with tourist traps and trendy cash-ins. There are three decent beers on the hand pumps – Adnam's Broadside and Explorer plus the far less often seen Bateman's Valiant, when we were last in. There's a reasonable wine list, a selection of other beers and spirits and plenty of cheap pub grub (mains under £8). It's a long, narrow pub, so it's quite easily filled, but, surprisingly, it's often emptier than surrounding venues. Service is prompt and polite and the atmosphere friendly – we're just surprised there aren't a lot more people in here.

FEATURES:   **HANDY FOR:** National Gallery, Trafalgar Square

Lamb & Flag

RATING:

33 Rose Street
WC2E 9EB
020 7497 9504

This pub is pretty famous in these parts, so it ought not to need much of an introduction. It's a genuinely old, higgledy-piggledy place, with bare floorboards, plenty of dark-wood panelling and little brass plaques commemorating previous punters. It's just the sort of Olde Worlde Englishe Pubbe that tourists expect to see (especially if they're here for the first time) and they love it. It might be a tourist cliché, but, even for the most cynical of hardcore pub-goers, it's a jolly decent pub. It serves well-kept Young's beer and decent pub grub and, as a result of its location and fame, you'll usually find it to be pretty packed. If you can fight your way up the narrow stairs you can find a quieter spot or, if you're lucky, even a seat. If you're in the area and it looks quiet, do go in and have a pint and a nosey around. And if you like cheery, crowded, old-fashioned pubs you won't be disappointed here.

FEATURES:  **HANDY FOR:** National Gallery, National Portrait Gallery

Marquis of Granby

RATING: 

142 Shaftesbury Avenue
WC2H 8HJ
020 7836 8609

We've known this pub for years, and have always had a bit of a soft spot for it after many an afternoon or evening spent here. Fit and working again after a recent refurb, the Marquis has been smartened up, its new décor evoking theatrical times past with a selection of theatre memorabilia (drapes, old opera programmes). Although, with an interior not too dissimilar to many a gastropub, you might expect the menu to be upgraded too, but you'd be wrong. On our last visit, the bar menu merely consisted of a list of quality sandwiches. The beer selection was decent enough and things are clearly governed over by a landlord of the old school. It is worth noting as well that this one fills up for the football and the rugby – it may not be what the tourists are after, but it does make a change for the area. All in all, the pick of the pubs around Cambridge Circus.

FEATURES:  **HANDY FOR:** National Gallery, Trafalgar Square

Moon Under Water

RATING:

28 Leicester Square
WC2H 7LE
020 7839 2837

Nowadays, this is one of the smaller Wetherspoon pubs, which is especially surprising given the location. As ever, as it's a Wetherspoon pub, cheap booze and food are on offer, without the distractions of music, pool and TV. However, its claustrophobic interior (low ceilings) means it is a very, very noisy place to inhabit. The service is incredibly prompt and attentive and it's easy for your out-of-town mates to find – you could do far worse in the immediate vicinity.

FEATURES:  

HANDY FOR: National Gallery, Trafalgar Square

The Roundhouse

RATING:  

1 Garrick Street
WC2E 9AR
020 7836 9838

Located slap bang in the middle of town, the Roundhouse manages to serve a decent pint in the midst of the madness that is Covent Garden without leaving you feeling like it's the End of Days. For those of us not members of the nearby Garrick Club, this place offers a handy spot for meeting up and moving on from after an introductory pint. Although not the sort of place you'd want to spend all night in, it offers a warm welcome and a big-screen TV for sports events.

FEATURES:   

HANDY FOR: National Gallery, Trafalgar Square

Salisbury

RATING: 3/3

90 St Martin's Lane
WC2N 4AP
020 7836 5863

The Salisbury is an ornate, well-preserved gin palace, built at the height of Victorian extravagance. The interior is a wonder of etched glass, mirrors and mahogany. Coupled with some charming ornate art nouveau light fittings, you begin to appreciate there aren't many of these once commonplace pubs left in such good nick. The past touristy excesses of the pub have been thankfully toned down (we didn't see any of the tacky T-shirts which were once sold here) and the focus seems to have shifted in the right direction – it was a pleasant surprise to find no fewer than six ales on offer. If you visit at busy times (after work, pre-and post-theatre) the chance to get the best seats is rather limited, but, considering our visit found the place with an agreeable atmosphere, very good service and a surprisingly mixed crowd, we didn't begrudge propping up the bar for a pint.

FEATURES:  

HANDY FOR: National Gallery, Trafalgar Square

Salvador & Amanda

RATING: 3/3

8 Great Newport Street
WC2H 7JA
020 7240 1551

Not a pub, but given this area doesn't have many great pubs we don't have a problem recommending a decent bar. Taking its name from Senor Dali and his muse of the 60s, this basement bar doubles as a Tapas venue, though it's hardly the sort of place that you'll stand out in if you just stick to a drink. This place prides itself on sangria and cocktails, though a decent range of spirits and bottled beers are also available. It's a fair-sized space, darkly lit with an array of tables to cope with small or large groups. Heartening too, they haven't gone overboard on the Dali theme – a few black and white photos of the man and his muse. That sort of subtlety works in its favour and, although it's got some of the bar features we're not keen on (your change on a tray, for example), it doesn't go too far down that route. A cut above your average West End bar then, but it manages to evade the exclusive nature of London's swankier drinking holes. Stylish yes, pretentious no. And if you're after a late night, this one's open till 2am Mon–Thur and 3am at weekends (though you'll have to pay to get in after 9pm).

FEATURES: 

HANDY FOR: National Gallery, Trafalgar Square

Spice of Life

RATING:

37–39 Romilly Street
W1D 5AN
020 7437 7013

This a large pub in a in a prime location, which, of course, is what brings it down – it's smack bang in the heart of the theatre district, bringing through a constant tide of people flowing in and out as they make their way to and from the shows. Especially in the evenings, when all the regulars have gone home to suburbia. Being a McMullen pub, the choice of beers is not your usual West End selection and they've got a good pub grub menu. This pub's OK, and a good place to meet because of its prominent location, but it's not necessarily one you would go out of your way for. And there's live music (jazz features heavily in the schedule) in the basement every night of the week.

FEATURES:    **HANDY FOR:** National Gallery, National Portrait Gallery

Three Greyhounds

RATING:  

25 Greek Street
W1D 5DD
020 7494 0902

The Three Greyhounds is a mock-Tudor extravaganza that's been lovingly restored by its owners to its former glory. There's a good range of well-kept beers on the hand pumps and an extensive food menu which is heavily promoted. We'd like to give it a higher rating, but the size of the pub works against it – you only need little more than a handful of people to make the place feel pretty crowded and, given where this pub is, it's easily achieved. Nevertheless, it's a Nicholson's and, with the excellent beers on offer, this place is a pretty good pub.

FEATURES:    **HANDY FOR:** National Gallery, National Portrait Gallery

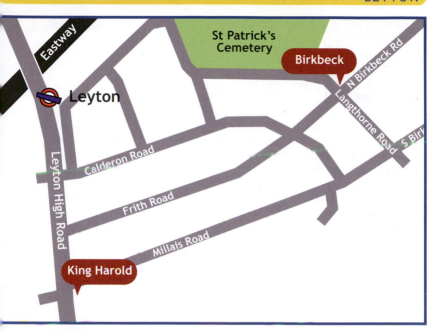

St Patrick's Cemetery
Birkbeck
Eastway
Leyton
N Birkbeck Rd
Langthorne Road
S Birk
Calderon Road
Leyton High Road
Frith Road
Millais Road
King Harold

Birkbeck

RATING:

45 Langthorne Rd
E11 4HL
020 8539 2584

This imposing locals' pub hasn't really changed much since we started going here almost a decade ago, which is no bad thing. Made up of a large public bar and a smaller room at the front with a pool table, it's a decent pub. It still sells 'Rita's Special', a bitter named after a previous landlady, apparently, as well as a rotating line-up of guest beers which don't stick around very long. The local darts team meets here, as evidenced by the trophies in the cabinet over the door to the front bar. One of the dart boards is placed near the doorway to the large, kid-friendly, beer garden, and requires good timing to get outside if there's a game on. Populated by friendly locals and genial bar staff, it's got a lot going for it. Now, if they only did Sunday lunch...

FEATURES:         

LEYTON

King Harold

RATING: 3

116 High Road
E15 2BX
020 8558 3635

This large, lively, friendly local shows how it should be done. OK, the beer won't have CAMRA members creaming their jeans, although the only ale appears to be Toby (we've not seen that anywhere else for years), but there's enough of a range to keep all but the most fussy drinkers happy and the service is friendly, prompt and attentive. The locals are more than fine with outsiders being in their pub – possibly down to its nearness to Leyton Orient's ground – and there are loads of activities to keep people happy (even a large beer garden in case we get something resembling a summer). Any time of day it seems to have a buzzing clientele. Long may it last. Cheers!

FEATURES:     

LIMEHOUSE (DLR)

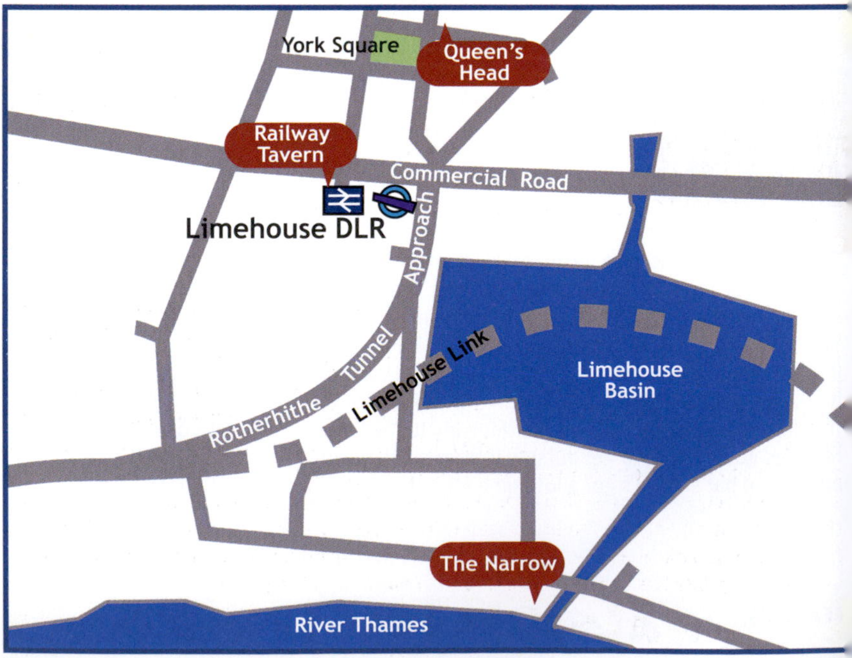

The Narrow

RATING:

Narrow Street
E14 8DP
020 7592 7950

When it seems all the pubs around London are turning into pub-themed restaurants, Britain's no. 1 foodie, Gordon Ramsay, turns the Narrow Street from a below-par gastropub into a genuine pub with a separate restaurant serving good food. The Narrow's principal attraction is its location at the mouth of Limehouse Basin and a large terrace with a great view of Limehouse Reach. Previously, this didn't compensate for a bad experience, but things have changed for the better. The beers on offer feature a couple of old faithfuls on the hand pumps and the usual suspects on tap, plus a fine range of bottled beers and ciders, along with a pretty fair wine list. The menu is as expected – upmarket traditional British food, and, although prices are more than average, many gastropubs charge comparable amounts for less. Service is friendly and the décor pleasantly understated. The clientele mostly hail from luxury apartments and offices nearby, but it's more mixed than you might imagine. If you just want a drink, you'll find a good atmosphere. This is the most attractive incarnation of the place and long-standing local pubs have a real challenger in their midst.

FEATURES:    

Queen's Head

RATING:  

8 Flamborough Street
E14 7LS
020 7791 2504

Ever been in a Young's pub and wondered where that photo of the Queen Mum pulling a pint comes from? Well, it was here that Her Maj looked the East End in the face (well, midriff) from behind the bar and worked a pump. The pub's changed a bit since then. Externally it's still a traditional Victorian pub in a rather nice Victorian square, but internally it's had a makeover – and not for the better. The walls are now predominately red, with a cream ceiling, the old bar is still there, but there's now an abundance of 21st- century technology, flat-screen TV and projector for the sport, MP3 jukebox, super-cold beer pumps etc. It continues to serve Young's beer on the hand pumps, but the locals nowadays seem to prefer something of a much lower temperature. It's still a friendly enough place and everyone seems to know everyone else, but for the casual visitor the update has removed some of the charm from the place.

FEATURES:    

HANDY FOR: Ragged School Museum

Railway Tavern

RATING:

576 Commercial Road
E14 7JD
020 7790 2360

Being both on the busy and grimy Commercial Road and located more or less underneath a railway bridge, the Railway does have a rather off-putting air to it. However, it's a fairly decent locals' haunt, appealing to both a gay and straight clientele. It's the sort of place where the bar staff greet their regulars as soon as they walk in the door and start pouring drinks in anticipation of their orders. Even with Pride on the hand pumps and Sky TV for the sport, it doesn't have too much to offer the passing pub-goer, but, given the paucity of venues in these parts, it will have to suffice.

FEATURES: 

HANDY FOR: Ragged School Museum

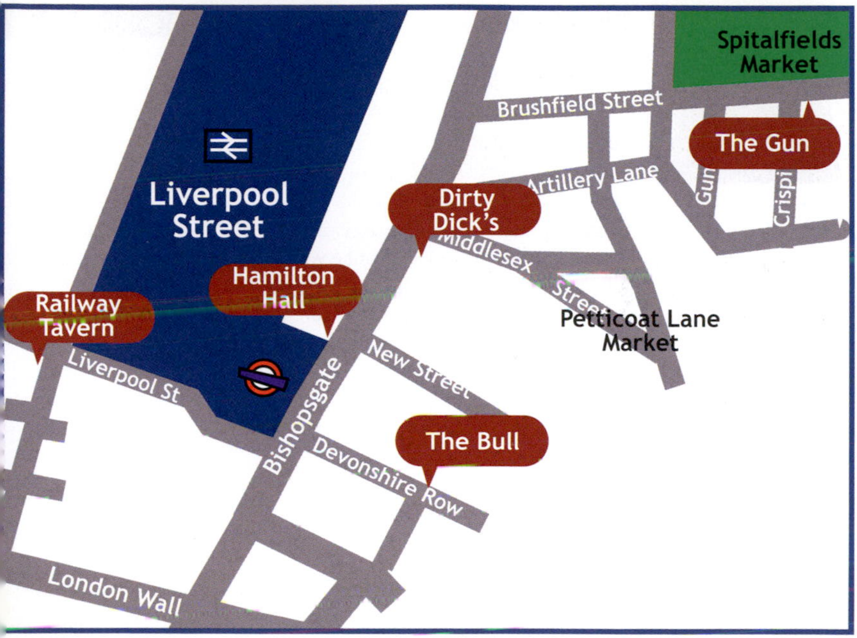

Spitalfields Market
Brushfield Street
The Gun
Liverpool Street
Artillery Lane
Gun
Crispin
Dirty Dick's
Middlesex Street
Hamilton Hall
Railway Tavern
Petticoat Lane Market
Liverpool St
New Street
Bishopsgate
The Bull
Devonshire Row
London Wall

The Bull

RATING: 3 out of 3 beer glasses

2 Devonshire Row
EC2M 4RH
020 7247 6792

The T & J Bernard signage is still intact, but with this pub now firmly tied to the restaurant opposite, this 'bar and restaurant' is just that – a restaurant that serves drinks. What you'll first notice on entering is the interior: a makeover has attempted to pack a mix of contemporary styles into a small, one-roomed space. The leather settles have gone, with tables (mostly set for lunch) taking up most of the space, though a ledge does make its way through the middle of the room for vertical drinkers to lean an elbow upon. The new owners have tried to make this as grand a space as possible. As for the food and drink on offer, gone is the old pub's reliance on real ales: a guest beer Brain's SA was alongside the London Pride pump fighting for space next to premium lagers like Peroni. The food looks as good as you'll get in a pub in these parts and, for City folk wishing to fill up before a 9 o'clock meeting, this one opens at 8am.

FEATURES:    **HANDY FOR:** Petticoat Lane Market, Spitalfields Market

Dirty Dick's

RATING:

202 Bishopsgate
EC2M 4NR
020 7283 5888

This notorious City pub and tourist attraction underwent a facelift a few years ago, unfortunately eradicating all traces of the dive it once was. Its proximity to Liverpool Street Station makes it a popular last stop before getting the train home for many office workers. They serve vast amounts of lager, but can also pour a pint of Guinness and have the usual range of Young's excellent beers on tap. It tends to be very busy around lunch and immediately after work, but quietens down later. The downstairs bar, where all the interesting stuff used to be, can be hired and it now seems to be open at the weekends. There's also an upstairs bar which tends to be a bit quieter.

FEATURES:     

HANDY FOR: Petticoat Lane Market

The Gun

RATING: 

54 Brushfield Street
E1 6AG
020 7247 7988

Many pubs in the Spitalfields area are reinventing themselves as 'bohemian' bars with crappy furniture, louder than usual music, candles, foreign-sounding menus, Smirnoff Ice and all that. Thankfully, this pub has stuck to its guns and presents itself as that increasingly hard-to-find venue – the traditional boozer. It's a regulars' pub, with blokes (mostly) from the offices nearby being ably catered for with decent beer – Broadside, Bombardier, IPA and Deuchars on the hand pumps – food and service with the occasional sporting event on the telly. The upstairs restaurant seems to do a roaring trade at lunchtimes – and the Masons used to meet here, which makes the place all the more interesting.

FEATURES:    

HANDY FOR: Spitalfields Market, Petticoat Lane Market

Hamilton Hall

RATING:

Liverpool Street Station
EC2M 7PY
020 7247 3579

This pub seems to have it all in one package: a dazzlingly ornate interior which was originally a part of the old Great Eastern Hotel (some say it was a banqueting hall, some say a ballroom, it all depends who you ask); and, being Wetherspoon, it has a large range of decent, well-priced beer (especially for the City) and cheap pub grub. Unfortunately, nothing is ever quite as it seems. During the week, it does get very busy with braying City commuters and slightly lost tourists making it difficult to get a drink, much less a drink in peace. It does quieten down later in the evening, however, and we have to give the staff credit – they do a pretty good job and make the best of the circumstances. Weekends make it one to avoid, however; once you've found the weekend crowds and thrown in a soupçcon of pissed footy supporters, you'll have a pretty close approximation of some people's idea of hell.

FEATURES:        

Railway Tavern

RATING: 

15 Liverpool Street
EC2M 7NX
020 7283 3598

Not many pubs in the Square Mile have an ivy-clad exterior; even fewer display the crests of the old railway companies, but then given this pub's name that shouldn't come as a surprise. Shame, then, that this one hasn't many other touches of originality to it. As it's bang opposite the station, it's busy when you'd expect it to be with City commuters and other disparate transients. The beer selection's not bad and there's Sky Sport on the TV, should one feel so inclined. One plus point: it's open at weekends, and so offers an alternative to the nearby Wetherspoon for the weary traveller (safe and sound pub grub too). It does a job, but not quite enough to disprove the old dictum: the closer you get to a mainline train station, the worse the pub. At least it's not as close as Hamilton Hall though...

FEATURES:     

HANDY FOR: Petticoat Lane Market

The Britannia

RATING: 4

44 Kipling Street
SE1 3RU
020 7403 1030

The Britannia is a charming and sympathetically renovated pub around the back of Guy's Hospital. Despite the stripped floorboards, a couch or two and a scattering of statuettes (including Betty Boop), this still feels like a proper pub. Good lighting, quality music and great service are the first things which grab your attention, but the positives don't end here. Accompanying the reasonable choice of ale on tap and some decent grub is a simply staggering list of whiskies. We know a number of pubs in London offer a good selection of whiskies, but the blackboards here indicate that more than 100 are on offer, even if the number of bottles on the shelves behind the bar seem somewhat short of this figure. Despite Borough not being short on excellent places to drink, this relaxed and cosy pub is still one of the better in the area and happily fulfils the description of 'hidden gem'.

FEATURES:  

HANDY FOR: London Dungeons, HMS Belfast

Bunch of Grapes

RATING:

2 St Thomas Street
SE1 9RS
020 7403 2070

This handsome pub (a Grade II listed building) offers the decent selection of beer and food that you would expect from Young's. It also has a pleasant split-level garden to the rear which is ideal for a relaxing drink, and is particularly convenient for meeting people near London Bridge station. Being situated on a busy junction, and in the path of many commuters, means it can get pretty noisy in here, so you're unlikely to linger at commuting times. And don't come here on Sunday, it's closed.

FEATURES:    **HANDY FOR:** London Dungeons

George Inn

RATING: 

77 Borough High Street
SE1 1NH
020 7407 2056

This well-preserved galleried coaching house (owned by the National Trust) off Borough High Street serves a loyal following as well as the innumerable walking/coach tours that visit it. It serves a number of guest beers, including its own George Ale (brewed by Adnam's). All the usual suspects on tap and wines in little bottles of wine are available too. When the weather's good, the outdoor area's one of the best attractions of this pub, as it's a great place to sunbathe and people-watch while having a pint. The George Inn tolerates children and the function room on the first floor is available for hire. These are all plus points, of course, but, in terms of a drinking experience, the George can be disappointing. The bars are often very crowded and it can take an age to get served (and then the service can be pretty haphazard), let alone find a seat. The George seems to be a victim of its own high profile. The cosy room at the far end of the pub, with a fire in winter, retains an antique atmosphere but the other bar areas have been modernised in a rather anonymous way. The historical significance of the George notwithstanding, there are several other pubs that we prefer in this area.

FEATURES:     **HANDY FOR:** London Dungeons

Horniman at Hay's

RATING:

Hay's Galleria, Counter Street
SE1 2BA
020 7407 1991

The Horniman is a huge pub built in a refurbished wharf renamed Hay's Galleria. It's quite picturesque in an Olde Worlde industrial way and consequently captures a lot of the tourists passing on the way to Tower Bridge or the Globe. The pub is large and sprawls over the ground floor of one side of the wharf on the riverside. It's all been done up in a tiled, Victoriana Turkish-bath style which doesn't quite convince you that it's for real (which it isn't). However, the pub and its surrounding area manage to accommodate the crowds without feeling too stuffed so it doesn't get too uncomfortable, although Fridays are usually pretty manic. As well as the main bar, the pub has two extra areas, the downstairs Wharfside Cellar Bar and the upstairs Mezzanine for dining, along with a spot outside with views of the Thames. Service can be slow at busy times, resulting in a thirsty wait; at least the range of drinks is solid, with us counting five ales on tap. If you can find it during a quiet moment, it's worth popping in when you're passing it on the way to the nearby tourist attractions.

FEATURES:       

HANDY FOR: HMS Belfast

The Market Porter

RATING:

9 Stoney Street
SE1 9AA
020 7407 2495

This is a gem of a pub – it's got something for everyone no matter what time or day of the week you choose to visit. It's a lively place on Friday and Saturday nights with a mixed crowd and a real pub atmosphere. The food is OK, there's a restaurant upstairs, and the drink is excellent. There's an interesting and very well-kept range of beers on the hand pumps – the regular is Harvey's and some unusual beers and old favourites make up the rest, changing pretty regularly. A great pub that's worth going out of your way for and what with the recent refurbishment and extension of the back room there's now more chance of getting a seat. But it does get very, very busy when Borough Market is on (Fridays and Saturdays), with traders and visitors alike piling in.

FEATURES:    

HANDY FOR: Borough Market, London Dungeons

Miller of Mansfield

RATING:

96 Snowsfields
SE1 3SS
020 7407 2690

Nestling behind Guy's Hospital, the Miller of Mansfield is a welcome change from London's gastro makeover circuit, offering drinkers a great space to park themselves. There are no surprises on the beer front, but the Miller has an ample and affordable wine list, with cocktails offered should you need to let your hair down. The spacious ground floor offers a nice mix of bigger tables for groups, and smaller set-ups for a more intimate level of conversation. It attracts hospital staff, well-behaved King's students and workers from the local environs. Food is on offer and, as the menus say, 'basically we cook food we would like to eat'. Judging by the punters chowing down, they agree. It's reasonably priced, well presented and will fill you up without wishing you'd asked for a pack of McCoy's on the side. The excellent staff are another bonus, getting through the thirsty hordes and keeping everything else ticking over nicely. There's a good-sized function room upstairs, available for hire, with regular music and comedy nights in place. And if you fancy your chances as the next Fast Eddie Felson, there's a rather good red pool table downstairs. Plenty of outdoor seating awaits you when the weather gets a bit warmer, too.

FEATURES:     

Old Thameside Inn

RATING: 

Pickfords Wharf, Clink Street
SE1 9DG
020 7403 4243

The Old Thameside Inn has become well established on the tourist trail; this once overlooked Nicholson's pub is now a hive of activity most of the time. And why not? With fine views of the city from the riverside terrace (if you can get onto it) and a decent range of drinks and food on offer, it's certainly a place you'd give a try if you came across it on holiday. But its very popularity is what lets it down: when there's a crowd in – which is more often the case nowadays – it can be a thirsty wait.

FEATURES:    

HANDY FOR: Tate Modern, Globe Theatre

The Rake

RATING:

14 Winchester Walk
SE1 9AG
020 7407 0557

In addition to being the only pub actually in Borough Market (for at least 100 years), The Rake also claims to be the smallest pub in London and, in our experience, that claim seems to have some substance. The addition of some decking with outdoor seating adds another 200% or so to the available drinking space, which in summer is handy, but a little less useful on a wet and windy winter's evening, although the heaters help. However, it is certainly worth risking a crush to experience some of the exotic and esoteric beers on offer. Founded by the beer specialists Utobeer, who have traded in the market for a few years, you'd expect something special and you won't be disappointed. The range on tap changes very frequently – so it's pointless listing any here as the likelihood is it will have changed by the time you read this – but rest assured, if you like beer, you'll find something you'll like. There's always something that's a cut above average and well kept and, if the pumps don't tempt you, there's an extensive range of bottled beer. Even if you don't fancy a beer, you can always sample the range of ciders and genevers that's also on offer.

FEATURES:   **HANDY FOR:** Borough Market, London Dungeons

Southwark Tavern

RATING: 

22 Southwark Street
SE1 1TU
020 7403 0257

Victorian outside, predominately 1930s and later inside, the Southwark Tavern is a large pub prominently located on the periphery of Borough Market. The ground-floor bar is a typical mix-and-match-furniture affair, with a central bar serving a wide range of drinks – with ales such as Old Hooky, Pride and Abbott on the hand pumps and a good few continentals (e.g. Leffe, Hoegaarden, Fruli) on tap. There are wine and spirits (with a £10 per bottle deal on wines on Mondays) if beer doesn't take your fancy and plenty of food. The Debtors bar downstairs has all sorts of nooks and crannies where you can hide away for those more intimate moments and it's also the location for a popular quiz on Tuesdays. It usually gets pretty crowded immediately after work and you can also find it open early in the day (weekdays – it's not usually open at weekends) to cater for the market crowd.

FEATURES:       **HANDY FOR:** Borough Market

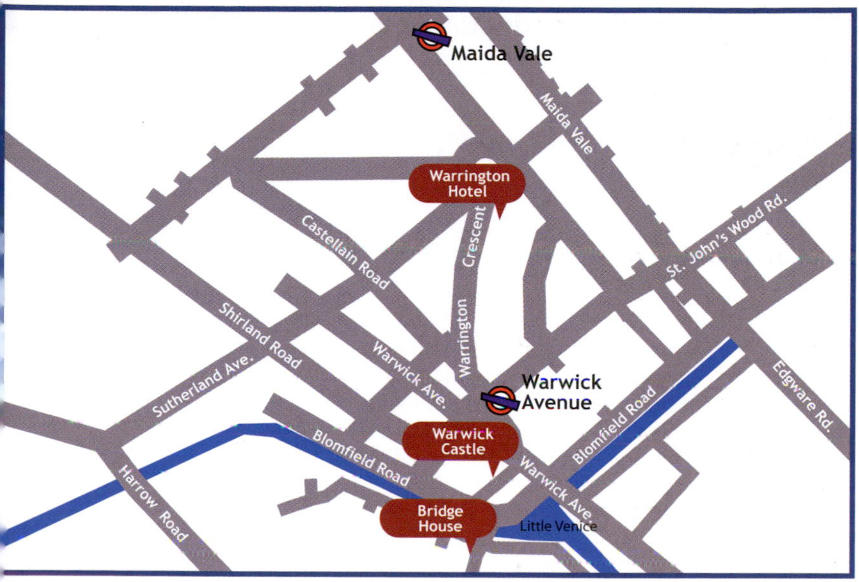

Maida Vale
Maida Vale
Warrington Hotel
Castellain Road
Crescent
Warrington
St. John's Wood Rd.
Shirland Road
Warwick Ave.
Sutherland Ave.
Warwick Avenue
Edgware Rd.
Blomfield Road
Warwick Castle
Blomfield Road
Harrow Road
Warwick Ave.
Bridge House
Little Venice

The Bridge House

RATING: 

13 Westbourne Terrace Road
W2 6NG
020 7432 1361

This place is just great, it must have one of the nicest canalside settings in London, but, when you're in here, all thoughts of narrow boating and other navigational pursuits are quickly forgotten. Set in a grand Neoclassical terrace, you'll easily recognise its 21st-century gastropub aspirations from the interior décor. But this place is not your run-of-the-mill, give it a pretentious name and overcharge for a bit of rocket and focaccia place. It's a place where you come to enjoy good drink, food and company. There's an excellent range of booze on offer on the hand pumps with a number of contintental beers on tap. There's a decent wine list and a choice of champagnes, cocktails and liqueur coffees – all alcoholic preferences seem to be catered for. The food is pretty decent – relatively unpretentious and reasonably priced – the service is good and the atmosphere pretty relaxed. If that's not enough for you, there's *Newsrevue* in the Canal Café Theatre upstairs. The only downside is there are a load of offices round here (with more on the way) and for obvious reasons this is the place of choice for office leaving dos around here. Who could blame them?

FEATURES:    

The Warrington Hotel

RATING:

93 Warrington Crescent
W9 1EH
020 7592 7960

Walking up to the majestic exterior of the Warrington Hotel Pub and crossing the mosaic portico is daunting, and inside is much the same. Acres of new plush crimson carpet, exotic woods, fierce gilt crown mouldings and veined marble columns make one wonder if this is indeed a pub at all. A magnificent Tiffany window sheds calm light on semi-nude art-nouveau nymphs frolicking overhead, framed by chubby cherubs. This is a pub for the discerning imbiber. The thick, engraved drinks menu lists an excellent selection of real ales, draught beers, ciders, bottled beer, wines, spirits and liqueurs. Although recently redone by noted gourmet Gordon Ramsay, his talents are not really visible here. There is a very small menu of bland 'bar snacks' on offer at lunchtime only: the good food is evidently reserved for the upstairs restaurant. In fact, other patrons were asking where the 'real' menu was – they were promptly directed upstairs by the attentive, helpful bar staff. The Warrington is not the place to put up your feet and watch rugby – it's a destination pub for special occasions when you want excellent drinks in a truly splendid atmosphere.

FEATURES:     

Warwick Castle

RATING: 

6 Warwick Place
W9 2PX
020 7432 1331

The Warwick Castle is a nice, old pub in a posh, leafy suburb on the Maida Vale/Paddington border. It does decent beer, with Deuchars, Sharp's Doom Bar and Adnam's on the hand pumps and there's food (pub grub). The service is friendly as is the mood of the clientele; it can get a little crowded at times, but it's all good-humoured. With its pleasing, old-fashioned pub décor and a few seats and tables outside, it's ideal for that out-of-the-way, quiet pint with the newspaper.

FEATURES:   

Harringay Green Lanes
Oakdale Arms
Lothair Rd
Beaconsfield
Endymion
Hermitage Road
Finsbury Park
Green Lanes
Woodberry Gr
Seven Sisters Road
Manor House

The Beaconsfield

RATING: 

357-359 Green Lanes
N4 1DZ
020 8800 2153

The Beaconsfield is a welcoming locals' pub, which is mostly geared towards the area's sports fans. There are huge screens at either end, which are often tuned to different channels to allow greater choice, and a series of smaller flat-screen TVs to ensure there is no excuse for missing that vital goal or wicket. It is near impossible to end up in a blind spot, but with a large bar and two pool tables taking up a lot of space it can sometimes be tough to find a seat to watch the action. It is a friendly place for a couple of pints at other times and the pub retains a raft of original features, including glass panelling on the walls and carved wooden doorframes. The dark ceiling may not be to everyone's taste, but is certainly striking. It's got efficient service and a good variety of clientele, while it is worth mentioning the small yard at the rear is now kitted out with three tables to keep the smokers happy.

FEATURES:     

MANOR HOUSE

The Oakdale Arms

RATING:

283 Hermitage Road
N4 1NP
020 8800 2013

The Oakdale is an honest suburban local run by the Milton Brewery, which also draws in real ale fans. There's usually half a dozen ales on offer, mainly from the Milton range, along with 'real' ciders, Belgian beers and some great single malts. A decent cross-section of locals are usually in place, all relieved to have a decent pub in an otherwise barren area. A Thursday quiz night, pool table and a simple food menu try to lure in the regulars, whilst excellent beer festivals – offering up to 30 ales and ciders – bring in the CAMRA members. However, our repeated visits have found the focus to be more on the beer than the atmosphere. The lighting is pretty harsh and the décor still looks like a half-finished DIY project years after first opening – we assume it's not going to change dramatically now. It's also been rather cold here more than once – the games room only had one radiator on during one chilly visit, for example. Nonetheless, with the sword of Damocles perpetually hanging over the Oakdale (in the form of an approved application to turn it into flats), a trip here is worthwhile.

FEATURES:       

MANSION HOUSE – *see Cannon Street, page 85*

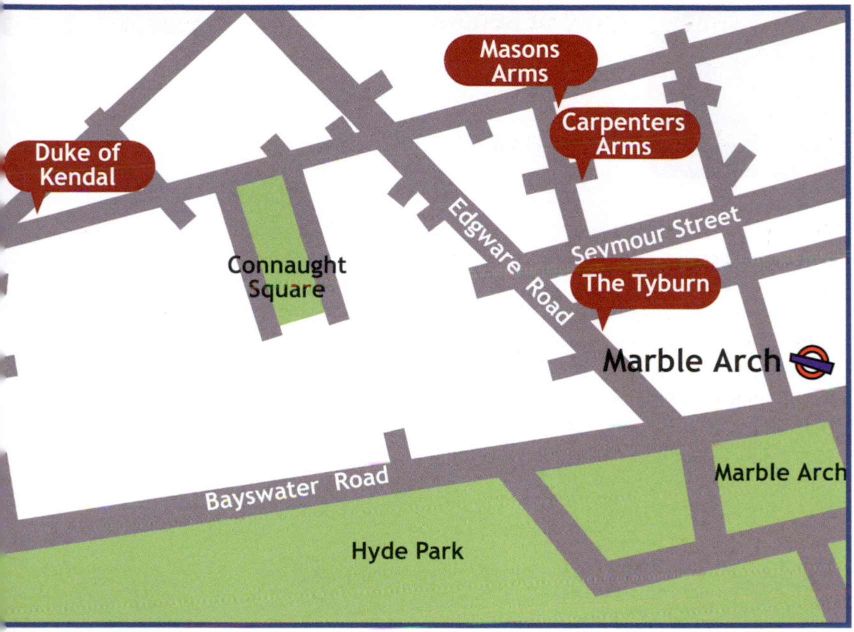

Masons Arms
Duke of Kendal
Carpenters Arms
Connaught Square
Edgware Road
Seymour Street
The Tyburn
Marble Arch
Bayswater Road
Marble Arch
Hyde Park

Carpenters Arms

RATING: 4/4

12 Seymour Place
W1H 7NE
020 7723 1050

This is a pleasant old, traditional-looking boozer a little off the beaten track in a heavily touristed area. Dark and cosy with lots of stuff on the walls (including some nice Victorian tilework) and an excellent, varied and ever-changing range of beers on the hand pumps. Service is good and the grub looks decent and cheap, although we still haven't tried it. Saturday afternoons are great if you want to while away an hour or two with the sport on the TVs, though it can get a bit crowded if a big match is on.

FEATURES:    

Duke of Kendal

RATING:

38 Connaught Street
W2 2AF
020 7723 8478

One of the closest real locals' pubs to Oxford Street, it's possible to get a decent seat here, even at busy times like Friday teatime. Considering its size and location though, this is quite an achievement. The beer ranges from Directors to Adnams but also proving popular on our visit was the Thai food in the back bar (there's also a takeaway service for locals). Note, too, the upright piano in the front bar: if you're after a sing-a-long of a Sunday evening, then be sure to pop by. This one's also close to Tony Blair's London pad, but whether he'll be found propping up the bar now he's moved on from Downing Street can't be guaranteed. Though there's always the Thai takeaway if Cherie fancies a night off from the cooking.

FEATURES: 

The Masons Arms

RATING: 

51 Upper Berkeley Street
W1H 7QW
020 7723 2131

A small pub with great beer – Tanglefoot, Badger and Sussex. With its open (albeit gas) fires and tongue and groove boarding up to the ceiling, it's a very comfortable and cosy boozer. This pub is definitely worth a visit for any pub aficionado; it does traditional grub, has friendly locals and prompt and friendly service. It's also got a sort of snug if you want to get away from the rest of the bar, but you have to be lucky enough for it to be free. One word of warning: it does tend to fill up with tourists in the summer, but there should be plenty of room for all.

FEATURES:   

The Tyburn

RATING: 2 pints

18 Edgware Rd
W2 2EN
020 7723 4731

Like most Wetherspoon pubs, the one great strength of this pub is cheap booze. The allure added to by the fact that this is one that serves cheap booze just off Oxford Street, which is something of an attraction come the 29th of the month. Apart from that there's not much to say – the atmosphere is rather lacking, but that's no great surprise in the heart of tourist land. The décor is a bit odd but we think it's trying to be American diner *circa* 1960. It has a nice picture window from which one can watch the world go by up Oxford Street of a summer evening or watch the new York Building complex take shape. Apart from that, there's not much to say: it's a bog-standard Wetherspoon.

FEATURES:  

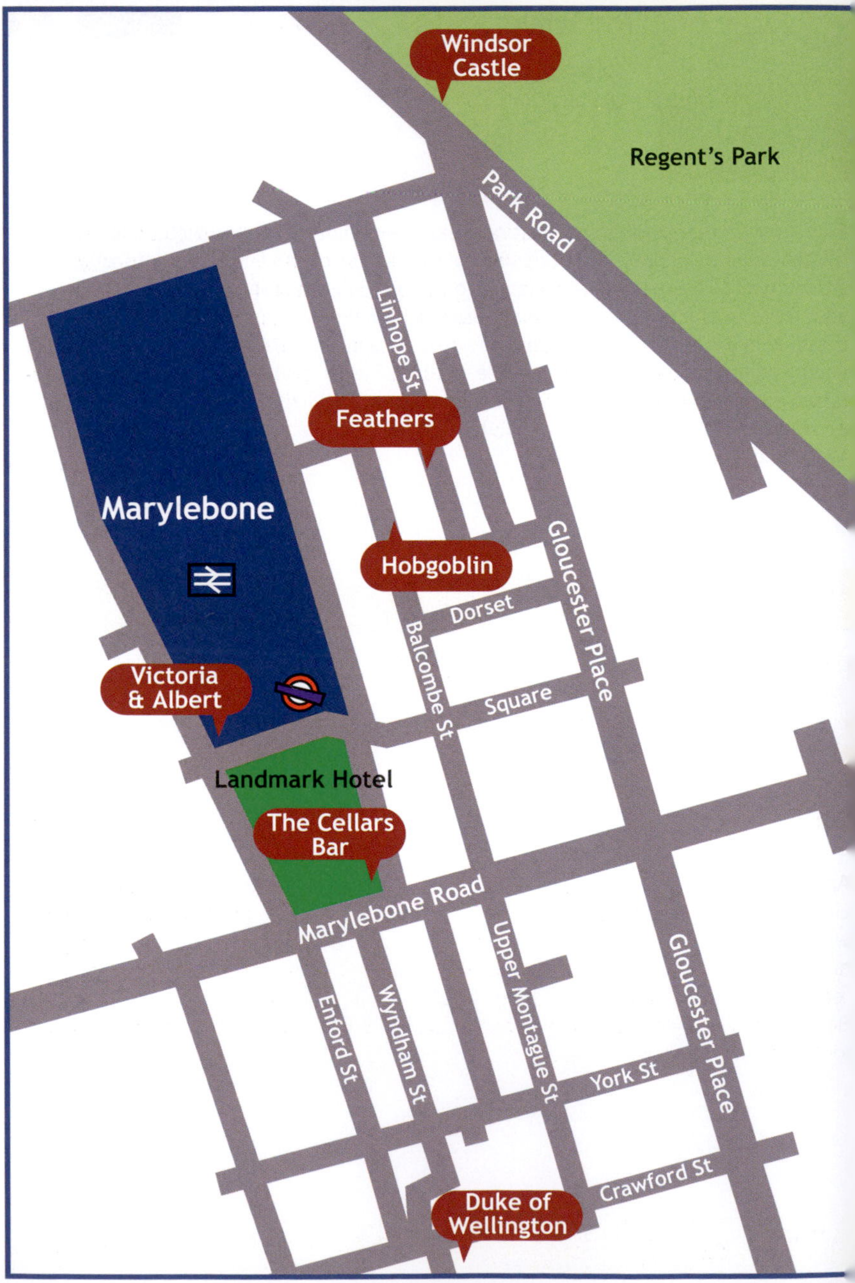

Windsor Castle

Regent's Park

Park Road

Linhope St

Feathers

Marylebone

Hobgoblin

Dorset

Balcombe St

Gloucester Place

Victoria & Albert

Square

Landmark Hotel

The Cellars Bar

Marylebone Road

Enford St

Wyndham St

Upper Montague St

York St

Gloucester Place

Crawford St

Duke of Wellington

The Cellars Bar at the Landmark

RATING: 3

222 Marylebone Road
NW1 6JQ
020 7631 8000

Every so often at Fancyapint? we have a desire for grander surroundings than those offered by the average boozer and the Landmark's Cellar Bar fits the bill perfectly. A grand hotel of the old school, possessing one of the finest lobbies of any, anywhere, you might feel that a pint here would prove to be a wallet-busting experience, but it isn't. The wine, spirits and cocktails certainly do carry a premium price but the beer is only a tad more expensive than many of the pubs in the area. Couple this with five-star table service, spicy nuts and excellent air con and you've got a comfy place to while away a relaxing hour or two before the commute home. Cheers!

HANDY FOR: Madame Tussauds, Wallace Collection

Duke of Wellington

RATING: 3

94a Crawford Street
W1H 2HQ
020 7224 9435

Another pub in the confluence of Marylebone that has made the move more upmarket. Like the Beehive nearby, it's aiming for a more adult and sophisticated crowd, though with a slightly quirky feel to it. More bistro than pub, perhaps. The staff are friendly and the beer's good – Deuchars was on when we were in last. The wine list looks reasonably priced for the area, too. The menu's more gastro than the aforementioned Beehive, but it looks good and reasonably priced, too. We know it's early days, but it looks like this one's worth a look.

FEATURES:  

HANDY FOR: Madame Tussauds, Wallace Collection

The Feathers

RATING:

43 Linhope Street
NW1 6HL
020 7402 1327

If you wanted to define a back-street boozer – look no further. Quite possibly the smallest pub in London, coming here feels like stepping into someone's living room. The area around Marylebone station has an air of forgotten London, and that's certainly the feel you get here. Staff chat away to customers old and new alike, and an easy-going atmosphere permeates and if the landlord's on form you'll hear the whole, tragic story of his life and the pub. The jukebox might seem a tad incongruous, but there's some space outside if you need to escape the music. Tribute and Doom Bar were on tap last time we were in. The sort of pub you wished was at the bottom of your street.

FEATURES:   HANDY FOR: Madame Tussauds, Wallace Collection

The Hobgoblin

RATING:  

21 Balcombe Street
NW1 6HB
020 7723 0352

Having had a lick of paint and new signs put up, this pub no longer looks so dark and foreboding from outside. Step inside and you'll find a jolly traditional pub – owned by Wychwood – and one that houses a happy mix all round. It sits on a quiet corner of this delightful area, just two minutes from Marylebone station and the unstoppable A40. It's on a road that mixes Georgian charm with the calling card of the Luftwaffe, the latter the fate of the pub's earlier building. The pub caters equally well for a good mix of locals and suits, and offers Thai food and real ale from Wychwood. For those in party mood there are jugs of Vodka Red Bull or Pimm's, and you can even hire the cellar bar. The staff were friendly and helpful and encourage you to sample the beers, before deciding and, though pretty full on our visit, it's usually quieter than a pub like this deserves to be.

FEATURES:      HANDY FOR: Madame Tussauds

Victoria & Albert

RATING:

Marylebone Station, Melcombe Place
NW1 6JJ
020 7402 0676

Hardly the most desirable accolade you can bestow but this one is probably London's best mainline railway station pub. Given the relatively small size of Marylebone station – and the quality of the competition – that's probably not a surprise, but judged on its merits this one pretty much does the business. Sure, it's mostly chaps in suits delaying their evening journey back home, but not too many station pubs have two pool tables available or a range of six beers on tap. Best of all – just like the station that houses it – a slightly wistful air can dominate. What with its sepia photographs of steam trains or the hat stand and (disused) fireplace in the side bar, this one harks back to times past and feels slightly out of kilter with your average pub. Although, unless you're departing to locations like Amersham or Banbury, it's doubtful that you'll be beating a path to this one's door. However, if you do find your way here, you'll find it to be a decent enough spot and one that might even suggest attempting a London-stations pub crawl. Don't bother though – just stick with this one.

FEATURES:  

HANDY FOR: Madame Tussauds, Wallace Collection

Windsor Castle

RATING: 

98 Park Road
NW1 4SH
020 7723 9262

Located on the edge of Regent's Park, this one's carved a niche for itself in the local area. Leaning towards the gastro end of things, the prices for food and the beer reflect that accordingly. They do have a nice, and regular, selection of guest ales and some Belgian beers and the food looked very nice. It's got comfy sofas upstairs – and you can reserve this area – and it seems pretty relaxed overall. Just to warn you that, as it's located practically next door to the London Business School (not to be confused with the London School of Business, mind), it does get staff and students visiting on a regular basis. Nonetheless, it's worth a visit for a lovely pint. And, if you've gone for a walk in the park, it's a good place for a sit down.

FEATURES:  

HANDY FOR: Madame Tussauds

MILE END

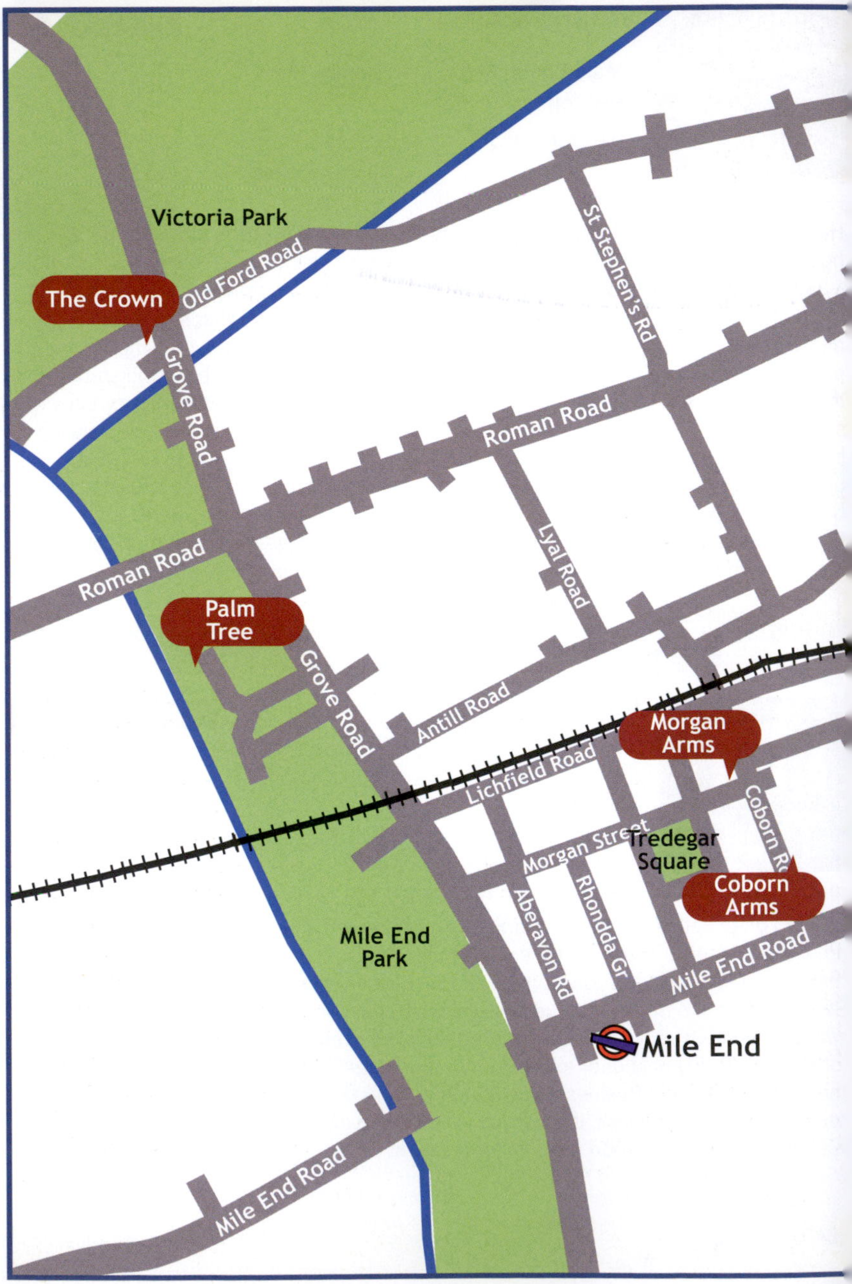

Victoria Park

The Crown

Old Ford Road

Grove Road

St Stephen's Rd

Roman Road

Roman Road

Lyal Road

Palm Tree

Grove Road

Antill Road

Morgan Arms

Lichfield Road

Coborn Rd

Morgan Street

Tredegar Square

Coborn Arms

Aberavon Rd

Rhondda Gr

Mile End Park

Mile End Road

Mile End

Mile End Road

Coborn Arms

RATING:

8 Coborn Road
E3 2DA
020 8980 3793

The Coborn Arms is a decent Young's pub serving Young's excellent beers and food. A favourite with the locals, it's a pretty large pub with a dedicated darts room (resplendent with trophies) and beer garden. If you're in the area, it's definitely worth popping in. Serves food – proper pub food – lunchtimes and evenings weekdays and Sunday lunch.

FEATURES:     

HANDY FOR: Ragged School Museum

The Crown

RATING: 

223 Grove Road
E3 5SN
020 8880 7261

The Crown is set in a handsome Victorian building, on a prime site next to one one of Bow's premier attractions, Victoria Park, and you'd think it would be a runaway success; unfortunately, in recent years this hasn't been the case. However, after a year or so of uncertainty, the Crown is open once again and this time the new owners – Geronimo Inns – not only know how to run pubs, they also know the area well and have turned another local lame duck into something rather more successful. The place has been spruced up, modernised and rationalised somewhat – the interior downstairs being divided into a trendy, loungey area, slightly separate from the bar, with a more formal dining room upstairs. A layout that will not be entirely unfamiliar to previous visitors, but this time around it seems to make a lot more sense. The drink on offer is the usual high-quality range you'd expect from Geronimo – Pride, Adnam's and Sharp's excellent Doom Bar on the hand pumps, with Aspall's Cider and more regular lagers etc. on tap. The wine list is pretty decent and there are plenty of spirits. The food looks good – a now familiar modern British pub menu – we've still to try it but, given our experience with other pubs in the group, it should be of a good standard, we'll let you know soon. Pricing is about what you'd expect – higher than average, but then that's also to be expected. As ever, towards the end of the week in the evening, you'll find the place pretty crowded with bright young things up for a night out, but, earlier in the day and in the week, you'll find it a pretty chilled-out experience.

FEATURES:    

Morgan Arms

RATING:

Morgan Street
E3 5AA
020 8980 6389

The relentless gentrification of parts east continues and the Morgan Arms hasn't been left out. Having had a bit of an up-and-down career (mostly down) in days gone by, it became a gastropub. We're a little surprised it took so long for this to happen around here, there are some pretty posh houses nearby, many of the original inhabitants having taken the money and run. So what's the pub like? Got your gastropub checklist handy? Let's begin – comfy settees, check. Butcher's block tables, check. Other *objets* from recent decades, check. Art on the walls, check. Extensive wine list, check. Cool vibe, check etc. etc. It's OK, especially for the area, and there's decent beer on the hand pumps plus Aspall's cider and the service is good. Friday and Saturday nights will see it filled with the bright young things of Bow. And its elevation to stardom has been accompanied by an elevation in tariff. We suppose it keeps out the riffraff.

FEATURES:   

Palm Tree

RATING: 

Haverfield Road
E3 5BH

The Palm Tree is a great traditional East End pub, with regular music from Thursday to Sunday night. At first glance it's not so different from many pubs in the East End, but the people who play and sing here do it with gusto and there's some real talent too; it's a great night out. The pub is hidden away in Mile End Ecology Park, so it's not terribly easy to find, although it is one of the few surviving buildings in the area. In fact, due to its attractive exterior and authentic interior it's appeared on telly quite a few times. There's usually a decent guest beer on the hand pump and, though the food really only amounts to sausage rolls and sarnies for the darts teams, along with occasional seafood at the bar, it doesn't detract. It's got atmosphere and everybody knows everyone else in the pub, but that doesn't mean strangers aren't welcome – just don't ask for tap water. It's especially lively at the weekend, when everyone goes for a sing-song. The Palm Tree's not changed much over the years and we sincerely hope it stays that way.

FEATURES:   

MONUMENT – see Bank, page 29

MOORGATE

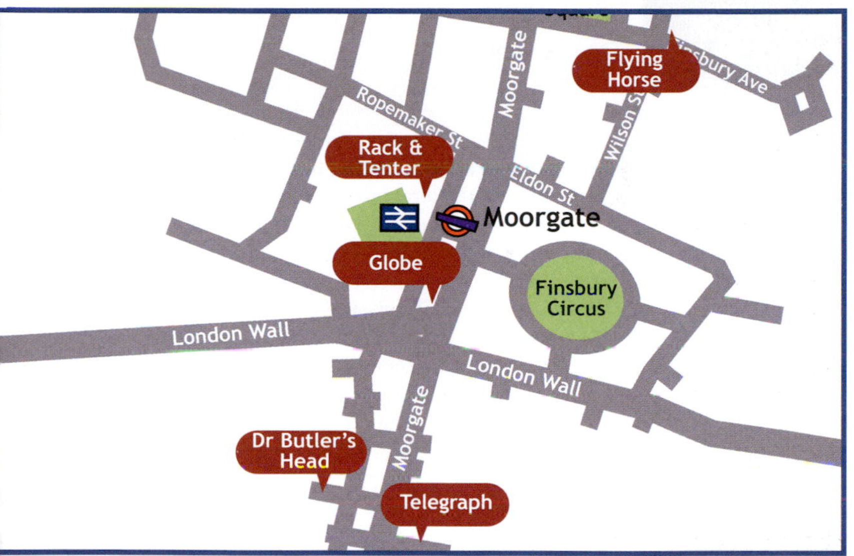

The Flying Horse

RATING:

52 Wilson St
EC2A 2ER
020 7247 5338

After donkey's years with very little change, apart from maybe a thicker layer of dust on top of the picture frames, The Flying Horse had a major update a couple of years ago. Well, that may be pushing it a bit, but out went all the pictures of horses, jockeys and the dear old Queen Mum, allowing the walls to see daylight again. It even appeared that someone had used a paintbrush on the inside of this place. What the owners have managed to do is update it (some new furniture and a large TV) without losing track of what made it work before. This is like a traditional pub in an area where City bars devoid of personality rule the roost, but the continued presence of six real ales serves to illustrate that no major changes are afoot here. They have retained the old food counter at the end of the bar and can rustle up a hot roast sandwich for you at lunchtime, while there is an upstairs function room available with darts and a pool table. Also, there's a fairly decent jukebox.

FEATURES:        

The Globe

RATING: 3

199 Moorgate
EC2M 6SA
020 7374 2915

Originally two pubs, one the Globe, the other the John Keats. Now just called 'The Globe', the John Keats is relegated to a bar, though it has an upstairs that appears to be largely ignored – it's obvious from the strange connections between the two pubs upstairs that they weren't the same building originally. There is some speculation John Keats was actually born here in 1795, in a pub known as the Swan and Hoop, but the sources are vague. Sadly, neither pub appears to be that old, with modernised Victorian interiors in both. Owned by Nicholson's, there is a good range of well-kept beer on tap and the food is pretty good, too. It can get crowded at lunch and commuting times – though try the upstairs bar at the Keats if you're trying to get away from it all.

FEATURES:       **HANDY FOR:** Barbican Centre

The Old Doctor Butler's Head

RATING: 4

2 Masons Avenue
EC2V 5BT
020 7606 3504

When you encounter this pub for the first time it's hard not to be taken by it. It's a handsome olde worlde, dark-wood pub, situated in a narrow, hard-to-find alleyway in the heart of the City. Nowadays it's surrounded on all sides by modern office buildings, but it's not difficult to imagine what it must have looked like a few decades ago when the adjacent buildings were of similar vintage. And more recently than that, the interior was as evocative as the exterior with its dark wood, dingy decoration and gas lighting. But, as is the way, it's been brought up to date: the illumination is now electric light bulbs, the décor's been spruced up and the interior is nowhere near as dark and moody as it once was. The clientele is cliché City – crowds of dark-suited blokes. It's a Shepherd Neame pub so no surprises on the beer front – Spitfire, Bombardier etc. on the hand pumps and the usual, limited range of other beers on offer, which is a bit of a two-edged sword if you're not in the mood for good bitter. You can try to experience the pub out of busy times, but be warned: if it's quiet, it often closes early – and it's never open at weekends. The Old Doctor Butler's Head may have lost its atmosphere in recent times, but it's still worth popping in if you're in the area.

FEATURES:   **HANDY FOR:** Barbican Centre

Rack and Tenter

RATING:

45 Moorfields
EC2Y 9AE
020 7628 3675

A large pub situated under an office block in the 60s development around the old London Wall. We've known this pub for quite a while now, and it's had a couple makeovers in the last few years trying to keep up with the local wine bars. And now it's been taken over by Marston's. This isn't necessarily a bad thing, as you get Marston's and Jennings beers on the pumps in addition to the lager selection and wine list, and a pretty good food selection at the same time. As you'd probably expect, the main source of punters are the surrounding office buildings, meaning it does a pretty good trade at lunchtimes and immediately after work. The main thing it's got going for it in the summer is the two outdoor seating areas, which are such a scarce commodity in the City. Be warned, however, that it's closed on weekends.

FEATURES:    

HANDY FOR: Barbican Centre

The Telegraph

11 Telegraph Street
EC2R 7LL
020 7920 9090

Installed in one of a bunch of buildings, arranged according to a medieval street plan, this 'modern' bar is where Fuller's take on All Bar One, head-to-head. The ales, beers, wines, staff and clientele are slightly more upmarket than those of its rivals and, it must be said, so are the prices. The atmosphere is correspondingly more refined, but not overly appealing. And it's obvious where they make their money as the majority of the pub was set for food at lunchtime when we went in last. You can still get a drink, and there are Fuller's beers on, but it's not strictly that kind of place. If you're looking for a modern take on the City wine bars of old, this might be for you.

FEATURES:   

HANDY FOR: Bank of England, Museum of London

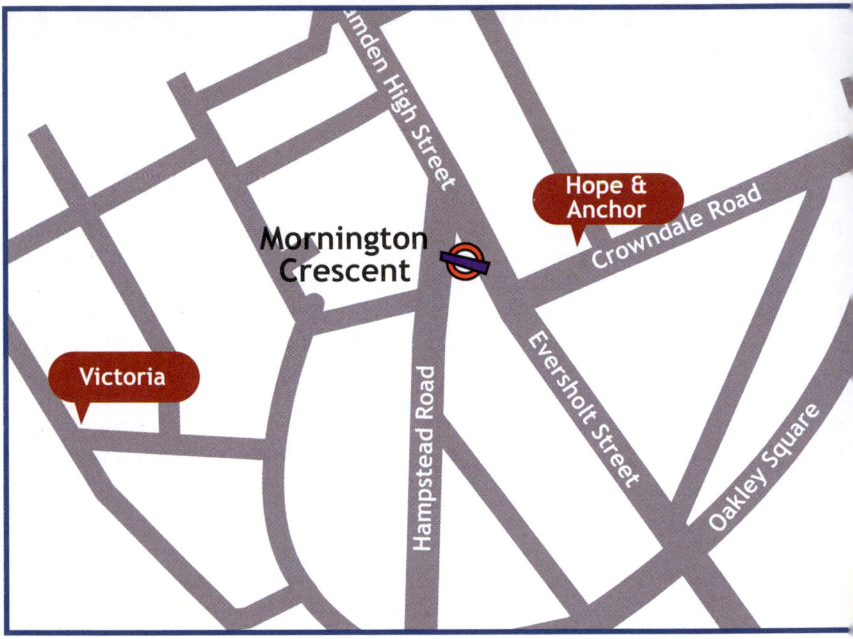

Camden High Street
Hope & Anchor
Crowndale Road
Mornington Crescent
Victoria
Hampstead Road
Eversholt Street
Oakley Square

Hope & Anchor

RATING:

74 Crowndale Road
NW1 1TP
020 7387 9506

The Hope & Anchor sports a splendid tiled exterior, which is probably the most architecturaly interesting feature of the pub. The interior's nothing spectacular, with stripped-wood floors and a large central bar on two levels. It tends towards a local clientele when there aren't gigs on at Koko (formerly the Camden Palace) next door, and it feels pretty local. The upper level of the pub is dominated by a pool table, and there's a jukebox as well. The only ale on tap was off last time we were in, so the selection tends towards lager and Guinness. It does get pretty horrendous before gigs, which is worth remembering, unless you like that sort of thing. The rest of the time, it's an unpretentious local and, as a previous reviewer said, almost timeless, making it a decent enough place for a drink.

FEATURES:     

The Victoria

RATING: 3 pints

2 Mornington Terrace
NW1 7RR
020 7387 3804

Midway between Camden and Euston, in its way this is as good a pub as any in these areas. It's a smart redevelopment of an old pub, but in this instance it's been done with care and a bit of style. The interior gives off the air of a room in a smart country house, and the beer garden has a pleasant feel to it too. It's the atmosphere that wins you over here – even at night there's a relaxing air. Maybe the punters enjoy it so much they don't want to let everyone else in on the secret. It's got a decent menu, and a couple of real ales on the pumps, friendly staff and punters (and an even friendlier pub dog), making this one to head for if you're in the area. It's not far from Koko, and provides a welcome alternative to the pubs nearer the venue, particularly if you're going to a gig.

FEATURES:       

MUDCHUTE – *see Island Gardens, page 216*

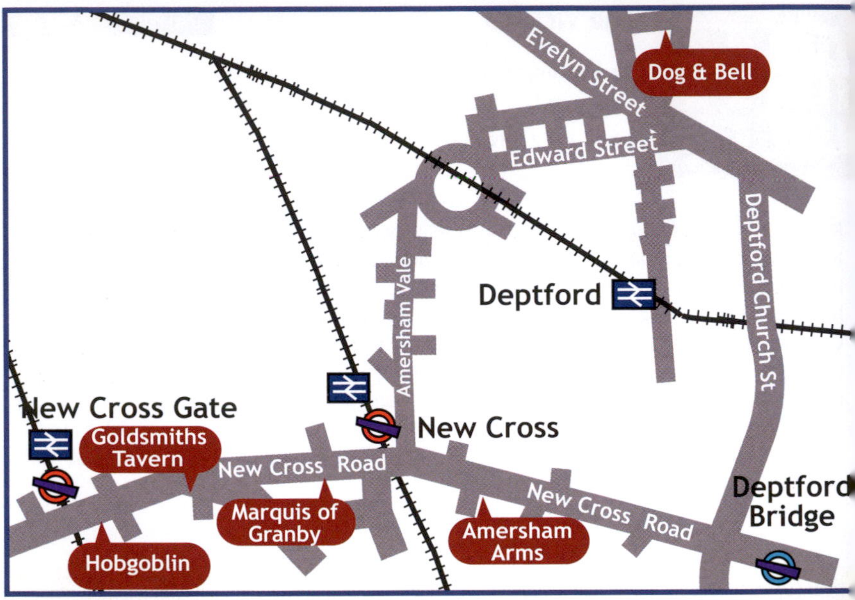

Evelyn Street
Dog & Bell
Edward Street
Deptford Church St
Amersham Vale
Deptford
New Cross Gate
New Cross
Goldsmiths Tavern
New Cross Road
Marquis of Granby
Hobgoblin
Amersham Arms
New Cross Road
Deptford Bridge

Amersham Arms

RATING: 

388 New Cross Road
SE14 6TY
020 8692 2047

The Amersham Arms – a long-time favourite of students and locals alike – has recently been refurbished by the people behind the Lock Tavern in Camden. They've done a good job – low lighting, retro couches and junk on the walls create a bohemian air. Cocktails are displayed on a greasy spoon café-style pinboard and named after classic cars – fancy a Jensen Interceptor, perhaps? A little too clever for its own good, we admit to being secretly impressed. They're also smart enough to keep food prices down; this is a student-heavy area, so a well-made burger only costs £5.95, while the beer choice includes Spitfire on tap. Service was good, but the more busy it became – and it became pretty darn busy – the more the queues backed up, in no small measure due to the preparation required for the aforementioned cocktails. It was also good to see that the back room still plays host to musical entertainment – the Horrors have done DJ sets here – plus there's a lot of live acts. Overall, we really like it here and just hope it doesn't suffer the fate of its older brother by taking itself too seriously.

FEATURES:    

Dog & Bell

RATING:

116 Prince Street
SE8 3JD
020 8692 5664

Should you find yourself thirsty in Deptford, this place is indubitably your best bet. Unlike quite a few of the pubs in the area, the Dog & Bell is neither grubby nor intimidating. It's a well-kept establishment with quality real ales on tap and superb bottled beers in the fridge. Friendly service and a relaxed atmosphere amongst the locals are the order of the day. A bar billiards table adds to the charm and there's a rear terrace for those rare sunny days. A decent menu is offered and a changing range of art adorns the walls.

FEATURES:

Goldsmiths Tavern

RATING: 

316 New Cross Road
SE14 6AF
020 8692 7381

Is this the new face of New Cross? The Goldsmiths is a spare, modern place with colourful décor and lots of natural light. It serves a decent range of beer (no real ale out of the pumps but Spitfire and Bishops Finger in bottles) and lagers on tap. With tasty burgers and pizzas for under a fiver (during the week), this is one of the best New Cross pubs for food. The pub's diary is full too: salsa on Thursday, RB Fridays and DJs on Saturday nights. The large dance floor at the back makes all this possible, and the big-screen video jukebox is worth a punt too.

FEATURES:

Hobgoblin

RATING: 

272 New Cross Road
SE14 6AA
020 8692 3193

The Hobgoblin seems to do things on a big scale. There's a sizeable beer garden at the back for summer weather and smokers, which draws locals and students for sunshine and jugs of lager. There's an extensive range of real ales on the hand pumps and it's not just Wychwood's own, with Landlord, Young's and others also available. In addition, there's Thai food on the menu – with every main dish costing the princely sum of £5 – Monday to Thursday, poker nights on Tuesday and BBQs in summer. The service is usually good and there's a 20 per cent student discount on offer. In a pretty mixed area for drinking, this place seems to keep everyone happy.

FEATURES:    

Marquis of Granby

RATING: 

322 New Cross Road
SE14 6AG
020 8692 3140

This pub is also known as Kelly's Bar, which makes more sense given its Irish identity. Giant photos of the auld country, harp signs and a fittingly sentimental jukebox complete the picture. Greene King IPA and London Pride are on offer at the bar, as well as the black stuff, obviously. It's a typical example of the dimly lit, cavernous Irish pubs you find all over London, but a good mix of older locals and Goldsmiths students keep it lively.

FEATURES:    

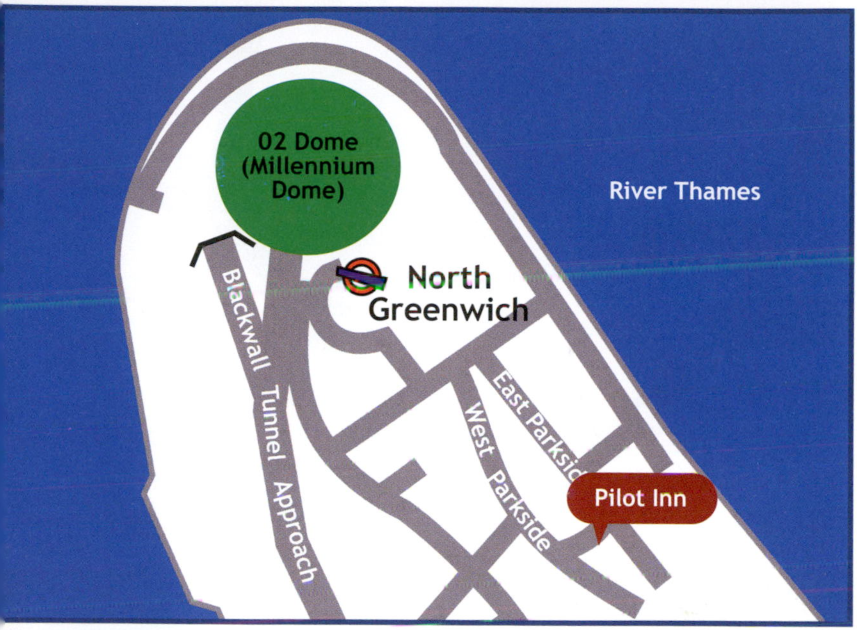

02 Dome (Millennium Dome)
River Thames
North Greenwich
Blackwall Tunnel Approach
East Parkside
West Parkside
Pilot Inn

Pilot Inn

RATING: 

68 River Way
SE10 0BE
020 8858 5910

The Pilot Inn is a lovely old pub that only narrowly missed being demolished to make way for the Greenwich Peninsula revitalisation. It's got something for everybody, good beer (Fuller's), an enormous range of food, a bit of history – the pub, and the terrace in which it sits, are just about the only old bits left in these parts, beer garden, TV, accommodation – the lot. It's a cheerful, well-kept place and just far enough from the O2 to escape the attentions of stray Take That fans – phew.

FEATURES:     

HANDY FOR: O2 Dome

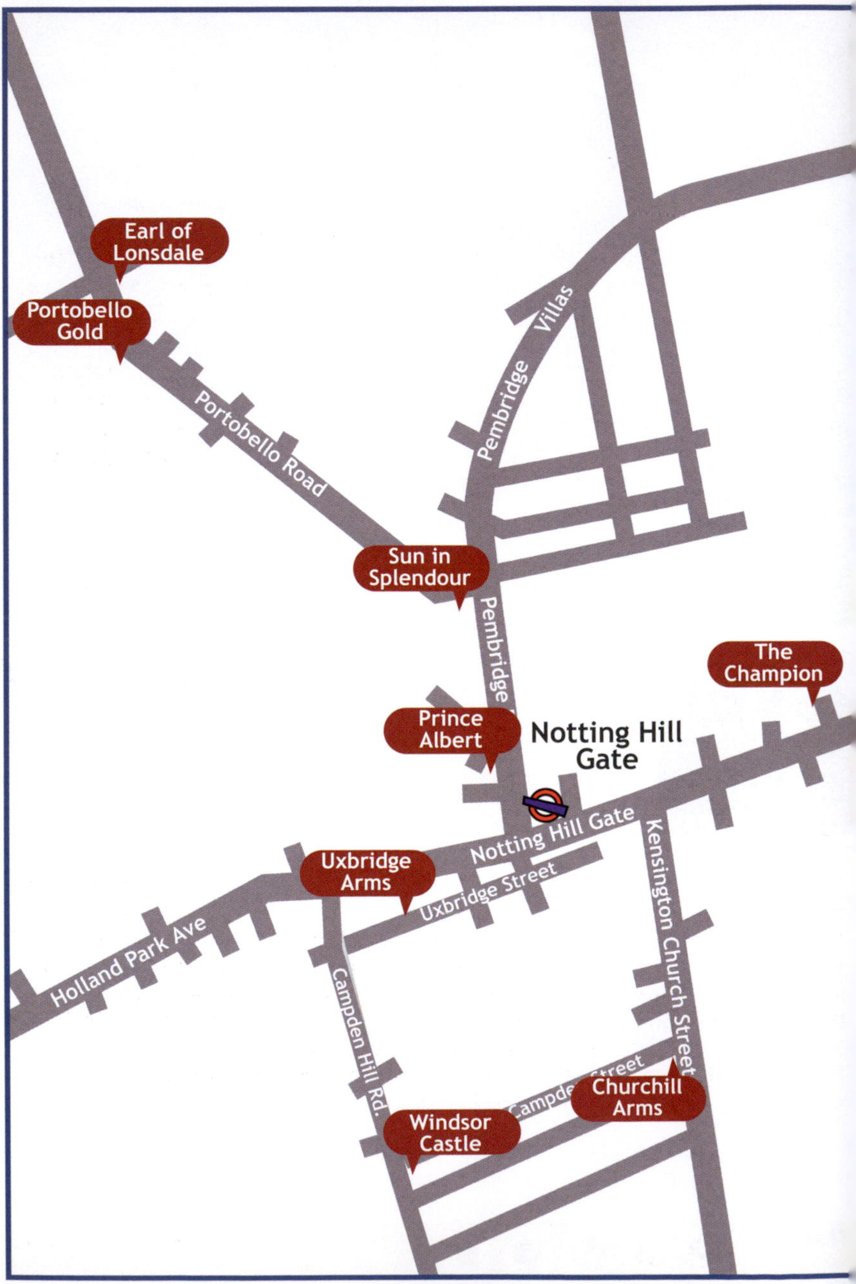

NOTTING HILL GATE

Earl of Lonsdale

Portobello Gold

Portobello Road

Pembridge Villas

Sun in Splendour

Pembridge

The Champion

Prince Albert

Notting Hill Gate

Notting Hill Gate

Uxbridge Arms

Uxbridge Street

Kensington Church Street

Holland Park Ave

Campden Hill Rd.

Campden Street

Churchill Arms

Windsor Castle

The Champion

RATING: 3

1 Wellington Terrace
W2 4LW
020 7792 4527

Walk the Bayswater Road from Marble Arch to Notting Hill and the pubs you pass (unsurprisingly) fit the image of the olde worlde London pubs that the majority of the area's hotel guests expect to find. It's a different story at the Champion though. One of those Mitchells & Butlers unbranded pubs, there's no sign advertising 'Our Famous Fish & Chips', but a selection of beer pumps of all shapes and sizes and a mishmash of loungey furnishings. We're also rather taken with the secluded basement garden (a fine spot to nab early on a summer's day) and any pub that displays a prominent picture of Debbie Harry wins a place in our heart straight away. Europe's most expensive street is (allegedly) just across the road, but don't expect too many of the residents to be in here getting a round in.

FEATURES:  

HANDY FOR: Kensington Palace

Churchill Arms

RATING: 5

119 Kensington Church Street
W8 7LN
020 7727 4242

One of the great pubs in London and it's been consistently one of the greats for a long, long time. You get a good pint of Fuller's, one of the best pints of Guinness around town, traditional food and one of the first (if not the first) pubs to serve Thai food. Eclectic decoration and winner of the 'Boozers on Bloom' award, a mixed clientele and a genial landlord go together to make one of the best pubs in London. And they keep winning awards, receiving Fuller's coveted Griffin Award for the third time and Stella's 'Love Your Local' award. The only downside, if there is one, is that so many people have cottoned on to the Churchill that it gets very crowded, especially if you want to eat. Still, if they're open, what are you hanging around for?

FEATURES:  

HANDY FOR: Kensington Palace

Earl of Lonsdale

RATING:

277–281 Westbourne Grove
W11 2QA
020 7727 6335

Nowadays, when most pubs get around to doing a refit, you know the 'stripped-out' look isn't far away. Sam Smith's, not being ones to follow fashion (it's Yorkshire after all), have tried something different. Having found the original Victorian plans, they've turned back the clock in the Earl of Lonsdale. Now once where the large open bar was is a succession of snug compartments, with tiny interconnecting gates; definitely not for the elderly or infirm. Even more etched glass can be found than before and it seems like the dark wood has been given a needed revarnish. The cynical would say it was all for the benefit of attracting tourists looking for an olde pubbe experience; after all, they already feel the need to provide beer menus on all the tables, for those who might struggle ordering from the exclusively Sam Smith's range. Nevertheless, the place looks more cared for and feels considerably more cosy than before. For those who find the whole thing a little too claustrophobic or twee, the large back room is still open plan, with plenty of couches and two open fires and the beer garden has been greatly improved, albeit at the expense of sacrificing the conservatory. In an area where pubs are going the way of the Dodo, this place is a welcome relief, especially as on the Saturday afternoon we visited it wasn't as heaving as other places in the area.

FEATURES:  

HANDY FOR: Portobello Road Market

Portobello Gold

RATING: 

95 Portobello Road
W11 2QB
020 7460 4910

Fit and working again after a fire a while back, this place packs a lot in – internet access, guest rooms, conservatory and a roof garden. Oh, and a bar and restaurant. Somehow, despite the intriguing decor and reasonable beer, we've never quite warmed to this one. It can be a handy stop on a Portobello Road crawl, but it just seems more cafe-bar than bar-pub. Unduly cruel perhaps? Give it a go and see what you make of it.

FEATURES:    

HANDY FOR: Portobello Road Market

Prince Albert

RATING:

11 Pembridge Road
W11 3HQ
020 7727 7362

An old theatre pub that's been kicked into the 21st century: the formula is certainly not new – there's a large island bar of which half is a grill/kitchen to show where your chosen dish was assembled. One, possibly original, feature is a lovely wall of stained glass at the end of the pub. It's a bit gastro, but obviously does the job for the regulars and locals that go in there. The decor invites loungers, and candles, well, burn. The bar offers a mix of beers to suit the Notting Hill set – continental lagers and beers alongside a couple of real ales on the pumps. Even when it's quiet, the service can be a bit slow. When there's a show on upstairs (at the Gate) it's even worse. It's better if you're in the mood for lounging and reading the paper with a quiet pint in the afternoon.

FEATURES:   

HANDY FOR: Portobello Road Market

Sun in Splendour

RATING: 

7 Portobello Road
W11 3DA
020 7313 9331

Another one of Mitchells & Butlers loungey refits, you'll find a decent range of beers from both the UK and the continent, and a reasonable menu of modern British pub grub, priced for the area. And that is the problem. Anyone going to Portobello Road from Notting Hill tube will pass this attractive-looking pub and as a result it suffers the consequences. Weekday evenings aren't too bad though. Should be a three pinter, but the crowds force us to downgrade it (sorry). Though if you do follow the crowds in, do sneak a peek at the secret garden (which is where you'll find the smokers).

FEATURES:   

HANDY FOR: Kensington Palace, Portobello Road Market

Uxbridge Arms

RATING:

13 Uxbridge Street
W8 7TQ
020 7727 7326

A jolly decent local tucked away in a back street just a short distance from Notting Hill Gate. The Uxbridge sports a good range of good beers – Tribute was well kept on the last visit – and, despite its posh address, an unostentatious and welcoming atmosphere. It's a traditional local through and through and, with the rise of the gastropub, there aren't many of those around nowadays. Being on the southern side of Notting Hill Gate, it's well away from the hordes of tourists and Quixotic bargain-hunters aiming for Portobello Road. It seems to us that there are quite a few little gems in these parts, away from the main drags and largely neglected by the tourists – true local watering holes. Interesting.

FEATURES:  

HANDY FOR: Kensington Palace

Windsor Castle

RATING: 

114 Campden Hill Road
W8 7AR
020 7243 9551

A fine old pub that wouldn't be out of place in a much more rural setting, the Windsor Castle has been a favourite with the Fancyapint? reviewers for years. It's a rambling, higgledy-piggledy place, with the sort of pub interior you'd expect to find in *Treasure Island* – including forehead-bashing little doors in the partitions. The beer is pretty good with excellent well-kept real ales on the hand pumps – Pride, Landlord, Sunchaser and Old Rosie (OK, so that one's cider) – and the food's also pretty good too. True it is pricey, but that's hardly a surprise considering where the pub's located. There's a very agreeable enclosed beer garden out the back, but it's unlikely you'll find a seat on a warm summer's evening, such is its popularity, but for a leisurely weekday lunch it's an excellent spot. The Windsor Castle's a very pleasant place when it's not crowded and, when it is, it's often a jolly crowd.

FEATURES:  

HANDY FOR: Kensington Palace

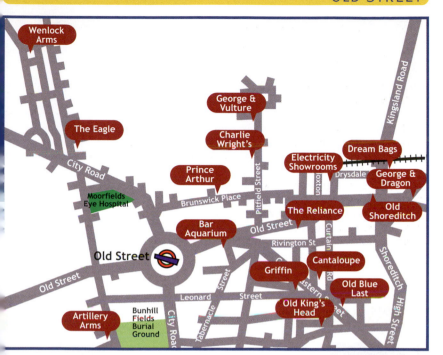

Wenlock Arms
The Eagle
George & Vulture
Charlie Wright's
Prince Arthur
Electricity Showrooms
Dream Bags
George & Dragon
Old Shoreditch
The Reliance
Bar Aquarium
Cantaloupe
Griffin
Old Blue Last
Old King's Head
Artillery Arms
Kingsland Road
City Road
Moorfields Eye Hospital
Brunswick Place
Pitfield Street
Drysdale
Hoxton
Old Street
Rivington St
Curtain Rd
Old Street
Shoreditch High Street
Great Eastern Street
Leonard Street
Tabernacle Street
Bunhill Fields Burial Ground
City Road

Artillery Arms

RATING: 3

102 Bunhill Row
EC1Y 8ND
020 7253 4683

The Artillery is one of the real pubs in the Square Mile and hasn't really changed in the last decade. Oh, it's had a bit of a tidy-up and a lick of paint, but it hasn't lost its appeal. It's old, kind of small, serves a good range of Fuller's beers, as well as decent pub grub – the fish-finger sarnie is a particular favourite of ours. It's still an oasis on the fringes of the City, and one of the few in this neck of the woods you'll find open at weekends. And, if you're interested in London history, particularly cemeteries, it's right across the road from Bunhill Fields (hence the address) where several notables are buried, including Daniel Defoe, William Blake and John Bunyan.

FEATURES:   

HANDY FOR: Barbican Centre

Bar Aquarium

RATING:

262–264 Old Street
EC1V 9DD
020 7253 3558

When the people behind the Aquarium club next door took on this pub, we thought Bar Aquarium would be a pure pre-club hangout, all expensive sofas and loungey trimmings. However, despite a new dining room and redecorated interior (including the eponymous aquarium), there's still a pub feel – with a games room on the first floor including a dart board, pool table, table football and a proper pinball machine as well as Sky Sports on the telly. It's not a small place either: you should be able to find a bit of space in the main bar, or failing that there's another bar – and a roof terrace – upstairs. Catering as much for those winding down after work as for those gearing up for a big night out, Bar Aquarium attracts a mixed crowd and manages to stand out in an area brimming with pubs and bars.

FEATURES:      

Cantaloupe Bar and Restaurant

RATING:

35 Charlotte Road
EC2A 3PD
020 7613 4411

The strident, heady days of the dot-com boom are well behind this locale now, but the whole area is still trendy-bar city. Cantaloupe can lay fair claim to being one of the bars (if not *the* bar) that established the area as the capital's capital of cool. Things are somewhat more tranquil than they used to be – although the weekend evenings are still pretty busy – and it is a decent place to relax on a weekend afternoon (actually, it can get very quiet sometimes). There aren't any real beers on tap – it's not that sort of place, but there are plenty of continental beers (including the original Bud) and not a bad pint of Guinness. Wine and spirit drinkers have far more choice, which after all is the main thrust of the place. The restaurant's OK too. If you can bag the squashy settees in the back room, you can have a pretty chilled afternoon – and that's what we tend to do here.

FEATURES:      

Charlie Wright's International Bar

RATING: 

45 Pitfield Street
N1 6DA
020 7490 8345

A pub that puts together a combination of Belgian beers and Thai food doesn't sound original, yet this one manages to stand out, even in a part of town overloaded with bars. The décor is spartan to say the least – one room divided up into spaces for diners and drinkers (and dancers). It all clicks into place though: the aforementioned Mr. Wright keeps a cheery eye on proceedings and DJs keep things lively till the small hours. You'll have to part with a couple of quid to get in after 10pm at weekends (but it is open until 4am), but that sounds fair enough to us. The pub/club hybrid isn't always a winner but this one does it as well as any other.

FEATURES:     

Dream Bags Jaguar Shoes

RATING: 

34–36 Kingsland Road
E2 8DA
020 7739 9550

The proprietors had a great concept. Whether it was to cut expense, or a flash of inspiration, the place looks like almost no renovation was done to turn it into a bar. Even the original signs from when it was two separate wholesaler's shops (hence the name) are present. Inside, it's a stripped-down sort of place, with only pieces of artwork decorating the walls, old leather sofas in place and a pretty utilitarian bar. In the basement, a brick fireplace is the only decoration and the only thing hinting at the building's Victorian past. Its dark ambience makes it feel like a Beatnik hangout, only the philosophical discussions about Sartre are replaced by conversations about haircuts. Musically, its a mixed bag: we've heard everything from ironic 80s power ballads to blues here, but it usually hovers somewhere in the indie section of the musical spectrum. Ultimately it's a great place, erring on the right side of pretension and one of the better bars in Hoxton.

FEATURES: 

The Eagle

RATING: 4

2 Shepherdess Walk
N1 7LB
020 7553 7681

'Up and down the City Road, In and out the Eagle, That's the way the money goes. Pop! goes the weasel.' For those who like a bit of history, not many pubs can lay claim to being mentioned in a nursery rhyme – an old cautionary tale of spending all your money on booze. Times have changed (perhaps) and, although the Eagle was Islington-ised a while back, at heart it's still a pub. The staff are friendly and there's a fine choice of drink – guest ales on the hand pumps and plenty of fine continental beers on tap. In addition, the ivy-covered garden is pretty and there are barbecues in summer. Although often eerily quiet on Saturdays, its location off Old Street roundabout means during the week it's full with what can be an oil-and-water mix of local office workers, flat sharers, council-estate dwellers and Hoxtonites. Overall, not bad at all.

FEATURES:     

Electricity Showrooms

RATING: 3

39a Hoxton Square
N1 6NN
020 7739 3939

A pleasant surprise, this one. We seem to remember a previous incarnation which was all black leather furnishings and cubed seats – well, there's been a refit which has turned the place back into (yikes!) a pub. So, enter through the revolving doors and take your pick from a fine drinks selection (Sleeman's India Pale Ale being worth a try). The menu also offers up traditional fare and, by the time we noticed the bar billiards table, we though some heavy exercise in Shoreditch irony was underway. It's not – just like the Owl and Pussycat not too far from here, this is a modern pub with a traditional feel and – judging from our visit – it's one that's proving popular. We haven't sampled this one at weekends yet, though it's safe to say the multicoloured downstairs dance floor gets some action. Midweek, though, this is one of the best in the area.

FEATURES:  

George & Dragon

RATING: 3

2–4 Hackney Road
E2 7NS
020 7012 1100

The George & Dragon could be aptly described as where Hoxton bohemia meets the East End. Rescued from near dereliction, the owners kept what they could of the old place (after all, it was falling to bits) and added a dash of the early 21st century (i.e. 70s and 80s retro). The bizarre and eccentric décor all works very nicely and it creates a relaxed ambience. There's a CD jukebox playing pretty decent tunes earlier in the day and a couple of decks come to life in the evenings knocking out an eclectic, often retro mix. It's a very small place and only takes an average-sized party to pack the place out, but even so the atmosphere is usually genial – even when people are dancing around. It's always a good sign when you're sorry the evening has to end at closing time. The beer no longer includes anything on hand pumps, which is a pity for the ale drinkers and, on recently asking what wine was available, we received the answer 'red or white' (we couldn't tell if the barman was trying to be amusing). But don't let that put you off, it's a fun pub – handy for kicking off a weekender in the area.

FEATURES:  

George & Vulture

RATING: 2

63 Pitfield Street
N1 6BU
020 7253 3988

Formerly a solid, locals' pub, a recent refit has seen things being altered here, with the pool table – and we think some of the bar furnishings – removed. An old L-shaped Fuller's boozer, there's still a decent pub at its core, but there's just the sense its wings have been ever so slightly clipped since the refit. It feels a tad more formal than before – especially now there's a baby grand piano in the corner. Even with that addition, we're not too sure there'll be too many sing-songs at this one.

FEATURES:   

Griffin

RATING:

93 Leonard Street
EC2A 4RD
020 7739 6719

People might feel sorry for this pub because it looks so rundown, standing on the corner of a largely barren plot in an otherwise built-up area. We love it for this: it's a good antidote against other nearby pubs and bars which are slowly being refurbished and sanitised, formularising the heart and soul out of the pub-going experience. For us, it's eccentric places like the Griffin that make going to the pub worthwhile. We hope it stays that way and given its popularity with a mix of regulars and Hoxtonites, we can't see any good reason to change it. Indeed, it goes to show you don't need to strip a pub out to attract a young, lively crowd. The range of drinks on offer is usual pub fare – a couple of ales (sometimes on, sometimes off) and the usual lagers. Service can be brusque at busy times, but we forgive them. Decent jukebox, too – when there isn't a DJ on, at least.

FEATURES:    

The Old Blue Last

RATING: 

39 Great Eastern Street
EC2A 3ES
020 7739 5793

An average boozer in a prime site on Great Eastern Street? It couldn't last. One of the last remaining old-school drinking dens in Hoxton was taken over a while ago and the Hoxtonites have descended. But fear not. For despite a fair few new wave and new romantic wannabes, the hair-care-product-heavy atmosphere and (rather good) obscure electro-punk/rock nights on the first-floor bar, it seems devoid of much of the annoying judgemental preening clientele who permeate other nearby venues. Be who you wanna be seems to be the mantra. Perhaps it's this slapdash approach which has kept them away; the pub looks pretty untouched from the outside since its olden days – rough and little sleazy – and inside all they've done is swap the chairs for sofas and remove the carpet. It looks like a student flat from 1991. The only criticism is that the beer, including the lager, tastes poorly kept – but hopefully that'll improve. A cool pub in Hoxton that isn't annoying? It can't last.

FEATURES:  

Old King's Head

RATING:

28 Holywell Row
EC2A 4JB
020 7246 0658

This firmly locals' pub has had a makeover – though perhaps one better suited to Goths than trendies, as the blood-red walls and dark-stained wood evoke a certain atmosphere. It's tempting to surmise that the walls were painted to match the leather sofas, but that's probably not fair. And, despite the fact it's surrounded by designers and other trendy types, this is still very much a locals' pub. If you fancy a pint without the crowds and don't mind a few stares, it does the job. The fact that horse racing was on the big screen instead of the cricket says something about the clientele, but they seem to keep the regulars happy.

FEATURES:  

The Old Shoreditch Station

RATING:  

1 Kingsland Road
E2 8AA

A diminutive, fairly new addition to the Hoxton scene, the Old Shoreditch Station is a café/bar unsurprisingly set in the original Shoreditch railway station building. It's a tiny place and until recently there was seating for as little as 20 or so people, but they've now expanded into the shop next door increasing capacity by 100%. Even so, it can get rather crowded later in the evening, but, if you're able to get a seat and space on one of the great 1950s coffee tables to rest your drink, there's a very comfortable and unrushed atmosphere. The choice of drink isn't spectacular, focusing mainly on spirits (although the Stella Artois Bock went down nicely), but on the whole we warmed rather nicely to the place. With many try-too-hard, perpendicular anodyne bars around (i.e. Jam), for us, the Old Shoreditch Station provided a refreshing antidote. Oh, and if you're a railway-enthused Hoxtonite, you can see (en route to the toilet) the original staircase leading up to a non-existent platform for a train station long since gone.

FEATURES:  **HANDY FOR:** Geffrye Museum

Prince Arthur

RATING:

49 Brunswick Place
N1 6EB
020 7253 3187

There are not too many pubs left with an old-style visible hot grill for lunchtime bar food, nor one that gives so much of its limited floor space over to dart players, but this place proves there's still a market for all that. Add Shepherd Neame's fine ales to the equation and you've got a thoroughly old-school pub, enjoyed by one and all. We've seen this one packed with office staff, media workers and locals from the flats next door – though rarely at the same time. An 'andsome, busy little boozer.

FEATURES:    

The Reliance

RATING:  

336 Old Street
EC1V 9DR
020 7729 6888

A mainstay of the Old Street drinking scene for a number of years, the Reliance is popular throughout the week with the after-work crowd, with Friday and Saturday nights bringing even more punters through the doors. This pub is all about clean lines not clutter but has enough character about it to recommend, especially with the excellent eclectic jukebox providing aural stimulation. It looks quite compact from the front, though an upstairs section doubles capacity and is probably a better option for larger groups. A seat next to the window upstairs is a perfect vantage point for counting the number of blokes walking down Old Street who've opted for wearing unnecessary hats. A lucky few can also slouch on a couch in a dimly lit corner at the back downstairs. Ale drinkers are well catered for and there are two strengths of Czech Litovel on tap, with quite a large selection of bottled offerings from Belgium. The staff can be a bit hit and miss, but if it's the former you should have a good time.

FEATURES:  

HANDY FOR: Geffrye Museum

Wenlock Arms

RATING:

26 Wenlock Road
N1 7TA
020 7608 3406

On paper this pub could be awful: hidden off the City Road and hard to find, it's in an area filled with factories, warehouses and a council estate. Once part of the Wenlock Brewery Co, which used to be situated in this road, the décor doesn't appear to have been updated since the brewery was closed by Bass in 1962. It's full of locals who know each other's names, and even has its own football club! But, once you've found it, it's a gem. Boasting the largest selection of real ales in North London, you'll easily find quirkily named, rare brews from obscure companies. The turnover is pretty high, so the selection could well entirely change between visits – even in the same week. Weekend nights are especially popular, with a trio of elderly gents usually in residence playing some fine jazz, while the Thursday quiz night attracts the crowds to an already very busy pub. The locals create a genuinely friendly atmosphere, just like a real pub should. Highly recommended – just don't flash your laptop around on the way there.

FEATURES:     

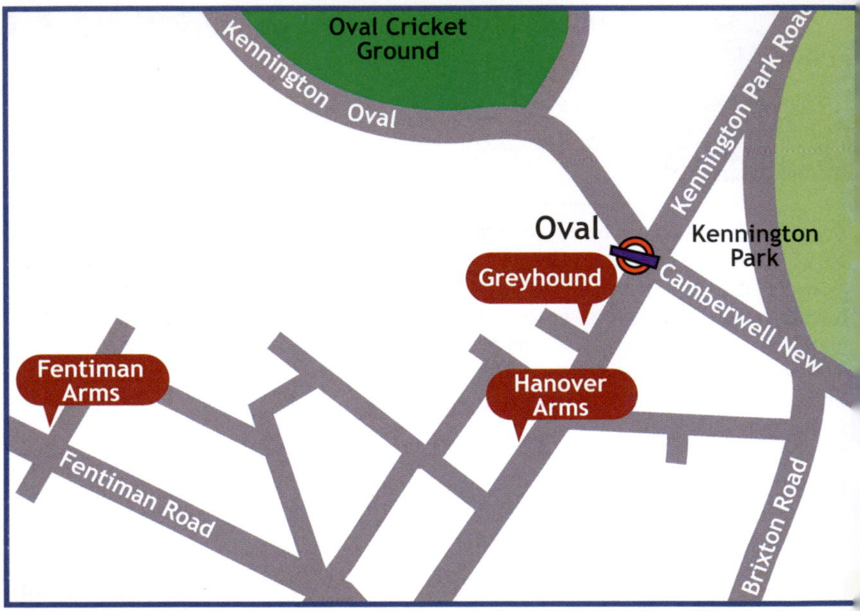

Fentiman Arms

RATING: 

64 Fentiman Road
SW8 1LA
020 7793 9796

Stepping out from Vauxhall station into the grim urban chaos which greets you, you'd never think you were only ten minutes or so walk from a smart gastropub. Though once you start passing the large Victorian houses of Fentiman Street you realise Geronimo Inns did their homework and that there are enough local takers for their brand of loungey pub-bars. Even the most hard-bitten fan of the traditional pub experience has to admit that this place does what it does effectively (you sense there's as much thought been put into the décor as into the food and drink). A few real ales on the hand pumps (Deuchars, Bombardier, Tribute and Greene King IPA), though most of the clientele were opting for wine to accompany their modern pub grub choices. The service is excellent and all in all it's a pretty relaxed place. The split-level beer garden is a handy feature for smokers and warmer days, even if the use of decking makes you wonder if Titchmarsh and Dimmock have just passed by. It's all very nice, very tidy – very Geronimo Inns.

FEATURES:    

HANDY FOR: The Oval

The Greyhound

RATING: 

336 Kennington Park Road
SE11 4PP
020 7735 2594

Another old-school pub which has escaped the gastropubification of many such places. There's a good choice of beers and Irish whiskies in stock and the staff seem to take care to keep their wares in good condition. For this reason (and the live racing) we would give it a slight edge over its neighbour. But they are both agreeable places and much of an unfashionable muchness.

FEATURES: 

HANDY FOR: The Oval

Hanover Arms

326 Kennington Park Road
SE11 4PP
020 7735 1576

The Hanover's a big, noisy, uncomplicated place. Perfectly well suited for a Saturday afternoon reading the *Sun* and watching the big-screen sport over a pint or two. There would appear to be one or two characters among the clientele, including one fellow at the table next to us with a stock of Shane McGowan anecdotes (and they're just what you'd imagine they'd be).

FEATURES: 

HANDY FOR: The Oval

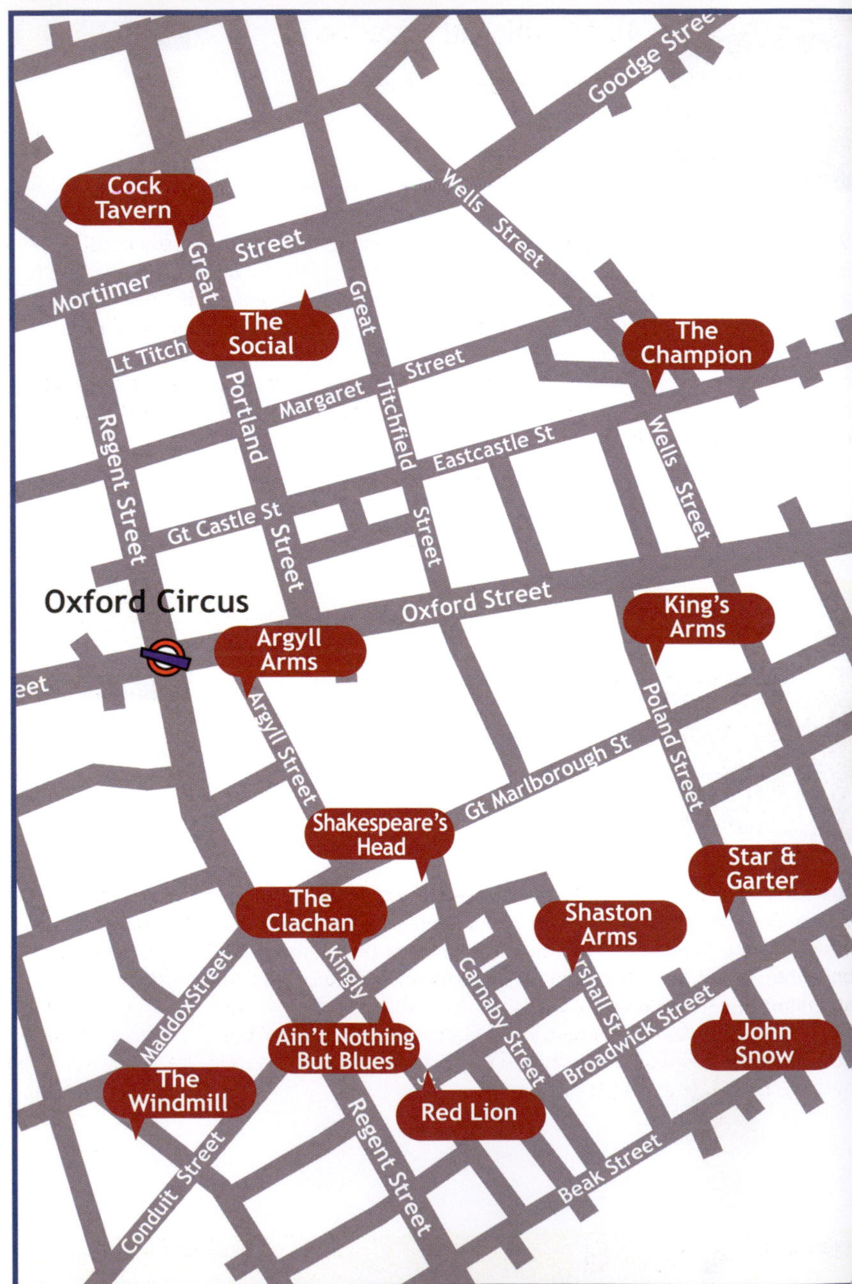
Goodge Street
Cock Tavern
Wells Street
Mortimer Street
Great
The Social
Lt Titch
Great
The Champion
Margaret Street
Portland
Titchfield
Regent Street
Eastcastle St
Wells Street
Gt Castle St
Street
Street
Oxford Circus
Oxford Street
King's Arms
Argyll Arms
eet
Argyll Street
Poland Street
Gt Marlborough St
Shakespeare's Head
Star & Garter
The Clachan
Shaston Arms
Kingly
Carnaby Street
rshall St
Maddox Street
Broadwick Street
Ain't Nothing But Blues
John Snow
The Windmill
Red Lion
Regent Street
Conduit Street
Beak Street

Ain't Nothin' But Blues Bar

RATING: 4

20 Kingly Street
W1B 5PZ
020 7287 0514

Something a bit different for Soho – or indeed London – a dedicated blues bar. There's live music most nights of the week (with the add-on of a late licence) but, if the blues ain't your thing, it's still a handy one to meet up in before a night out in Soho. The walls are filled with posters and sheet music from various blues players, all of which adds to the authentic atmosphere. It fills up quickly these days as it's justifiably popular, but if you're here early it's possible to get a seat, a bit of grub and a fine pint of ale. If you're after something a bit different from the more run-of-the-mill drinking dens of the area, give it a look.

FEATURES:   

Argyll Arms

RATING: 

18 Argyll Street
W1F 7TP
020 7734 6117

The Campbells are coming, the Campbells are coming, right after they've visited the shops, the Palladium and Carnaby Street. Any place this close to Oxford Circus is bound to have the trappings of a tourist... erm... trap. It naturally gets incredibly busy because it's in this location. The place is very much an olde English pub in appearance, albeit one with a transitory feel – this pub doesn't have much in the way of regulars. Still it's not that bad, with a good range of ales, solid pub grub, nice décor, some nice old prints on the walls and friendly staff. It can be a useful place to meet, if nothing else – if you can get in.

FEATURES:   

The Champion

RATING:

12–13 Wells Street
W1T 3PA
020 7323 1228

If you're worn out by the shopping hordes of Oxford Street and need a drink, the Champion is the place to go. It's a beautifully appointed pub with a lovely exterior and fantastic champion-themed stained-glass windows. It seems that Sam Smith's is annexing the West End for Yorkshire and taking the best-looking pubs to boot. The service is excellent, even when it's busy, and on a warm evening towards the end of the week it can get very, very busy. During shopping hours, however, it's a fairly relaxed place and, if it's crowded downstairs, there's always the upstairs bar. One other good point to note is that (like a good number of other Sam Smith's in the area) you can find that most traditional of pub games: a dart board.

FEATURES:   

The Clachan

RATING: 

34 Kingly Street
W1B 5QH
020 7494 0834

If you go into a Nicholson's pub and don't find an opulent Victorian interior, you should be disappointed. But don't worry, you definitely won't be disappointed here – the fixtures and fittings are everything you would expect of the brand and if that's all you're looking for you'll be happy here. Owing to its prime location, the clientele can be unpredictable: it can be crowded with tourists and after-work drinkers – usually Friday nights – or occupied by a few regulars and shoppers. The food's decent, with service both downstairs and in the upstairs Liberty Bar (which is often empty, and a better place for a conversation). The fare is Nicholson's so expect a good range of beers on the five hand pumps, well kept and well served. You can even try the beer before you buy in their 'Sip before you sup' promotion – very nice.

FEATURES:    

The Cock Tavern

RATING:

27 Great Portland Street
W1W 8QG
020 7631 5002

This terrific-looking pub has large glass lanterns outside and a wonderfully ornate interior. It has plenty of seating and serves the usual range of Samuel Smith's beers. Like all the other pubs in this area, it can at times (usually Friday evenings) be packed, but is certainly worthy of your patronage.

FEATURES:  

John Snow

39 Broadwick Street
W1F 9QJ
020 7437 1344

Rather than celebrating the life of the newsreader (Jon) famed for his garish ties, this Victorian pub in the heart of Soho is named after the doctor who established that cholera was a waterborne disease – and nothing to do with vapours or miasma. The site of the original water pump, which was key to his discovery, is marked by a granite kerb slab outside the pub (it's not where the mock water pump is, just down the road). It serves decent cheap pub grub and all the standard Sam Smith's beers. Unfortunately, the drink is served in cheap plastic glasses, even if you stay inside – apparently to avoid the the wrath of the Republic of Westminster. It's the only pub we visited in these parts that did this – why the council appears to have it in for the John Snow, we've no idea – and the heavy-handed eviction tactics at closing time only heaped insult upon injury. What Snow, who was said to be teetotal would make of this, we don't know, but for us the John Snow's no longer the pub we used to enjoy.

FEATURES: 

King's Arms

RATING:

23 Poland Street
W1F 8QJ
020 7734 5907

This gay pub in Soho isn't bad at all, being more trad pub than trendy bar. Selection of beer is nothing to shout about, but what they do have is well kept. Guess it gets busy on weekends, but can be a good place to go for a quiet drink during the day. It has some interesting attributes left which may or may not be original, but the quote on the wall is quite interesting: 'In this Old Kings Arms tavern was the Ancient Order of druids revived 28th November 1781'.

FEATURES:    

Red Lion

RATING: 

14 Kingly Street
W1B 5PR
020 7734 4985

The Red Lion is a fine old oak-panelled pub hidden behind Carnaby Street. Despite a small frontage, it's deceptively large with three bars in total, including one upstairs. Our personal preference is for the tiny front bar which sports a real open fire – we saw a couple of coal buckets so we assume it's in use during colder days, too. It seems to attract a fair few younger media types, but perhaps due to its slightly hidden location it's easier to find a seat here than other nearby places. It serves the usual Sam Smith's range of fare but no one seems to object and there's a pretty jolly atmosphere all round. A word of warning, however: watch out for the dart board – not because it's such a rare sight in Soho these days – but because of its potentially hazardous position next to the bar; if you're unlucky, a double top could take on a different meaning altogether.

FEATURES:    

Shakespeare's Head

RATING:

29 Great Marlborough Street
W1F 7HZ
020 7734 2911

Any pub called the Shakespeare's Head in an area as touristy as Carnaby Street would just have to be an olde worlde building with leaded-glass windows and, true to form, this one is. It hasn't changed at all in recent years. The only critical recent addition being the chairs and tables on the pavement outside, for the smokers and just in case the weather turns nice (it does occasionally). The pub does get chock full on weekends and in the evenings, with a mixture of local workers and tourists. There is an upstairs restaurant serving pub food, and it seems to do it well enough as it's always busy. It's not a bad place and well placed for Carnaby Street – it can be a great place to meet when it's not full, but that doesn't seem to happen very often.

FEATURES:  

HANDY FOR: Carnaby Street

The Shaston Arms

RATING:

4 Ganton Street
W1F 7QN
020 7287 2631

Although it feels like it's been there for years, this one is a comparatively new pub. A decade ago, Hall & Woodhouse took the wine bar on the site and did their best to make it look like a pub with a bit of history. So, expect a few mirrors, wooden floors and dividers in the décor. It's a reasonable effort given the layout of the place, with nooks and crannies in a relatively small space. There are decent Hall & Woodhouse beers – Badger, Tanglefoot – on offer accompanied by all the other booze you'd expect of a pub in the centre of town. However, its cramped layout and overwhelming popularity on weekend evenings (and towards the end of the week) means it's not always the place for a quiet chat over a pint or two – unless you're lucky enough to get one of the seats at the very back, that is. Oh, and it's closed on Sundays.

FEATURES:  

The Social

RATING:

5 Little Portland Street
W1W 7JD
020 7636 4992

Music has a big part to play at The Social, owned since '99 by Heavenly Records. Located between the glitzier end of London's rag trade and the consulting rooms of Harley Street, it offers drinks, music and food to a self-consciously fash-tastic crowd sporting ridiculous haircuts, obscure trainers and, God love them, studded belts. There are two levels to the place, the larger basement with a range of music events on the programme, and a smaller ground-floor bar. There are a limited number of brews on tap, balanced by a wide range of bottled beers from around the globe and an extensive range of spirits. Its central London location makes it a handy place to meet up; the food, including tasty fare from the Square Pie company, is reasonably priced – but why you'd want to eat spaghetti hoops on toast in a bar is beyond us. The amazing jukebox doesn't bleed you dry, offering a superb mix of classics and new music (so new two of the albums weren't even out in the shops on our last visit). And it's not played at earsplitting levels, so you can carry on a conversation. The place is relatively quiet and sociable (excuse the pun) during the week, but it gets absolutely rammed towards the end of the week (closed on Sundays); it can feel very impersonal, especially given the preponderance of loathsome asymmetric hairdos trying to outdo each other in the style stakes. However, if you like beats to complement your beer, this could be the place for you.

FEATURES:  

Star & Garter

RATING: 

62 Poland Street
W1F 7NX

This is a jolly decent little boozer that's ideal for a quick drink or a longer session (space permitting). Sporting not much more than a jukebox and a small TV, the pub has a great deal more character than many of the more renowned Soho pubs and, being just a little bit off the main drags, a little less crowded. The beer is decent, the service is good – the Star & Garter offers a welcome respite from the area's trendsetting stylistas and serves as a reminder that you don't need to do a lot, just do it well, to run a welcoming and hospitable pub. It's closed on Sundays.

FEATURES:   

The Windmill

RATING:

6–8 Mill Street
W1S 2AT
020 7491 8050

There are one or two pubs in the West End that aren't the usual tourist traps, theme pubs or restaurants in disguise you get in these parts – they're just good, honest pubs that would be a delight for any discerning pub-goer to call his or her local. The Windmill, just off Regent Street is one of the best of them. It's a fine, traditional, looking pub, just enough off the beaten track, to make it easy to get to, but not too easy to find and, as it's a Young's pub, you can be pretty damn certain that it has a fine range of beers on tap. Nowadays, Young's also offer a pretty reasonable wine list, for those days when ale just doesn't suit the mood, so of course that's an option here, but this pub's crowning glory is its award-winning pies. Accompanied by excellent chips (and, yes, chips can vary widely in quality) and mushy peas, they're simply amongst the best you can get anywhere – well worth a special journey. The front bar may be a little small, but there's a larger room at the back and a restaurant upstairs and, when you add the prompt and friendly service and the generally relaxed and civilised atmosphere, you've got a top pub experience.

FEATURES:   

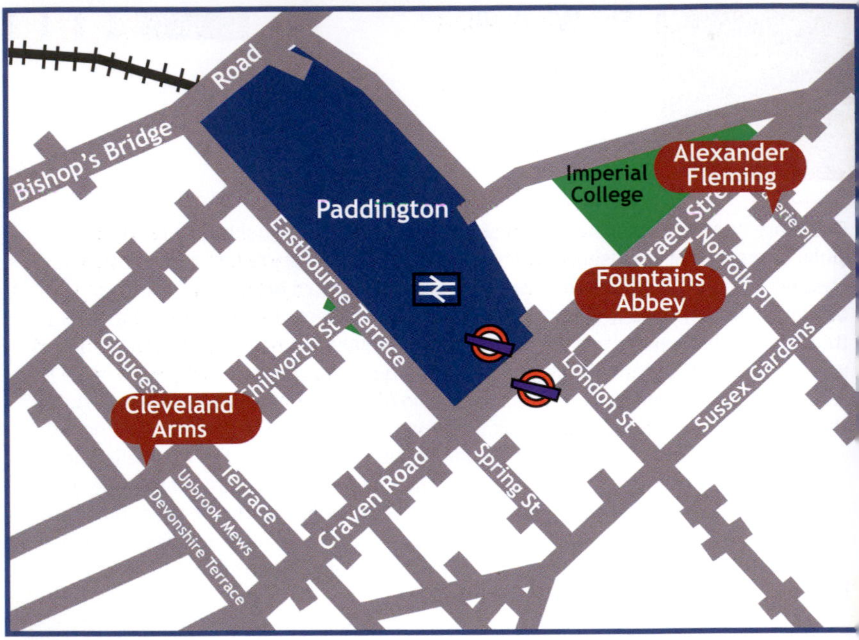

Bishop's Bridge Road
Paddington
Imperial College
Alexander Fleming
Praed Street
Norfolk Pl
Fountains Abbey
Eastbourne Terrace
Chilworth St
London St
Sussex Gardens
Gloucester Terrace
Cleveland Arms
Upbrook Mews
Devonshire Terrace
Craven Road
Spring St

The Cleveland Arms

RATING:

28 Chilworth Street
W2 6DT
020 7706 1759

A real find within spitting distance of Paddington station. The Cleveland Arms is a proper pub, eclectically decorated, nestling within an area full of large white Georgian townhouses. It is not particularly big, but people are often more than happy to make room – particularly on the quiz night, which is a friendly occasion, despite the gruffness of the quizmaster/landlord (we think he's just shy). There are three ales on tap (Greene King IPA, Bass and a guest ale), and more choice in bottles, plus the usual; all at decent prices, as befits a truly independent pub. The background music is just that – in the background. Plus, we should mention the food in this review: it is honestly and unashamedly microwaved in front of you on the bar, and not only tasty but excellent value.

FEATURES:       

Fountains Abbey

RATING:

109 Praed Street
W2 1RL
020 7723 2364

Fountains Abbey is a massive pub that's just a little bit too close to Paddington station. The transient clientele don't do it any favours, but the staff seem to cope pretty well with the churn and demands of a busy pub. It's got decent beer, kept to Cask Marque standards and standard pub grub. Despite many makeovers in its time, the interior still retains some of the original Victorian features – check out the tilework near the bar. While probably not a pub to write home about, it does the job in a reliable fashion. It gets busy, but that's no surprise this close to the station. Nonetheless, for a decent pint, this isn't a bad bet.

FEATURES:    

Sir Alexander Fleming

RATING:

16, Bouverie Place
W2 1RB
020 7723 6061

Despite a nice back-street location and a relatively attractive exterior, the Sir Alexander Fleming is a bit of a wasted opportunity. A change of ownership in 2006 cleared away the plants outside, along with the net curtains and apparently the rather scary clientele, only to replace it with essentially nothing. So it's pretty soulless overall – the unattractive bar sits at odds with an otherwise bland and forgettable space – we weren't expecting a penicillin-themed pub, but a better nod to the great man after whom the pub is named wouldn't have gone amiss. A recent Friday-night visit found a fairly lively mix of locals and a few people who'd obviously wandered in from the myriad of local hotels. It's a shame the two large-screen TVs were used to blast our eardrums with tunes from a middle-of-the-road music channel.

FEATURES:  

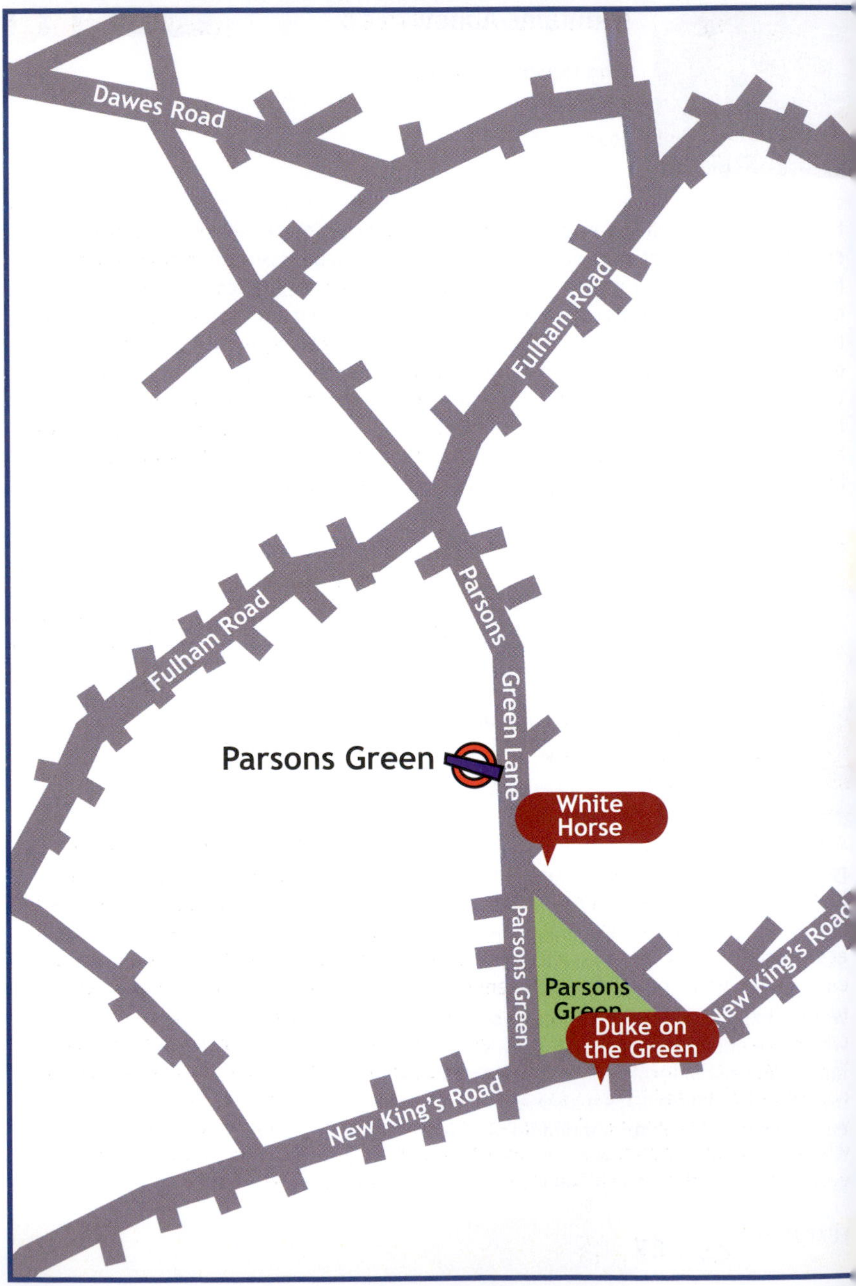

Dawes Road

Fulham Road

Fulham Road

Parsons Green Lane

Parsons Green

White Horse

Parsons Green

Parsons

Duke on the Green

New King's Road

New King's Road

The Duke on the Green

RATING: 4

235 New King's Road
SW6 4XG
020 7736 2777

Located across the Green from the more famous White Horse, this pub is proving competition for its more widely known compatriot. Long gone are the hordes of footy fans that rampaged through here on the way to Craven Cottage, and a much more civilised experience is on offer. Thankfully, the lovely Victorian tilework at the front of the pub has been left intact after the last refurb – it positively glows. There's an extensive international wine list, and the beers on the pumps are all Wells and Young's, hardly surprising as they had a massive presence just over the river until recently. The food looks good, if a little pricey (even for London), but that's probably a by-product of where it is. And it doesn't seem to stop the locals tucking in. Worth a look – particularly if you can't get into the pub across the way.

FEATURES:    

The White Horse

RATING: 3

1–3 Parsons Green
SW6 4UL
020 7736 2115

A bit of a landmark in Parsons Green, this was one of the last staging posts on the route in and out of London, with quite a bit of history surrounding the pub and its location – it definitely feels a bit rural, even with a tube station just around the corner. It's got a great Victorian interior and superb sun spot out in front that borders the actual Green. It's very easy to see why it's been listed in the *Good Beer Guide* as the eight hand pumps provide an excellent selection of real ales that are well kept and really hit the spot on a lovely afternoon. We don't often see Hobson's Mild in the capital, and it was very quaffable. It has had a reputation in the past as being a bit 'Sloaney', but we found little evidence of that on our last visit, elbow-to-elbow with a couple of builders at the bar and an older gentleman reading the paper across the way. It's got a very good-looking menu, if a bit pricey, and it does regular barbecues when the weather permits. It's an excellent place to go as a destination and we can easily imagine whiling away an afternoon or an evening here.

FEATURES:   

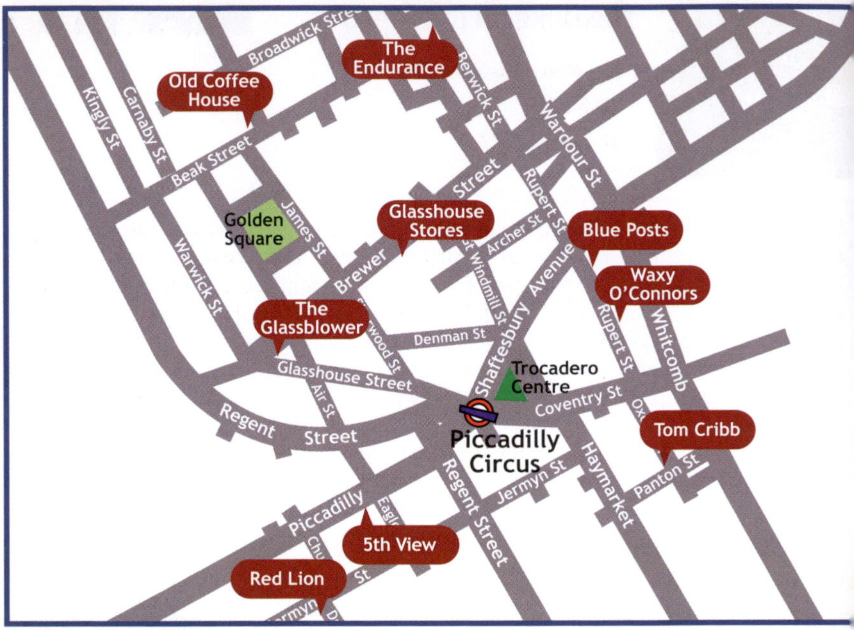

5th View

RATING:

203–206 Piccadilly
W1J 9LE
020 7851 2433

If you're in a literary frame of mind and feeling the need for classy surroundings in which to imbibe, you'll find the solution in the unlikely combination of old-style class, 21st-century book retailing and a museum caterer. The venue for all these needs is the venerable Simpson of Piccadilly department store, now a Waterstone's bookstore and host to 5th View – a bar/restaurant located on the eponymous 5th floor, run by Digby Trout, who run similar enterprises in a number of museums and galleries around the country. There's an indecently large beer menu, ranging from decent bitters to knock-you-out Belgian brews and they don't mind if you stay for just one. The wine list is also pretty decent and, if that won't do, you can always try a cocktail or two. The food is naturally pricey, but good and the table service is fast, friendly and polite. There's a fine view and, if it wasn't for the early closing (they say it's 10pm, but it's really 9:30), it would be a four pinter. One worth visiting.

HANDY FOR: The Royal Academy

Blue Posts

RATING:

28 Rupert Street
W1D 6DJ
020 7437 1415

For a pub so close to the tackfest that is the Trocadero Centre, this one makes a fair go at being a normal boozer. That a decent drop of Timothy Taylor Landlord can be had helps, as does the rather lived-in feel of the pub (you sense there's been some good nights celebrated here over the years). Not a stone-cold classic but, given the area, a pub with a welcome bit of atmosphere.

FEATURES:   

HANDY FOR: The Trocadero Centre

The Endurance

RATING: 

90 Berwick Street
W1F 0QB
020 7437 2944

Replacing The King of Corsica – a rather rough and ready boozer in Berwick Street Market – is this modern take on the pub experience. Even though it was a bit of a rough house, the old pub had a certain something. The old clientele has moved on to a new regular now, as this one is clearly aimed at a younger and trendier crowd. Smart and plush inside, it's worth noting that food is only served until 6pm. Once the plates get cleared away, attention shifts to the excellent jukebox – quite arguably the best in Soho. An above-average venue for this neck of the woods, it's just slightly odd that this self-styled 'traditional fish and game pub restaurant' is sited so close to most of Soho's strip joints – are they due for a Wallpaper-style makeover too?

FEATURES:   

The Glassblower

RATING:

40–42 Glasshouse Street
W1B 5DL
020 7734 8547

Located just off Regent Street, this one feels like it's trying to strike a balance between being a harmless tourist pub and a slightly trendy West End bar. It's more former than latter all told, with cheapish food but it still suffers from the old problem of its anti-tardis effect (it looks bigger on the outside than it does on the inside). As well as a choice of international bottled beers, it's got decent beer after a bit of a dry spell, with Butcombe's bitter and Shepherd Neame's Whitstable Bay two of the selections when we were in last. A smaller upstairs bar can often be a breathing space, but don't be too surprised if you find it hired out for a private function. Not a bad effort though: it certainly fits the bill if you're after somewhere to meet near Piccadilly Circus. You may even find yourself staying a bit longer than expected.

FEATURES:  

HANDY FOR: The Royal Academy

Glasshouse Stores

55 Brewer Street
W1F 9UN
020 7287 5278

A quirky Sam Smith's pub in the heart of the touristy bit of Soho. Some nice old features remain and give the pub an olde worlde atmosphere. It's larger than it looks from the outside, with a basement bar and space out the back to have a cigarette hidden away, along with a hugely enjoyable bar billiards table. There's usually a regular or two in the front part of the pub – it's that kind of place – along with the usual smattering of Soho media office workers. It's better than a lot of the tourist traps in the area, made even better by Sam Smith's (cheap) pricing. As long as you have a liking for Sam Smith's fare – and not everyone does – this one's a good place to meet up in if you're heading further into Soho. It's also one of the better pubs in this neck of the woods on Friday and Saturday nights.

FEATURES:    

HANDY FOR: The Royal Academy

Old Coffee House

RATING:

49 Beak Street
W1F 9SF
020 7437 2197

A traditional-looking pub, with loads of knickknacks hanging from the ceiling and pictures on the wall to impress the tourists – ranging from posters for prize fighters to recruitment posters from the Second World War to beer ads to a stuffed antelope head – but it doesn't have that forced olde worlde look some places do, because it's looked like this forever. Probably Victorian, it looks older, which is fine for visitors and it is, after all, a proper pub. After work, it's packed with local workers and, although some stay and some go, providing a steady turnover of people, the atmosphere somehow manages to stay relaxed. Every so often a bunch of tourists wander into the place, but the pub takes them in its stride. Inexpensive food in good quantity, plus Wadworth 6X, Deuchars and Pedigree were on draft last time we were in and, with prompt, attentive service, this pub would be a pretty decent local anywhere, especially remarkable in Soho.

FEATURES:  

The Red Lion (Duke of York St)

RATING: 

2 Duke of York St
SW1Y 6JP
020 7321 0782

The Red Lion is an old-style traditional pub. It's small, has great beers on the hand pumps (Cask Marque standard) and a stunning interior. This is a great pub to come to when you are out and about in the West End and fancy a quiet pub – unfortunately, the world and his mother has had the same idea so it's seldom one you'll get a bit of peace in. However, if you time your visit with precision you'll be suitably rewarded. Lethal stairs to the toilets though.

FEATURES: 

HANDY FOR: The Royal Academy

Tom Cribb

RATING: 

36 Panton Street
SW1Y 4EA
020 7747 9951

A small pub with a lovely tiled exterior, the Tom Cribb is hidden sufficiently behind Leicester Square that you should be able to enjoy a reasonable drink most of the time. Named after a 19th-century world champion English bare-knuckle boxer who owned a pub nearby, it can fill up after the Prince of Wales Theatre empties out. Even so, it's a friendly enough place and serves a nice pint, too. Our last visit found the barmaid more prone to serving the regulars she was chatting to before other customers, but we'll give the benefit of the doubt this time. A knockout pub this isn't, but it still clinches a three pint rating.

FEATURES: 

HANDY FOR: The Royal Academy

Waxy O'Connors

RATING: 

14–16 Rupert Street
W1D 6DF
020 7287 0255

More theme park than pub, this cavernous, never-ending pub is truly enormous. A full-grown tree in the middle of the pub adds to the Tolkien-esque air of the place. Still, it does serve a mean pint of (rather rare nowadays) Beamish and a decent enough pint of the other dark stuff. Overall, though, it's about as authentically Irish as an inflatable leprechaun.

FEATURES:   

HANDY FOR: The Trocadero Centre

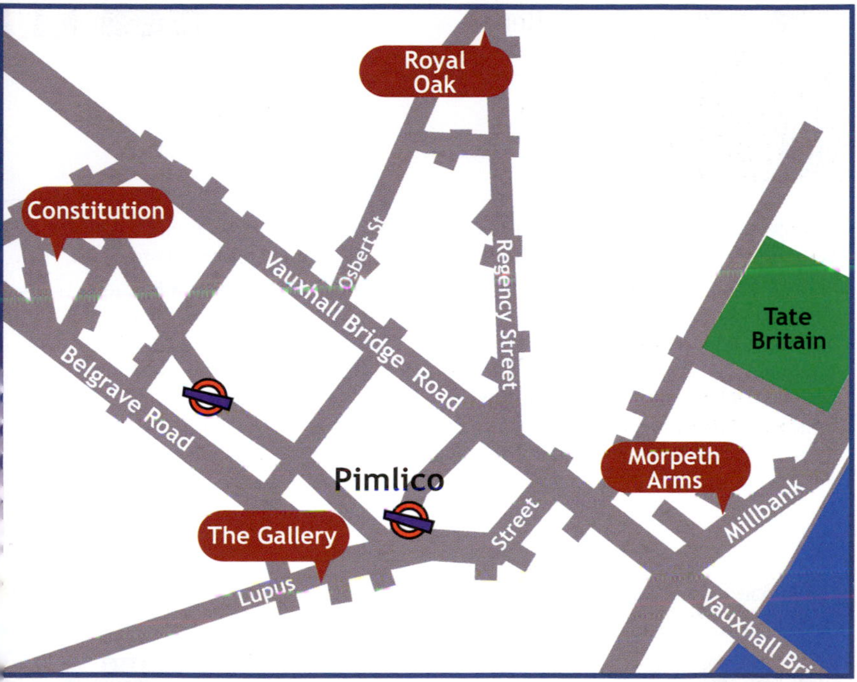

Royal Oak
Constitution
Osbert St
Regency Street
Vauxhall Bridge Road
Tate Britain
Belgrave Road
Pimlico
Morpeth Arms
Millbank
The Gallery
Street
Lupus
Vauxhall Bri

Constitution

RATING: 

42 Churton Street
SW1V 2LP
020 7834 3651

Nestled in the more charming villagey part of Pimlico, The Constitution is a butterfly of a pub. On certain visits we've found the clientele were resolutely of the local-men variety, all there to watch the football. However, at certain times, a metamorphosis occurs and, as the lone men wend their way home, they are replaced by younger, friendlier couples and groups all out for a quiet evening of socialising. As a result, the place magically becomes more inviting – unfortunately we just can't predict when this happens. Inside, the décor is pleasantly old school, the staff efficient, the food cheap and the ales well kept. We should also be grateful that it can provide a good place for a quieter drink on a Friday night: while other nearby pubs are filled to the rafters with after-work drinkers, The Constitution is usually a more pleasant place to be.

FEATURES:      **HANDY FOR:** Westminster Cathedral, Tate Britain

The Gallery

RATING:

1 Lupus Street
SW1V 3AS
020 7821 7573

Despite its proximity to Pimlico tube, The Gallery is often a lot less frenetic than the other workers' pubs scattered around the area. Indeed, it seems that it straddles, pretty successfully, a fine line between old-bloke local pub and after-work hangout. The interior is decked in a simple refurbished style, but it's comfortable enough and the nooks and crannies make it vaguely interesting. We also like the upstairs bar where you can grab a seat overlooking the street while simultaneously getting a bird's eye view of those sitting on the ground floor (with the help of the eponymous gallery). Nothing very exciting on the taps, but the pub grub is reasonable and the service considerably more cheerful than average. If you're after a normal pub and want to be as close to Pimlico tube as possible without actually being on the Victoria line, then The Gallery is your best bet.

FEATURES:   

HANDY FOR: Tate Britain

Morpeth Arms

RATING: 

58 Millbank
SW1P 4RW
020 7834 6442

A traditional Young's pub that's been given the redecoration and rebranding which so many other Young's pubs have had in the last few years. Probably the thinking is that the cultured visitors to Tate Britain wouldn't dream of setting foot in an old-fashioned pub, so let's give them something more modern. Whilst we're sad to see that this one's interior has been slightly altered to make room for more 'vertical drinkers' (i.e. people standing up), a noticeable change is now the level of service here. The Morpeth always seemed to have all the right ingredients for a great pub, but in our experience it never was. The refurbished Morpeth won't be for everyone, but the alterations aren't as wholesale as in some other Young's pubs and they haven't resulted in the Morpeth ending up as a wannabe gastropub. The beer is as good as it ever was and the service from the staff has definitely improved: reason enough then for this one to be promoted to a three pint rating.

FEATURES:    

HANDY FOR: Tate Britain

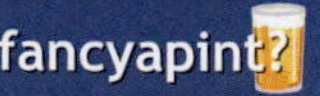

The Royal Oak

RATING: 3 pints

2 Regency Street
SW1P 4BZ
020 7834 7046

The Royal Oak is one of the more decent pubs in this area. The beer and food are good, bar staff friendly and the atmosphere is relaxed. It is busiest at the usual lunchtimes and few hours after work, but there appear to be enough locals to keep it pleasantly ticking over at other times. Worth a visit if you're in the area.

FEATURES:  

HANDY FOR: Tate Britain, Westminster Cathedral

PUTNEY/PUTNEY BRIDGE

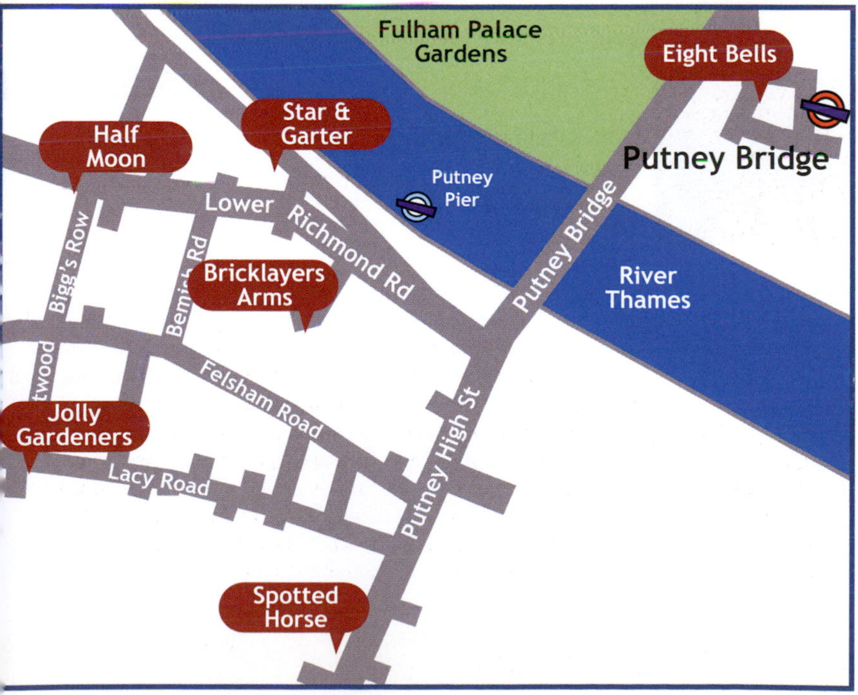

The Bricklayers Arms

RATING:

32 Watermans Lane
SW15 1DD
020 8789 0222

A slice of Yorkshire in Putney, this pub regularly has three, four and occasionally five Timothy Taylor's beers on tap. This makes it a rarity indeed, but the pub is more than just a flag waver for the brewery. The Bricklayers has a rather idiosyncratic approach to décor and hanging from the ceiling we noted a sledge, ice skates and party balloons, along with an Astroturfed beer garden. There's also a real local friendly feel to the place, so don't be too alarmed if you're brought into the conversation of your fellow drinkers or your gaze is caught by a game of shove ha'penny or bar skittles. There aren't many places like this in Putney – or in London for that matter – so give it a look if you're around. Well worth it.

FEATURES:   

The Eight Bells

88 Fulham High Street
SW6 3JS
020 7736 6307

This is a great traditional pub just across the bridge from Putney and when it's not packed with weekenders – footy, boat race, similar stuff – it's a real locals' place. That said, the locals are pretty friendly and happy to share. There's a couple of decent beers on the hand pumps, with Hogsback Brewery's T.E.A. on the pumps when we were in last, and ordinary pub grub for the lunchtime locals and friendly service. Pleasant enough place to spend an afternoon when it's quieter, its location means its handy to meet in as it's so near the station. And, as a result, it's a place many people start Putney pub crawls from.

FEATURES:  

Half Moon

RATING:

93 Lower Richmond Road
SW15 1EU
020 8780 9383

Pub that makes a lot of its musical heritage – U2 and the Stones both played here in their early days – with nods in that direction in the rota of covers bands which play here (Limehouse Lizzy, Achtung Baby – no sign of Half-Sister Sledge though). Still, the stage is removed enough from the pub if you're not here for a gig, and out of hours it's a relaxed sort of place with comfy sofas, a good jukebox, a decent selection of Young's beers and an oddly Mediterranean menu (lamb burger anyone?). It's competent and non-threatening – a bit like their musical bill. And worth a visit if you're in the area.

FEATURES:     

Jolly Gardeners

RATING:  

61–63 Lacey Road
SW15 1NT
020 8780 8921

Situated in the quiet suburban road of Lacey Street, SW15, the Jolly Gardeners is a rather good gastropub. In keeping with other such establishments, this one's all dim lighting, comfy leather seats, blackboards and coffee-table mix tapes on the stereo. Still, a nice, roomy, welcoming place, and not a bad selection of beers: when we visited Hopback Summer Lightning and Adnams were on and well kept. We can't speak for the food unfortunately, as we were too lazy to get out of our leather sofas near the cosy fire and order any. Still, it looked pretty much par for the course with mozzarella, olives, ciabattas and the like in abundance. If you're in the area and fancy that kind of thing you could do far worse.

FEATURES:  

The Spotted Horse

RATING:

122 Putney High Street
SW15 1JN
020 8788 0246

Another Young's pub that's 'benefited' from a makeover. We can hear you sigh from here. But it's not that bad, honest. OK, it's more of a lounge bar now, but it's comfortable (think squishy sofas and chairs, alongside butcher's block tables) and welcoming with decent beer on the taps and a good menu to go along with it. Add to that genial locals and a nice fire (best in winter, obviously) and it's just the sort of place to settle in for an evening. There's lots going on here, with Monday-night poker and the Wednesday-night quiz, but other times it's just a decent place with a dining area at the back. The pub has a tiny frontage, giving the misguided notion that it's not very big – even with the back converted largely to dining, the place still feels pretty massive once you get in, and we were pleasantly surprised how much we liked it. We'll no doubt be going back again soon.

FEATURES:       

Star & Garter

RATING:

4 Lower Richmond Road
SW15 1JN
020 8788 0345

We remember this place from way back when it used to be packed on hot summer nights with the young and trendy from the area and hordes of SW rugger-buggers. Saturday nights were always a bit lively and the area in front of it teemed with happy drunkards, trying not to get their feet wet. And we always stayed away on boat race day. Now this huge place is more bar than pub – no common pub grub here, they've put in a 'Cheese Room' and serve plates of charcuterie and cheese to the clientele. Gone are all the remnants of the pubs past, replaced with comfy chairs and conversation groups, albeit with great views over the river. There's an extensive wine list with an international flavour (including some rarities), but fear not: you can still get a decent pint from one of the two hand pumps. And, if you're stuck for a place to hold that knitting circle, there's a rather large room downstairs that's for hire. Don't get us wrong, it's welcoming enough and an excellent place for a pint during the week. We just wonder how they'll cope with the boat race now.

FEATURES:     

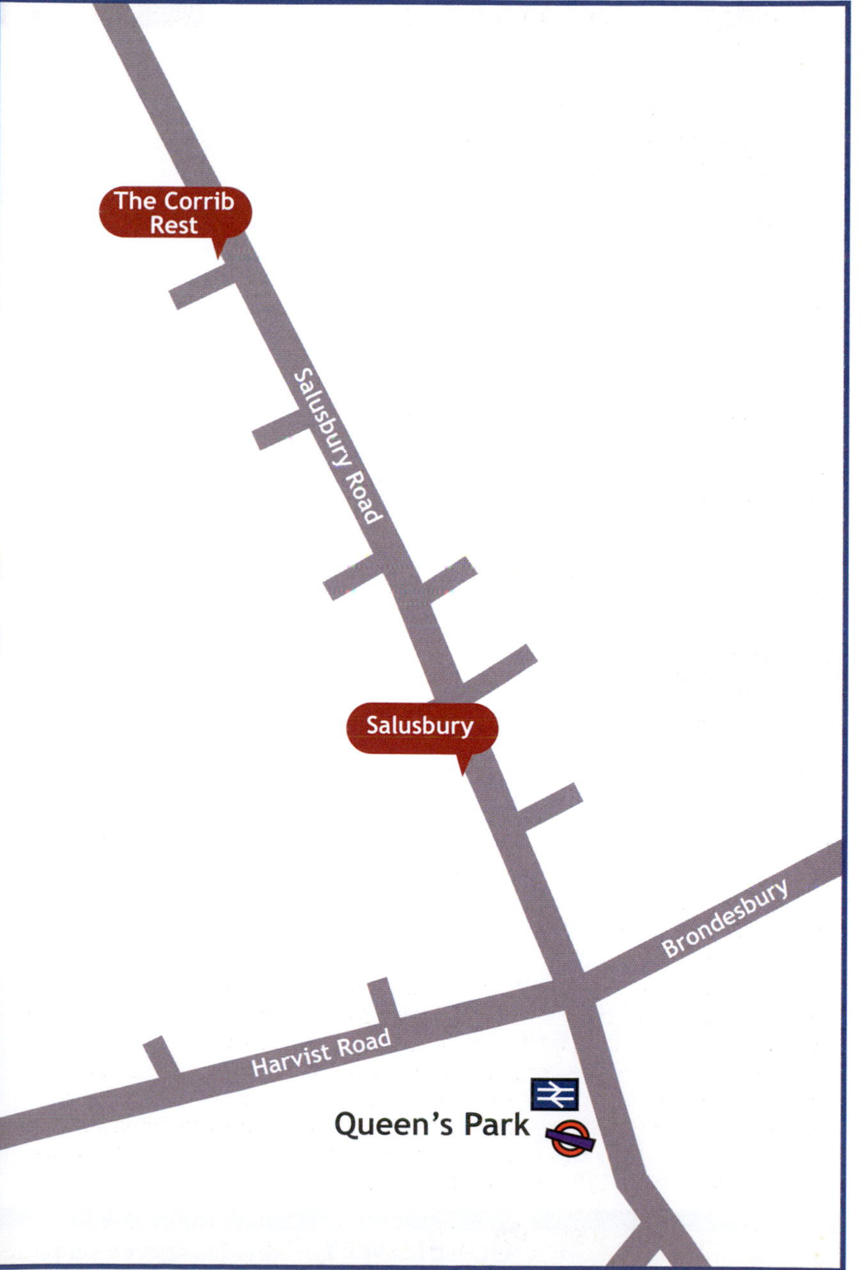
The Corrib Rest
Salusbury Road
Salusbury
Brondesbury
Harvist Road
Queen's Park

QUEEN'S PARK

The Corrib Rest

RATING:

76–82 Salusbury Road
NW6 6PA
020 7625 9585

When drinking in this pub, it's quite easy to believe you are in Ireland (especially as there are few windows to see London through). The pub is huge and wood-panelled with open fires and plenty of knickknacks on the walls but this is no theme pub – it has a traditional two-room bar/lounge design, you have to wait the proper length of time for your Guinness and the emphasis is definitely on drinking. Most tellingly, virtually all of the staff and customers at our visit were Irish. Live music at the weekends and the food's decent too. Interestingly, they offer regular Salsa and Irish dance classes – we can understand the Irish dance classes, but Salsa?!? In this day and age, whatever works...

FEATURES:        

Salusbury Pub & Dining Room

RATING:

50–52 Salusbury Road
NW6 6NN
020 7328 3286

Is this a gastropub or just a pub with a restaurant attached? However you describe it, the separation of pub from dining area here means you're not getting in the way of the diners and vice versa. Whereas most pubs limit the reggae they play to having Bob Marley's *Legend* on the jukebox, it's nice to find a place rather more in thrall to lesser known Jamaican artists. Covers of classic reggae albums adorn the walls, and on our visit some Ska and rock-steady sounds were being aired. It certainly adds to the relaxed air of the place. There was a wide selection of lagers as well as two Adnams beers on tap (and tasting fine). We thought the food smelled pretty good – we still can't vouch for the Dining Room (nor the Salusbury's organic food shop down the road), but the pub part of the equation works well.

FEATURES:    

QUEENSWAY – *see Bayswater, page 40*

Anglesea Arms
Paddenswick Road
Andover Arms
Ravenscourt Park
Bradmore Park Rd.
Glenthorne Roa
Ravenscourt Park
Dalling Road
Salutation
King Street
Great West Road
The Dove
Old Ship Inn
Furnival Gardens
River Thames

Andover Arms

RATING:

57 Aldensley Road
W6 0DL
020 8741 9794

Visit a pub between Hammersmith and Shepherd's Bush and it's probably a boozer bordering on scuzzdom, or a conversion aimed at the gastro market. If you're really unlucky, an Australian bar. The Andover Arms doesn't fit into any of those categories – even if its menu has been given a gastro tweak of late – being a decent, well-run locals' pub. Good Fuller's beers, friendly staff and a pleasant atmosphere make this one of the best drinking holes in W6. It's the sort of comfortable pub where 'popping in for one' may stretch to an afternoon session. If you like your pubs in London to be hidden away with a 'village' air to them, hunt this one down.

FEATURES: 

Anglesea Arms

RATING:

35 Wingate Road
W6 0UR
020 8749 1291

The Anglesea Arms is a very popular gastropub that caters for the well-spoken trend-setters of W6. It's a pleasant place when it's quiet, but it can get horribly busy when it's feeding time at the zoo. Furnished in the archetypal gastropub style of stripped floors, wooden chairs and assorted mixed furniture, this is a much more comfortable place to drink in than most of the dives on the nearby Goldhawk Road – and a real fire adds cosy charm in the winter. There's Pride and Landlord on the hand pumps, a good range of other beers, lager and cider and, of course, a pretty extensive wine list. Dining is predominately carried out in the large area at the back of the bar, but a word of warning – if you are after food here, it's first come first served, so you may have to wait an age for a table.

FEATURES:  

The Dove

RATING: 3 pints

19 Upper Mall
W6 9TA
020 8748 9474

A pleasant old pub on the river, a short walk from Hammersmith Bridge. It looks like a good British pub should – situated in a narrow alleyway, a low door opening into dingy interior with nooks and crannies furnished with old wooden chairs, stools and benches. The pub opens at the back into a riverside terrace which has had a couple of extra ad hoc extensions. That might give you a clue as to why we don't rate this pub any higher than a three – quite simply it's almost always packed. If you like jostling shoulder to shoulder with people and doing the furtive vacant table search as you chat to your mates, then this is the pub for you. Although, as one might expect, if you choose a sunny weekday afternoon rather than a weekend, you'll stand a much better chance to relax here, at which point it easily becomes a four pinter. The beer is well kept (it doesn't exactly have far to travel) and the food is good British pub grub.

FEATURES:    

HANDY FOR: Riverside Studios

Old Ship Inn

RATING: 

25 Upper Mall
W6 9TD
020 8748 2593

The Old Ship is a large pub located on the north bank of the river, just down from Hammersmith Bridge, with a handy, grassed, open space just to the side of it. You don't have to be Einstein to surmise that on a warm day this area proves to be very popular. And indeed it is, so much so that a sunny bank holiday will find little available space for latecomers to park their picnics and grab a pint. There's an elevated terrace too, but you have to be a very early bird to get a place. Recently taken over by Young's, the Old Ship doesn't yet appear to have changed that much – only one pump with Young's bitter in operation and decidedly un-Young's Erdinger present amongst the gas-propelled brigade when we visited. Food is heavily promoted – something the owners seem to be doing rather a lot of nowadays, it's also family-friendly, got a function room and has WiFi if you just can't stop Twittering. The old Old Ship never really was our cup of tea (can you say that about a pub?) – the weekend hordes put paid to that – and, in its latest guise, we can't really see that opinion changing.

FEATURES:    

HANDY FOR: Riverside Studios

RAVENSCOURT PARK

Salutation

RATING:

154 King Street
W6 0QU
020 8748 3668

The Salutation is a pretty decent pub, with a rather unusual Edwardian tiled facade. It serves excellent Fuller's beers accompanied by basic pub grub. It has an airy feel, helped by the conservatory and sizeable beer garden at the back. There's a big screen with Sky for the footy (and other sports). It's a jolly good pub (especially to while away a Saturday afternoon) in an area lacking in them – proving it can be done.

FEATURES:   

REGENT'S PARK – *see Gt Portland Street, page 169*

RICHMOND

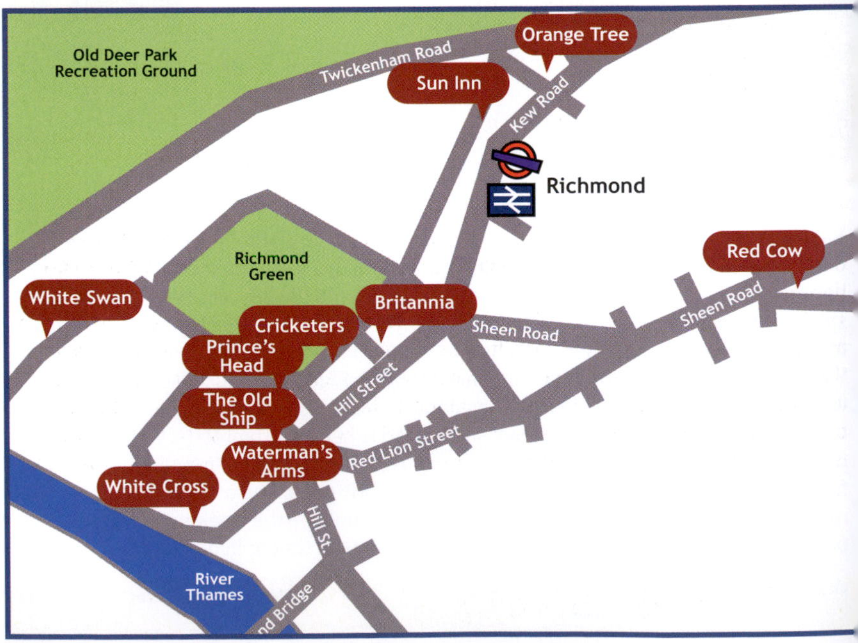

Old Deer Park Recreation Ground
Twickenham Road
Orange Tree
Sun Inn
Kew Road
Richmond
Richmond Green
White Swan
Cricketers
Britannia
Red Cow
Prince's Head
Sheen Road
Sheen Road
Hill Street
The Old Ship
Waterman's Arms
Red Lion Street
White Cross
Hill St.
River Thames
nd Bridge

The Britannia

RATING:

5 Brewers Lane
TW9 1HH
020 8940 1071

Promisingly situated down a side-street called Brewers Lane, this is possibly the best of the cluster of pubs just off Richmond's George Street. All bases seem to be covered: decent food, fair drink and an atmosphere conducive to enjoying them. The TVs for the sport don't seem to get in the way of nattering locals, and, when the weather allows, there's a good-sized garden and roof terrace at the back to sample. As an optional extra there's also a comedy club upstairs on a Sunday night. Back to the drink, the wine list seemed well chosen, whilst ales offered included Sharp's Doom Bar. In showing there's more to the Massive pub brand than Identikit Tup pubs, this one has a rather singular air to it – which is probably why photos of Sean Connery (as Bond with his Aston, naturally) and hirsute rakes Charles Rennie Mackintosh and Graham Hill fit in nicely on the wall.

FEATURES:      

The Cricketers

RATING: 

The Green
TW9 1LX
020 8940 4372

The Cricketers is a handsome pub in a picturesque British setting. It's very much the tourist ideal of the English pub, especially in summer when there's cricket played on the Green out front. In fact, The Cricketers is so true-to-type, it has even appeared on TV once or twice. It's a Greene King pub so the drink and food are usually up to scratch and the service polite and efficient. It can get pretty packed on a summer's day when the sun's out and there's cricket on the Green and occasionally things can get a little fraught here when the crowds overwhelm the staff. And should the British weather behave as you expect you can always go indoors and watch the rain from the handy upstairs room, or the sport on one of the TVs. A popular place and understandably so.

FEATURES:   

The Old Ship

RATING:

3 King Street
TW9 1ND
020 8940 3461

With stylish wood panelling and beams, there's an appropriate ship-like feel to this pub that's been serving ale since at least 1735, when it was a major coaching stop. But it's not all olde worlde charm, the 21st century is represented by three substantial screens for the big sports events; understandably it's popular for the rugby and free WiFi for those who can't live without their hourly Facebook fix. The pub is much bigger than the exterior suggests, there are two bars served by the central island as well as an upstairs bar which can be hired out. The drink's good – it's Young's so you'd expect it to be – and ambience for all and thankfully it's not been given the Young's 'modern' treatment. The only (minor) negative we can attribute here is the quality of the food, which we found to be rather basic and unimaginative tourist fodder. Still, worthy of stopping by for a pint or two.

FEATURES:    

Orange Tree

RATING: 

45 Kew Road
TW9 2NQ
020 8940 0944

One of the more famous pubs in the area, the stylish 19th-century exterior would lead you to believe the interior is of a similar vintage. Unfortunately this is not the case, it appears the All Bar One people sneaked in and redesigned it when Young's weren't looking. So here we have another one of those bare-floorboard and sofa venues, designed to appeal to the same punters you'll get down at the Pitcher & Piano on Richmond's riverfront and the City. It's very close to the station and, when you add big-screen TV, this pub naturally gets pretty busy when the rugby (or cricket) is on. Expect to pay Richmond prices (i.e. not cheap) for the usual (admittedly good) Young's food and drink. Unfortunately, it all adds up to a so-so experience.

FEATURES:   

Prince's Head

RATING: 

28 The Green
TW9 1LX
020 8940 1572

The Prince's Head is a pretty straightforward local. It's a Fuller's pub, so you know the beer will be good, the food is unpretentious pub grub, there are plenty of screens for the sport (which is not always rugby – a rarity in these parts) and you can always sit outside if it's a nice day. It's a reasonably sized place, so when it's busy if you don't get at seat at least you're not being elbowed out of the way and you can always sit on the benches in the nice paved area outside, or stroll across to the Green for the full picnic experience. Balancing the weekend crowds with the after-work crowds quite nicely, the Prince's Head is a decent honest boozer in a very handy location.

FEATURES:  

The Red Cow

RATING: 

59 Sheen Road
TW9 1YJ
020 8940 2511

The Red Cow has been serving beer to the locals of Richmond for over 200 years and continues to do a fine job today. Being a Young's pub, it has the usual excellent range of ales, which can help you wash down home-cooked food from a menu that changes daily. It's had a bit of a refurb in recent times, with the addition of some tall tables and bar stools plus loungey furniture that have added a touch of the Casbah at the rear of the pub. The pub's splendid Victorian decoration remains intact and, with the big screens for sport around the pub, it adds up to an interesting but comfortable mix. If beer, food or sport isn't enough for you, there's usually live music at the weekend and, if the prospect of a walk down to the station seems too much like hard work, you can always stay in one of the bedrooms here. All in all, The Red Cow is a jolly fine pub for locals and visitors alike.

FEATURES:      

Sun Inn

RATING:

17 Parkshot
TW9 2RG
020 8940 1019

No surprise to find a pub with such strong rugby ties here, but there is such a proliferation of Union rules photos, drawings, shirts, and even boots, that the ceiling has been pressed into action to accommodate it all. Of course, it can get rammed on the usual match days, and has big and small screens throughout to show them, but, somehow with the handful of outside tables, a big back seating area and determined service, it seems to cope quite well. Despite this, outside the rugby calendar it functions competently as a decent side-street local. They offer pub grub, and seem to play easy listening which was, well, easy to listen too. The small central bar had hand pumps offering Pride et al and a standard range of lagers etc.

FEATURES:   

Waterman's Arms

RATING: 

12 Water Lane
TW9 1TJ
020 7093 2883

Hidden away on the approach to the river, this Young's pub is slightly overshadowed by its bigger relation, the White Star Hotel, just around the corner. On first impressions it seems like a solid little locals' pub, and entering confirms those impressions. A friendly local then, with a regular crowd, very possibly those of a river-faring nature. If you don't fancy nursing a pint of ordinary while you search for a corner that isn't already taken, you can pop upstairs and get a fine and reasonably priced Thai meal. If you don't feel up to the rough and tumble of crowded bars filled with thick-necked, collars-up rugger-buggers, this could be the sensible option.

FEATURES:  

White Cross

RATING:

Riverside
TW9 1TJ
020 8940 6844

In Richmond, on a warm summer's evening, everyone wants to be by the river and the White Cross is where they go. Drinkers mill between the water's edge and the pub, occupying a space that gets steadily less accommodating as the tide comes in – there's even a high side entrance, should the tide swamp the front of the pub. A pair of terraces also help contain the crowds, but these fill up quickly. Inside the pub, there's a central bar where the staff work quickly, politely and efficiently to service the demand for the excellent Young's beer. Ironically, if it is a fine day it's usually not difficult to find a seat inside. The kitchen works non-stop to keep the hungry sated and there's a paging system to let you know your food's ready, wherever you may be. The White Cross is a well-known and easy-to-find pub in a picturesque setting so its popularity was never in doubt, but it's particularly pleasing that it continues to be a proper pub and not the cliché tourist trap it could so easily be.

FEATURES:   

White Swan

RATING: 

Old Palace Lane
TW9 1PG
020 8940 0959

Tucked away on a little lane between Richmond Green and the river, this old pub, built 1777, is more of a locals' place than some of the neighbouring establishments. Being just off the beaten track means, on days when the rest of Richmond is bursting at the seams, this place is a welcome oasis of calm. There are three decent beers on the hand pumps and the wine list is good, but here at the White Swan there's a stronger emphasis on food. The menu looks a little pricey at first glance, but the quality is right up there. And the fact it's often fully booked at the weekend is testament to the quality – especially in view of all the surrounding competition in Richmond town. There are a couple of tables out front and a nice sheltered beer garden and conservatory at the rear for those rare fine days. The occasional rattle of trains on the embankment at the back does little to disturb this haven of calm. When you add polite, friendly service and amiable locals you have the perfect recipe for a relaxing summer's afternoon.

FEATURES:    

ROTHERHITHE – *see Canada Water, page 78*

RUSSELL SQUARE

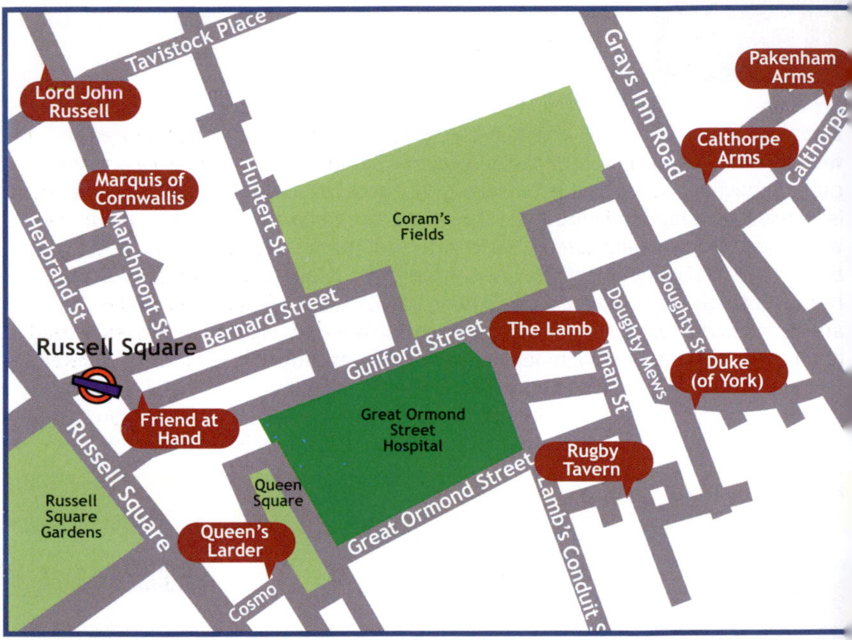

Calthorpe Arms

RATING:

252 Grays Inn Road
WC1X 8JR
020 7278 4732

This is a fairly quiet and comfortable pub not far from King's Cross, with a local crowd enjoying its traditional atmosphere. A nice pint of Special is to be had (all of the Young's range is usually on offer) and they do food all day too – including a hearty Sunday roast. There's also an upstairs bar which is available to hire. This is a fine pub and, if you're in the area, give it a look in. We're just hoping it's not on the list of pubs to be 'fixed' in Wells and Young's latest spasms of pub regeneration.

FEATURES:    

Duke (of York)

RATING:

7 Roger Street
WC1N 2PB
020 7242 7230

Slightly off the beaten track, this gastropub has a local feel and caters for local workers. The pub forms part of a handsome Art Deco building. The striking bar area catches the eye – Formica tables, bold red and black lino flooring – and the dining area is wood panelled with private, dark leather booths: the kind of place you can picture Wyndham Lewis sneering at you over lunch. Full marks for the décor then, though the beer selection of continental lagers and the odd ale is slightly less impressive; however, the bar snacks are tasty and cheap. Still, when we last looked in, the atmosphere was relaxed and inviting, so much so one of the other punters felt moved to take to the piano. Definitely worth a look if you want something a little bit different.

FEATURES:  

Friend at Hand

RATING: 

4 Herbrand Street
WC1N 1HX
020 7837 5524

We remember this pub when it used to have a bit of a seafaring theme (the pub sign was of a lifeboat rescue) and the interior was done up to look like the inside of a capsized sailing ship (or at least that's how it appeared to us). More recently, the interior was returned to a more sensible, Victorianesque style of décor, more befitting the exterior and the sign now depicts a Saint Bernard. Basically, it's back to what it should be, an honest boozer, in a very touristy location, serving regular drink (Bombardier, Pride and Courage Best) and food to a thirsty and hungry clientele – local workers at lunchtime and tourists the rest of the time. All this offered with a genial smile on its face and plenty of sport on the telly.

FEATURES:      

The Lamb

RATING: 

94 Lamb's Conduit Street
WC1N 3LZ
020 7405 0713

The Lamb is a genial old boozer, with lots of Victorian charm – and that's just the locals. This place has been one of the top pubs in London for a long, long time and it still continues to maintain its high standards. The beer's good (Young's), the food's pretty decent, it's got some quaint Victorian fixtures and fittings, without it being too olde worlde – it gets the balance just right. The clientele are the genial pub-going type and even the drunks are polite and apologetic, they seem to operate a shift system just to make sure there's always one in. The Lamb is in an easy-to-get-to location, but it's just far enough away from the tourist trails to deter all but the determined and appreciative. Oh, and there's an upstairs function room if you need that kind of thing.

FEATURES:   

Visitors' Award – Overall Winner 2008

Lord John Russell

RATING: 

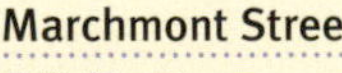

Marchmont Street
WC1N 1AL
020 7388 0500

The Lord John Russell is a pub with few pretensions, other than to be a no-nonsense locals' boozer. It's quite small and bright with large picture windows on two sides. It has a few tables outside too – although you may well find yourself sitting alongside the bins. There is a good range of drinks on tap (Wadworth 6X, Deuchars and John Smith's Barrel were on last time we were in) and the lunchtime food is of a decent quality and reasonably priced. We've had some varied service in this one over the years, but, when we last looked in, the quality of drink, range of punters and relaxed feel of the pub all added up to a decent experience. One to go a little out of the way for.

FEATURES:   

HANDY FOR: British Library

The Marquis of Cornwallis

RATING:

Marchmont Street
WC1N 1AP
020 7923 5961

Now that the Brunswick Shopping Centre has been relaunched as a centre for high-gloss retail, it's no surprise that this nearby pub – part of the cheap-as-chips world of the Goose chain – has had a makeover too. It's now one of Mitchells & Butlers unbranded pubs, which fits perfectly with how the Brunswick is marketing itself. The M&B ethic is in full effect here, with traditional ales (Spitfire, Timothy Taylor Landlord) and continental beers (Bellevue Kriek, Fruli etc.) sharing equal billing at the bar, and a mix of furnishings filling up both the ground-floor and upstairs bars. All very friendly, all very unthreatening – it has to be when your nearby competition includes a Carluccio's – but its hardwood floors means this one can get pretty noisy when there's a crowd in. The pub has been an immediate hit with local workers (and shoppers), although there's still one or two of the old regulars in attendance. As the area also attracts a fair few of our American cousins, we'll be intrigued to see if they'll be enticed to a pub named after a British commander in the American Revolutionary War...

FEATURES:   

Pakenham Arms

RATING: 

1 Calthorpe Street
WC1X 0LA
020 7837 6933

This pub is still a bit of all right, with loads of well-kept, interesting beers on the hand pumps (Doom Bar and Broadside were on when we were in last), loads of great cheap pub grub, loads of screens to watch the sport and a matey atmosphere (and we don't mean bubble bath). Its proximity to the Mount Pleasant sorting office probably has something to do with this, especially as the pub does breakfasts 9–11:30 – but, whatever the reason for the way it is, we like it. A refurb in the last little bit hasn't affected the quality of the place, just tidied it up a bit. It's even got decent toilets, though the steps in and out might prove a bit of a challenge after a couple of pints.

FEATURES:    

Queen's Larder

RATING:

1 Queen Square
WC1N 3AR
020 7837 5627

A tiny, tiny pub that's been here a long time. You can expect decent, well-kept beer, a quite nice olde worlde décor with theatre posters on the walls, a dining room upstairs, and a huge throughput of clientele (who always seem to be on their way somewhere else). However, it's not a bad place at all, being a cosy little spot in the depths of winter and a handy one for a seat outside in the summer. It shares a space on Cosmo Place with two restaurants and another pub and it's a bit of a touristy area, so, if you do chance an alfresco pint, be prepared to be serenaded by chancers with accordions. That aside, it's one of the best in the area. The name, as you'll know doubt find out if you take the time to read the plaque outside, comes from the time of King George III (yes, the mad one). He apparently stayed nearby under the care of his doctor and his consort, Queen Charlotte, rented the cellar beneath the current pub to store delicacies to help his recovery. It was then named in her honour.

FEATURES:    

Rugby Tavern

RATING: 

19 Great James Street
WC1N 3ES
020 7405 1384

What a decent pub this is. The clientele are a jolly and friendly crowd, and it's got good drink and food – after all, it is a Shepherd Neame pub. It's in a quiet, leafy location with some outdoor seating and it's right in the centre of London. It's recently(ish) been sympathetically refurbished, not stripped out like so many pubs today (don't get us started), and it has a pretty nice atmosphere. It's very well done all round, we say and we're hoping it doesn't change – it's one of the reasons we keep going in. Just watch out for the nights when all the corporate sporty types are in. It's got the feel of a good local, and that's what keeps us coming back.

FEATURES:    

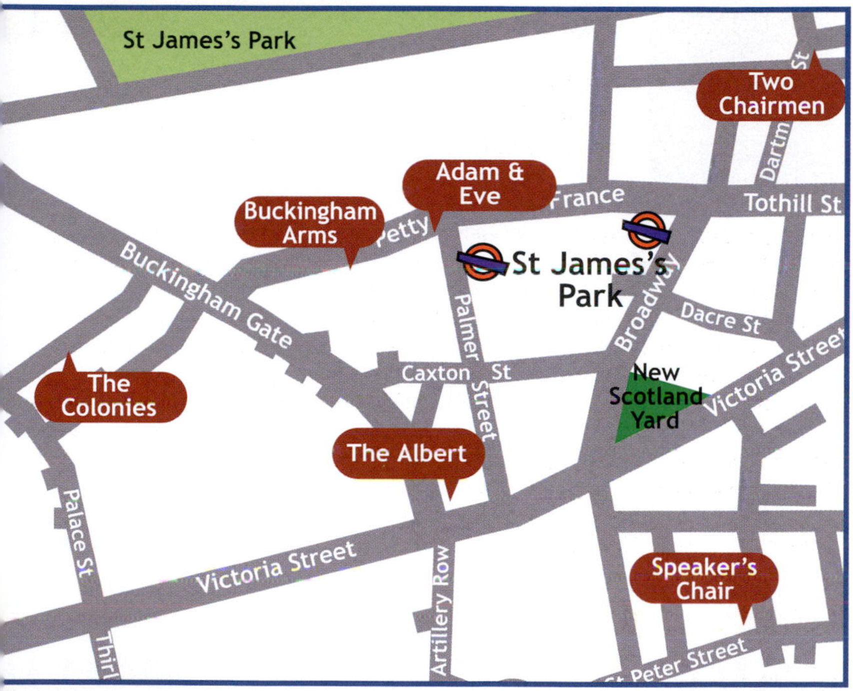

St James's Park
Two Chairmen
Dartm St
Adam & Eve
Buckingham Arms
Petty France
Tothill St
St James's Park
Buckingham Gate
Palmer Street
Broadway
Dacre St
Caxton St
The Colonies
New Scotland Yard
Victoria Street
The Albert
Palace St
Victoria Street
Artillery Row
Speaker's Chair
Thirl
St Peter Street

Adam & Eve

RATING:

81 Petty France
SW1H 9EX
020 7222 4575

The Adam & Eve is fairly standard for the area around St James's Park. It's pleasant enough, with standard refurbished wood décor, standard beers, standard food and standard prices, the Adam & Eve is busiest at lunchtimes and after work. A rebranded T&J Bernard pub, the beer here is well kept (as it always was in T&J pubs) and there's a reasonable choice, but the downside to this is, like others in this chain, it lacks a convincing pub atmosphere. And, as it's one of the two 'default' pubs on the walk back to the tube station from the offices roundabout, there are no prizes for guessing who comprises most of the clientele.

FEATURES: 

HANDY FOR: Cabinet War Rooms, Buckingham Palace

The Albert

RATING:

52 Victoria Street
SW1H 0NP
020 7222 5577

This huge Victorian pub is well placed for what it does – it's what all tourists expect from an English pub, so it's popular with them (and Chelsea Pensioners, apparently). But that doesn't mean it's not for the avid pub-goer. There's a good range of bitters on the hand pumps, with regulars such as Bombardier, Deuchars and IPA plus a guest beer – Theakston's Black Bull on our last visit – and decently kept. There's plenty of other drink on tap (including Leffe) and in bottles along with wines, spirits etc. It's a handsome building and, whilst the interior might be a shadow of its former self, the exterior amply demonstrates the palatial aspirations of the original builders. There's a strong emphasis on pub grub, which looks decent enough, although we haven't tried it, to fuel the tourist throngs. Surprisingly, considering where the pub is, the prices aren't sky-high and the service seems to cope admirably with the waves of visitors appearing at the usual times. As tourist pubs go, not a bad one at all.

FEATURES:   

HANDY FOR: Westminster Cathedral

Buckingham Arms

RATING: 

62 Petty France
SW1H 9EU
020 7222 3386

This handsome pub, dating from the early 19th century and situated in the back streets of Victoria, is one of only ten pubs to have appeared continuously in CAMRA's Good Beer Guide since its first publication. This wasn't enough, however, to exclude it from the relentless rota of owner Wells & Young's refurbishments. Having seen many other Young's refits which have erred on the trendier 'wine and food' side of the pub trade, we felt a certain amount of trepidation for the Buckingham. Thankfully, it's still a pub – after all, local civil servants still like a good pint (which you'll certainly get here). The original features are still more or less intact, with many gleaming after a good polish. The blue velvet bench seating is absent, replaced by additional chairs and tables, while the revamped menu still offers reasonable prices; £5.50 in change will give you a sandwich (*sans* the chips), while main courses float around the £8 mark. We rather liked the old Buckingham, but the newest version is perfectly acceptable too.

FEATURES: 

HANDY FOR: Cabinet War Rooms, Buckingham Palace

The Colonies

RATING:

25 Wilfred Street
SW1E 6PR
020 7834 1407

The best pubs in this area all tend to be tucked away in side streets and The Colonies is no exception. It's a vibrant place that's tailor-made for the after-office jar, and consequently fills up with local workers in the early evening. A good range of well-kept beers are all on the hand pumps – Pride, Young's bitter, Thwaite's Shuttle and Bateman's Jester when we were last there, accompanied by a standard range of lagers and wines. Nice old wood panelling and cosy décor make for a warm atmosphere, but the laminate flooring looks and feels a little out of place. It's also a fine place to go on a sunny day, as the beer garden out the back proves very popular with the local workers. Don't bother coming here at the weekend though – like many places round here, it's closed.

FEATURES:  

HANDY FOR: Westminster Cathedral, Buckingham Palace

The Speaker

RATING: 

46 Great Peter Street
SW1P 2HA
020 7222 1749

Despite The Speaker's proximity to Parliament, Civil Service HQs and Channel 4's offices, this is a cosy little pub ideal for a few jars on a dark night. It has the feel of a friendly local, mostly due to the cheery landlady who treats everyone as if she's been serving them for years. It's one of the best in the area, with an ever-changing supply of beer, this one's well worth hunting down. The only downside is the pub can get very busy at times (after work, towards the end of the week), although we suppose it just proves that a fervently traditional boozer such as this one can still rake in the customers.

FEATURES: 

HANDY FOR: Westminster Abbey, Houses of Parliament

Two Chairmen

RATING:

39 Dartmouth Street
SW1H 9BP
020 7222 8694

Hidden away in a secluded and exclusive area close to St James's Park, for many years the Two Chairmen remained the classic, cliché 'hidden gem'. Inevitably it was finally being 'discovered', by local civil servants, tourists and conference attendees. It does, however, still manage to retain some of the old local feel – quite a few of the clientele are regulars and know the barmen (and vice versa) and the interior is a cosy, old-fashioned, wood-panelled affair perfectly in keeping with the area. For beer-lovers, there's a good selection of well-kept beer on the hand pumps and the rest of the drinks menu is what you'd expect for an upmarket area such as this. Obviously early evenings and lunchtimes can see the place pretty crowded, so get here later (or earlier) if you want a seat. There is an upstairs room with a bar (which can be hired), but the bar itself is frequently not open, so you'll often have to negotiate the narrow stairs with your precious pints if it's your round. Like the City, it's rather quiet in these parts at the weekend, so unfortunately the pub isn't open then. But should you find yourself midweek, mid-afternoon in the area, you'll find the Two Chairmen a welcome detour.

FEATURES:   **HANDY FOR:** Cabinet War Rooms, Westminster Abbey, Downing Street

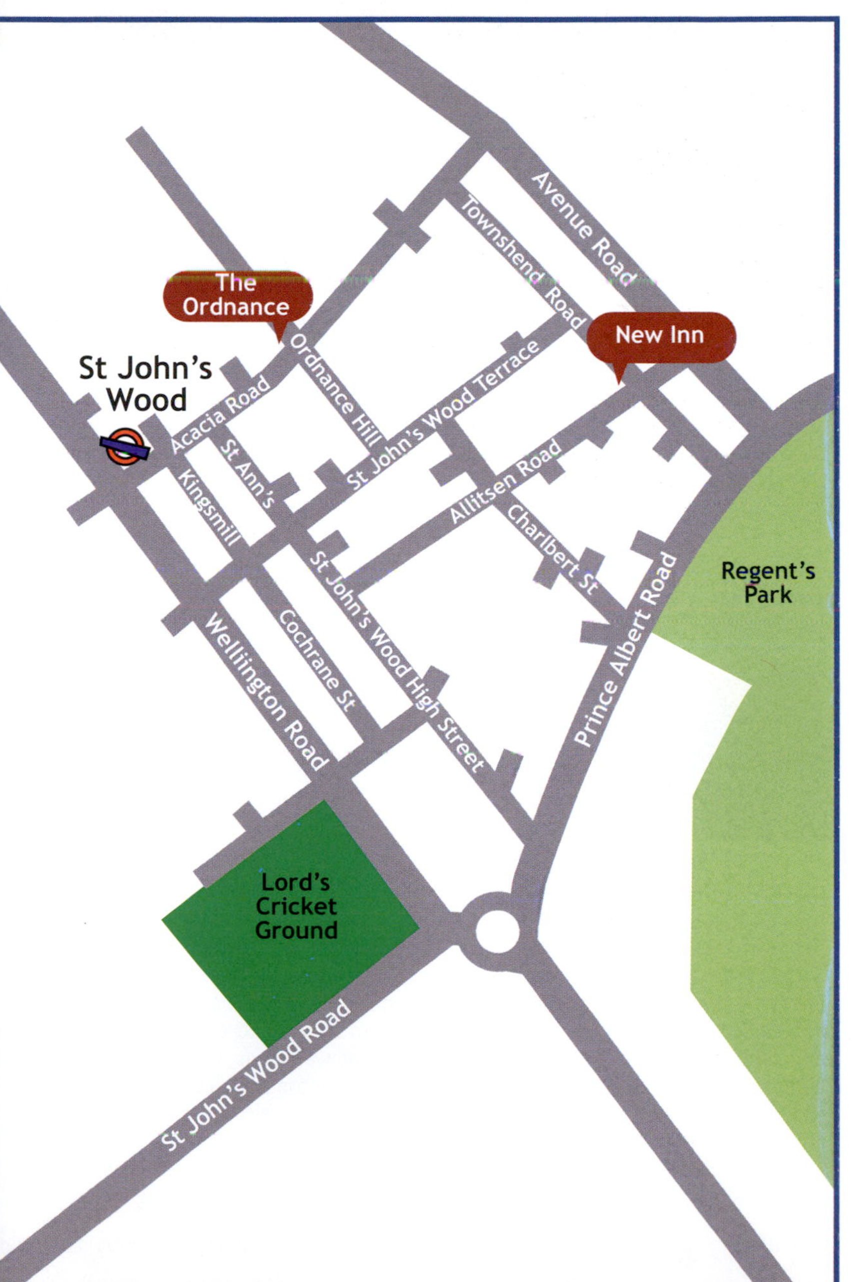
The Ordnance
New Inn
St John's Wood
Avenue Road
Townshend Road
Acacia Road
Ordnance Hill
St John's Wood Terrace
St Ann's
Kingsmill
Allitsen Road
Charlbert St
Prince Albert Road
Regent's Park
Wellington Road
Cochrane St
St John's Wood High Street
Lord's Cricket Ground
St John's Wood Road

New Inn

RATING:

2 Allisten Road
NW8 6LA
020 7722 0726

The mental image conjured up by St John's Wood might well consist of elegant Georgian houses, upmarket boutiques and ladies who lunch. But in a rare moment of light relief only minutes away from this potential Richard Curtis film location lies the New Inn. Sitting at the edge of a perfectly nice council estate, anywhere else this would be described as a stripped-out affair. Here, however, monikers aren't needed; its simply a very good pub. The predominantly older locals, all looking unusually dressed up, clearly didn't mind us interlopers in their pub. So while we sat, eating our rather good food, we listened to the excellent live over-60s blues band 'George & Friends' and looked around us; there was laughing, joking and chatting – all friendly and genuine. Did we find the New Inn on an unusually good day? Maybe, but we wish more pubs were like this.

FEATURES:        **HANDY FOR:** Lord's Cricket Ground

The Ordnance

RATING:  

29 Ordnance Hill
NW8 6PS
020 7722 0278

Located on this quiet tree-lined road, you'd imagine that, if The Ordnance is as good on the inside as it looks on the outside, a rather nice pub lies within. Well, it is and it isn't. Somewhat upmarket and with St John's Wood prices to match, this is an unpretentious Sam Smith's pub, away from their usual W1 territory. With a predominantly wooden interior, a couple of settees and interesting lighting, there is a warm, homely atmosphere, even in the conservatory. There's also a conscious effort on the food front and although pricey, it's reasonable for the area and well made. Finally, a small leafy garden extends around two sides of the pub. It's never too crowded – presumably, the wealthy locals aren't pub fans. It's a shame then that the welcome from the staff is never exactly enthusiastic and the sometimes inappropriate, chain-wide 'no-music' policy can kill the atmosphere as it does here. Alas, these last two quibbles almost make The Ordnance a two pinter; but we still have a soft spot for drinking here.

FEATURES:   **HANDY FOR:** Lord's Cricket Ground

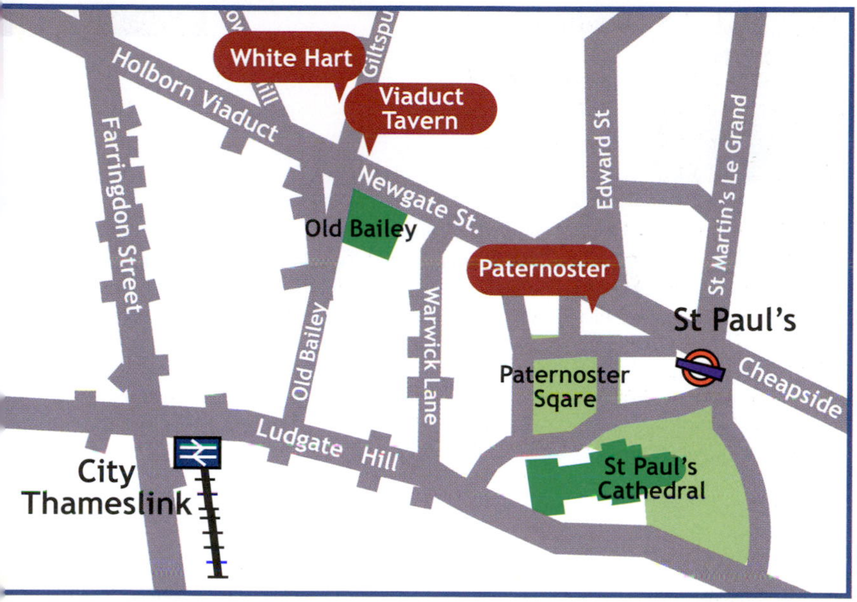

White Hart
Viaduct Tavern
Paternoster
Holborn Viaduct
Giltspur
Farringdon Street
Newgate St.
Old Bailey
Edward St
St Martin's Le Grand
St Paul's
Cheapside
Old Bailey
Warwick Lane
Paternoster Sqare
Ludgate Hill
City Thameslink
St Paul's Cathedral

Paternoster

RATING: 

2–4 Queen's Head Passage, Paternoster Square
EC4M 7DX
020 7248 4035

Settling in nicely as a replacement – but never a replica – of the genial old dump that was the Master Gunner, the Paternoster has found its feet as a modern, comfortable bar in keeping with the 21st-century recreation of the whole square. Young's were right not to keep the name and not to try to rival the excellent traditional pubs nearby. It's a businesslike place, serving businesslike people in a businesslike way. It's bigger than it looks from the outside and the raised central seating area helps break it into separate areas which include comfortable armchairs or spacious tables for dining – or lining up the glasses. The food is good quality and interesting, if a trifle pricey and the Young's beer – also confidently priced – is well kept and served. And the wine passes muster, too, although it would have to in this location. Suits and city workers in abundance but also a place for dignified old coves in blazers and medals to gather and quietly remember after attending memorials at St Paul's. (Open weekends until 5pm – food until 4pm)

FEATURES:   

HANDY FOR: St Paul's Cathedral

Viaduct Tavern

RATING:

126 Newgate Street
EC1A 7AA
020 7600 1863

The Viaduct has been a Fuller's pub for a couple of years now, but to be honest you don't really come here for the beer (even though it's good), but to take in the Victorian interior. Built on the site of an old jail (there are still a couple of surviving cells in the basement), the Viaduct Tavern is a well-preserved pub with some glorious touches of 19th-century decor. The fare on offer does its best to live up to the opulent surroundings, and this one's worth popping in if you happen past. It tends to get crowded with the highly paid punters from the nearby offices and, less frequently, journalists, witnesses and spectators from across the road; it's worth a visit outside of the busy times if you want a nosey round the interior. (Closed Sunday.)

FEATURES:  **HANDY FOR:** Old Bailey, St Paul's Cathedral

White Hart

RATING: 

7 Giltspur Street
EC1A 9DE
020 7248 6572

The White Hart soldiers on, apparently oblivious to the whims and caprices of the pub-going market in these parts. It sticks to its long-standing, tried-and-true, simple pub formula – there's decent beer on the hand pumps (we especially liked the Flowers IPA), simple pub grub, decent, friendly service and that's really about it. The pub is simply furnished, mostly wooden barstools and tables, with a squashy settee and some upholstered furniture at the rear (the only nod to modern pub furnishing trends). And when you add very reasonable prices charged here (a £2.50 pint in the City – amazing for the area and a pub that's not a Wetherspoon) you've got all you need for lunchtime or evening with your mates or work colleagues. The world's complicated enough, especially in the world of high finance, and we believe this pub's refreshing simplicity to be the perfect antidote.

FEATURES:   **HANDY FOR:** St Paul's Cathedral, Old Bailey, St Bart's Hospital

Cable Street
Cann
Shadwell
Dellow
Shadwell DLR
Cable Street
The Old Rose
The Highway
Pennington St
Tobacco Dock
Glamis
Wapping Lane
Garnet Street
Prospect of Whitby
Wapping Wall
Wapping
Wapping
Town of Ramsgate
High Street
Captain Kidd
River Thames

Captain Kidd

RATING:

108 Wapping High Street
E1W 2NE
020 7480 5759

This is a pretty respectable pub in a good location. It's built in an old warehouse and you wouldn't believe it hadn't been there for a hundred years but it really dates from the 80s – the 1980s, that is. It's a Sam Smith's pub so there are no surprises with the drink: it's well kept and reasonably priced and the service is good. The bar food is average at best and there's a restaurant on the top floor – untried as yet by us, it needs to be better than the bar food to make it worthwhile. There are usually two floors you can drink on (the restaurant is on the 2nd), but sometimes the upstairs bar hosts private parties as do other bits of the bar and it's a good place for a party too. All the rooms have splendid views of the river, with large windows that open up in summer to provide a cooling breeze, and there is a large terrace at the side of the pub.

FEATURES:      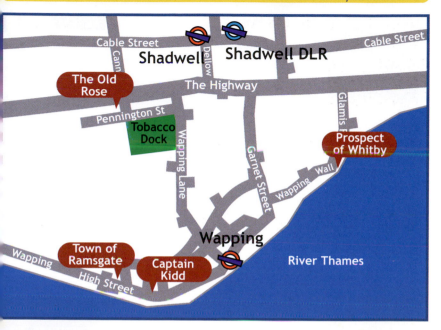

The Old Rose

RATING: 

128 The Highway
E1W 2BX
020 7481 1737

A long, long time ago, there were dozens of pubs around here serving the dockworkers in Wapping, but, now the docks have been filled in and planted with dozens of brick apartment blocks, there are precious few pubs left around here. It seems that the new inhabitants are not the big drinkers of old. Fortunately, amongst the remaining few is the Old Rose – a decent, traditional local, serving good beer, cheap food and with good service. We often find that, when you get these drinkers' deserts, as Wapping has now become, a lack of competition leads to complacency, but the Old Rose, thankfully, bucks this trend.

FEATURES:  

Prospect of Whitby

RATING:

57 Wapping Wall
E1W 3SP
020 7481 1095

The Prospect of Whitby should be no stranger to any visitor to London, as the coachloads of tourists are testament to its worldwide recognition. It bills itself as the 'oldest riverside pub in London' and we can find no reason to disbelieve this. It's an attractive old place, with an unusual pewter bar, cute olde worlde nooks and crannies and extensive riverside views, but its once dominant presence on Wapping Wall has been diminished in recent years by the developments towering around it. The pub's only nods to the 21st century are a couple of squashy settees and an ATM, which hardly affect the historic atmosphere. All in all, it's a pretty good pub, there are decent beers on the hand pumps – Broadside, Speckled Hen and IPA, when we were last in. The food is OK and the location and views make it well worth a visit, but the pub's popularity does mean a premium price and a jostling session with bunches of tourists.

FEATURES:      

Town of Ramsgate

RATING: 3 pints

62 Wapping High Street
E1W 2PN
020 7481 8000

Popular with the people who live roundabout, this old pub has had its up and downs, but has settled down in the last few years to become a jolly decent boozer. Whilst it is, by and large, a locals' pub, it's not at all unwelcoming. The pub is an old, narrow building next to one of the first warehouses to be converted into apartments (well before the 80s property boom) and backs onto the Thames where it has a small terrace with a limited view of the river. It's well looked after and a relatively recent redecoration has done nothing to spoil the old-world (as opposed to olde worlde) atmosphere. There are all sorts of historical claims made about the place (e.g. Judge Jeffreys was captured here attempting to flee to the continent) so it often appears on the tourist map, but not many of them manage to seek the pub out. Despite the fact that this area was the heart of the old London docks – and at one time there were 36 pubs on Wapping High Street alone – this area is nowadays a pub desert and, of the few pubs that are left, this is certainly one of the better ones.

FEATURES:    

SHEPHERD'S BUSH – *see Goldhawk Rd, page 160*

SHOREDITCH HIGH STREET (OPENS 2010)

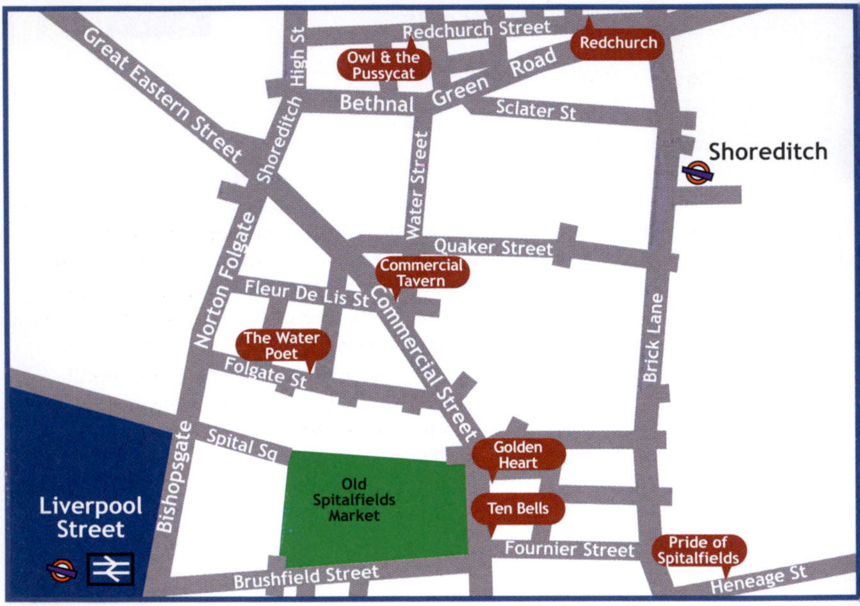

Great Eastern Street
Shoreditch High St
Redchurch Street
Redchurch
Owl & the Pussycat
Bethnal Green Road
Sclater St
Shoreditch
Water Street
Quaker Street
Commercial Tavern
Norton Folgate
Fleur De Lis St
Commercial Street
The Water Poet
Folgate St
Brick Lane
Bishopsgate
Spital Sq
Liverpool Street
Old Spitalfields Market
Golden Heart
Ten Bells
Fournier Street
Pride of Spitalfields
Brushfield Street
Heneage St

Commercial Tavern

RATING:

142 Commercial Street
E1 6NU
020 7247 1888

Well, guv, the old Commercial Tavern's been knocked on the 'ead and been replaced with a much artier affair. The exterior is much as it was, the most obvious clue to its changed identity being the plants outside, but much of the Victorian interior has been painted baby blue. Motifs cut out of magazines have been pasted onto the furniture, chairs adorned with poetry and walls panelled with various ephemera, including a panel of *Interview* covers and scraps of wallpaper. Look up and you'll see a scattering of chandeliers and a collection of cuckoo clocks. On the drinks front things look interesting too, with real ales usually offered (e.g. Black Sheep) even if their condition is sometimes variable. After a quiet start, trade is in full swing now and they've opened the upstairs, providing much needed additional capacity. We like the idea of mixing the arty and traditional and in these times, when it's increasingly hard to distinguish even some independent bars from each other, there are few places with such a unique and innovative approach.

FEATURES:    

HANDY FOR: Spitalfields Market, Brick Lane

The Golden Heart

RATING:

110 Commercial Street
E1 6LZ
020 7247 2158

The Golden Heart is in the right location to draw in punters walking between Brick Lane and Spitalfields Market. There's a decent range of beer available, a more than adequate jukebox and, when it's not too busy, an altogether agreeable atmosphere. The smaller wine bar section on the left-hand side, which is done up as an old-school all-wood-fittings, subdued-lighting Truman Brewery pub, with a pub dog that likes curling up next to the log fire (in winter), is especially nice. If you're not a fan of Hoxtonites, however, you might want to avoid Friday and Saturday nights, when even getting inside the pub to order a drink can be a laborious affair.

FEATURES:    

HANDY FOR: Spitalfields Market, Brick Lane

The Owl & The Pussycat

RATING:  

34 Redchurch Street
E2 7DP
020 7613 3628

A pub between the City and Shoreditch conjures up images of suited gents haranguing Hoxton fins, but there's none of that here. Just a fine pub. The well-kept interior has loads of space, and the inviting bar area glitters away at you in a welcoming fashion. There are good ales on tap and favourably priced pub food. Add on a garden for summer drinking and you've got all the ingredients of a fine pub. As an added bonus, there's a carvery upstairs of a Sunday. Sure, it's a bit hidden away, but it's certainly as good as anything between Liverpool Street and Old Street. Give it a try. Unfortunately, its 'discovery' by the occupants of the nearby Tea building, means that Thursday and Friday nights here are not quite so often the jaunty occasions they used to be.

FEATURES:    

SHOREDITCH HIGH STREET (OPENS 2010)

Pride of Spitalfields

RATING:

3 Heneage Street
E1 5LJ
020 7247 8933

The Pride of Spitalfields is a lovely old boozer just off Brick Lane. Formerly the Romford Arms, this place is warm and cosy with a pleasingly wooded interior, old pictures and hundreds of beer bottles lining the walls. The staff are friendly and offer up a good range of well-kept beers (Fuller's, usually – and guests). It can get pretty crowded at night with punters drawn from all shades of East End society – old Cockneys, Bangladeshi restaurant staff and artsy types – but it's all very friendly and harmonious. Away from weekend nights, it's less busy and consequently rather more relaxing, but either way it's definitely worth a visit whenever you're passing. If only the real world was more like this.

FEATURES: 

HANDY FOR: Brick Lane, Whitechapel Gallery

The Redchurch

RATING:

107 Redchurch Street
E2 7DL
020 7729 8333

Where do the beautiful people of Shoreditch go after hours these days? It would appear some of them gravitate towards The Redchurch – one of the more recent late-night E1/E2 haunts. Unlike other nearby places, it doesn't seem to be favoured exclusively by the nearby City folk, nor the Hoxtonites, but is still frequently busy with a good-natured crowd. And don't be put off by the sea of heads in the entrance of this 70s-styled bar – although it often looks full to capacity, the long, thin nature of the place makes the available space seem less than it actually is. A recent refurb has replaced the now-unfashionable grubby, student, bedsit furniture, with something rather more plush – and red. With its late licence, as long as you don't mind sharing the toilet sinks with members of the opposite sex, you could find yourself having a rather fun time here into the wee small hours.

FEATURES: 

HANDY FOR: Brick Lane, Whitechapel Gallery

Ten Bells

RATING: 3

Commercial Street
E1 6LY
020 7366 1721

This old boozer, formerly a stop-off on the Ripper tour, has been given the Bohemian bar treatment. It's retained the ornate Victorian tilework on the walls, but now it's been filled with a load of old settees, low tables and candles etc. The atmosphere is pretty lively, but nowadays all Spitalfields is like that, there's nothing remarkable on the booze front – it's one for the bright young things, rather than hardened drinkers – they'll be in the murkier places round the corner.

FEATURES: 

HANDY FOR: Spitalfields Market, Brick Lane

The Water Poet

RATING: 3

9–11 Folgate Street
E1 6BX
020 7426 0495

If you're looking for a smart boozer, you've come to the wrong place, this pub has thrown its heart and soul into the scruffy Bohemian trendy bar look and pulled it off. It's a huge place with rooms seemingly in all directions and even a large outside space – obviously devoted to smoking with the ban. The beer's pretty good with offerings such as Flower's and Landlord on the hand pumps and the usual bar-type stuff you expect in a place like this. The clientele are very mixed, but they seem to mix happily, nevertheless, as everybody's here for a good time and, by Jove, they get one. There's just one caveat – it can get pretty crowded in the evenings, particularly when some enterprising soul books one of the back rooms or a section of the garden. As we said of its previous incarnation, the old Pewter Platter Tavern, you could do far worse in this neck of the woods.

FEATURES:     

Visitors' Award – Winner 2008

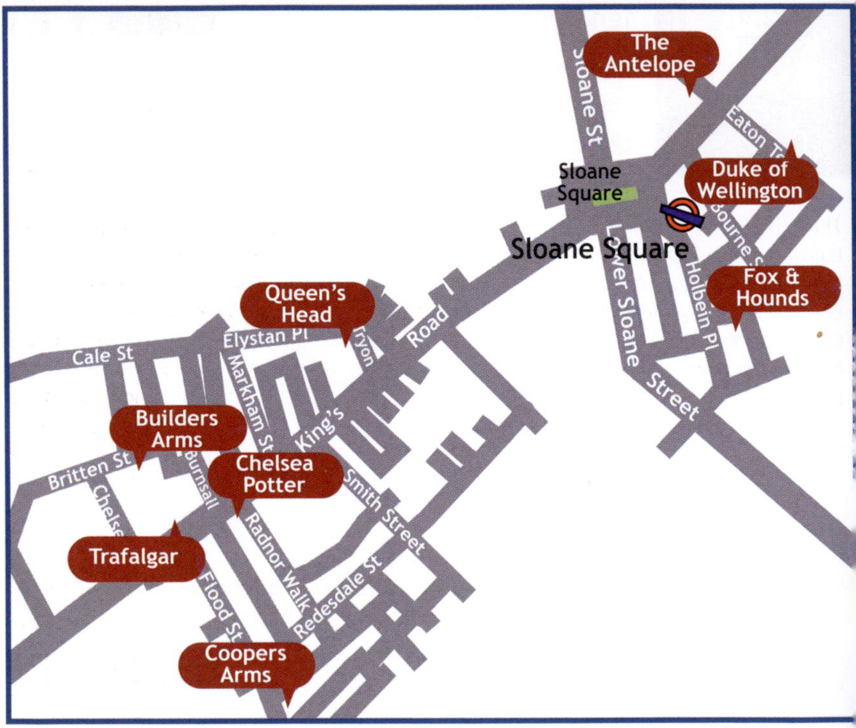

The Antelope
Sloane St
Eaton Te
Sloane Square
Duke of Wellington
Bourne S
Sloane Square
Lower Sloane Street
Holbein Pl
Fox & Hounds
Queen's Head
Elystan Pl
Tryon
Road
Cale St
Markham St
King's
Builders Arms
Britten St
Burnsall
Chelsea Potter
Smith Street
Chelsea
Radnor Walk
Trafalgar
Flood St
Redesdale St
Coopers Arms

The Antelope

RATING:

22 Eaton Terrace
SW1W 8EZ
020 7824 8512

As with many a pub in this part of town, there's an air of gentility about The Antelope, what with the wooden interior and the photos of the pub cricket team. It's also a bit cosier than your run-of-the-mill pubs, with an open fire in the back for those cold, dark evenings. For those in need of a little privacy, there are some booths and large sofas tucked away in the corners. If you're just after a reasonable pint, four well-kept Fuller's ales are available, with seasonal variations. A good cross-section of locals and an inexpensive, if slightly eccentric menu (when was the last time you saw beans on toast on a pub's menu?) make this one to seek out if you are in the area. And it's rather more down-to-earth than its location may suggest.

FEATURES:  

Builders Arms

RATING:

13 Britten Street
SW3 3TY
020 7349 9040

The Builders Arms is a trendy, modern gastropub, with real ales, continental-style cool lagers, wines and spirits. It's had a reputation for excellent food, though in recent times it's been suggested the quality's deteriorated, but the number of people eating when we were in last indicates it's back on course. The slightly quirky interior is pleasant enough – check out the Mona Lisa montage with fish – with an open fire and a long zinc bar in the main pub area. The locals seem to like it and the prices are pretty reasonable for the area, which is probably why the posties were sitting outside on our last visit. It's got three pumps with regular guest beers (St Austell's Tribute was on last time we were in) as well as the aforementioned lagers. And, while it can get packed on the weekends, it's very civilised on a weekday afternoon.

FEATURES:   

Chelsea Potter

RATING:  

119 King's Road
SW3 4PL
020 7352 9479

This boozer certainly feels like it hasn't changed in years, though there is fresh evidence of a lick of paint and the sticky old carpet's been replaced. It's still a stalwart of the area and shows no sign that it's going to be turned into a trendy wine bar or restaurant. It's got a reasonable beer selection, food during the day and a fairly usual Chelsea crowd of locals and workers from the surrounding area. Part of the popularity of this pub has to do with its location – it's the first pub on the King's Road coming down from Sloane Square, which makes it a good pub for meeting people. Worth a look in if you're in the area.

FEATURES:   

Coopers Arms

RATING: 

87 Flood Street
SW3 5TB
020 7376 3120

The Coopers Arms is a spacious, well-kept pub offering the usual excellent range of Young's ales. The large windows bring plenty of light into the pub, giving it a refreshingly open feel. A relaxed atmosphere pervades the pub and, with its ample seating and open fires for a winter's day, this is a great place to nurse a drink or two with the Sunday papers. Popular with locals, especially towards the end of the weekend as a meeting place before going on to other, later things. The beer is Young's, the food is excellent and, especially for the area, even the prices aren't bad. Jolly good show.

FEATURES:  

The Duke of Wellington

RATING:

63 Eaton Terrace
SW1W 8TR
020 7730 1782

Small but perfectly formed, this busy little Shepherd Neame house offers a glimpse of how great pubs can be. With a good mix of punters and a warm atmosphere, it's just the sort of place made for a cosy drink on a dark winter's night. There are three good ales on tap and simple, old-school pub grub on offer – sandwiches don't come with meticulously arranged hand-cut wedges here. Indeed, the price of food is equally old school, in some cases half that of nearby Chelsea gastropubs. Sadly the first-class landlord who used to greet people with that simple yet increasingly rare question 'How are you?' has now moved on, but service is still friendly and attentive. Although it sports a Belgravia postcode, it's a lot more down-to-earth than its location suggests and, along with the nearby Antelope, is worth seeking out.

FEATURES:    

Fox & Hounds

RATING:

29 Passmore Street
SW1W 8HR
020 7730 6367

The Fox & Hounds – a tiny pub on a tiny SW1 back street – has an interesting past. Until 1998 its was the last 'beer only' pub in London but, once that changed, it felt rather bare here. Thankfully, things improved and for a while now it's been consistently great. With a profusion of wood, a gas fire and only two small windows at the front, it's warm and glowing – the perfect pub for cosy winter evenings. Despite its size they even managed to fit a couple of Chesterfields at the back without the place becoming claustrophobic. The mix of customers is good, too; apart from the bar-propping regulars, there are customers from all walks of life meeting for a pint or three. On one visit we spied a troupe of musicians, along with their instruments, having popped in for some post-performance imbibing. One of the best in the area and a fairly handy meeting spot for Sloane Square tube as well.

FEATURES: 

Queen's Head

RATING: 

25 Tryon Street
SW3 3LG
020 7589 0262

The Queen's Head is a popular gay pub just off the King's Road in a fairly ordinary Victorian shell. It's friendly and well served by the bar staff with a decent selection of beer on the pumps. Local workers tend to congregate in here at lunchtimes, taking advantage of the good food deals on offer and they don't seem to mind the TVs showing videos rather than sport (Take That appeared to feature prominently when we were in last). There are lots of activities on ranging from the weekly quiz to karaoke to 'Strictly Bingo with Jaqui D' on the first Sunday of the month. While this may not be everyone's cup of tea, we've always found it welcoming and friendly. And its location that little bit further off the main drag – pun intended – means it can be a little quieter, too.

FEATURES:         

SLOANE SQUARE

Trafalgar

RATING:

200 King's Road
SW3 5XP
020 7349 1831

The designers have worked hard on the Trafalgar. There's not only a new grey exterior, but we have a new, mad interior – a mishmash of sofas and chairs, as if someone's made a collage out of back issues of *Wallpaper*. Oddly enough, it somehow works. Once you get it out of your head you're trapped in some kind of lounge furnishings version of *The Crystal Maze*, you can relax and enjoy some decent food and drink. There's excellent beer on the taps, ranging from real ale and a selection of continental and international beers, and the eager staff help add a friendly air to the place. We've commented on the prices in here before, but nowadays they're merely in line with the rest of London now. The Trafalgar's next door to the Chelsea Cinema, so don't be surprised to overhear earnest discussions of the latest art-house films close to chucking-out time.

FEATURES:    

SOUTH ACTON – *see Acton Central, page 1*

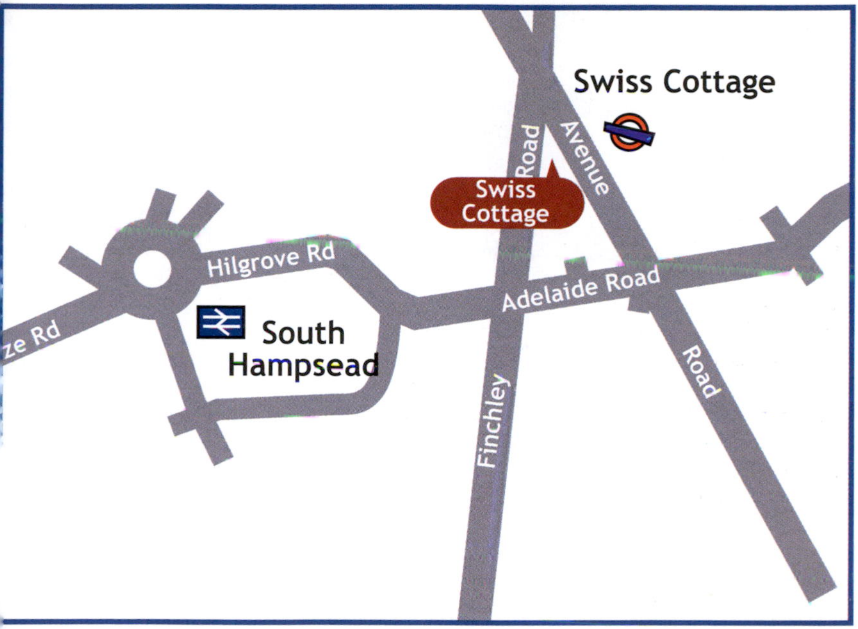

Swiss Cottage
Finchley Road
Avenue Road
Swiss Cottage
Hilgrove Rd
Adelaide Road
ze Rd
South Hampsead

Ye Olde Swiss Cottage

RATING:

98 Finchley Road
NW3 5EL
020 7722 3487

Externally, at least, this is one of the more eccentric pubs in London. Having taken its name literally, it has the appearance of a Swiss chalet. A Swiss chalet on the apex of a multilane traffic island, with the back of a cinema looming in the background, like a metaphorical Matterhorn. Inside, it has several large rooms, all of which are fairly comfortably laid out, including a Pool Club with six tables. A bit of a labyrinth inside, with a number of not necessarily connected bars, and the atmosphere is a bit hotel lobbyish, but that may be an unfortunate side-effect of its size and shape. The food is fine and, being a Sam Smith's pub, the beer is reasonably priced. It's probably the cheapness of the beer and the absence of a nearby Wetherspoon that attracts a fair few local older gentlemen. Still, it's a lively place and has got better since Sam Smith's took over. It also has a beer garden, which in most cases would be a bonus, but in this instance is more of a warning, due to its position on one of the busiest roads in North London.

FEATURES:    

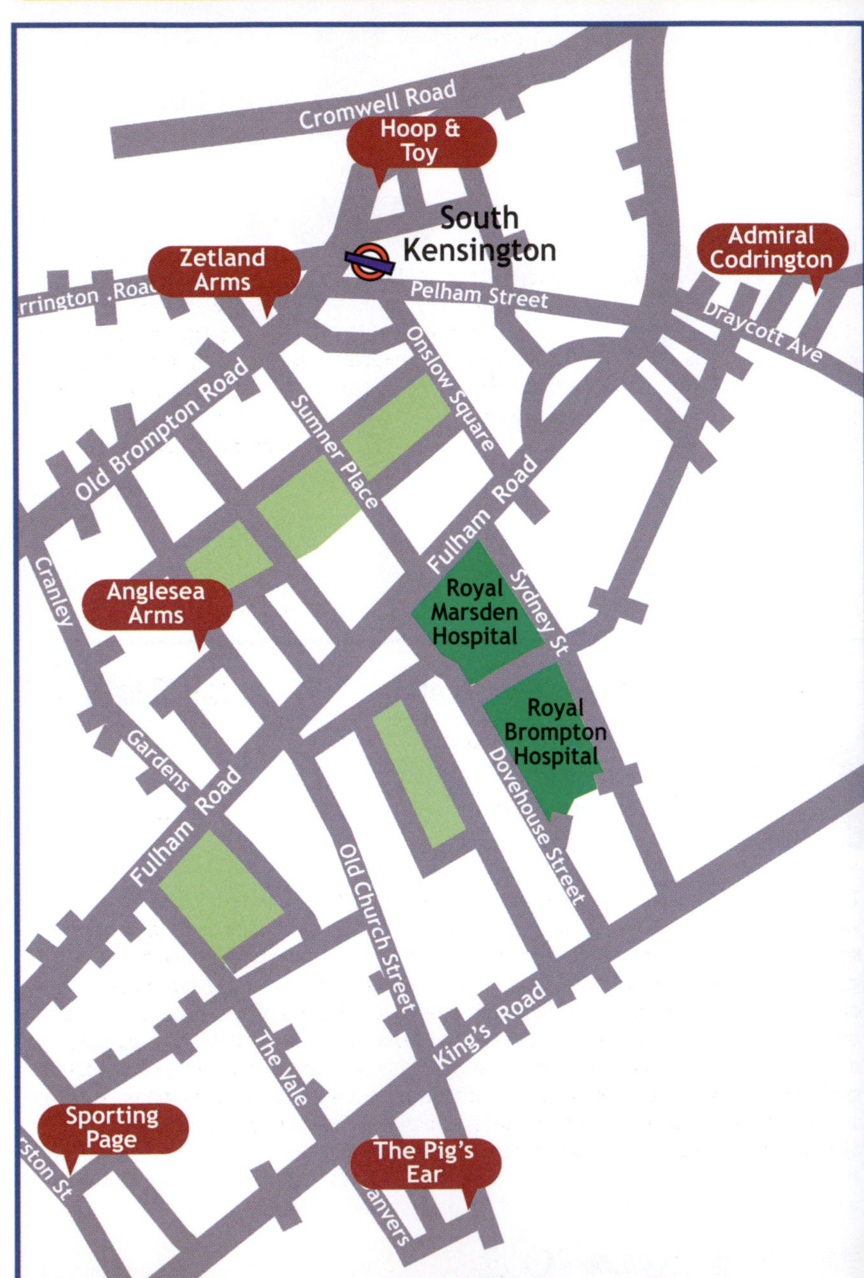
Cromwell Road
Hoop & Toy
South Kensington
Zetland Arms
rrington Road
Pelham Street
Admiral Codrington
Draycott Ave
Onslow Square
Old Brompton Road
Sumner Place
Fulham Road
Cranley
Anglesea Arms
Royal Marsden Hospital
Sydney St
Royal Brompton Hospital
Gardens
Dovehouse Street
Fulham Road
Old Church Street
King's Road
The Vale
Sporting Page
rston St
The Pig's Ear
anvers

Admiral Codrington

RATING:

17 Mossop Street
SW3 2LY
020 7581 0005

On the outside, this place looks rather like a pub you'd find on a council estate, but inside turns out to be a trendy pub/restaurant chock-a-block with people who we used to describe as Sloanes. Apparently Fergie used to enjoy a tipple in here, but these days, probably, Weight Watchers keeps her at bay. Unlucky for her, as you sense some of the clientele might be in her dating range. The pub has a light, airy feel to it, much aided by the adjoining restaurant, with a small patio-esque outdoor seating area to its side. Only a couple of beers on offer last time we were in – Black Sheep and Spitfire – and, perhaps unsurprisingly, a wide selection of wines and lagers.

FEATURES:    **HANDY FOR:** Victoria & Albert Museum, Science Museum

The Anglesea Arms

RATING: 

15 Selwood Terrace
SW7 3QG
020 7373 7960

The sort of classy, slightly tweedy, pub you'd expect in this neck of the woods, it's still worth a look even if you don't have a flat in Chelsea Harbour or a nice mews house in Kensington. There's a cosy main bar for the dark nights of winter; a tree-lined beer garden for the summer. And, if you're feeling especially swish, there's an elegant dining room at the back. The fine range of ales – there's usually Adnams, Pride and a range of regular guests on call on the six hand pumps – and excellent bar meals are the focus of attention here: no jukebox or games machines in sight. The pub can fill up rapidly with bright young things at the weekend, often spilling out onto the pavement, so it's maybe not ideal for large groups. Definitely one of those pubs that's worth nicking off from work to visit out of peak hours though.

FEATURES:     

Hoop & Toy

RATING:

34 Thurloe Place
SW7 2HQ
020 7589 8360

If we hadn't been in the day before the Hoop & Toy closed for a recent refurb, we might have missed it – such is its understated nature. Granted, the place looks cleaner and smarter, but the owners have thankfully stuck to the tried and tested formula that makes this pub work – an excellent choice of beer on the hand pumps (County, Pride, Abbott and Spitfire), experienced bar staff who provide polite and friendly service, even when it's crowded, and decent and relatively cheap pub grub. However, the trouble is the pub is so very close to the tourist mecca that is South Kensington tube. It's a very handy place to meet if you're coming to the area – and, as a result, it suffers. Unlike some places we can think of, this pub doesn't set out to be a tourist pub, but the tourists do pile in and, like every pub we know with such a transient clientele, it rather spoils the enjoyment of what should be a relaxed and competent pub. It's a pity, but that's the pub business for you.

FEATURES:     

HANDY FOR: Victoria & Albert Museum

The Pig's Ear

RATING: 

35 Old Church Street
SW3 5BS
020 7352 2908

There's a whiff of the continent about The Pig's Ear – helped along by an adaptation of that old Toulouse-Lautrec poster of the chap in the hat and scarf on the sign outside – yet there's still a traditional pub at the heart of things. The interior's somewhat eclectic, with non-gastro paintwork and Formica-topped tables – there's almost a queue in winter for the seats around the real open fire. Carrying on the porcine theme, trying a pint of Pig's Ear beer from the Uley Brewery in Gloucestershire is almost de rigueur. The bar menu is fairly priced and pretty French in orientation (we can't remember the last time we saw bone marrow on a pub's menu), as is the extensive wine list. There is a dining room upstairs which can be hired for private functions. This is one of the more impressive pub reworkings we've seen recently and one that thankfully doesn't live up to the cockney interpretation of its name.

FEATURES:   

The Sporting Page

RATING:

9 Camera Place
SW10 0BH
020 7349 0455

Perhaps surprisingly for where it's located, The Sporting Page is a fairly normal sports pub with decent beer, friendly (if a bit posh) locals and reasonably priced food. There are four hand pumps with regular guest beers as well as the usual selection of Eurolagers. If you're not into sport, it's worth avoiding when the footy, rugby or other sport's on, as it tends to fill up with sporty types, but it can be a bit quiet during the week – a great place for a pint and a paper with the slightly eccentric locals. It's not even vaguely pretentious and is far enough away from the hustle and bustle of the main roads to make it a pleasant alternative at any time except for match days.

FEATURES:    

HANDY FOR: Chelsea Football Club

Zetland Arms

RATING: 

2 Bute Street
SW7 3EX
020 7589 3813

Although this Victorian pub is in the heart of a very touristy area, it's not just for tourists – it's also aimed at sports fans and locals. There are screens scattered around the place and big televised sporting events can draw big crowds. And it does a pretty decent job of catering for tourists, with food – unpretentious, honest pub grub – available most of the time (part of the upstairs focuses on dining, but you can eat anywhere) and it offers a reasonable range of well-kept Cask Marque beers to wash it all down. The service is fast and friendly and it's almost always busy, so it's probably not the place for a cosy pint and the crossword, but the Zetland Arms is a handy place to meet and/or watch the big match.

FEATURES:    

HANDY FOR: Victoria & Albert Museum

SOUTH QUAY – *see Canary Wharf, page 82*

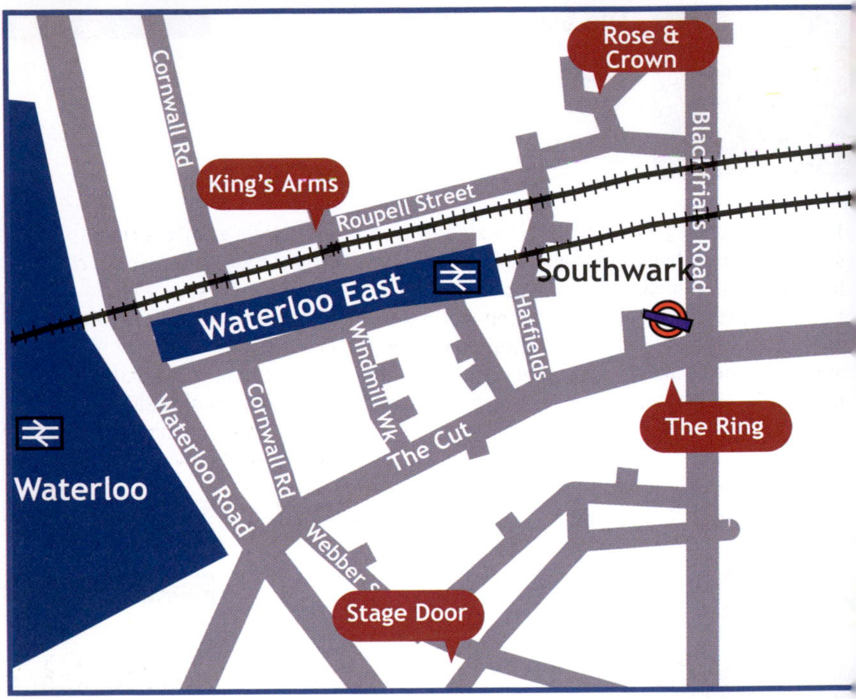

Rose & Crown
Cornwall Rd
King's Arms
Roupell Street
Blackfriars Road
Southwark
Waterloo East
Hatfields
Windmill Wk
Waterloo Road
Cornwall Rd
The Cut
The Ring
Waterloo
Webber St
Stage Door

King's Arms

RATING:

25 Roupell Street
SE1 8TB
020 7207 0784

An excellent local in a quaintly picturesque area (especially if you like industrial Victoriana) just at the back of Waterloo East Station. We're sure we've seen the nearby blackened terraced houses in many a period drama and this pub just fits right in. That's not to say it's an olde worlde, touristy pub-going experience – it's not. Weekdays finds a mix of office workers and a wide selection of locals and the atmosphere is usually excellent. There's usually a decent selection of ale on, some good Thai food and efficient service (it has to be on busy Friday nights). We like this place a lot – so much so we gave it not one, but two awards.

FEATURES:    

Visitors' Award – Winner 2008

The Ring

RATING:

72 Blackfriars Road
SE1 8JZ
020 7928 2589

The Ring has moved with the times, evolving from an old-fashioned boozer into something more in tune with modern tastes. It attracts a smart youngish crowd of local workers who enjoy the laidback music and relaxed atmosphere. A link with tradition is maintained in the hundreds of framed boxing photographs (some of them signed) which adorn the walls, although their spotless condition feels a little antiseptic. There are a couple of hand pumps offering beers such as Courage Best and the usual Guinness, lagers etc. on tap and, if you're feeling peckish, there's Thai food available most of the day. It's a non-too-large, one-roomed pub so it can get crowded pretty quickly, especially evenings towards the end of the week. A handy place for meeting up on a night out in these parts, or for a few jars with your friends, nowadays, the only claret you'll see spilled here comes out of a bottle.

FEATURES: 

HANDY FOR: The Old Vic Theatre

Rose & Crown

RATING: 

47 Colombo Street
SE1 8DP
020 7928 4285

The Rose & Crown is a lovely, well-kept old boozer frequented by locals, workers from the offices from roundabout and a few sporty types from the sports ground just across the way. It effuses a local and homely atmosphere aided and abetted by the prompt, polite and friendly service. It's just off the beaten track, so it means it doesn't get too crowded and in summer a large beer garden out back adds significantly to the available space. It serves a pretty good pint of Shepherd Neame ale and decent, cheap pub grub. Opening times can be a little unpredictable, we've yet to find it open at the weekend. But it's a very nice place to pop into during the week.

FEATURES:    

HANDY FOR: The Old Vic Theatre

SOUTHWARK

Stage Door

RATING:

28–30 Webber Street
SE1 8QA
020 7928 8964

The Stage Door is a lively, friendly back-street pub, a stone's throw from Waterloo tube station and appropriately tucked around back of the Old Vic Theatre. The service is friendly and the relaxed atmosphere helped by subtle lighting. There's a good-looking, late-serving, un-gastroesque menu (featuring burgers) and a couple of real ales on tap. A pretty standard range of beers and lagers sits alongside wines and spirits. Off to one side, they've managed to squeeze a pool table into the tightest possible space, which must be tricky for those long shots. There are a few TVs dotted about, showing football on our visit (we hear it gets busy for the important footy matches, as well as the cricket). Filled with after-work people on weekdays, the weekends finds it a more local affair – with live music featuring most weekends, but, if this was your local, you'd be happy to spend time here. Who knows, maybe local man Kevin Spacey does, too?

FEATURES:       

HANDY FOR: Old Vic Theatre

STAMFORD BROOK

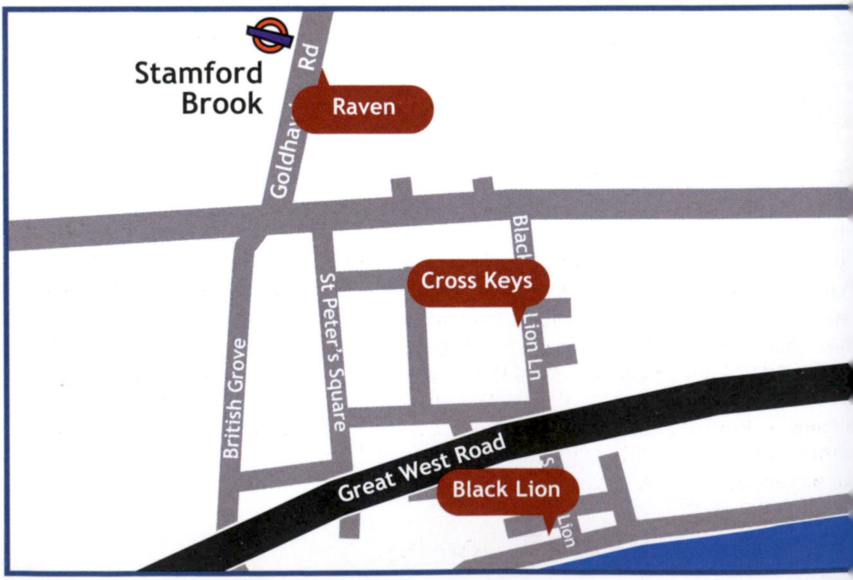

Stamford Brook
Goldhawk Rd
Raven
Black Lion Ln
Cross Keys
St Peter's Square
British Grove
Great West Road
Black Lion

Black Lion

RATING: 3

2 South Black Lion Lane
W6 9TJ
020 8748 2639

This part of the Thames has quite a plethora of pubs and on hot sunny days the inhabitants of Hammersmith and Chiswick swarm here en masse. The tendency is to get as close to the river as possible, but, if you're willing to forego a waterside view, you'll find the Black Lion offers the most pleasant pub-going experience in these parts. It's a large pub that's been here for a couple of hundred years or so and consequently has the olde worlde low ceilings, exposed beams, bare floorboards etc. that perfectly fits our traditional image of a British pub. Like many other pubs nowadays, there's a strong focus on dining, including a barbecue in the huge beer garden when the weather's nice (hard to resist when you're walking past), but that doesn't mean that the beer's been neglected. There's an excellent and varied selection of real ales on the hand pumps as well as all the other wines and spirits you'd expect of a modern gastropub. Kid-friendly, dog-friendly and with live music most Thursdays and a quiz on Sunday, this pub has something for everyone and, apart from the times there are so many people that the service is rather slow, the Black Lion offers a relaxed and friendly experience.

FEATURES:       

Cross Keys

RATING: 

57 Black Lion Lane
W6 9BG
020 8748 3541

The Cross Keys is a Fuller's house that's ideal if you're finding the bright lights of the Chiswick High Road too much of a strain. Our last visit found a fairly busy locals' pub, predominantly – but not exclusively – filled with men in their 50s and 60s. There's a choice of four pumps – bizarrely all serving London Pride – although bottled ales can be found behind the bar, alongside the usual lagers. Traditional in style, you'll find plenty of wooden panelling, along with a larger back section, complete with a vaulted ceiling. A good back garden with a smoking den and a simple pub grub menu (priced around the £8 mark) add to the positives. Ultimately, this is a good, homely and unpretentious pub – just the way we like them.

FEATURES:        **HANDY FOR:** Tabard Theatre

STAMFORD BROOK

The Raven

RATING:

375 Goldhawk Road
W6 0SA
020 8748 6977

By day, The Raven is a jolly nice old pub – a low-level, rambling sort of place, with a number of small rooms laid out in a semi-open-plan way, furnished with wooden seats and tables (plus the occasional settee) and there's a little yard out the back crammed with more tables and chairs for the smokers. The beer choice is decent, including a few real ales, and the food is simple modern British pub grub. The service is friendly and it all adds up to a pleasant place to enjoy a pint or two over a long lunch – especially with two courses for £10 early in the week. But, as darkness falls, the sleepy daytime atmosphere dissipates and the pub becomes far more boisterous, as the bright young things from hereabouts gather and the (often live) music is cranked up to industrial levels – especially at the weekend. So, if you pardon the mixed metaphors, here we have a Jekyll and Hyde sort of pub with a bit of a Marmite flavour. If you like the relaxed daytime atmosphere you probably won't appreciate the freneticism of a Friday night and, if you like things lively, you might find daylight hours somewhat enervating. It's an interesting mix that works – as long as you know when to go.

FEATURES:   

STEPNEY GREEN

Half Moon

RATING:

213–233 Mile End Road
E1 4AA
020 7790 6810

This place starts off very well – an impressive conversion of one of the previous homes of the Half Moon Young People's Theatre, it's well designed, spacious, looks interesting and serves an enormous range of well-priced drink, including Cask Marque ales and cheap food. And, unfortunately, that's as good as it gets. The Wetherspoon pricing policy (we're talking provincial prices in the centre of London here) makes this place very attractive to groups, that, whilst we would not consider them to be undesirable (and we won't name names), tend to be over-enthusiastic about the booze (especially at these prices) and, as a result, end up bringing the tone of the place down. It's just unfortunate we guess, transplant this pub to a location with a classier catchment area and you'd be looking at a four pint rating – alternatively raise the prices (but that would never do). A Catch-22 made manifest.

FEATURES:     

HANDY FOR: Ragged School Museum

Old Globe

RATING:  

191 Mile End Road
E1 4AQ

Astronomical objects abound in this area, what with the New Globe at Mile End, just up the road and Half Moon along the block, but, this pub, the Old Globe, has precedence – it is the oldest of them all. It's a lively, solidly local, local, not unfriendly, like some we could mention, offering all the amenities you could ask for – Charles Wells beer on the pumps, lagers, spirits etc., darts, pool, quizzes and Sky TV for the sport (and the music when there's nothing to watch). It offers a bit of something for everyone who lives hereabouts. Just the ticket.

FEATURES:    

HANDY FOR: Ragged School Museum

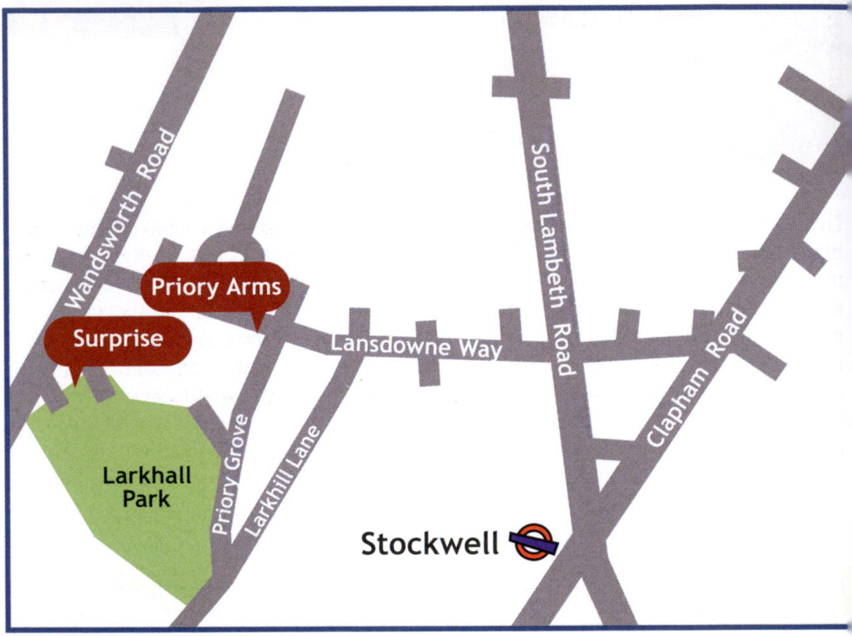

Wandsworth Road
Priory Arms
Surprise
Lansdowne Way
South Lambeth Road
Clapham Road
Larkhall Park
Priory Grove
Larkhill Lane
Stockwell

Priory Arms

RATING:

83 Lansdowne Way
SW8 2PB
020 7622 1884

Just as the Wenlock Arms is the real ale mecca in North London, here's its equivalent south of the river. Going by the beer mats plastered round the pub they've had more ales guesting here than you'll probably taste in your life. You'll always be guaranteed an excellent pint – there were five real ales on the pumps when we last looked in, well kept and rather tasty. As you've probably guessed, the food is of the traditional variety and the service is warm and friendly. Frankly, the smell of Sunday roast was nearly overpowering when we were last in, and we nearly got trampled by the locals coming in for their lunch. The beer alone would make this one worth it, but the whole package makes it definitely one to make the trip for.

FEATURES:       

Surprise

RATING:

16 Southville
SW8 2PP
020 7622 4623

Living up to its name, this place is not the sort of pub you'd expect to find off the busy Wandsworth Road. Being on the edge of Larkhall Park adds a certain rural touch which the cosy size and amiable atmosphere of the pub build on. The usual Young's fare and lived-in interior is on offer – let's hope they don't decide to change this unreformed boozer – though no sign of their seasonal beers being on tap. The back bar is adorned by caricatures whom we take to be locals (we're sure we matched up the picture to the drinker for at least one customer). It's the sort of neighbourly pub where knocking out illustrations of your fellow drinkers doesn't seem out of the ordinary. A little charmer in an otherwise dour environment.

FEATURES:    

STONEBRIDGE PARK/WEMBLEY CENTRAL/WEMBLEY PARK

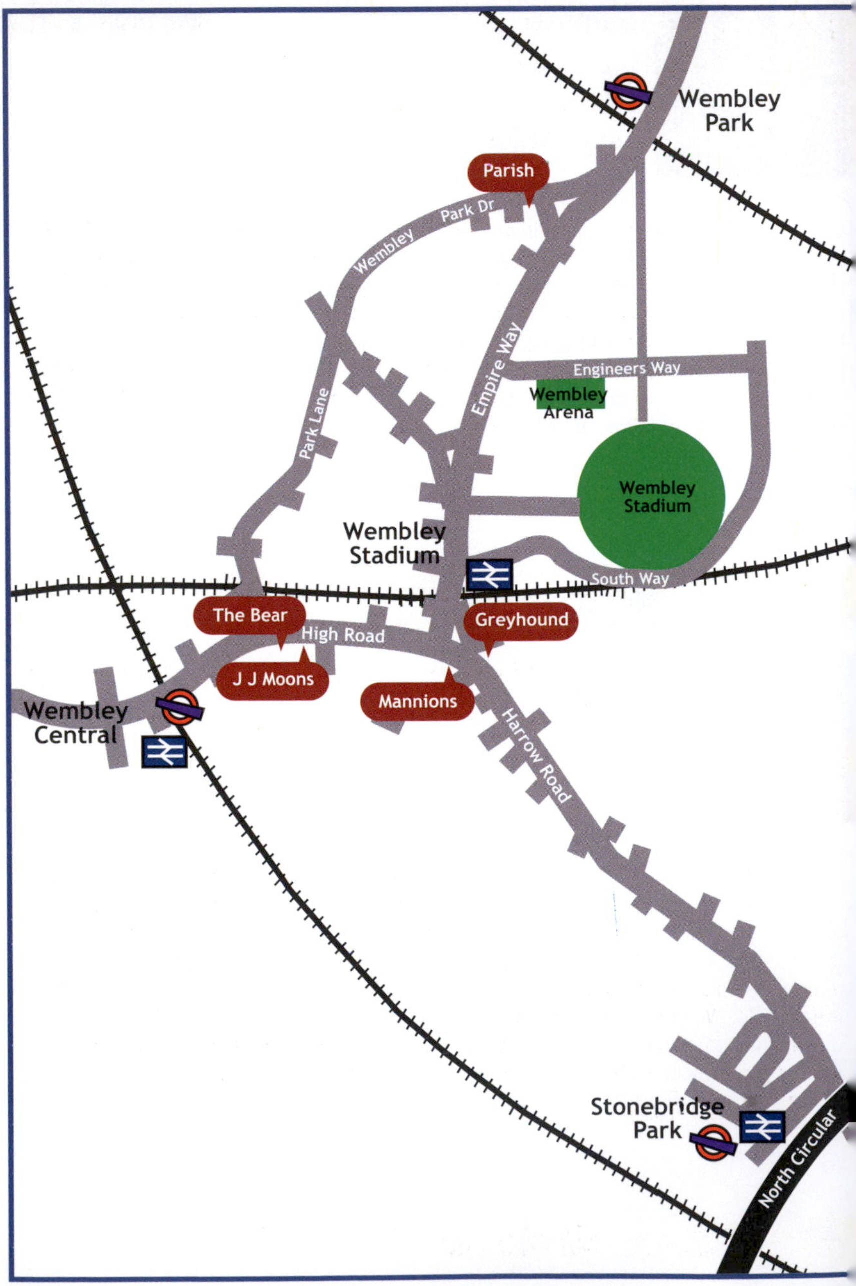

Wembley Park
Parish
Wembley Park Dr
Empire Way
Engineers Way
Wembley Arena
Park Lane
Wembley Stadium
Wembley Stadium
South Way
The Bear
High Road
Greyhound
J J Moons
Mannions
Wembley Central
Harrow Road
Stonebridge Park
North Circular

The Bear

RATING:

379a High Road
HA9 7DT
020 8795 1768

This one's obviously in competition with the Wetherspoon next door – not necessarily a bad thing, as the price of a pint is competitive and reasonably priced. It's not an identikit pub, though, with lovely leather banquettes against the wall and several levels of seating, combined with a pool table. True, as well as the cheap beer, it has a reasonable menu, several screens and plenty of room for the hordes that arrive for matches and events at the nearby Wembley Stadium and Arena. It's also got plenty of lager and assorted spirits for those who don't like beer. All that aside, it's still a good place to go and very civilised it is, too.

FEATURES:      **HANDY FOR:** Wembley Arena, Wembley Stadium

The Greyhound

RATING: 

324 Harrow Rd
HA9 6LL
020 8900 0819

This is a grand-looking pub from the outside, so we were expecting something rather different from what we found inside, once we'd walked through the door. It's obviously seen better days on the inside, and could do with a bit of love and attention. No doubt the clientele have helped determine the direction this pub's gone, as there's a distinct emphasis on shooters and extra-strength lager. This one suffers from the influx of fans heading for Wembley, no doubt, but it has to have a regular crowd to fill its echoing (well, it would be if not for the sticky carpet) interior. Part pool parlour, part slightly grotty boozer, this one's a bit schizo and probably serves its regulars well – we're just not going to hurry back.

FEATURES:      **HANDY FOR:** Wembley Arena, Wembley Stadium

J J Moons

RATING:

397 High Road
HA9 6AA
020 8903 4923

Now, we know Wetherspoon pubs get a lot of stick on our site and elsewhere – but that's generally not down to the pub, more often than not it's the clientele they attract. Wetherspoon pubs get a lot of things right: decent staff (and well trained), regular guest ales at a price that doesn't break the bank, inexpensive and generally tasty food, and the pubs are usually well maintained. This one's no exception. There's nothing wrong with the place itself – and it won a Best Bar None award at the first awards in Brent – but the selection of pensioners killing a Friday afternoon and dole-boys on the lash does put one off a bit. Even the cheerful staff seemed to be flagging, and we commend them for their patience with one particularly difficult customer of a certain age. Combined with one of those sink hand-dryer options in the men's loo (you know the sort, they're the ones you find in public toilets that're expecting vandalism), it doesn't bode well for this establishment. All that said, it's still a pretty reasonable option in the Wembley area – though we might give it a miss on Friday or Saturday nights.

FEATURES:       **HANDY FOR:** Wembley Stadium

Mannions

RATING:  

313 Harrow Road
HA9 6BA

A tiny Irish bar just off the High Road, this is a welcoming, if peculiar, bar. When we were in last, racing was on all the TVs, including racing from somewhere in the Middle East. It has been painted recently, but the odd ornaments on the ceiling – consisting of several ploughs and a couple of old rifles dangling down – still give it a somewhat rural air. The photos on the walls and the awards for shinty give it a homely feel, and the locals are pretty welcoming too. Don't expect real ale in this bar, it's Guinness or lager and maybe cider. Our guess is this gets pretty busy at the usual times, but, if you can get in, give it a go.

FEATURES:     **HANDY FOR:** Wembley Arena, Wembley Stadium

The Parish

RATING:

120 Wembley Park Drive
HA9 8HP
020 8903 8119

This tiny Irish pub does pretty much what it says on the (Guinness) tin – good beer and good craic. When we say it's small, any cat swinging has to be taken out of doors, otherwise you might damage the wallpaper or the glassware. Like most of the Irish pubs around this way, the Guinness (regular and cold) is excellent, but there's little to choose from in the real ale department unless you like John Smith's. This used to be one of those smoky Irish pubs you used to see on telly, but the smoking ban's put paid to that and it's practically liveable, regardless of the stale-fag smell. It appears to have a dance floor down one end, but that may be in aid of the darts team as much as anything. There's Sky on all the tellies and a decent jukebox with a pretty comprehensive selection. Unsurprisingly, its location just down from Wembley Park and near the main road does mean it fills with gig- or match-goers prior to any events in the area, but it doesn't seem to get quite as manic as others nearby.

FEATURES:    

HANDY FOR: Wembley Arena, Wembley Stadium

Railway Tavern
Angel Lane
Great Eastern Road
Stratford
Stratford Centre
Stratford Bus Station
Great Eastern Road
King Edward VII
Broadway
Ye Olde Black Bull
Builders Arms
High Street

The Builders Arms

RATING: 3 pints

302 High Street
E15 1AJ
020 8534 1598

This is a large locals' pub on the edge of Stratford with a lot going for it. The interior's a mix of traditional pub features (think horseshoe-shaped bar) and more trendy pub couture, which works somehow. Prints of old Stratford line the walls – and, bizarrely, the front page of a newspaper from the day of the *Titanic* disaster – comfy chairs and stripped floors, none of which detracts from the ambience. With cheap beer on tap (if mostly lager, there was only one ale on tap when we were in last), stalwart and friendly regulars, and large tellies, it's a bit of a haven from the bars and clubs nearby. It's got seats outside to enjoy any good weather in the East End, if you don't mind being inches from the busy High Street. Still, it's a good place to watch the sport or play a little pool without any hassle and have a few beers.

FEATURES:     

King Edward VII

RATING: 4 pints

47 Broadway
E15 4BQ
020 8534 2313

The King Edward VII – or King Eddie's as they like to call themselves – has the proud honour of being the best pub in Stratford. Compared to the post-war shopping centre over the road, the pub's Victorian exterior positively stands out, with low doors and bay windows. Indeed, as you step down into the pub, you're greeted with a warm, dark and traditional pub, boasting a host of features dating from its last refurbishment in 1914; check out the cosy fireplaces and the tiled hallway which links the public and saloon bars. Initially it can seem rather small, but the labyrinthine nature of the layout means you'll soon discover two further bars, plus a decent back garden. Despite the size, our recent midweek visit found it busy enough that it was hard to find a seat; we can imagine it picking up even more for the Thursday live music night, or the Sunday quiz. The food and drink don't disappoint either: there were four well-kept ales on tap, complemented by a good range of bottled beers and a decent wine list. Meanwhile, if you're hungry, although the food isn't the cheapest around, it is freshly prepared and worth the money. If you're after a traditional pub which offers a genial and friendly atmosphere, then look no further than King Eddie's.

FEATURES:       *Reviewers' Award – Winner 2008*

STRATFORD

The Railway Tavern Hotel

RATING:

131 Angel Lane
E15 1DB
020 8534 3123

This one's been upgraded to a hotel – it's been done up and nine en-suite rooms added to it (well, we suspect they were already there, just not being used or functional). We can only assume this has been done to capitalise on the area's up-and-coming status as the home for the Olympics in 2012, as we can't find any other compelling reasons to stay in the Stratford area. It's decent enough, with a reasonable crop of regulars, OK beer on tap and inexpensive pub food. With the range of activities on offer, it's obviously meeting a niche need for the area, and it's hard to fault the owners for taking advantage of the gentrification of the area. Apparently, it's been owned by the same family for 40 years now, and we can only say that the steady ownership has been a good thing. If you're looking for an excellent freehouse in the area, you could do a lot worse.

FEATURES:           

Ye Olde Black Bull

RATING:

13 Broadway
E15 4BQ
020 8519 6720

Gutted and refurbed throughout, this one's changed a bit. Gone is the slightly grotty Irish bar that was, in comes the chrome and glass and framed photos on the walls. They've spent a bit of money on the refurb, including the Bull on the outside of the building. But don't let that put you off – while the old Black Bull had its charms, it wasn't that conducive to pulling in the punters and now we can't see that they'll have much trouble. It serves decent beer, with Deuchars, Bombardier and IPA on when we were in last and there's the promise of reasonably priced food, too. The garden at the back is a bit of an oasis, and far enough from Stratford's one-way system to keep the hydrocarbons down. The racing on a Saturday afternoon suggests it's still a bit of an Irish pub, but the punters definitely didn't mind. Give it a go.

FEATURES:      

SURREY QUAYS – *see Canada Water, page 78*

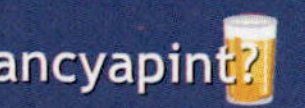

SWISS COTTAGE – *see South Hampstead, page 367*

TEMPLE

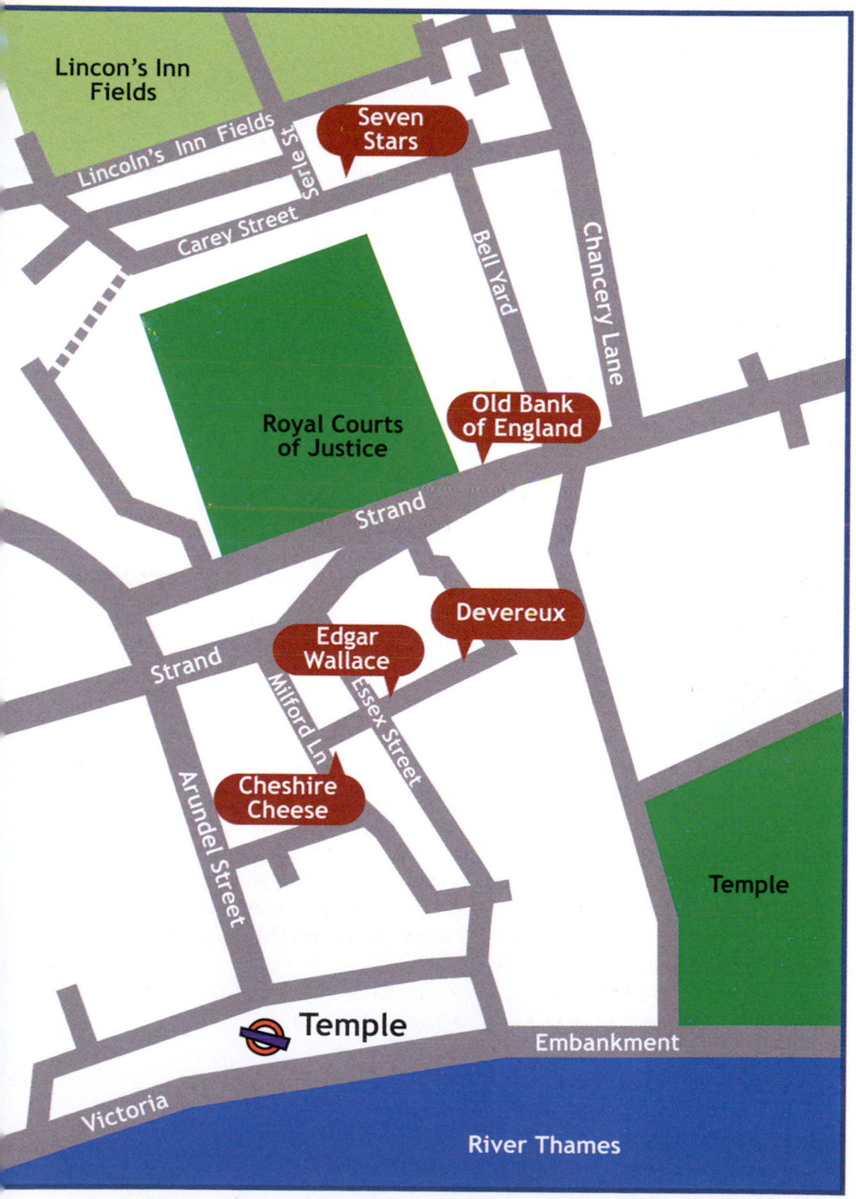

Cheshire Cheese

RATING: 

5 Little Essex Street
WC2R 3LD
020 7836 2347

Not to be confused with the nearby, much more famous 'Ye Olde' Cheshire Cheese on Fleet Street, this pub quietly goes about the business of providing local workers in the surrounding legal establishments with sustenance and relaxation. It's a quiet pub, being hidden in the back streets just off the Strand, almost villagey in feel, but without the territorial attitude that comes with some village pubs. It has several hand pumps with a couple of standard beers and a guest, a decent enough wine list and it also provides pub grub lunches and evening meals. You won't find this place in the guides to great pubs, but, if you want decent fare, with decent service at a decent price (especially for this area), you'll be OK here. Be warned, it can close early and isn't open at the weekends.

FEATURES:   

HANDY FOR: Sir John Soane's Museum

The Devereux

RATING: 

20 Devereux Court (just off Essex St)
WC2R 3JJ
020 7353 7534

Well off the beaten track in one of the quiet, quaint alleyways which are a feature of the Inns of Court, the Devereux is a pub enhanced by its atmospheric location. We've had our ups and downs in this one over the years, with the quality of service and fare on offer ranging from decent to terrible. Things seemed slightly more stable on our last visit, but with one downside: the pub was very, very quiet. Quite possibly this was down to its being the summer months, so we'll try to get back to this one when the lawyers are back from their holidays.

FEATURES: 

HANDY FOR: Sir John Soane's Museum

Edgar Wallace

RATING:

40 Essex Street
WC2R 3JF
020 7353 3120

A handsome, but deceptively pokey pub once you get inside, which gets crowded pretty quickly at the usual post-office-hours times. Given the area, the number of suits was not a surprise but it's not unbearable and they head off to their homes pretty quickly after work. There is an upstairs function room with bar (which can be hired) offering some breathing space, but expect this to be occupied on Friday evenings. There's a good range of decent beer and a pretty standard range of pub grub on the menu; add to this table service – even when the pub is very busy – and you've got a very nice pub indeed.

FEATURES:   

HANDY FOR: Sir John Soane's Museum

Old Bank of England

RATING: 

194 Fleet Street
EC4A 2LT
020 7430 2255

The Old Bank of England is another of Fuller's fine banking hall conversions. Despite the name, it isn't the original Bank of England – that one's been in its familiar location since 1734. This one was built as a branch of the Old Lady to serve the nearby law courts. When it was built in 1888 the one thing the Victorians didn't do was stint on the décor and when it's the Bank of England you'd expect it to be built to impress – and it certainly does. Fuller's spent a fortune restoring the building when they took it over in the 90s and, more recently, it's had a bit more renovation work. Nowadays, you get is Fuller's excellent beers, accompanied by a jolly decent wine list, served in an interior that's easily opulent enough for any wannabe dictator (or football star). Of course, it's popular in these parts so expect it to be very crowded at lunchtimes and early evenings, especially towards the end of the week, but, if you can get in at a quieter time, it's a great place to sip a good pint of bitter and admire the scenery.

FEATURES:  

HANDY FOR: Sir John Soane's Museum

TEMPLE

The Seven Stars

RATING:

53 Carey Street
WC2A 7JB
020 7242 8521

The Seven Stars is an ancient, tiny little pub that's a great place for a pint when it's not packed (to do this you need to avoid lunchtimes and early evenings). It's a charming and olde worlde pub and would be just the thing for the tourists if it wasn't already packed with people from the surrounding law courts. The excellent selection of well-kept ale on the hand pumps, decent pub grub and friendly service make this one well worth a visit if you're in the area. Watch out for the precipitous stairs to the toilets (especially when you've had a few) and for the resident pub cat Tom Paine – once seen sporting a white ruff. Oh, and it's also one of the few pubs in the Square Mile that you'll find open seven days a week.

FEATURES: 

HANDY FOR: Sir John Soane's Museum

TOTTENHAM COURT ROAD

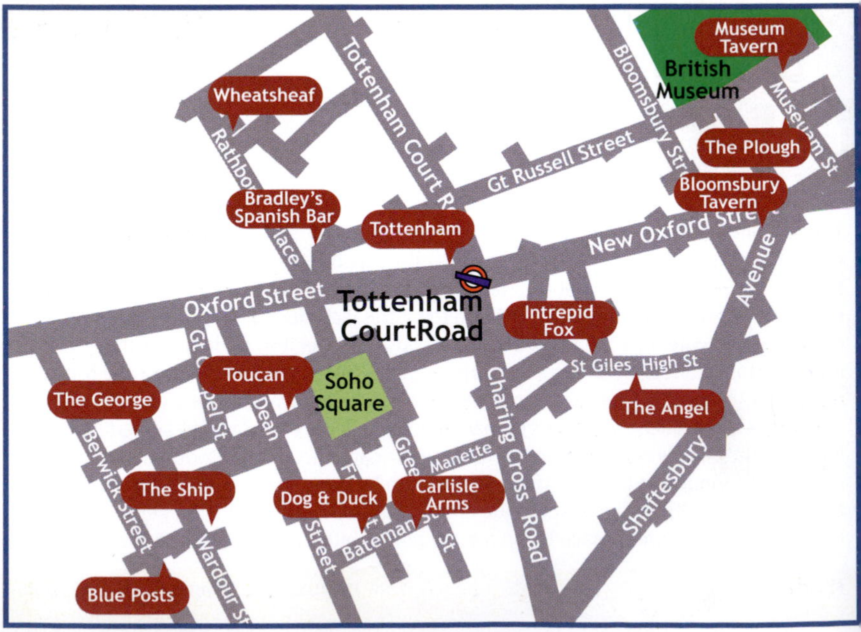

Museum Tavern
British Museum
Wheatsheaf
Tottenham Court Road
Bloomsbury Street
Museum St
Rathbone Place
Gt Russell Street
The Plough
Bloomsbury Tavern
Bradley's Spanish Bar
Tottenham
New Oxford Street
Avenue
Oxford Street
Tottenham CourtRoad
Intrepid Fox
St Giles High St
Toucan
Soho Square
The George
Gt Chapel St
Dean
Charing Cross Road
The Angel
Berwick Street
Greek St
Manette
The Ship
Dog & Duck
Carlisle Arms
Shaftesbury
Frith Street
Bateman St
Wardour St
Blue Posts

The Angel

RATING:

61–62 St Giles High St
WC2H 8LH
020 7240 2876

This is a lovely Victorian pub in the grey area between Covent Garden (Shaftesbury Avenue) and Tottenham Court Road. Because of its location, it can be a great place to meet/drink in town. It's got a lot of original Victorian features – including tilework – and has been refurbished with great care and attention. It does food, which is a bit basic, and not the best representation of a Sam Smith's pub. It serves the usual Sam Smith's fare and is very reasonably priced for central London. It's obviously had complaints from local residents, as the beer garden now closes promptly at 5.15pm. The bar staff can appear a little miserable, but apparently that's par for the course when you work for a brewer from Yorkshire. Anyway, don't let that put you off though – definitely worth a look.

FEATURES:  

HANDY FOR: British Museum

Bloomsbury Tavern

RATING: 

236 Shaftesbury Avenue
WC2H 8EG
020 7379 9811

This pub is one that most shoppers and tourists in London will have spotted, being a distinctive, handsome, late-Victorian pub, in the busy area, just to the north of theatreland and on many a bus route, and it hasn't changed in years – good. The fayre is Shepherd Neame's usual range of beers (a good thing in our view) and there's a decent wine list should you feel so inclined. The service is fast, polite and friendly and there's Shepherd Neame's pub grub too. It's a rather small place but there is another room upstairs where you can usually find extra space. The TVs are usually showing some sporting event or another, but it's not very obtrusive. It's a handy refuelling stop betwixt shopping and a night out at the theatre. (Closed Sundays.)

FEATURES:     

HANDY FOR: British Museum

Blue Posts

RATING:

22 Berwick Street
W1F 0QA
020 7437 5008

A lively pub at the top end of Berwick Street Market. The surrounding area with the market and shops is still a bit of old London (although changing fast) and this pub is just what most pubs in the area used to be like. There are a couple of real ales on the hand pumps and the rest is what you'd expect from a proper boozer. Most of the clientele are regulars, supplemented by the usual Friday and Saturday nighters. Enjoy it while it lasts.

FEATURES: 

Bradley's Spanish Bar

RATING:

42–44 Hanway Street
W1T 1UP
020 7636 0359

This is quite a unique venue; bang in the West End, it appears (to this non-Hispanophile) every bit as authentically Spanish as its name might suggest, perhaps with the principal exception that no Tapas is served. There are two bars: a tiny bar at ground level, where there is a vinyl jukebox with a grand selection of (Anglophone) tunes from the 50s to the 90s and a (slightly) larger, cavern-like bar downstairs. There are a lot of Iberian knickknacks all around, Spanish magazines available and a wide range of lagers from that country and others. It is a bit expensive, and at times rather too crowded for comfort, largely because of its minuscule scale. Nonetheless, it's charming enough, and there's a mixed range of regulars both Spanish-and English-speaking; given its location – highly visible from (the scummy end of) Oxford Street – other passers-by and tourists are liable to drop in too. We heard a slightly inebriated chap enter and announce loudly to all around that he was 'going out on the pull tonight'. We've no idea how successful he was, or if he was welcomed here, but it's not a bad place, and an institution of a kind.

FEATURES: 

HANDY FOR: British Museum

Carlisle Arms

RATING:

2 Bateman Street
W1D 4AE
020 7287 5533

The Carlisle Arms is a well-loved Soho pub, which we thought we'd waved good-bye to when it closed at the end of 2006. We're happy to report that it's open for business again and not too much seems to have changed. It always was a straightforward little pub, often overlooked amongst the more famous pubs and bars in the area. One lone pump of Pride won't have beer fans making a beeline here, but if what you're after is a quieter pub in the middle of Soho then – as before – give this one a go.

FEATURES: 

Dog & Duck

RATING:

18 Bateman Street
W1D 3AJ
020 7494 0697

The Dog and Duck is a tiny, popular pub with a very well-preserved ornate Victorian interior and it's well worth a visit at quiet times (mid-afternoon) to have a shufty. (Most of the time the place is pretty crowded, so it's hard to view the décor.) The beer's good – it is a Nicholson's after all – with a good range of well-kept ales on the hand pumps and there's a pretty decent wine list. There's food too with the sausage sarnies particularly recommended. The crowds are generally convivial, adding to the atmosphere and, if it gets too much for you, there's a little relief if you pop upstairs to the George Orwell room – he used to drink here. One of the better places in Soho for a pint.

FEATURES:  

The George

RATING:

1 D'Arblay Street
W1F 8DN
020 7439 1911

A late-Victorian pub it may be, but this one is starting to look a little frayed around the edges. The bar staff are pleasant and efficient but there's not that great a range of choices on offer and the overall feel is of a pub that needs a little TLC. Fingers crossed it gets it, as this little one-roomed boozer has a degree of old-school charm to go with the lovely interior (though the insertion of an electric fire in the old fireplace was an interesting choice). Being slightly grubby doesn't stop it being a popular place with the denizens of Soho, and you still get a few characters in, rubbing shoulders with lost tourists. At the moment, though, it's a pub that doesn't completely win us over.

FEATURES:  

The Intrepid Fox

RATING:

27 Museum Street
WC1A 1LH
020 7636 7964

When Goth and Rocker hangout the Intrepid Fox closed its doors in 2006 (a victim of a calculated M&B pub cull), we thought it was the end for this Soho institution. But then we discovered that it moved – lock, stock and barrel – to a new venue in Tottenham Court Road, having taken over the under-performing Conservatory bar. Ugly as sin from the outside, inside you'd think the place had been there for years. Tunes are of the hard-rock variety while piercings and tattoos abound. The trip down to the loo was covered in death-metal posters and don't be surprised when they draw a pentangle in your Guinness. We heard ties are a no-no if you want serving, and indeed a couple of besuited types at the bar were very much tie-less. It made us wonder if that meant Angus or Nick wouldn't get a pint, so we donned our best gothic apparel – complete with black tie – and had no problems; it seems it's not necessarily what you wear, but how you wear it. Anyway, if anything, the increase in space has made this a better place to drink than the original and it seems that the Intrepid Fox MK2 will have a bright (well, dark) future.

FEATURES:  

HANDY FOR: British Museum

Museum Tavern

RATING: 3 pints

49 Great Russell Street
WC1B 3BA
020 7242 8987

This lovely pub located across the road from the British Museum has managed to maintain its standards over the years and, despite having a regular tourist clientele – something that doesn't always work to the benefit of the pub – it still manages to be a decent pub, which is a rare occurrence in our opinion. There's usually a decent guest beer or two on – with seven pumps to choose from, you're bound to find something you like. And the quality and standard of service overall is pretty good, with friendly and attentive staff. It can get busy at lunchtimes, but that's no surprise as it serves reasonably priced food during the day. There are also a fair few after-workers, so if you want it quieter give it a go in the afternoon or later in the evening. It's also a fantastic place to meet to go to the British Museum; or, if one is coming out of the museum and needs a place to rest one's feet and quench that thirst, it's still a winner.

FEATURES:  

HANDY FOR: British Museum

The Plough

RATING:  

27 Museum Street
WC1A 1LH
020 7636 7964

Quite a handsome Victorian pub (particularly after a recent lick of paint) that's in an area overrun with tourists going to the British Museum. The results are what you would expect – no matter how hard the management try, and they do pretty well considering, it will always be a tourist pub. 'Famous for our fish and chips' gives an indication of the market their aiming at. But, that said, it's worth a pint or two if you can get into it when it's quiet. And as it's got outside seating with a little pedestrianised area, it's a good place to meet on a nice day. The beer selection's pretty good too, including Pride, Landlord and Old Speckled Hen last time we were in. It's got to be a nice little earner though – we're just jealous.

FEATURES:    

HANDY FOR: British Museum

The Ship

RATING: 

116 Wardour Street
W1F 0TT
020 7437 8446

Apart from the odd lick of paint here and there, this pub has not changed much over the years. No bad thing in this area, where you only have to turn round for ten seconds and yet another style bar has opened up to cater for the media luvvies. A good, solid pub: the beer's excellent – the Fuller's range – and, with the eclectic music on the PA (a bit on the heavy side for some tastes, but we like it) and a good atmosphere any time of the day, it's definitely a pub to seek out.

FEATURES: 

The Tottenham

RATING: 

6 Oxford Street
W1D 1AR
020 7636 7201

Like most of the Nicholson's pubs in the West End, this one's gleaming after a polish and general tidy up. It's doing its best to stand out from the general madness of this part of town: unfortunately it's still all you'd expect from the only pub on London's busiest road. It serves an ever-changing throng of shoppers, tourists and chancers and quickly fills up. The Victorian décor hints at past glories, but, unless you enjoy hopping over shopping bags then a scrum at the bar before you get served, head downstairs for a slightly more peaceful drinking environment.

FEATURES:  

Toucan

RATING: 

19 Carlisle Street
W1D 3BX
020 7437 4123

A tiny, tiny Irish pub, with quite a good atmosphere, good Guinness (of course) and good service (when you can get to the bar), but way too easily overcrowded. When you can get in it's OK, otherwise, you will be standing on the street with the rest of the media types. Welcome to Soho.

FEATURES: 

HANDY FOR: British Museum

Wheatsheaf

25 Rathbone Place
W1T 1DG
020 7580 1585

Back in the 1930s when beer was 6d a pint, George Orwell, Dylan Thomas and other assorted bohemians drank in the panelled room that makes up the main bar. These days, the beer has gone up in price and the pub always seems oddly, and pleasantly, quiet (except for just after work, towards the weekend). It's a very traditional-looking pub, with a large section of stained glass completing the picture, and it makes no attempt to pretend otherwise. The local workers who go there don't seem to mind, either. There are a couple of real ales and a lunchtime menu on offer. If you have a soft spot for atmospheric old boozers, give it a try.

FEATURES:   

TOWER HILL/TOWER GATEWAY (DLR)

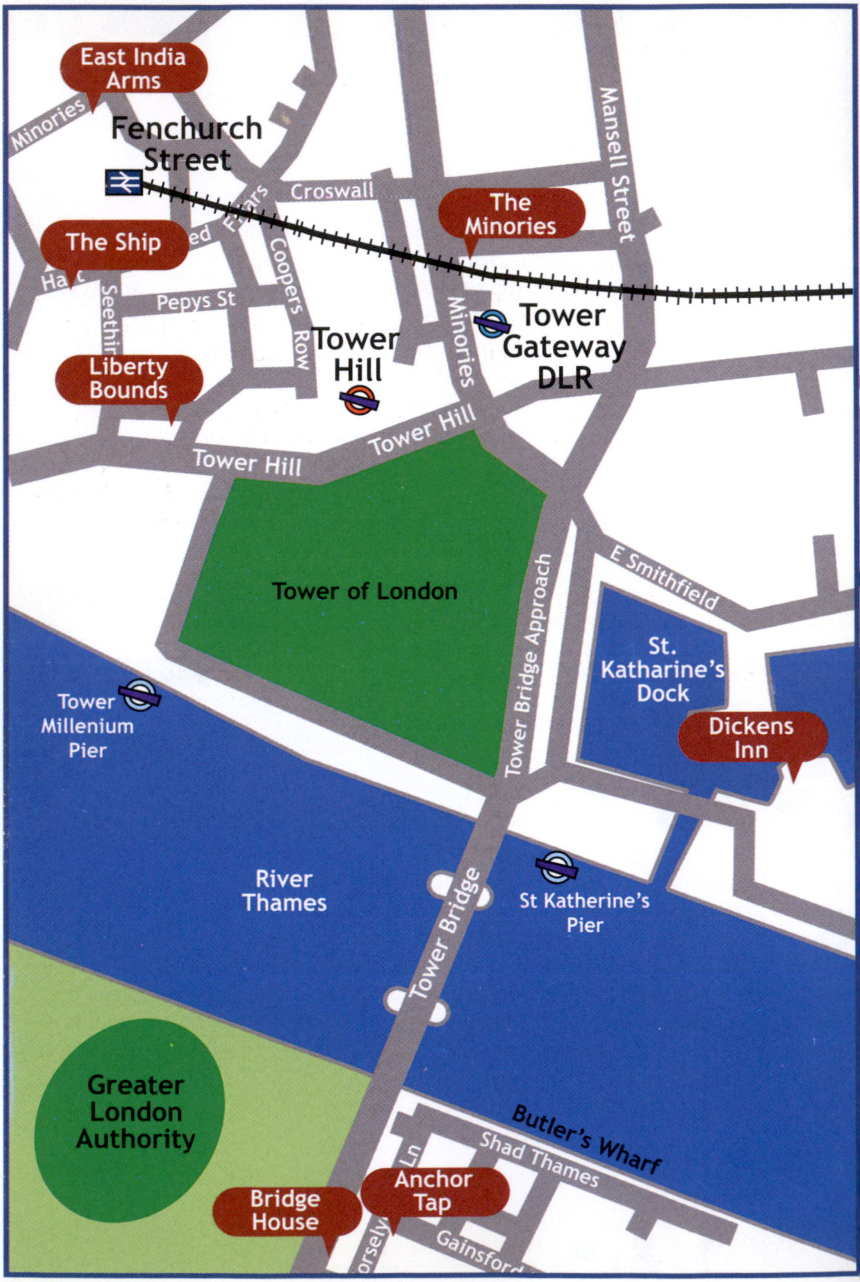

East India Arms
Minories
Fenchurch Street
Croswall
The Minories
Mansell Street
The Ship
Pepys St
Coopers Row
Liberty Bounds
Tower Hill
Minories
Tower Gateway DLR
Tower Hill
Tower Hill
Tower of London
E Smithfield
Tower Bridge Approach
St. Katharine's Dock
Tower Millenium Pier
Dickens Inn
River Thames
Tower Bridge
St Katherine's Pier
Greater London Authority
Butler's Wharf
Shad Thames
Anchor Tap
Bridge House
Gainsford

The Anchor Tap

28 Horselydown Lane
SE1 2LN
020 7403 4637

The Anchor Tap is an old pub right in the middle of Conran land (Butler's Wharf), but don't get the idea it's a trendy designer pub – it's not. Inside, it's a bit of a ramshackle place, with numerous small rooms heading off in different directions, but the overall effect can be quite cosy, especially in winter. Still, this is exactly what you'd expect from traditional pub owner Sam Smith's who have usually eschewed the trend to make it open plan, which often happens when pubs get refurbished. There's a small beer garden/terrace at the back for fine weather (and smokers). And, despite its proximity to two of the major tourist attractions in the capital, it rarely gets packed with visitors. The Anchor Tap offers the usual standard of drink you would expect from a Sam Smith's pub and with cheapish pub grub means that, if you like Sam's fare, it's not bad here at all – and it's considerably better than some nearby places.

FEATURES:    

HANDY FOR: Tower Bridge, Design Museum

The Bridge House

218 Tower Bridge Road
SE1 2UP
020 7407 5818

If the phrase real ale style bar sounds like an oxymoron to you, maybe you should come and have a look at the Bridge House as it's probably the best way to describe this Adnams house on the southern end of Tower Bridge. There are excellently kept Adnams and guest ales in an interior well in keeping with the converted warehouse flats of the area. So, here you can enjoy a decent pint and ponder laying down a deposit on one of the displayed works of art... hmm. Yet, somehow it works: it helps that the food's very good and the landlord is a friendly soul. Even if the racked magazines seem a bit Toni & Guy, the fare on offer is impressive making their four pint status inevitable. A good spot for some refreshment whilst walking along the Thames, visiting the Tower or an inspection of the GLA space oddity.

FEATURES:   

HANDY FOR: Tower Bridge, Tower of London

Dickens Inn

RATING:

St Katharine's Way

E1W 1UH

020 7488 2208

This pub, situated in St Katharine's Dock, is next to one of the biggest tourist attractions in London and, consequently, has a huge number of visitors. As a result, we hardly ever venture near the place. It has two restaurants (one's a pizza place), a large terrace (not as big as it used to be since the residents complained) that closes at 9:45 (for the same reason). The building itself was once the structure of a brewery, which was then incorporated into a spice warehouse and subsequently restyled as a coaching inn, when it reopened as a pub in the 1970s. The location is great, picturesque and historic, and everyone else seems to think so too – this pub is just too crowded for our tastes.

FEATURES:   

HANDY FOR: Tower Bridge, Tower of London

East India Arms

RATING: 

67 Fenchurch Street

EC3M 4BR

020 7265 5121

A rather handsome, but, unfortunately, smallish pub in the heart of the City, en route to Fenchurch Street station. Unsurprisingly this pub's clientele is mostly the lunchtime and commuter crowd and, accordingly, is thronged at these times. It's not a bad place at all outside peak times, as the beer is pretty decent – plenty of Shepherd Neame's ales on the hand pumps – and the service is good (when you can get to the bar).

FEATURES:  

HANDY FOR: Tower of London

Liberty Bounds

RATING:

15 Trinity Square
EC3N 4AA
020 7481 0513

Another Edwardian commercial property gets converted into a Wetherspoon pub, hardly a newsworthy item nowadays, an almost everyday occurrence in the City it sometimes seems. As ever, there's the range of well-priced, well-kept, hand-pumped beer and the cheap food to accompany it. And, as ever, the place is packed with people throwing cheap drink down their necks as if they're going to get their throats cut very soon. All predictable stuff, but at least it gives tourists in the area a chance to sample something approaching the British pub experience without having to sell their offspring into slavery in order to pay for it.

FEATURES:  **HANDY FOR:** Tower Bridge, Tower of London

The Minories

RATING:  

64–73 The Minories
EC3N 1JL
020 7702 1658

Largish pub catering to local City workers that hasn't really changed in years. It comes into its own on Thursdays and Fridays when a 'party atmosphere' descends. Cheesy as hell, often with a DJ (who probably does weddings as well) proffering big shouts out to the homies in Accounts (with fine tunes from Kenny Loggins and Bruce Springsteen). Not the place you come for a quiet drink but if you're in the right mood (i.e. plastered) there's entertainment to be had. If the thought of a pub based on an office party appeals, come on down...

FEATURES:     **HANDY FOR:** Tower of London

TOWER HILL/TOWER GATEWAY (DLR)

The Ship

RATING:

3 Hart Street
EC3R 7NB
020 7481 1871

Not so long ago, there used to be dozens of little pubs like the Ship around the City, pleasant drinking holes where local workers meet for a spot of lunch, or gather after work for a quick pint or two before the weary, dreary commute home. Nowadays, there aren't very many of them left, space is at a premium in the Square Mile, so turnover has to be high just to break even, so most of them have either disappeared completely, or been replaced by much larger bar-type experiences such as Fine Line and All Bar One. Thankfully, though, The Ship is still here, recently refurbished and still offering the traditional pub experience; good beer (Butcombe Bitter and Sharp's Doom Bar for instance), unfussy pub grub – a range of burgers, including Thai fish, are a feature, but there are also sandwiches and pies – and polite, friendly service. It's a real haven and a reminder of a less frenetic and more relaxed way of doing business. We need more, not fewer, pubs like The Ship and it's surely our duty as pub fans to frequent them in order to keep them in business.

FEATURES:   

HANDY FOR: Tower Bridge, Tower of London

TUFNELL PARK – *see Gospel Oak, page 166*

TURNHAM GREEN – *see Chiswick Park, page 110*

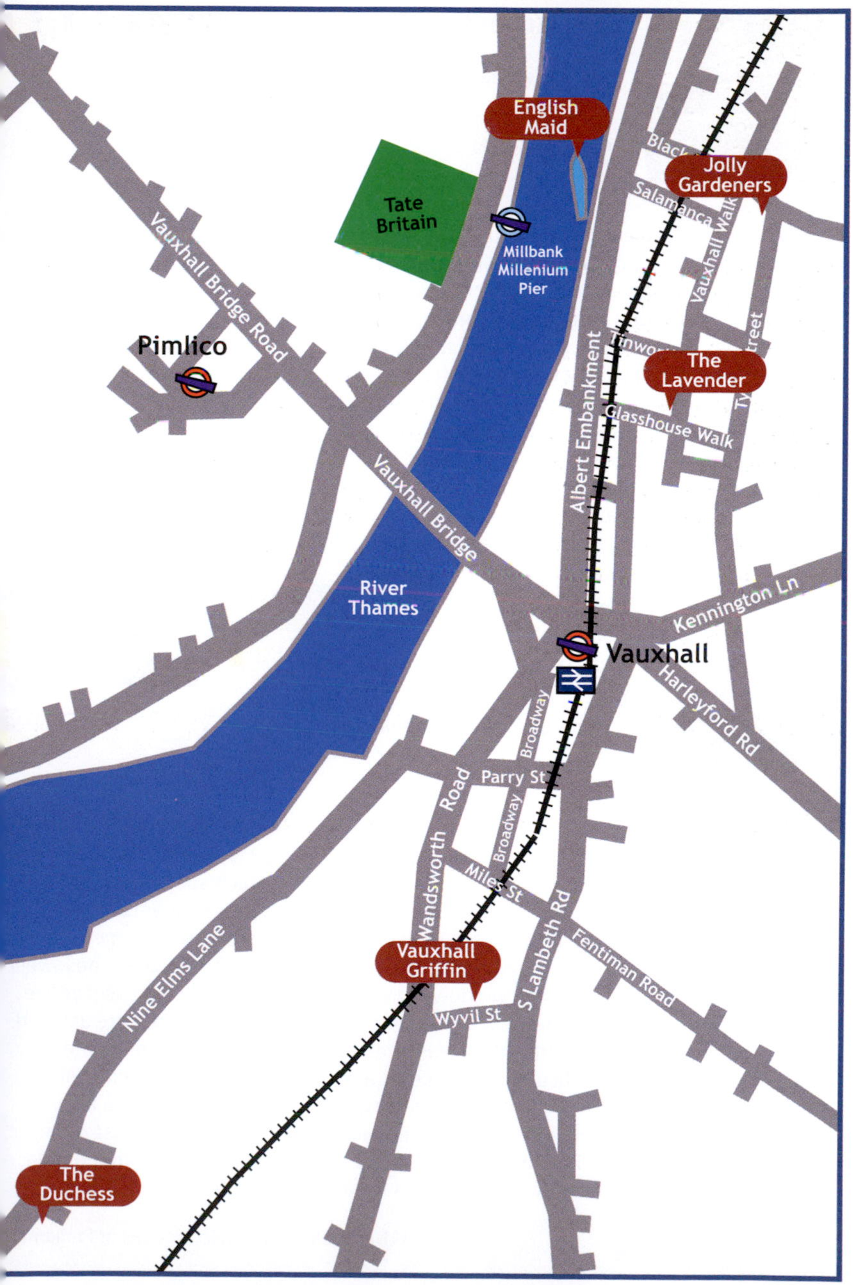

English Maid
Jolly Gardeners
Tate Britain
Salamanca
Vauxhall Walk
Millbank Millenium Pier
Vauxhall Bridge Road
Pimlico
The Lavender
Glasshouse Walk
Albert Embankment
Vauxhall Bridge
River Thames
Kennington Ln
Vauxhall
Harleyford Rd
Broadway
Parry St
Wandsworth Road
Broadway
Miles St
Fentiman Road
S Lambeth Rd
Nine Elms Lane
Vauxhall Griffin
Wyvil St
The Duchess

The Duchess

RATING:

101 Battersea Park Road
SW8 4DS
020 7627 4711

Until recently a run down postie haunt, The Duchess of York managed to survive long enough to be taken over by some bright young things, presumably hoping to capitalise on the long-awaited regeneration of the area. Having dropped 'of York' from its name, it's been well refurbished, creating a comfortable and relaxed atmosphere. Décor flutters between differing eras, Georgian through to the 1960s. It actually works well, helping accentuate the grandeur inherent in this old Victorian pub. And, if you're a fan of industrial architecture, you'll be in seventh heaven as it boasts unrivalled views of Battersea Power Station, especially from their excellent roof terrace. There are a couple of Greene King ales on the hand pumps, but real aficionados will go for the great range of whisky and vodkas available. With friendly service, live music, a good pub quiz and great food, this is a more relaxed place than its nearest trendy rival and deserves to reap the rewards. Certainly, this is a place we visit whenever we can.

FEATURES:      *Reviewers' Award – Most Improved 2008*

English Maid

RATING: 

Anna G, Albert Embankment
SE1 7TP
020 7582 1066

The *English Maid* is a rather ironic name for a Dutch barge which spent much of its life sailing up and down the Seine. We're glad it's permanently moored near Lambeth Bridge for life as a bar. Apart from the deck with stunning views of the Thames and Parliament, there are two floors inside, filled with plenty of comfy couches. The lowest level is rather disconcerting, with windows at water level, making it seem as if you're bobbing about in the water; a cracked pane of glass didn't help, but we were assured that a low-budget Poseidon Adventure wasn't about to unfold. Not much of note on tap, but it *is* notoriously difficult to keep ale on a boat and a reasonable selection of bottled beers made up for it. Cheap food aplenty, too, with burger and chips a very competitive £6. It's a shame our visit found it considerably quieter than most of the other pubs around, even if it did mean seats were easy to come by. With impeccable service and a warm, genuine welcome, this is by far our favourite pub in the area.

FEATURES:    **HANDY FOR:** Tate Britain, Houses of Parliamen

Jolly Gardeners

RATING:

49–51 Black Prince Road
SE11 6AB
020 7840 0426

The Jolly Gardeners describes itself as London's first German pub and, considering the German love of beer, it's surprising there aren't more places like this. Just south of the river, it's rather intimidating from the outside. High windows prevent you seeing in, while the black paint job makes it look like a funeral parlour. Inside, the black theme continues, with modern elevated bench seating sitting uneasily with the last vestiges of this Victorian boozer. It feels sparse, with the scattering of high tables and chairs looking like a forest after a visit from an over-enthusiastic lumberjack. Still, as a German pub, the most important thing is the beer, which doesn't disappoint. With both dark and wheat beers amongst the 20+ selection, you'll find Bitburger, Paulaner, Erdinger and Warsteiner. While not groundbreaking if you've ever propped up a good bar in Berlin, the choice is still impressive by London standards. They also show German footy, which was proving popular with the ex-pats present. The food, as expected, was meat heavy, with plenty of sausages and meatloaf dishes to chose from at reasonable prices, but the quality needs improving. There are a few niggles, but it doesn't stop us coming here for a pint.

FEATURES:  

HANDY FOR: Tate Britain

Lavender

RATING:  

112 Vauxhall Walk
SE11 5ER
020 7735 4440

Vying for trade with the nearby Rose, these two smartened-up Victorian pubs battle it out daily for the lunchtime and after-work crowds (well, apart from those who prefer the more sleazy delights of the Queen Anne over the road). Of the two, the Lavender is the more pubby. Sure, its bare-floorboarded intentions are easy to categorise and we spotted a couple of reserved signs, but there's a couple of ales on tap – Young's Special and Spitfire last time we were in – and plenty of space to spread out and relax. We didn't sample the gastro-style food menu but we nonetheless enjoyed an agreeable time here.

FEATURES:  

HANDY FOR: Tate Britain

Vauxhall Griffin

RATING:

8 Wyvil Road
SW8 2TH
020 7622 0222

Pubs that try to please everybody can sometimes be found lacking, but credit to the Vauxhall Griffin – they pull it off pretty successfully. Tucked off a side street a few minutes' walk from the unpleasantness of Vauxhall station, and once an underwhelming pub called 'Wyvil's', the new owners seem to know what they're doing. Nicely decorated in a slightly shabby bohemian style, a central bar separates the comfortable main bar from the back area where you can find board games-a-plenty and a pool table. The latter space is also impressively filled with music-related articles pasted over the walls, which also gives you a clue that the jukebox is above average (we'll assume E17's *Greatest Hits* are ironic). Ale fans have to make do with bottles from the fridge, and a simple pub grub menu is offered at lunchtime, along with Tuesday nights (which complements the lively pub quiz). Friday and Saturday usually offer a late licence with DJs playing alternative tunes, but be warned this can sometimes make the pub a bit of a venue for gaudily dressed 'pre-loaded' revellers, passing time until the local clubs open. Nevertheless, at other less frenetic times, the Griffin is arguably the best pub in Vauxhall.

FEATURES:          

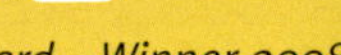

Reviewers' Award – Winner 2008

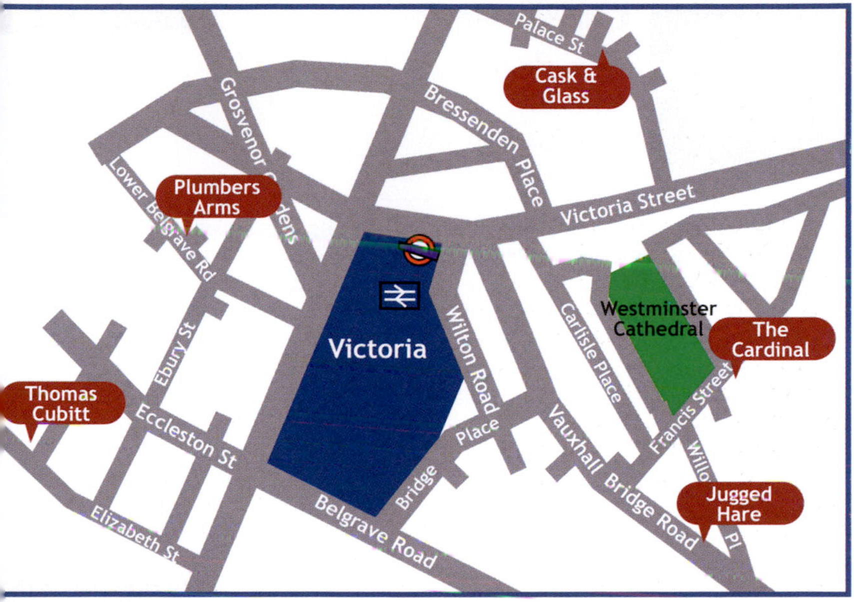

Palace St
Cask & Glass
Bressenden Place
Grosvenor Gardens
Lower Belgrave Rd
Plumbers Arms
Victoria Street
Victoria
Wilton Road
Westminster Cathedral
Carlisle Place
The Cardinal
Francis Street
Ebury St
Thomas Cubitt
Eccleston St
Place
Bridge
Vauxhall Bridge Road
Willow Pl
Jugged Hare
Elizabeth St
Belgrave Road

The Cardinal

RATING: 

23 Francis Street
SW1P 1DN
020 7834 7260

We like this place – it's a very comfortable Sam Smith's pub almost right next to Westminster Cathedral, well actually in the very shadow of that venerable London landmark. Its proximity to the cathedral means that the walls are covered in portraits of popes, cardinals and various other papist royalty. We've yet to see any of the neighbours in here, but it does attract a regular following. As is usual for Sam Smith's, there is little or nothing else on offer than their own beers – if you want something else, we're afraid you're stuffed. It has an extensive menu, with good, inexpensive food, and a lovely Victorian interior. This one is definitely worth a look if you're in the area, and it is open at weekends too. Give this one a go before mass, if nothing else – not that we recommend going to mass pissed (though it might make it go a bit more quickly).

FEATURES:    

HANDY FOR: Westminster Cathedral

Cask & Glass

RATING: 

39–41 Palace Street
SW1E 5HN
020 7834 7630

The Cask & Glass is a cosy, friendly, little pub that is just far enough away from the main drag to avoid the hordes of local office workers as they wend their weary ways back to Victoria station and thence to suburbia. The pub appears to be a particular favourite of Home Office employees who linger for a pint or two before going home (and usually a few more than that towards the weekend). The beer on the hand pumps is, of course, from Shepherd Neame (including regular, seasonal ales) and is everything we've come to expect of Britain's oldest brewer.

FEATURES:  

HANDY FOR: Buckingham Palace, Westminster Cathedral

The Jugged Hare

RATING: 

172 Vauxhall Bridge Road
SW1V 1DX
020 7828 1543

Fuller's started putting their Ale and Pie Houses in former banks a few years ago with some success – and this one's no exception. It's a lovely building with vaguely opulent décor and very high ceilings. The front area is predominately for vertical drinking, but there's a seated back section to hide away in, as well as an upstairs balcony area. It's a little bit further away from a lot of the attractions in the area, so tends not to attract many tourists. The pub can get busy with local civil servants and office workers, however, so we'd recommend arriving sometime after lunch and before home time if you want to appreciate drinking one of the good choice of ales here in relative peace.

FEATURES:   

HANDY FOR: Westminster Cathedral

Plumbers Arms

RATING:

14 Lower Belgrave Street
SW1W 0LN
020 7730 4067

A busy one-roomed affair that's near enough to Victoria station for in-the-know commuters, but just far enough away from the busloads of tourists. With a fair selection on tap, this one's a decent enough pub with a livelier atmosphere than you might expect from a Belgravia boozer. It also played a small role in the Lord Lucan saga, and you'll find an old newspaper report of the case on one of the walls if you're interested in learning more about it. We've heard rumours that this pub was on the brink of closure before the *Daily Telegraph* moved to its new headquarters in Victoria and adopted the place as a preferred house pub. We haven't spotted Simon Heffer in here yet – but there are a lot of journos in here of an evening. You may or not find this off-putting, but the regular custom might just have saved the place. (Closed weekends.)

FEATURES:    

HANDY FOR: Buckingham Palace

The Thomas Cubitt

44 Elizabeth Street
SW1W 9PA
020 7730 5437

It's always heartening to see a pub trying this hard, and it's obvious from its popularity they're succeeding at what they do. It's funny how quickly the standard of things change as you leave the tatty hotels and cheap shops clustered around Victoria station – this place is more upmarket and is probably more bar than pub. The staff are friendly and efficient – when it's crowded the fact they do table service is fantastic. The atmosphere is pretty frenetic of an evening, but it's still possible to converse with your friends . Cocktails are available, as is well-kept beer and a good selection of mostly European wine. Now that a lot of things have bedded in, it's a pleasure to go to. They've also dispensed with a lot of the gastropub frou-frou stuff: sausage and mash is called sausage and mash, a sign the chef's comfortable with the food he's serving. And, thank God, all the tables on the ground floor are available in the evenings for drinking – you can still order food, it's just not expected. The food is pretty good, with their organic beefburger being our particular favourite. You can also get sandwiches and fish and chips alongside that steak. While this isn't a cosy old boozer, it's still a pretty good place to go.

FEATURES:    

HANDY FOR: Westminster Cathedral

WAPPING – *see Shadwell, page 355*

WARREN STREET

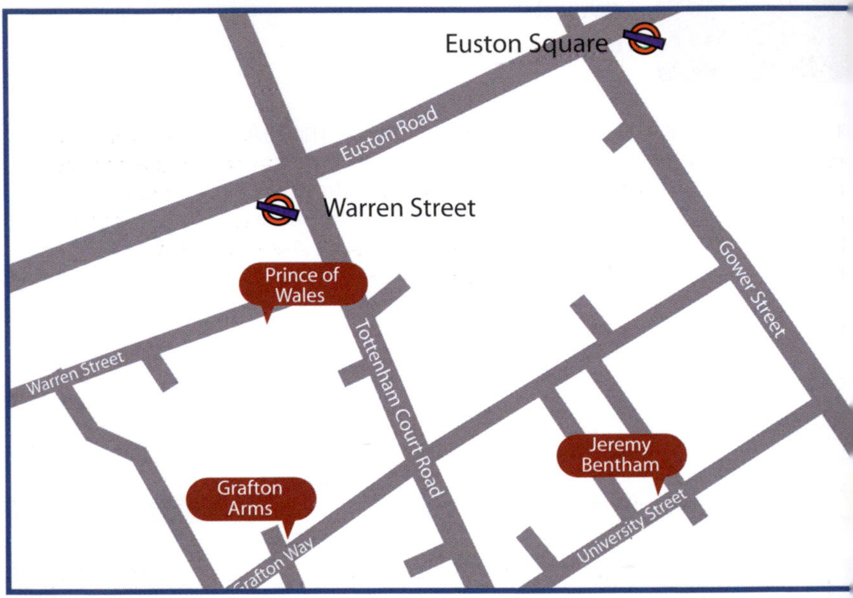

Euston Square
Euston Road
Warren Street
Gower Street
Prince of Wales
Warren Street
Tottenham Court Road
Jeremy Bentham
Grafton Arms
University Street
Grafton Way

Grafton Arms

RATING:

72 Grafton Way
W1T 5DS
020 7387 7923

The takeover of this pub by Greene King has certainly raised the standards, which is particularly important in Fitzrovia as you're spoilt for choice when it comes to pubs. The refurb has made a lot of difference, as the downstairs pub is more welcoming than it used to be. The friendly staff make all the difference, too. It also has an upstairs bar which doubles as a private function room (making it frequently closed) and topping it all off is a handy roof garden. The upstairs room is a good size and its central location means it's ideal for those birthday and works dos, hence it's pretty popular. Now relegated to smoking-room status, the roof terrace is still a welcome relief in summer. The pub does get busy at lunch and commuter times, but it's ideal for a quiet drink in the afternoon should you be in the area, or for a relaxed evening drink.

FEATURES:    

WARREN STREET

The Jeremy Bentham

RATING:

31 University St
WC1E 6JL
020 7387 3033

This pub's proximity to University College Hospital (and University College London) means it can often be crowded with students and medics, but don't let that put you off. This pub has a pretty impressive range of guest ales supported by a standard range of pub grub, which is adequate, but unlikely to win Michelin stars. If you've been pounding the streets of London, looking for that elusive – electronic, round here – bargain, you might find this pub a welcome respite.

FEATURES:  

Prince of Wales Feathers

RATING:

8 Warren Street
W1T 5LG
020 7255 9911

While the outside of this pub across the road from Warren Street is pretty traditional looking (it's even been used in a period drama not so long ago), the interior is definitely in the vein of that modern pub style: wood floors, overstuffed furniture and a couple of plasma screens to edge things into the 21st century. It's one of those solid and consistent pubs that might not have you crossing London to visit, but given its proximity to Warren Street is never going to be short on punters at commuting times, and the clientele tends to be a little on the transient side. It also does the job as a handy meeting spot, certainly as a starting (or finishing) spot for a Fitzrovia pub crawl.

FEATURES:   

WARWICK AVENUE – *see Maida Vale, page 269*

Waterloo Bridge
Stamford Street
Cornwall Road
White Hart
Whittlesey Street
IMAX Cinema
Wellington
Hole in the Wall
Exton Street
Waterloo East
Mepham Street
York Road
Waterloo Road
Waterloo

Hole in the Wall

RATING:

5 Mepham Street
SE1 8SQ
020 7928 6196

Pretty much an institution in these parts, this pub is actually quite a large hole in a wall, being situated in railway arches in front of Waterloo station and has been a watering hole of choice for commuters for many a year. Never a place one would ever describe as spick and span and with conversation drowned out by the trains rumbling over head every few minutes, the appeal of the place is not easy to identify. But, when you consider its proximity to the station and the excellent range of beers on the hand pumps, the penny drops. Not a great place for a romantic tête-à-tête, but a handy one to put right the evils of another day in the office.

FEATURES:   

HANDY FOR: London Imax Cinema, National Theatre

The Wellington at Waterloo

RATING: 

81 Waterloo Road
SE1 8UD
020 7928 6083

The Wellington at Waterloo is a giant of a pub that also provides accommodation. There's a decent range of beer on the hand pumps, with more unusual beers such as Jennings Biggest Liar on offer. There are plenty of screens for watching sport and there's pub grub if you're hungry. The trouble is it's an over-bright characterless place, often crowded (making it hard to find a table, despite its size). It's handy for meeting up before heading into town (especially if you're meeting friends from the south and south-west), but that's honestly about the strongest recommendation we can make for it.

FEATURES:   

HANDY FOR: London Imax Cinema, The Old Vic Theatre

White Hart

RATING:

Cornwall Road
SE1 8TJ
020 7401 7151

The formula's becoming more and more familiar as M&B converts more pubs to this winning format, but that doesn't mean we're getting tired of it. And why should we, when you are offered excellent hand-pumped beers, a very extensive range of continental beers (with all kinds of exotic stuff such as Fruli) a decent wine list and decent food? Add to this a comfortable, friendly environment and decent service and you don't mind that bit extra on the price for the extra you get in return. If it does have a downside, that's the fact that this pub is even more popular than it used to be. But if you get in early and snaffle a settee or corner table, you're going to be happy here.

FEATURES:  

HANDY FOR: London Imax Cinema, The Old Vic Theatre

WEMBLEY CENTRAL/WEMBLEY PARK – *Stonebridge Park, page 380*

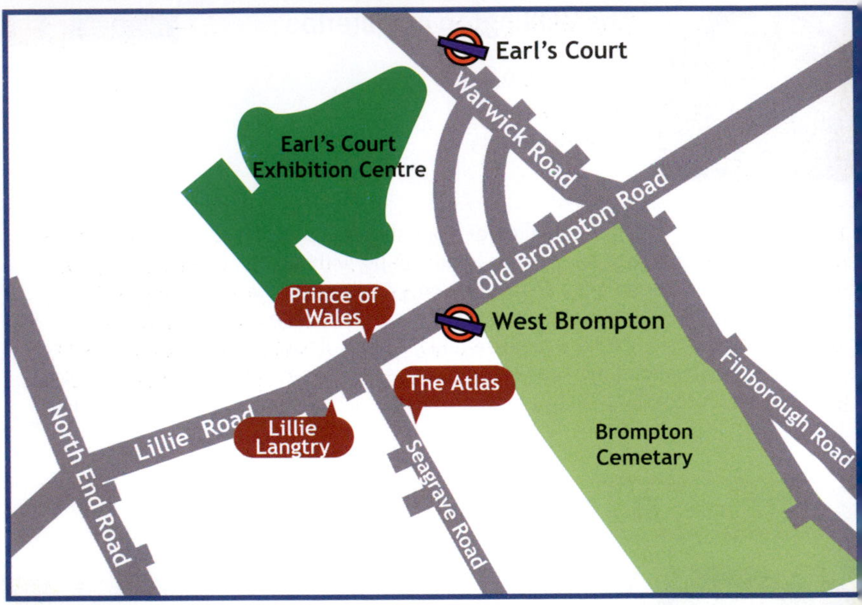

Earl's Court
Warwick Road
Earl's Court Exhibition Centre
Old Brompton Road
Prince of Wales
West Brompton
The Atlas
Finborough Road
Lillie Road
Lillie Langtry
North End Road
Seagrave Road
Brompton Cemetary

The Atlas

RATING: 

16 Seagrave Road
SW6 1RX
020 7385 9129

It's nice to see some things don't change and this hasn't changed. The mix 'n' match wooden tables and chairs are de rigueur for this gastro conversion, this one's still a pub first and foremost. One thing you can count on is that it usually has decent beers on tap and they're well kept. The excellent food is reasonably priced, if a bit gastro, and a proper coffee contraption takes up one end of the bar. There's a nice suntrap at the side too, for the occasional, pleasant evening drink. It's also got a function room that's available to hire, with a large telly in it, but they only show big games on terrestrial as there's not enough demand for the pub to fork out for Sky, even though it's close to Earl's Court for a pre-concert/post-exhibition drink and accordingly busy. It is popular in the evenings – the outside has an awning which they use at nights to double their space. Definitely worth a visit. The only complaint we've heard is that they don't do bubbly by the glass – well, if you're that tight...

FEATURES:     

HANDY FOR: Earl's Court

The Lillie Langtry

RATING:

19 Lillie Road
SW6 1UE
020 7385 3605

This pub is a bit of a fixture of the area around West Brompton tube and, beyond the odd lick of paint, hasn't changed in years. It's warm and friendly, with cheerful staff and a pretty comfortable local feel. And the locals aren't scary either, happily sharing their pub with one and all. There isn't any real ale on – two kinds of Guinness don't count – but it's still a great place to watch the sport and chill out of an afternoon. The chances are good it probably suffers the influxes of concert and conference attendees, but it's pretty reasonable otherwise.

FEATURES:    

HANDY FOR: Earl's Court, Chelsea Football Club

Prince of Wales

14 Lillie Road
SW6 1TU
020 7385 7441

In the shadow of Earl's Court, this is a great place to go when the weather is agreeable, as it has a large garden in the back and a substantial terrace on the front. It's proven popular with local workers and conference attendees for a decent lunch and a pint. While it's not necessarily one to go out of your way for, it does most things right, and the friendly staff cope with crowds pretty well, no matter how busy it gets. It does have real ale, but only Pride was on the four hand pumps when we were in last. Just a warning, it gets pretty heaving if there's a gig on next door, but you shouldn't have any trouble getting a drink – just finding somewhere to drink it might be a problem.

FEATURES:      

HANDY FOR: Earl's Court

WEST HAMPSTEAD

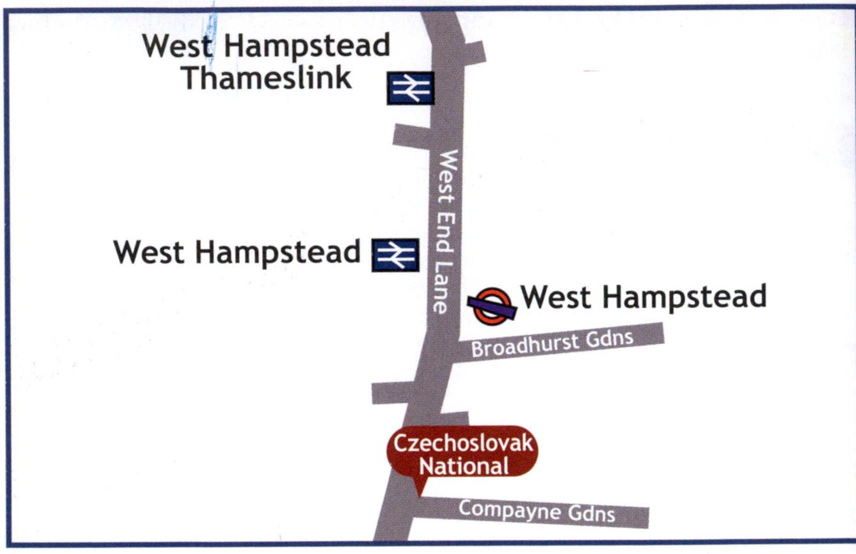

Czechoslovak National House

RATING:

74 West End Lane
NW6 2LX
020 7328 0131

The bar is just one part of this club for exiles from Czechoslovakia (as was) which has been going since the late 1940s, apparently. There's also a restaurant open to all comers, but for our purposes the most important thing is beer. Czech beer. Which is why we go here and, of course, it's excellent stuff. There are bar snacks too, such as herring and bread if you feel peckish. The ex-pats still predominate but there are plenty of other visitors. During one visit, instead of meeting, say, a group of gorgeous young ladies with impossibly long legs, we encountered a group from Glasgow and Belfast exchanging Republican and Unionist slogans. This sums up our lives too perfectly to dwell on further. Instead, we should warn readers that, apparently, they won't serve halves because (in true Eastern bloc spirit) 'if I gave you one, then I'd have to give everyone one'. They do some spirits, but, if you come here, just drink pints, hey?

FEATURES:   

WEST INDIA QUAY – *see Canary Wharf, page 82*

WEST KENSINGTON – *see Barons Court, page 38*

WESTBOURNE PARK

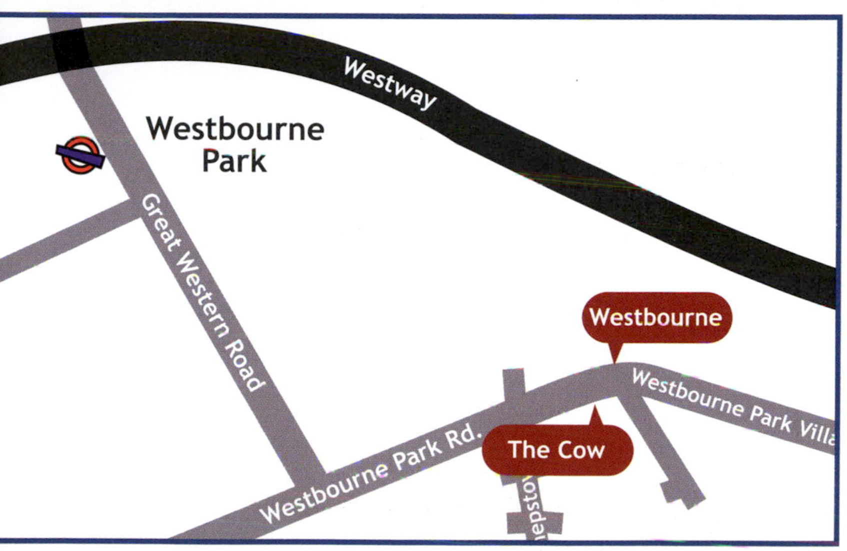

The Cow

RATING:

89 Westbourne Park Road
W2 5QH
020 7221 0021

The Cow is a trendy little pub, complete with a restaurant upstairs. It's pretty small and always crowded with beautiful people (well, at least they seem to think they are). Perhaps there is an ironic allure going to a pub that has red Formica tables and the sort of lighting you get in working men's clubs. For us, though, it's pretty homely, reminding us of former haunts. The food in the bar's pretty good, with a good chunk of the menu devoted to shellfish (the oysters have a deserved reputation). Be warned it can be on the expensive side – particularly for a pub – but this isn't terribly surprising at it's part of Tom Conran's empire, son of the famous Terence and brother of Jasper. The beer on the pumps is good and a fine drop of Guinness is poured here too, if you fancy a drop of the black stuff with your oysters. Sadly for us, the sometimes overbearing clientele usually make the novelty wear off before too long and, usually, we wend our way somewhere else.

FEATURES:   

Westbourne

RATING:

101 Westbourne Park Villas
W2 5ED
020 7221 1332

A large Victorian pub that's been gutted to turn it into a trendy bar with an extensive and very good-looking menu. Though, with the Cow across the road, it's probably got to work that little bit harder to attract customers in the area. While it's far more in the category of a bar, you can still get a decent pint here, with two ales on the pumps. Decent beer, WiFi and a menu you can sink your teeth into are probably the main attractions, though celeb spotting (the ones who couldn't get into the Cow) may be another. It's not a place to go that extra mile for, but it does provide a viable alternative if you're in the area.

FEATURES:   

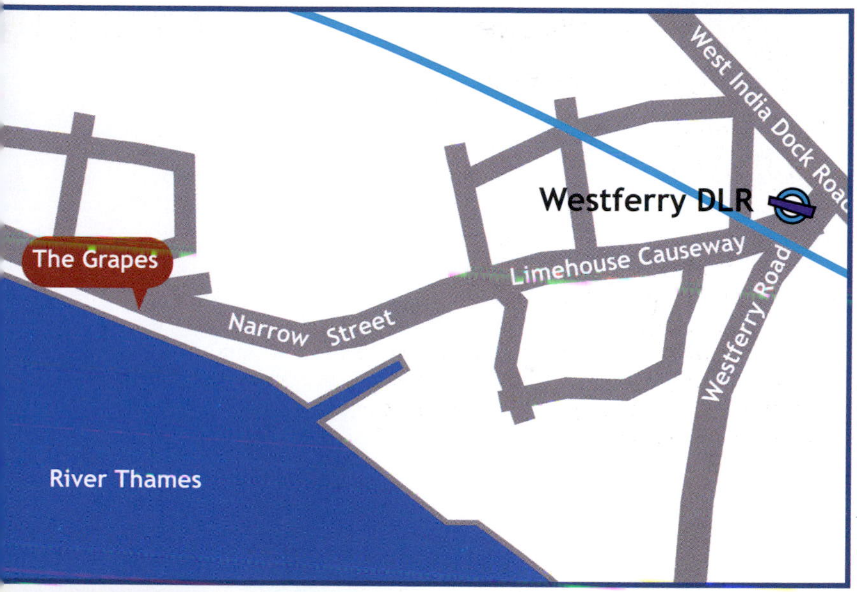

West India Dock Road
Westferry DLR
Limehouse Causeway
Westferry Road
Narrow Street
The Grapes
River Thames

The Grapes

RATING: 5 pints

76 Narrow Street
E14 8BP
020 7987 4396

We like this place – it's a quaint, narrow, little pub in a very old terrace on the north bank of the river at Limehouse. There's a tiny terrace at the back that you can squeeze onto, if you're lucky, and enjoy views of Limehouse Reach and Rotherhithe. The beer's pretty good and the décor old and genuine. But there's more to it, there's a sort of timeless traditional atmosphere about the place in an area where property booms and yuppiedom have wreaked their worst. The restaurant upstairs specialises in fish and it's pretty good too. If you do go, try to book the table that looks out over the river (you need to book anyway, it's pretty popular). The food is traditional seafood and is entirely dependent on what is good at the market that day. It's well presented, but can be a little pricey. The service is friendly and prompt and, with the fare on offer, what more could you want? It just looks, acts and feels like a proper English pub. It's just perfect for the area.

FEATURES:       

Reviewers' Special Award – Best London Pub 2004–2008

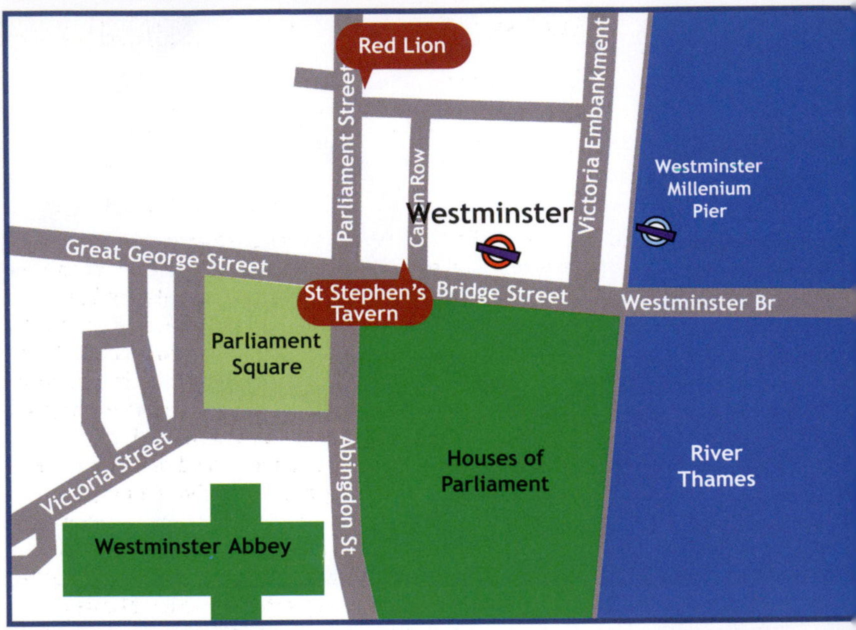

Red Lion
Parliament Street
Cannon Row
Victoria Embankment
Westminster
Westminster Millenium Pier
Great George Street
St Stephen's Tavern
Bridge Street
Westminster Br
Parliament Square
Victoria Street
Abingdon St
Houses of Parliament
River Thames
Westminster Abbey

Red Lion

RATING:

48 Parliament Street
SW1A 2NH
020 7930 5826

Often cited as the most popular pub name in the UK, the most famous Red Lion of them all is probably this one in Westminster. This isn't for its attractive turn-of-the-century features, etched glass or surfeit of mahogany, but because it's the nearest pub to Downing Street. So often is it frequented by MPs and various politicos that its televisions show the BBC Parliament channel, instead of the usual sport. Apparently, it even rings a division bell to alert the more right honourable customers of an upcoming vote. In usual media attention-grabbing style, it was also the place where Culture Secretary Tessa Jowell happily announced an end to UK's antiquated licensing laws (even if ironically the Red Lion was refused a late licence itself). The pub's small size and quantity of besuited regulars means it's often very busy, even if a cellar bar and upstairs dining room help alleviate the pressure. Still, it's worth a look out of peak times and you never know when some tidbit of political gossip might be overheard.

FEATURES:    **HANDY FOR:** Downing Street/Whitehall, Cabinet War Rooms

St Stephen's Tavern

RATING: 3 pints

10 Bridge Street
SW1A 2JR
020 7925 2286

This Grade II listed pub was one we didn't think would ever open again. Having been closed for the best part of 15 years, it quietly reopened its doors just before Christmas 2003. From our research, it appears that this 125-year-old watering hole has been frequented by many notables, including prime ministers such as Baldwin, Churchill and Macmillan. The results of the refurbishment are fantastic – they should be after a multimillion pound restoration done with the help of English Heritage (or interference, depending on whom you talk to). Apparently, many of the fittings are from the original pub, having been stored since the pub closed. So now it's mellowed nicely into a distinguished pub. One thing to note, the chairs chosen have curved backs, making the small rooms feel more crowded than they actually are – sometimes ending up feeling rather cramped. It is very popular straight after work, with political hangers-on and civil servants standing around and chatting, shoulder-to-shoulder, until around 8.ooish, when things start to quieten down. There's a good range of well-kept beers on the hand pumps – Tanglefoot and Badger's Best amongst them. Outside of crush times, this is a fine place and well worth a visit if you're in the area.

FEATURES:   

HANDY FOR: Houses of Parliament, Westminster Abbey

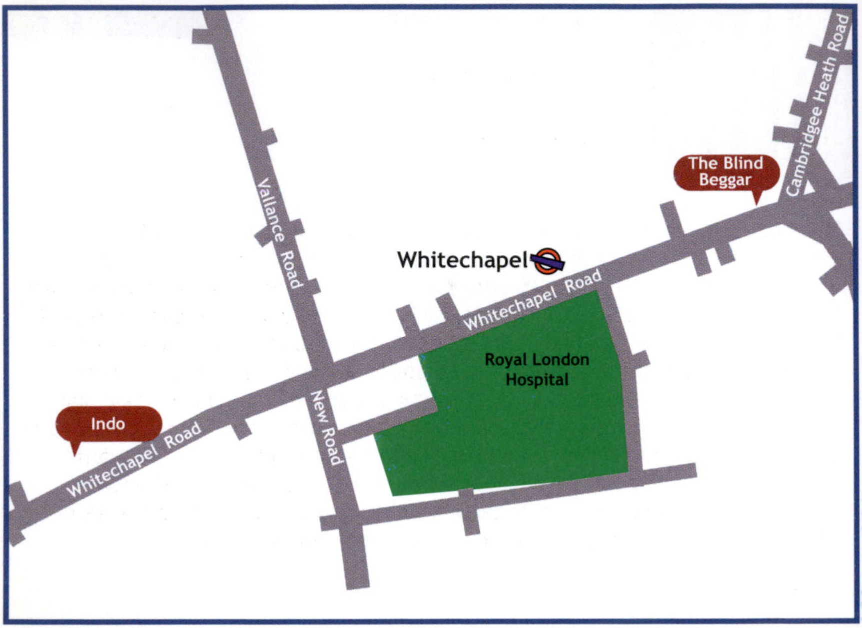

Vallance Road
Cambridgee Heath Road
The Blind Beggar
Whitechapel
Whitechapel Road
Royal London Hospital
Indo
Whitechapel Road
New Road

Blind Beggar

RATING:

337 Whitechapel Road
E1 1BU
020 7247 6195

Most people have heard of this pub, thanks to an infamous incident in 1966 and some even make a trip to see it just for that reason. When they get here, they will find a decent, ordinary boozer that serves the locals well, but it's nothing out of the ordinary and certainly there are no bloodstains – or stains of any kind, for that matter. The fare on offer is pretty unremarkable, it's OK, but nothing special and the accommodation offers a little bit of something for everybody – you can choose from large beer garden, conservatory, comfy chairs (by the gas-coal fire), bar stools etc. Popular with locals, pop in if you're in the area, but it's not worth a special effort to get here.

FEATURES:  

Indo

RATING: 3 pints

133 Whitechapel Road
E1 1DT
020 7247 4926

While other nearby pubs seem to appeal to one or other of the various tribes that dominate this edge-of-the-City location, Indo offers one of the more refreshing and eclectic experiences. It's a long, thin place and not particularly large, so it doesn't take a lot for it to become busy – but despite this it's still a chilled-out experience; even the handful of Hoxtonites and Trustafarians who wandered too far from home were more or less behaving themselves. There's a very good choice of beers on tap – Budvar Dark, Konig Ludwig and Mort Subite amongst those offered – and the music is also well chosen. Wine buffs are slightly less well accommodated being offered a choice of red or white in varied quantities. The décor is simple, with rickety furniture offset against some bits of art and a few well-priced snacks (a good range of pizzas) are available to those who ask the nice people behind the bar. Suffice to say we like it here – just arrive here early (or early in the week) if you want a seat.

FEATURES: 

Index

INDEX

INDEX

INDEX

Erratum – changes to the book

Things change – we all know that. This book is a snapshot of the last year, and it's bound to have changes almost as soon as it's printed.

So, to help our users we've decided to create an online 'erratum' page which will have any changes to pubs or other destinations that affect the content of this book. To see the list of changes, simply go to

www.fancyapint.com/book

You can also view the list while you're out and about by using the internet browser on your mobile phone, by keying in

www.fancyapint.mobi/book

We'll do our best to keep this list up to date, but, as always, if you find we've missed something or that it's changed, email us at editor@fancyapint.com and we'll update the website.

Notes

NOTES

fancyapint?

THE LONDON UNDERGROUND

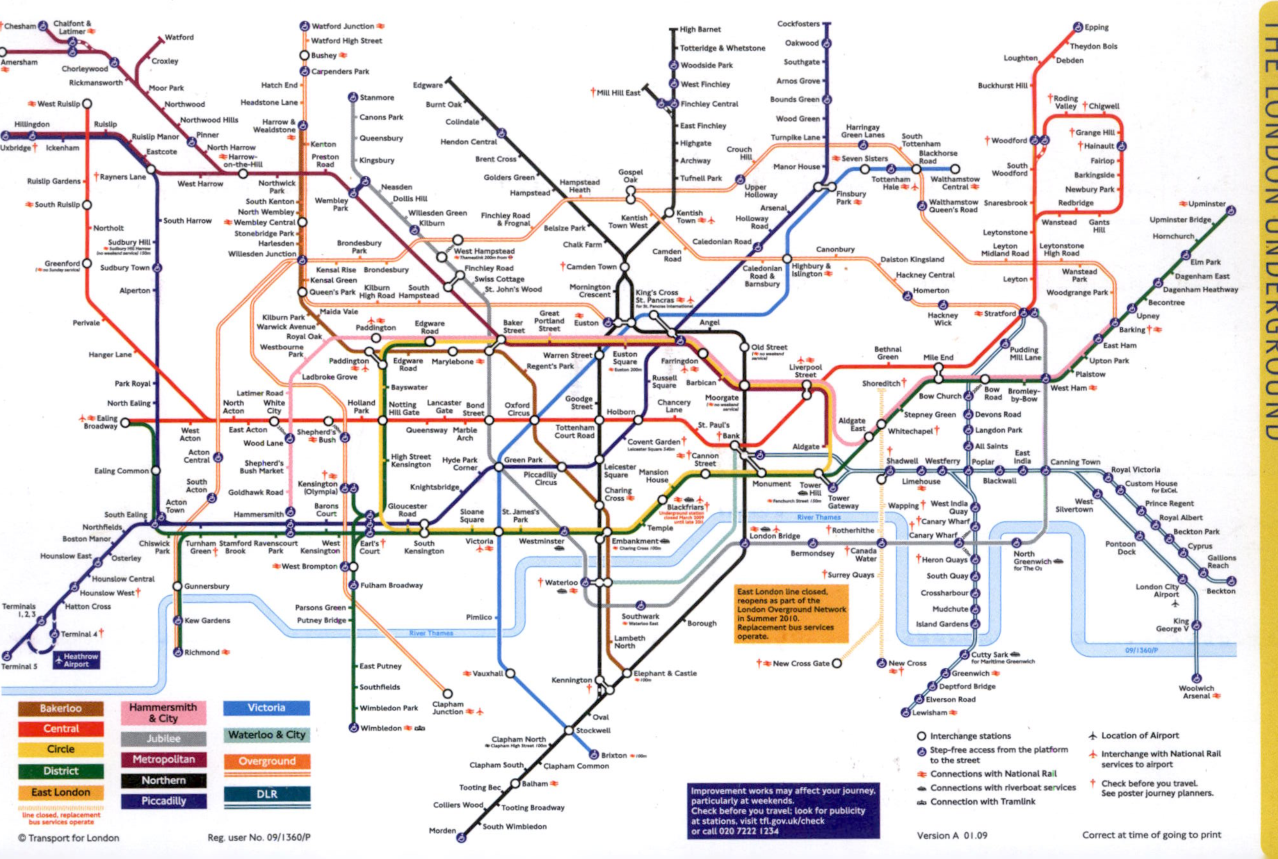